The Irish World Wide
History, Heritage, Identity

Volume 2 **The Irish in the New Communities**

The Irish World Wide
History, Heritage, Identity

Edited by Patrick O'Sullivan

The Irish World Wide
History, Heritage, Identity

Volume 2
The Irish in the New Communities

Edited by Patrick O'Sullivan

Leicester University Press
London and Washington

Leicester University Press
A Cassell imprint
Wellington House, 125 Strand, London WC2R 0BB, England
PO Box 605, Herndon, VA 20172

First published 1992
Reprinted in paperback 1997
© Editor and contributors 1992

British Library Cataloguing in Publication Data
A catalogue record for this book is available from the British Library

ISBN 0 7185 0116 0

Typeset by Florencetype Ltd, Kewstoke, Avon
Printed and bound in Great Britain by
Biddles Ltd of Guildford and King's Lynn

In memory of Jane Catton O'Sullivan

Contents

List of figures

List of tables

List of contributors

Donald Harman Akenson is Professor of History at Queen's University, Kingston, Ontario, and is the author of numerous books and articles on aspects of Irish history and Irish migration history, including *Small Differences: Irish Catholics and Irish Protestants, 1815–1922.*

Mervyn A. Busteed is Lecturer in Geography at Manchester University, England. He is the author of books and articles on the human geography of Ireland and a regular contributor to Irish Studies courses.

Karen P. Corrigan lectures in English Language and Linguistics at the University of Newcastle, England, and has held similar posts at the Universities of Edinburgh, York and University College Dublin.

Nessan Danaher is co-ordinator of the Irish Studies Workshop at Soar Valley Community College, Leicester, England. Since 1983 he has organised and co-tutored an annual Irish Cultural Studies programme, which includes Irish Studies, Irish Language, set and ceili dance and traditional music. He organises the Workshop's annual national conference on Irish Dimensions in British Education, and is an executive member of the British Association for Irish Studies.

David M. Emmons is a Professor of History at the University of Montana. He is the author of *The Butte Irish: Class and Ethnicity in an American Mining Town, 1875–1925,* a volume in the Statue of Liberty/Ellis Island Centennial Series and winner of the Robert G. Athean Award of the Western History Association.

Gordon Forth is Senior Lecturer in Australian Studies at Deakin University, Warrnambool, Victoria, Australia. He has published articles and books on Australia's pastoral history and a series of articles on Australia's Anglo-Irish colonists.

Laurence M. Geary is Wellcome Research Fellow in the History of Medicine, Royal College of Surgeons, in Ireland. He has held academic appointments in Ireland, Britain and Australia and has published on the history of these three countries.

Liam Greenslade is a research associate at the Institute of Irish Studies, University of Liverpool. He is currently conducting research on the health of first and second generation Irish migrants to England and is the author of a book on the Soviet semiotician V.N. Volosinov to be published by Routledge in 1993.

Ellen Hazelkorn is a Lecturer in Politics at the Dublin Institute of Technology. She is co-author of *The Dynamics of Irish Politics* (London, 1989), editor of *Irish Communications Review* (Dublin) and a contributing editor to *Science and Society* (New York). She has published widely on Irish politics, clientelism, labour history and migration.

Robert I. Hodgson is Lecturer in Geography at Manchester University, England. He has published articles on the early industrial revolution in North-east England (the subject of his PhD thesis) and on the history of Manchester.

Thomas F. Kennedy is a graduate of the Department of Geography, University of Manchester. Before taking up a teaching post in Singapore in January 1992, he taught Geography at Manchester Grammar School. He has widely researched and written about the growth of nineteenth-century Manchester.

Roger Swift is Director of Victorian Studies at Chester College of Higher Education, a Fellow of the Institute of Irish Studies at the University of Liverpool, and a Fellow of the Royal Historical Society. He has published widely on the history of the Irish in Britain.

Introduction to Volume 2: The Irish in the new Communities

Patrick O'Sullivan

This is the second volume of *The Irish World Wide* series, and is the companion to Volume 1, *Patterns of Migration*. Volume 2 continues the pattern of case studies offered by Volume 1. The Volume 2 case studies allow me to highlight key themes and areas of debate – notably themes and areas that have not been assigned their own volumes in the rest of the series. The most important of these is *work* – the movement of labour – the background theme to the first two volumes of this series. Volume 2 adds a number of historiographic and theoretical chapters, putting our case studies in contexts and encouraging further developments. Cumulatively, Volume 2 looks with a quizzical eye at the three elements of our series subtitle: 'history', 'heritage' and 'identity'.

The Irish World Wide series develops the first map or chart of inter-disciplinary, world-wide Irish Migration Studies – the series enables you to make your own assessment of 'the state of the art'. Because *The Irish World Wide* series is a report on the state of the art, you will at times in these Introductions see me back-pedalling furiously, as I try not to impose my own views and interpretations. But, as I explained in the General Introduction to the series in Volume 1, there are some ground rules.

This series is an academic publishing project – that is its special contribution to the study of the Irish migrations. As material about the Irish migrations is presented to us, we must think: methodology. Methodology, research technique, sources. What are the strengths and the limitations of this particular methodology? What special perceptions can only this methodology bring to us?

In the General Introduction I stressed the need for an inter-disciplinary approach to the study of the Irish migrations, and I insisted that the academic disciplines must learn from each other. That is a theme I will return to later in these pages.

I suggested two main ways that we might organise our material, so that we are not swamped by detail. I suggested we make better use of migration theory, in particular the 'Theory of migration' of Everett S. Lee, so that we can locate research gaps, compare the Irish experiences with the experiences of other migrant groups, and share our experiences with others.[1]

Developing some of the ideas of Gerda Lerner, the feminist historian, I suggested that writing about the Irish migrations tends to fall into the categories: oppression history, compensation history and contribution history. I saw the oppression/compensation/contribution approaches as a continuum. I was concerned that each approach hid or abandoned something of the Irish migration experience. For example, oppression history can conspire with the oppressor to let the oppressor shape our agenda, and, since there is a continuum, there is a possibility that the compensation and contribution approaches will also be so shaped.[2]

Nonetheless, I felt that Irish Migration Studies must embrace all three approaches. I did not explore the possibility of there being a fourth category – or any number of categories. Now, though I do not want to use these organising ideas in any heavy-handed way in *The Irish World Wide* series, I think you should be aware that they are in the background. Occasionally I will bring these organising ideas into the foreground, when I think that helpful.

In the General Introduction I said that, on the whole, I have tried to avoid jargon or technical vocabulary in these introductions – the series ranges across so many different academic disciplines that there is a danger of getting bogged down in a quagmire of competing jargons. And then, perversely, in the Introduction to Volume 1, I allowed myself to bring in a piece of private jargon – the notion of 'icons', iconic figures or themes, the sort of thing that immediately springs to mind in any pub discussion of the Irish migrations.

One of the achievements of *Patterns of Migration* was that our contributors showed how to develop, research and think about a number of those 'icons', and drew them into the coherent, developing study of the Irish migrations. We should not fear our icons. We even found some new icons: Irish accountants (our latter day 'Wild Geese'), and 'New Irish' 'illegals' in present day New York. So there was there the material to begin the study of that process of 'iconisation'.

Throughout *The Irish World Wide* series you will find that contributors give you jumping off points into the literature and the thinking on certain themes. I have not asked that these rough guides be exhaustive – quite the contrary. I think it more important that you be able to assess the methods used and the thoughts presented and not be, as I say, swamped by detail. Many of the editor's usual tasks have been farmed out and certain brave contributors have written more theoretical, background chapters. My task in these Introductions is then an unusual, and unusually interesting, one – to fill gaps, add to contexts and explore inter-disciplinary connections.

You can now begin to see *The Irish World Wide* project come together. You can, for example, also use the case studies from Volume 1 to add depth to your reading of Volume 2. Thus, King on the Murphy family and the Breen family, Chapter 4 of Volume 1, has already started us thinking about the migrant route, through Canada to the United States, which figures so largely in Akenson's analysis, Chapter 4 of this volume. Hanlon's chapter on graduate migration, Chapter 9 of Volume 1, can be put alongside Hazelkorn, Chapter 8 of this volume.

This volume begins with four linked chapters, two case studies each with a companion chapter of historiography. Together these chapters plunge you into two major areas of debate within the historiography of the Irish migrations. This juxtaposition means that, unlike the usual pattern whereby the chapter of historiography gives a critique of case studies, here in effect the two case studies allow you to critically examine the historiography. I know that this focus on the historiographies of the Irish in Britain and in the United States might mean that other parts of the world look neglected, but both our historiographers range widely.[3] I did want to foreground these two areas of debate. From my privileged position as the editor of this series, who has for some years been tracking the world-wide study of the Irish migrations, I can tell you that the themes and debates explored in our first four chapters do have world-wide significance for that study.

Engels' pig

The Irish community in Manchester, long established and constantly replenished from across the Irish Sea, is one of the most important in Britain.[4] But if the community is important in history, it is even more important in historiography. The first chapter in this volume is by Manchester's social geographers, Mervyn A. Busteed, Robert I. Hodgson and Thomas F. Kennedy. Their chapter carefully places itself within Manchester myths and realities, and Roger Swift's following chapter of historiography allows you to explore the wider contexts. I can be content here with a few observations.

There is an entire genre in writing about the Irish migrations that, in one of my few moments of bad temper, I have referred to as the 'Engels' pig school' of Irish migration studies. A heady mix of leftwing correctness and Irish quaintness, it dwells lovingly on that section in *The Condition of the Working Class in England* where Engels confronts 'The Irishman', and his pig: 'The Irishman loves his pig as the Arab his horse, with the difference that he sells it when it is fat enough to kill. Otherwise he eats and sleeps with it, his children play with it, ride upon it, roll in the dirt with it, as anyone may see a thousand times repeated in all the great towns of England.'[5] There is a lot to untangle here. As John Archer Jackson notes, in the 1830s and 1840s, 'Although this was not a practice limited to the Irish, much was made of the Irishman's "pig" by contemporaries.'[6] There are certainly questions, as the young Engels himself observed, about the appropriate place of livestock within our great cities, and the problems of garbage disposal if we do not have livestock within our cities.[7]

At one simple level there is an association of ideas, as, in the nineteenth century, horrified members of the middle classes became aware of the 'condition' of the working class. Koditschek, in his excellent study of the industrialisation of Bradford, Yorkshire, puts it thus: 'By the late thirties, the hope that workers might voluntarily embrace liberal individualist values was giving way to the fear that they had become so dehumanized as to have lost the capacity for values of any sort. Such fears, even when they were not explicitly articulated, were revealed by the language in which working–class modes of living were described.'[8]

The Irish migrant adds one word, 'Irish', to this English middle class association of ideas. Both Koditschek and I focus on the language of these lines from Angus Bethune Reach, writing in 1849: 'We proceeded first to see some of the low Irish haunts . . . the scene was perfectly savage. The floor was earth, covered with splints of wood produced in match making. The articles of furniture were two. . . . A woman with skin so foul, that she might have passed for a negress, was squatted on the ground, and a litter, I cannot call them a group of children, burrowed about her . . .'[9]

In such texts the metamorphosis is complete. Not only do the migrant Irish live like pigs, and live with pigs: here the Irish are pigs.[10] It is possible, I suppose, to use such material as straightforward evidence of industrial practices – the match splinters on the floor. But, before they are evidence of anything else, such texts are evidence of the writers' cast of mind. Engels shared these middle–class fears, seeing the migrant Irish as contributing to the degradation of the English working class. So, it is significant that Engels' perceptions of the Irish were influenced so much by Carlyle – Engels was very taken by Carlyle's account of the Irishman's rags – and, most important, by James P. Kay. Kay's influence, duly acknowledged by Engels, has been well analysed in Graham Davis' *The Irish in Britain*. Ultimately, there is no more influential account of the migrant Irish, whether directly or through Engels, than Kay's observations on 1830s Manchester. Kay's observations fed into and fed on nineteenth–century English discussion of 'the condition of England question', and the belief that there was an abyss, a moral cesspit, hidden from respectable society, but at all times threatening that society.[11]

What is remarkable is the way that belief has shaped the study of the Irish in Britain, and has shaped Irish perceptions of themselves – so that what was an admittedly important part of the Irish migration experience has some-how become the quintessential Irish migration experience. So that anyone of Irish heritage not fortunate enough to have spent a childhood in a slum somehow felt marginalised.

As Davis says: '. . . we have an image of the Irish in the ghetto that has lasted a century-and-a-half and has been accepted uncritically as a perma-nent and universal feature of Irish life in the great Victorian cities. In the circumstances, it is worth reminding ourselves of the immediate context in which Little Ireland was discovered and made infamous to a credulous world . . .' Kay's original pamphlet was written at the time of the 1832 cholera epidemic. His own influences are Malthus, Ricardo and Bentham. Kay became a sourcebook for many subsequent books on the subject. As well as influencing Engels he also shaped that literary fascination with Manchester we find in the works of the English novelists.[12] So, it is important that we develop a critical approach to Kay, and to Kay's heritage, as Davis does. But it would be nice to go further and throw new light on Kay, and that 150 years of historiography, by finding some way of going back to those Manchester communities and collecting data that does not come to us through that particular distorting glass. And that is what

Chapter 1 in Volume 2 begins to do, as our three social geographers start their assessment of the census-takers notebooks. They do not quite get alongside Kay and Engels, of course, but this is a good beginning.

With Swift's chapter here, and Graham Davis' book, you now have a baseline from which to begin studying, and developing, the history of the Irish in Britain. But note that both Swift's chapter and Davis' book focus on that important period, from 1815 to 1914.[13] As we saw in Volume 1 of *The Irish World Wide* the patterns of Irish migration to the sister island are long-established. And much remains to be done on the history of the Irish migrations in the twentieth century.

The mythopoetic city

Our second great area of debate has to do with the Irish in North America, and the focus within much Irish-American historiography on the Irish in the great cities of the United States. Volume 1 of this series accepted elements of that analysis, with studies of the Irish in Boston and New York – other great cities of America appear in later volumes of the series. It was suggested in Volume 1 that only in the cities could the Irish become America's 'political class'. But Volume 1 also offered material for a critique of much Irish-American historiography, through studies of the Irish in rural California, and of the frontier Irish of Argentina.

Pouring over my railway map of the United States in my search for the mythopoetic American city to put alongside our study of Manchester, England, I paused. I thought of the city that appears again and again in the itinerary of Irish travellers in the late nineteenth and early twentieth centuries.[14]

Butte, Montana, goes the legend, was the city where the Irish got there first, and later migrants had to accommodate themselves to Irish patterns – and, David Emmons tells us in *The Butte Irish*, in this case the legend is substantially true. '. . . Butte had advantages no other American city could match. It belonged to the Irish in almost the same way Salt Lake City belonged to the Mormons. They could build an Irish community to their own specifications. But more was involved in this proprietorship than the timing of the Irish arrival. Not only was Butte new, it was born industrial, or at least industrializing. '. . . the first Irish in Butte encountered none of the hostility that usually resulted when inexperienced immigrant workers moved into an area with an established native work force . . . They got there first, and theirs was the dominant culture. They were the host society, as responsible for Butte as it was for them.'[15] Butte's further claim to fame is that it is full of Sullivans.[16]

Every student of Irish migrations will understand the excitement recalled in the opening pages of Emmon's book, as he and his colleagues discover a mountain of 'Irish stuff' in the World Museum of Mining in Butte. They and he proceeded to mine that mountain, and, in a book that is full of rewards, Emmons showed us how the Irish people of Butte 'lived the big changes'.[17] One of the things Emmons makes clear, in his book and in his chapter here – something too easily lost sight of – is that this is a movement of working people. The hard rock miners went to Butte in search of work. His book is a study of class consciousness, of the organised working class of America.

His chapter here carries on the story told in his book, and is full of insights, again he shows the importance of work, he explores generational conflicts, he shows chain migration breaking down. What we want to know now is can David Emmons find a way of taking the story further and explore the Irish-American response, stunned, heart-broken, mourning, to the Irish Civil War of 1921–22?

Country and town

The simplest way to foreground the current debate within Irish-American historiography is to offer a rumbustious chapter of critical historiography and methodology by Donald Akenson. Ideally you should read this chapter alongside a similar piece by David Noel Doyle.[18] Together those two authors give you an excellent introduction to the present state of Irish-American historiography.

Now for a few personal comments. I have said that *The Irish World Wide* series is a report on 'the state of the art'. And because of the work I have done in developing the series, over the past few years, I can claim a special insight into the present state of world-wide (not only United States) Irish migration studies. And thus I have a special insight into the way the problem within Irish-American historiography has become a problem for all of us. The problem has two parts: observation of a phenomenon, and explanations of that phenomenon.

The observation is still best summed up in the bald statement of William V. Shannon: 'The Irish were a rural people in Ireland and became a city people in the United States.'[19] Now, you have only to read Akenson and Doyle to see how much that observation has been modified over the years. In many respects Akenson and Doyle are in substantial agreement, though their rhetorical styles do differ somewhat. And, at one level, the observation is an unsurprising one – that if Irish people, in search of work, came to a more urban or urbanising community, where work could best be found in cities – yes, they would become a city people. A feature of world history for at least the last two hundred years has been the growth of large cities, and the movement of population into them.[20] Also there are many things that can be best done in cities – like disappearing or hiding. The observation is, in effect, a comparative one – it implicitly contrasts the behaviour of the Irish in the United States with the behaviour of other immigrant groups. And Doyle concedes '. . . in the 1850–1870 period, the Irish-born were NOT comparatively more urban than other immigrants, even though dramatically more so than native born,' though he detects in the later period, around 1900, a more complex pattern.[21] Doyle also has a helpful section showing how much is known, and not known, about the Irish in the rural United States.[22] There are very real problems of interrogating the

United States material, problems of baselines and of definitions, including inclusive and exclusive definitions of 'Irish', as Akenson explores fairly thoroughly in his chapter here. Note that Doyle has to carefully speak of 'Irish-born'.

So, all in all, I find Shannon's comment an unremarkable one, and I am not convinced that his observation needs systematic comment, or at least not comment that focuses only on Ireland and the Irish, or assumptions about the nature of Irish Catholicism. By the way, Akenson's observation in his chapter on Irish Catholic economic success within the United States, as compared with the Irish Protestant lack of success, is also an unremarkable one, it is noticed, for example, by Marjorie Fallows, in *Irish Americans: identity and assimilation* in 1979.[23] On Irish-American Catholic success, Fallows says: 'It would be as valid to attribute their success to their religion as it was to attribute their presumed failure to the same cause.'[24]

A discourse on exile

So much for observations of the phenomenon. What of explanations? Akenson has chosen to build his critique of Irish-American historiography towards a discussion of Kerby Miller's 1985 book *Emigrants and Exiles*. This may be a little unfair to that painstaking and ambitious book, but on the world-wide stage it is the correct thing to do. For, I can report, there is a tendency to read the Irish-American-Catholic historiography as a unity, with *Emigrants and exiles* as its summation and justification.

Emigrants and exiles: Ireland and the Irish exodus to North America, attempts to build a transatlantic conceptual bridge between Ireland and America, between studies of Irish emigration and American immigration, guided, of course, by the then perceived patterns of Irish settlement within the United States.[25] It is an important work. In a work of such length there are bound to be tensions and ambiguities. Miller's very title lists three loaded ways of talking about the same phenomenon, 'emigrants', 'exiles', 'exodus': a prosaic movement of labour, a political ejection, and a journey towards a promised land. But, in the end, the fine detail of Miller's study is guided by a thesis whose chief charm and danger is that it can be simply stated – Akenson calls it, in his chapter, the 'Gaelic-Catholic Disability Variable'.

I come to these things through the study of literature and the arts and through the social sciences. There are elements of this United States historiographic tradition which have long puzzled me. The whole thing seems coloured by a specifically United States way of understanding its own history. For example, it seems to privilege one particular form of economic activity (called 'pioneering') when the reasons for such privileging are by no means self-evident.

I am constantly puzzled by the readiness with which historians seize upon purely psychological explanations of complex phenomena. Especially when the psychology employed is not psychology as anyone understands it who has studied that academic discipline, psychology – whether it be psychology in the more empirical forms of the English-speaking tradition or the more philosophical forms within other European intellectual traditions. The further difficulty for me is that I have found that throughout the world inexperienced scholars, studying the Irish migrations and thinking they are guided by Miller, assume that the most important thing they must assess is the psychological mood of their migrants. How depressed or not depressed were these people?[26]

Further, the whole thesis bears a very close resemblance to a strong theme within sociology, and in particular to a strand within empirical United States sociology, the work of the 'Chicago School': the study of the transition from the traditional, rural community to industrialised, urban society. The most powerful manifestation of that theme is the massive Thomas and Znaniecki project *The Polish Peasant in Europe and America*, published from 1918 to 1920.[27] This strand, within the United States sociology, focussed on issues around 'modernisation', urbanisation, industrialisation and their effects on the individual, the family and 'traditional' ways of organising everyday life. A 'traditional' family and community type was seen to be disintegrating under the pressures of American city life. The key themes are 'adjustment' and 'maladjustment'.[28]

Commenting on this trend within sociology C. Wright Mills has said: 'The idea of adjustment seems most directly applicable to a social scene in which, on the one hand, there is "society" and, on the other, "the individual immigrant". The immigrant must then "adjust" to the society. The "immigrant problem" was early in the sociologist's centre of attention, and the notions used to state it may well have become part of the general model for the formulation of all "problems".'[29] I think it is true to say that Thomas, Znaniecki and the other Chicago sociologists were impressed by the solidarity-bestowing quality of this family type – on the other hand the family was seen as an obstacle to the immigrants' adjustment to American life.[30]

You can see my problem when I see the Chicago School thesis enter Irish migration studies, and in a curious form. The basic ideas are all there: Durkheim, Tönnies, *Gemeinschaft/Gesellschaft*, Ogburn's 'cultural lag'. The whole sociology of 'modernisation' and the family within the American city seems to have transferred wholesale to the study of the Irish migrations. This might seem fair enough. You might disagree with the thesis, but there is nothing in principle wrong with trying to replicate for the Irish peasant what Thomas and Znaniecki, with their trans-atlantic research, did for the Polish.

But the thesis seems, within the discipline of history, to have lost its sociological roots and, no longer a thesis about 'modernisation' in general, has become a thesis about Irish people only. The thesis is that only the Irish suffered loss of community, only the Irish suffered cultural lag – that these are specific characteristics of Irish migrant culture. As soon as I introduce you to *The Polish Peasant* that thesis collapses. Further, the thesis seems to have been stood on its head. What was an explanation of why one group of peasants should be especially ill-suited to *city* life in the United States is now an explanation of why another group of peasants should be especially ill-suited to *rural* life in the United States.

The best critic of Kerby Miller remains Kerby Miller. There are two sections of *Emigrants and exiles* that I particularly admire. The best section of all is the 'Conclusion', Miller's poignant study of the 'American wake'[31] In another section of *Emigrants and exiles* which is too much ignored, Miller himself asks key questions about the notion of 'exile' – that is questions not only about the origins of this way of understanding departure from Ireland, but questions about the prolonging of that way of understanding.[32]

Miller has further clarified and developed these themes in a series of papers.[33] Essentially following Gramsci's analysis of hegemony, he shows developing in Ireland a way of talking about emigration – emigration as 'exile' – which was very convenient for Irish bourgeois nationalists and Catholic churchmen. 'Within this conceptual framework, clerics and nationalists could both oppose emigration and condemn the emigrants themselves . . . The emigrants must be either "traitors" or "fools"; indeed, Patrick Pearse stigmatized them as both.'[34] In *Emigrants and exiles* itself, Miller says: 'Indeed, sometimes the disjunctions between reality and interpretation were so great as to make post-Famine Ireland an almost schizophrenic, if not hypocritical, society.'[35]

The use of the word 'hypocritical' puts Miller alongside a critic of the culture of twentieth century Ireland, J. J. Lee. 'Few peoples anywhere have been so prepared to scatter their children around the world in order to preserve their own living standards.'[36] Considered thus, the traditional, and increasingly casual, Irish practice of referring to emigration as 'exile' is ideological, and is a mystification. And, since migration is so central to Irish history, the processes through which Irish society and culture mystify migration certainly bear studying.

The very concept of 'ideology' has been much criticised of late, notably by Foucault, for whom the main weakness with the category, 'ideology' is that 'it always stands in virtual opposition to something else which is supposed to count as truth.' With what has been called epistemological agnosticism, Foucault suggests that inquiry should concern itself with 'seeing historically how effects of truth are produced within discourses which in themselves are neither true or false.'[39]

So, we can regard 'exile' as an ideology, or 'exile' as a discourse – that is as a way of talking about, and a way of understanding, emigration from Ireland. But if 'exile' is a discourse, then it is only one of a number of possible discourses.

Identities

I want now to foreground another element in our series subtitle and begin to look at questions around migrant Irish 'identities'. The case studies so far have given material through which to explore the processes that go into creating and sustaining an Irish identity, and the circumstances in which an Irish identity survive or decays. In Volume 1 MacGurk chronicled the efforts of the 'Wild Geese' communities to hold on to one sort of Irish identity, and McKenna studied the maintenance and decline of an Irish identity in Argentina. In this volume we have Emmons on the Irish of Butte, Montana, and Akenson's chapter has suggested that there were, and are, entire groups, somehow 'secretly' Irish.

In the background is a large question: what is the relationship between the Irish identities we find inside Ireland and the Irish identities we meet outside Ireland? They are clearly not the same, as has often been remarked. 'What Americans, whether of Irish or non-Irish ancestry, usually find startling when they first visit Ireland is the soft speech, the gentle courtesy and the leisurely style of life. These characteristics seem startling because they are not the characteristics associated with Irish–Americans . . .'[38] But there are family resemblances.

A recent book by Dennis Clark, of Philadelphia, has a helpful chapter on the Irish–American identity, and the role of the family and story-telling in creating and sustaining a sense of self. In one section, taking the long view – as he can in Philadelphia – Clark looks back to St. Patrick's Day, March 17, 1771, and the founding of the Society of the Friendly Sons of St. Patrick, a society still active today. Through the more than 200 year history of the Friendly Sons, Clark shows the amount of mediation, negotiation and sheer hard work that has gone into maintaining that version of the Irish identity.[39] However, we seem to be reaching a stage where, for at least some North Americans, ethnic identity is a matter of personal choice, a matter of picking out the most attractive of the grandparents.

Within Ireland the notion of 'identity' demands intense exploration, especially when explanations of the present day conflicts in Northern Ireland can be couched entirely in terms of threatened or unrecognised 'identities'. John Whyte's admirable *Interpreting Northern Ireland* looks at this in detail, focussing in passing on Tajfel's 'social identity theory'.[40] Individuals belong to social groups, they strive to maintain or enhance their self-esteem, they do this mainly by distinguishing their group from neighbouring groups along some dimension which makes them feel superior.[41]

The historian T. C. Barnard has remarked that the concept of a 'colonial identity' is one of the few abstractions to have entered 'the historian of Ireland's scanty conceptual repertoire'. Though he thinks some uses of the notion uncritically interlink ideology, mentality and identity he still finds 'identity' an important tool for understanding the history of Irish Protestants.[42]

'I was brought up to think myself Irish, without question or qualification; but the new nationalism prefers to describe me and the like of me as Anglo-Irish'. Thus Stephen Gwynn begins his very readable autobiography.[43] One of the Irish identities is fortunate to have enough to have been the subject of that proud, elegant and thoughtful study, J. C. Beckett's *The Anglo-Irish Tradition*. Beckett qualifies his own title: 'The Gaelic revival of the later nineteenth century sharpened the sense of national distinctiveness and gave it a new quality. To be truly Irish now meant to be Gaelic; and any other claim to "Irishness" must be in some way qualified . . .' ' "Anglo-Irish", in ordinary usage, denotes the Protestant community that dominated Ireland in the eighteenth century and those who inherited and maintained its tradition in the changed and changing circumstances of a later age. It is in this sense that the term is used here. But it is used merely for convenience, without any of the apologetic connotation that it may seem to imply; and its use is not to be regarded as any concession to the racialism prevalent in a good deal of contemporary Irish thinking.'[44]

The 'Anglo-Irish' outside Ireland have been little studied and make few appearances, stage centre, in their own right.[45] Boylan's *Dictionary of Irish biography* finds it difficult to be interested in them: 'A large number of men of Irish birth distinguished themselves in the service of the British Empire. . . . The careers of these men exhibit a monotonous sameness and few had any relevance to Ireland.'[46] Thus the experiences of such people tend to be subsumed into 'Englishness', unless they are highjacked for 'Irishness'. Patrick O'Farrell notes that early studies of the Irish in Australia were built on the 'triumphalist "me too" principle', and were propagandist – that is to say, they were part of my oppression/compensation/contribution continuum. 'Critics scoffed at this kind of compulsory Erinism, and drew acid attention to the fact that most of these allegedly "Irish" public figures in Australia were Anglo-Irish . . .'[47]

So, our next contributor, Gordon Forth, from his base within the Australian Studies programme at Deakin University, Australia, takes one fairly well identified Irish identity, the Anglo-Irish identity, and looks at the extent to which it survived outside Ireland, in Australia. It is a fascinating story – it is essentially, and inevitably (given the nature of Forth's sources), a *male* story. It is the story of a class, or a caste, looking for a role. In the end it would seem that, despite the efforts of the 'Irish cousinage' the 'colonial identity' could not long survive in the new environment of colonial Australia.

Language and identity

I am a writer, and, like all craftspeople, like to keep my tools oiled and honed. This is an area where I have a special interest – I teach on language and writing. Since I have a special interest, I will have to be brief.

There is an issue around the Irish relationship with the English language. This project, *The Irish World Wide*, for example, was created and works within the English language – the project would not have worked this well if I had brought it to you within any other language. Preparing this project has brought home to me, yet again, the extent to which English is the current world language. I can write to scholars throughout the world, in a fairly standard style, and generally the expectation is that I will be understood. It is also striking that it has been comparatively easy to find scholars studying the Irish in the English-speaking countries, and rather difficult to find scholars studying the Irish in non-English-speaking countries. And I was eager, if only to clarify and make comparisons, to find studies of Irish migrations to non-English-speaking countries. In one such study, McKenna's history of the Irish in Argentina, you saw how an 'Irish identity' was maintained in a Spanish-speaking country through the medium of the English language. In general, in so far as an Irish identity is maintained outside Ireland it is an English-speaking identity.[48]

What are we to make then of the interest within Ireland in the maintenance and recovery of the Irish language? And the significance attached, by organized Irish communities throughout the English-speaking world, to the Irish language? We have had recently, from a very eminent source, one of the plainest possible statements of the necessary interconnection between the Irish identity and the Irish language. The section on 'Identity' in J. J. Lee' *Ireland, 1912–1985* is, mostly, about language: '. . . it is hardly going too far to say that but for the loss of the language, there would be little discussion about identity in the Republic. With language, little else seems to be required. Without language, only the most unusual historical circumstances suffice to develop a sense of identity. Those unusual circumstances existed in Ireland for perhaps two centuries. As that phase, broadly characterised by the reality, or the memory, of an obtrusive imperial presence, of a national revival, of a struggle for independence, draws to a close, the importance of the lost language as a distinguishing mark becomes more rather than less evident. As circumstances normalise, only the husk of identity is left without the language.[49]

'There is, in present circumstances, no substitute for the language. However exhilarating gaelic hurling and football may be at their best, however exhuberant the beat of the *bodhrán*, however enriching "the great resurgence of traditional music", these are only details in the overall design of a distinctive culture. The language is now, for practical purposes, the design.'[50]

J. J. Lee considers some of the reasons usually given for the Irish abandoning of the language: 'modernisation', economic development, and parents preparing their children for emigration.[51] He feels that the universality of English offers Ireland an opportunity, and a threat – 'It has made the Irish bad linguists.'[52]

'Substituting English for Irish is not an "ordinary" language shift', says J. J. Lee shortly.[53] The reasons for the quotation marks around 'ordinary' are not clear in Lee's text, but I suspect that he had been talking to a sociolinguist. And I think it fair to say that, for sociolinguists, there is not a more 'ordinary' language shift in the world than this, the move by Irish people out of the Irish language into the English as our next contributor, Karen P. Corrigan, a sociolinguist, makes clear. All the features associated with 'ordinary', 'normal' or 'usual' language shift are present: that is to say, political annexation or colonization, social prestige associated with one language rather than another, migration.[54]

There is no more striking example in this series than of the way that a change of academic discipline necessitates a shift of perspective, and discourse. For the historian of a national identity the loss of the language must be central and significant. For the sociolinguist this language loss is sad, but one of many and is precisely the sort of phenomenon Corrigan is studying. What she has bravely done is look anew, and indeed in some of her detail, for the first time, at some of the assumptions usually made, by historians of Ireland and by historians of Irish migration, about the connections between this migration and this language shift. Again, there is a change of perspective. As soon as we look at Ireland and the world, from the migrant's point of view, or the would-be migrant's point of view, all changes. The acquiring of English becomes a conscious endeavour – for God's sake teach the children English. Even though that may not be in the best longer term interests of those Irish who stayed at home to forge a new national identity.

The U-shaped hypothesis

You may recall, from the General Introduction to this series, that I briefly outlined and suggested we make use of Everett S. Lee's 'Theory of migration'. From a very simple schema Lee elaborated a series of hypotheses, and laid these hypotheses out in such a form that they could be tested against data. As an example, I now want to look at one of Lee's hypotheses in detail.

Lee's model identifies plus factors and minus factors for the migrant, in the place of origin and in the destination. In his section on 'Characteristics of migrants', Lee points out that migration is selective, but the ways in which it is selective vary over time, and vary from place to place. Next Lee suggests that migrants responding primarily to *plus* factors at *destination* tend to be, in Lee's terms, 'positively selected'. 'For example, highly educated persons who are already comfortably situated frequently migrate because they receive better offers elsewhere. Professional and managerial people are also highly mobile, and often because migration means advancement.'[55]

Migrants responding primarily to *minus* factors at the place of *origin* tend to be 'negatively selected'.[56] 'On the whole . . . factors at origin operate most stringently against persons who have failed economically or socially. Though there are conditions in many places which push out the unorthodox and the highly creative, it is more likely to be the uneducated or the disturbed who are forced to migrate.'[57]

It follows that, taking all migrants together, selection tends to be bimodal. At any given place of origin there will be some migrants responding to plus factors at destination and who therefore tend to be 'positively selected'. There will be others responding to minus factors at the place of origin, who will tend to be 'negatively selected'. 'Therefore, if we plot characteristics of total migrants along a continuum ranging from poor to excellent, we often get a J-shaped or U-shaped curve. Such curves are found, for example, where the characteristic is either occupational class or education.'[58] The U-shape makes the point most graphically, of course, and you will get the distinctive U-shaped curve if your graph expresses, not total numbers, but percentages of certain groups, from most advantaged to disadvantaged. Lee's model suggests that it is people in the middle of the U who tend to stay behind.

I find all Lee's hypotheses interesting, but this one especially so. I like to keep an eye out for studies whose research method and database can adequately test the U-shaped hypothesis. The database ideally must be such that it embraces both wings of the U – a difficult base to create from historical material.[59]

In the first two volumes of *The Irish World Wide* I have contented myself with presenting enough material about Lee's plus and minus factors, whilst offering three chapters about professional elite migration. In Volume 1 we read McGurk on the military elite of the eighteenth century and before, and Hanlon on the graduate emigration of the late twentieth century. Now, Laurence M. Geary, Wellcome Research Fellow in the History of Medicine, at the Royal College of Surgeons, Dublin, offers us a nineteenth century case study. Geary's study of Irish doctors in Victoria, Australia, can be put alongside Forth's study of the Anglo-Irish – two very different Irish elites making very different 'contributions' to their new homeland.

One response to this sort of material is to lament the loss of 'Ireland's best'. But elites are typically involved in service industries – you cannot keep your elites unless you keep your masses. In the section of *Ireland, 1912–1985* which laments the tiny 'market for ideas' in independent Ireland, J. J. Lee notes that 'The history of most professions has been . . . comprehensively ignored by Irish historians . . .'[60]

Geary's chapter here can be regarded as 'contribution history' in action – and the gift of so many trained medical personnel must be regarded as quite a significant contribution to Australia's development. I see Geary's chapter as itself a contribution to the historical sociology of the Irish professions. There is now the material to begin thinking about the Irish dimension to the history of the professions. This history would have to be migration-centred, and, it has to be said, would involve the search for space – creative, intellectual, professional space. For example, a recent book of Irish legal history suggested that in the nineteenth century Irish lawyers, with unsatisfactory experiences of unreformed common law within Ireland, contributed to the codification of American and Australian law, thus moving those legal systems closer to the European concept of codified civil law.[61]

The search for work

I said earlier that I wanted, in this Introduction, to foreground the search for work, the movement of labour. For if we are not looking at a movement of labour, what are we looking at? I am now going to offer two ways, neither of them entirely satisfactory, of understanding Irish migration as a movement of labour. The chapter by our next contributor, Ellen Hazelkorn, then offers a third way.

There is one 'iconic' figure that I have perhaps not been able to do justice to in this series, the wandering Irish navvy. But the navvy is important, for more than 'iconic' reasons, as are all seasonal workers. A number of commentators have noticed the build up of a culture of migration within Ireland in the late eighteenth and early nineteenth centuries – simply put, an expectation that some members of a household would have to go away for lengthy periods to find work.[62]

Ireland's seasonal migrants thus have a place within the pattern described by Lucassen in *Migrant Labour in Europe, 1600–1900*. Lucassen begins his study of migrant labourers by observing how often, throughout western Europe, the image of birds of passage is used to describe wanderers. In Spain they spoke of *golondrina*, the passage of swallows, in Sweden of *Sommarfågel*, summer birds, in Friesland of *Sneeuwganzen*, snow geese, in Germany Wanderfögel.[63] Hints of 'Wild Geese'?

Then, in an unusually dynamic, and comparative, use of push/pull analysis, Lucassen identifies push areas and pull areas throughout Western Europe. In the early nineteenth century a major pull area within the British Isles is the area around London, the 'Home Counties', and East Anglia – this attracted workers from as far away as Connacht, a push area. Other pull areas are the Paris basin and Castile and its capital, Madrid; push areas are the Massif Central and mountainous Galicia.[64]

Lucassen expects these migratory patterns to emerge when there is a free labour market and two regions within reach of each other with wage and price differentials: one a potential pull area, with capitalistic projects or single crop cultivation with seasonal peaks; the other a potential push area, with many small farmers unable to guarantee an annual income by domestic industry. These conditions he finds throughout western Europe, but not, in his period, in eastern Europe – where there was then no free labour market.[65]

Another way to approach the movement of labour is to take a long-term and a world view, as Lydia Potts does in *The world labour market: a history of migration*. Thus, in this world market for labour power, the transatlantic slave trade of 1700–1850 is a forced migration of labour. The Chinese and Indian 'coolie' systems of 1830–1920 are, in effect, a new form of slavery. Potts declines to look intensively at emigration from Europe, because 'Emigration from the leading countries of origin was not caused by outside interference (colonialism/imperialism), but resulted from those countries' own economic and social developments. It was basically a question of exporting social problems.'[66] This analysis might surprise some oppression history analysts of the Irish migrations. It would surprise the thousands of Irish people transported to the Caribbean by Cromwell's administration in the 1650s.[67] It would certainly surprise 'the black Irish of Jamaica'.[68]

Yet there is a place for the Irish experience within Potts' tentative 'Elements of a theory of the world market for labour power': 'The methods by which foreign labour power is and has been incorporated into the world market for labour power – beginning with the enslavement of the Indians [native Americans] and Indian forced labour, through African slavery and coolieism, to colonial forced and migrant labour, and finally labour migration and the brain drain – may be regarded and described as stages in that market's development.' In other words, there is a continuum, from slave to wage worker, with various forms of unfree and half-free labour along the way.[69] This analysis would allow us to look at the various movements of labour out of Ireland over the centuries, assessing their place in that continuum.

Ellen Hazelkorn now offers a third model, a core/periphery model, still firmly committed to the idea of a world market for labour, but her theme is the search for work. Her chapter looks at the world, and at that market for labour, from within Ireland, 'We can't all live on a small island', and brings our account of the patterns of Irish migration up to the present day.

Mental distress

In the semi-autobiographical novel, *The Fate of O'Loughlin*, the Australian novelist Dudley McCarthy has a long section in which he and his protagonist contemplate their shared Irish heritage. That heritage is by no means unproblematic. Some of it comes in a form that recalls Ned Kelly's letter, but the narrator quarrels with himself, even as he speaks. 'These Irish Roman Catholics were bitter clannish people, secretive except among themselves. They had reason to be, of course. They'd been persecuted for their religion (and done their own share of that, too, I suppose), driven off their land, starved in the famines. They'd been rebels on the run in Ireland and chased right out of the country, fugitives from want and poverty and the law, or transported felons. . . . The Irish were not alone in that, of course. Irish or English or anything, convicts were for flogging and shooting, hanging and hunting . . .'[70]

'What I can't understand about the Irish, though, is that when all this is behind them and they're free in a good new country, their country as much as anyone else's, they can't forget. Or they don't want to forget.' He broods: 'It's funny how the Irish never seems to breed out. You're born with it, even people like me. Gradually, as you grow, you know it's there . . . this damned Irish thing that never breeds out. It's going to keep you apart all your life, even when you're laughing and talking and singing and drunk. It's going to creep up on you suddenly sometimes in the night so you lie stiff as a board in bed . . . drowning in darkness and despair. Or you get up a couple of hours before dawn and look hopelessly around you feeling that you're damned for ever.'[71]

A curious and uncomfortable part of the heritage, this Irish thing that never breeds out – and McCarthy never really helps us to understand what it might be. It does not seem to directly connect with the opening scene of the novel, in which O'Loughlin helps supervise the hanging of five men – headhunters punished by the colonial power. For it is O'Loughlin's fate to be a young patrol officer during the period when Australia administered New Guinea. That opening scene is a straightforward confrontation between the colonized and the colonizer.[72]

Liam Greenslade's chapter for this volume is a an extended meditation on a fact, or an observation. It is a kindly meditation, but it is an uncomfortable observation: that there is some sort of relationship between Irishness and schizophrenia. I do have to tell you that all the obvious questions have been asked, and none of the answers have been found satisfactory. One of Greenslade's sources, E. Fuller Torrey, has said: 'If we could fully explain the high prevalence of schizophrenia in Ireland, we could probably explain schizophrenia.'[73] Torrey also reports a similar relationship in the United States and in Canada, amongst Irish-born immigrants, and amongst their children.[74] Greenslade, below, reports fully on recent research in England and Wales, including his own.

My own focus would be to look at the migration experience itself, which – it is well known – can be alienating and depressing. But that, as Greenslade observes, is not a sufficient explanation.

Greenslade's response, as his title suggests, is to place the Irish experience firmly within the colonial relationship as analysed by Martinique-born Franz Fanon. I write now as someone who has himself used some aspects of Fanon's analysis, to understand certain aspects of the English/Irish relationship, and as someone who has a professional interest in Fanon's themes.[75] What is often forgotten is that Franz Fanon practised as a psychiatrist, and that his analysis draws on his experiences as a psychiatrist. He found that oppressed people internalise oppression, taking the oppressor's hatred into themselves.[76] The origins of his insights lie in his psychiatric observations. So that there is a simple logic in applying those psychiatric insights to a mental health problem.

Greenslade's chapter, however, will please no one. There will be historians who find this analysis of Ireland's history simplistic. Mental health specialists will find irritating this resurgence of the double-bind theory of schizophrenia. This is the sort of material that compensation and contribution history would ignore, as would the kind of oppression history that likes oppression to have no real consequences. Yet Greenslade's chapter is oppression theory at its most dynamic, allowing some of the sadder realities of Irish experience to be shared with others, in a fascinating and, maybe, a helpful way. It is a study of inner exile.

Irish studies

In a recent brief article, in Philadelphia's *Irish Edition*, Dennis Clark mapped out what is essentially a development programme for Irish-America. He acknowledged, as is right, the work of the Irish American Cultural Institute and the American Conference for Irish Studies. But he added some sad thoughts about the present state of Irish studies and Irish migration studies: 'There are simply no organized media for educating Irish-American children about their heritage . . . we lack the materials and system for cultural formation of our young . . . At the college and university level, there are many courses in Irish literature and history, but none of these have really good institutional support, and none have endowments or sufficient funds for adequate staff and resources to stabilize them and make them permanent and admired features of third-level educational life.'[77]

You might ponder now to what extent Clark's sad summary applies to matters within your own country, state or academic institution. Inevitably I know the situation better in Britain, where we now have the Institute of Irish Studies, at Liverpool, and the British Association for Irish Studies.

The key, as the British Association for Irish Studies knows, is curriculum development – a long process of negotiation, clarification and, yes, institutionalisation. Anyone who has been involved in that kind of negotiation will understand the reasons for some of my ground rules, in particular my insistence on methodological clarity. It behoves us, who do the thinking, the research and the writing, to not send our negotiators naked into that council chamber. On that note, Nessan Danaher, our next contributor, certainly has some tales to tell.

It is really invidious to name just one person, but I really do think that no one person has done more to encourage the development of Irish Studies within British schools than Nessan Danaher. The most obvious manifestation of his efforts is his series of annual Irish Studies Workshops at Soar Valley, Leicester – what is striking about the Workshops, and all of Danaher's efforts, is the way they are designed to appeal to and help the working teacher. Amongst the things I have learnt from Nessan Danaher is that a course does not have to have the word 'Irish' in its title in order to contain Irish material – you could, for example, use this series, *The Irish World Wide* to teach a splendid course in historical and social science methodology.

In a wide-ranging chapter, which will be of interest to educationalists around the world, Danaher, an educationalist, explores the history of education. His chapter, quite independently, throws light on themes that have already emerged in this series, and will be explored further in later volumes – for example a tension between religious and cultural or ethnic identities, and a tension within different approaches to 'Irish Studies'.

What Danaher's chapter brings home is that the problems raised by Dennis Clark are nothing new – that is sad, but it is also helpful. We can begin to understand something of the nature of the problem. It is the nature of this sort of project to raise questions about established heroes – everyone has feet of clay, and heroes are no exception. But our project also gives us new heroes – Danaher tells us of Francis Fahy who, in 1880s Southwark, in south London, quietly got on with the job of giving Irish children something of their history, something of their heritage, and some feeling of identity. Now, go and do likewise.

Patrick O'Sullivan
Bradford
June 1992

Notes

1. Everett S. Lee, A theory of migration, *Demography*, 3 (1), 1966, pp. 47–57. For a lengthier discussion see my General Introduction, p. xvii, in *Patterns of Migration*, Volume 1, *The Irish World Wide*, Leicester University Press 1992, and note 5, p. xxii where I suggest we also look at the 1885 and 1889 papers of Ravenstein. R. P. Shaw, *Migration theory and fact: a review and bibliography of current literature*, Bibliography series 5, Regional Science Research Institute, Philadelphia, 1975, is helpful, particularly on questions around land use and migration. I like Everett S. Lee's model for many reasons, notably because it is a simple way of connecting Irish material with studies of other migrating peoples, and also because it allows a place for 'cultural products'.
2. Gerda Lerner, *The majority finds its past: placing women in history*, Oxford University Press, Oxford & New York, 1979, pp. 145–8. For a lengthier discussion see my General Introduction, pp. xviii–xx.

3. On the historiography of the Irish in Australia I would also recommend, Patrick O'Farrell, Writing the history of Irish-Australia, in Oliver MacDonagh and W. F. Mandle, eds, *Ireland and Irish-Australia: studies in cultural and political history*, Croom Helm, London, 1986; and Bob Reece, Writing about the Irish in Australia, in John O'Brien and Pauric Travers, eds, *The Irish Emigrant Experience in Australia*, Poolbeg, Swords, 1991. O'Farrell's chapter offers the personal reflections of the author of *The Irish in Australia*, New South Wales University Press, Sydney, 1987, explaining (p. 222) why he 'went for broke' and wrote a book that advanced the proposition that the Irish were the key dynamic factor in Australian history. Reece respectfully suggests new post-O'Farrell directions for research. Both men have interesting things to say about the strength and limitations of 'contribution history'.

4. I recall the autobiography of Anthony Burgess, and his graphic account of being not quite absorbed into the Manchester Irish, following his father's second marriage in 1922 – to widowed Maggie Dwyer, née Byrne, landlady of *The Golden Eagle*: '. . . the Dwyers were successful immigrants from Dublin. There was no Irish brogue left in them, and their speech was pure Manchester. The troubles of their native country – the heavy fighting in the capital, with the blowingup of the Four Courts, which followed on the setting up of the Irish Free State in 1921 – aroused little interest. . . . The Manchester Dwyers were adoptive Mancunians, though very Catholic in the Irish manner. The greatest member of the family is George Patrick Dwyer, who was to become Bishop of Leeds and then Archbishop of Birmingham. . . . The economic substructure of the Dwyer passion for turning sons and daughters into bishops and mother superiors was a flourishing greengrocery and poultry business. There was, however, a George Dwyer who went to Australia and became a millionaire. He was involved in sexual irregularities scandalous in a great Catholic family.' Anthony Burgess. *Little Wilson and Big God*, Heinemann, London, 1987, pp. 21–22.

5. Friedrich Engels *The Condition of the Working Class in England*, translated and edited by W. O. Henderson and W. H. Chaloner, Basil Blackwell, Oxford, second edition 1971, p. 106. Henderson and Chaloner are helpful on the importance of Engels' work in what was to become revolutionary Marxist thought (pp. xii–xiv, xxxiii) but, carefully probing Engels' sources, are less than respectful about use of the 24 year old agitator's book as social history (p. xx). Engels' lines about the Irishman's pig are also quoted by John Archer Jackson, *The Irish in Britain*, Routledge & Kegan Paul, London, 1963, p. 52.

6. Jackson, p. 52.

7. Earlier in his book Engels has commented (p. 63) on the numbers of pig breeders in Manchester: 'There are large numbers of pigs, some of which are allowed to roam freely in the narrow streets, snuffling among the garbage heaps, while others are kept in little sties in the courts. In this area, as in most of the working-class districts of Manchester, pig breeders rent the courts and build the sties there. In nearly every court there are one or more little nooks in which pigs are kept. The inhabitants of the court throw all their garbage into these sties . . .'

Compare: 'For all its fine trappings, New York had a coarse underbelly. Vagrant pigs acted as scavengers, and garbage thrown in the street was dealt with in this manner. On August 20., 1847, the New York *Sun* complained of "pigs dangerous as hyenas." An angry citizen wrote a letter to the editor about pigs he met "lounging up Broadway." A "Quaker lady" was chargd by a pig, knocked down and bitten right on Fifth Avenue . . .' Stephen Birmingham, *Real Lace: America's Irish rich*, Hamish Hamilton, London, 1974, p. 17.

What we have here are questions around the interlocking of rural and urban life. Engels objects, reasonably we now might think, to the practice of housing pigs so near to human living quarters (p. 63), but, caught up in an English association of ideas, later (p. 106) goes further: 'The Irish have brought with them the habit of building pigsties immediately adjacent to their houses. If that is not possible, the Irishman allows the pig to share his own sleeping quarters. This new, abnormal method of rearing livestock in the large towns is entirely of Irish origin.'

I will simply recall the short story, by Graham Green, in which a boy's life is ruined by the death of his father: ' "Your father was walking along a street in Naples when a pig fell on him. A shocking accident. Apparently in the poorer quarters of Naples they keep pigs on their balconies. This one was on the fifth floor. It had grown too fat. The balcony broke. The pig fell on your father" Mr. Wordsworth left his desk rapidly and went to the window, turning his back on Jerome. He shook a little with emotion . . .' 'A shocking accident', in Graham Greene, *Collected Stories*, Bodley Head/Heinemann, London, 1972, pp. 111–2.

It is, of course, possible to think, and write, in quite other terms about the pig:

Sorrowful and pale brother,
sister, sacrificed
countless times,

your name – sullied,
dragged through the mud
for thousands of years –
be praised.

Most generous of all creatures,
you give yourself totally.

Noble pig . . .

Eva Bourke, *Litany for the pig*, Salmon, Galway, 1989, p. 35.

8. Theodore Koditschek, *Class formation and urban-industrial society: Bradford, 1750–1850*, Cambridge University Press, Cambridge, 1990, p. 395.
9. Angus Bethune Reach, *The Yorkshire Textile Districts in 1849*, edited by C. Aspin, Helmshore Local History Society, Blackburn, 1974, pp. 18–19. These lines are quoted by Koditschek, p. 395, but without the reference to 'low Irish haunts' – Koditschek is using this source to make a point about class perceptions and relationships, when another researcher might use it to track ethnic perceptions. Reach, a young Scotsman (the name is pronounced Re-ach) was one of the special correspondents sent out, in October 1849, by the *Morning Chronicle* to investigate the condition of the British working classes. Reach's observations on Manchester are quoted later in this volume, by Busteed, Hodgson and Kennedy. One of Reach's colleagues was the more famous Henry Mayhew, the *Morning Chronicle*'s London correspondent, who continued with his investigations after leaving the paper and who is quoted by Swift, later in this volume.
10. I must admit that, from bad temper, I have somewhat mellowed. Because I have met this pig so many times, and perhaps feel some sense of social obligation to her, when she appears now I tend to greet her warmly. Why, it's Engel's pig! I cry. For example, she turns up in Chapter 7 of this volume, Laurence Geary's study of Irish doctors.
11. Gertrude Himmelfarb, *The Idea of Poverty: England in the early industrial age*,

Faber & Faber, London, 1984, p. 371. Thomas Carlyle derides the Irishman's 'suit of tatters, the getting off and on of which is said to be a difficult operation, transacted only in festivals and the high tides of the calendar', in *Chartism*, *English and other critical essays*, Everyman, London, 1915, p. 182. Engels quotes the passage, *Condition of the Working Class*, p. 104, while warning (p. 105) against Carlyle's bias. For Kay, see Graham Davis, *The Irish in Britain, 1815–1914*, Gill & Macmillan, Dublin, 1991, pp. 56–60 – but all the chapter on 'Little Irelands', pp. 51–82, is relevant.

12. Davis, p. 58. On the novelists, Davis (p. 57) lists Benjamin Disraeli, Elizabeth Gaskell and Frances Trollope.
13. And note the full title of David Fitzpatrick, *Irish Emigration, 1801–1921*, The Economic and Social History Society of Ireland, Dublin, 1984.
14. David M. Emmons, *The Butte Irish: class and ethnicity in an American mining town, 1875–1925*, University of Illinois Press, Urbana and Chicago, 1989, p. 86, lists the names of some of those travellers: 'The list reads like a roster of Irish and Irish-American political and literary notables', and includes Michael Davitt, John Boyle O'Reilly, Douglas Hyde, James Larkin, James Connolly, Eamon de Valera.
15. Emmons, pp. 63–64. The importance of getting there first, or at least of being there at the beginning, 'a founding people', appears also in Oliver MacDonagh, The Irish in Australia: a general view, in Oliver MacDonagh and W. F. Mandle, *Ireland and Irish Australia*, p. 170.
16. Emmons, p. 15. Emmons chapter for *The Irish World Wide* is one of our strongest examples of the pattern whereby Irish family names are used as evidence – see the discussion of this theme in my General Introduction, p. xx.
17. Emmons, pp. xi–xii.
18. David Noel Doyle, 'The Irish as urban pioneers in the United States, 1850–1870', *Journal of American Ethnic History*, Fall 1990–Winter 1991, Volume 10, Numbers 1 & 2, pp. 36–59.
19. William V. Shannon, *The American Irish*, Macmillan, New York, 1963, p. 27.
20. There is a brief discussion in Doyle, p. 53, which focuses, naturally, on the urbanization of European and American countries in the nineteenth century. But, given the comparison that is often made between Ireland and the 'Third World' countries, we could look at Third World urbanization, particularly in Latin American countries. For the comparison, see, as an example, Carol Coulter, *Ireland: between the First and Third Worlds*, Attic Press, Dublin, 1990. For urbanization, see Alan Gilbert and Josef Gugler, *Cities, poverty, and development: urbanization in the Third World*, Oxford University Press, Oxford, revised 1983 edition, in particular Chapter 3.
21. Doyle, pp. 51, 53.
22. Doyle, pp. 44, 48.
23. Marjorie R. Fallows, in *Irish Americans: identity and assimilation*, Prentice-Hall, Englewood Cliffs, N. J., 1979, Chapter 5, especially pp. 65–73.
24. Fallows, p. 68.
25. Kerby A. Miller, *Emigrants and exiles: Ireland and the Irish exodus to North America*, Oxford University Press, Oxford and New York, 1985.
26. Some take it even further, and develop the thesis that migrant depression is a specifically Irish phenomenon – which is absurd. But there are questions around the mental health of the Irish, at home and abroad – questions which are explored in Chapter 9 below, by Liam Greenslade.
27. W. I. Thomas and F. Znaniecki, *The Polish Peasant in Europe and America*, 5 vols., Boston, Badger, 1918–20.

28. I think I can be forgiven for wondering if the ability to 'adjust' to modern city life is a good test of anyone's mental health.

29. C. Wright Mills, *The Sociological Imagination*, Penguin, Harmondsworth, p. 103, 1970 – original edition 1959.

30. 'This latter perception was dominant in the thinking of educators and social workers, for whom Americanization (the 'melting pot') was a powerful and then hardly questioned ideal. Again, this ambivalence about the ethnic family has remained a continuing theme, manifesting itself later on once again in the controversies about the black family.' Brigette and Peter L. Berger, *The war over the family: capturing the middle ground*, Penguin, Harmondsworth, 1984, p. 22.

31. Miller, *Emigrants and exiles*, pp. 556–568. Though, even here, whilst moved by Miller's writing I cannot help wondering, Is not the 'American wake' itself an example of traditional Irish peasant culture responding *creatively* to changed circumstances?

32. The section I have in mind runs from p. 427 to p. 492. It is called 'Section 3. Emigration as "Exile": Tradition and Expediency in Post-Famine Ireland' in the 'Contents' and that is the sub-chapter title on p. 427 – but the more helpful running title is 'The Interpretations of Post-Famine Emigration'.

33. For example, Kerby A. Miller, 'Emigration, Capitalism, and Ideology in post-Famine Ireland', in Richard Kearney, *Migrations: the Irish at home and abroad*, Wolfhound, Dublin, 1990; and 'Class, culture and immigrant group identity in the United States: the case of Irish-American ethnicity', in Virginia Yans-McLaughlin, *Immigration reconsidered: history, sociology, and politics*, Oxford University Press, Oxford & New York, 1990.

34. Miller, Emigration, capitalism and ideology, p. 102.

35. Miller, *Emigrants and Exiles*, p. 435. The use of the word 'schizophrenic' here I find poignant – in the light of Liam Greenslade's chapter, Chapter 9 below.

36. J. J. Lee, *Ireland, 1912–1985: politics and society*, Cambridge University Press, Cambridge, 1989, p. 522.

37. Michel Foucault, 'Truth and power', in *Power/Knowledge: selected interviews and other writings, 1972–1977*, Pantheon Books, New York, 1980, p. 118.

38. William V. Shannon, 'Starvation, struggle and success', Chapter 8 of Brian de Breffny, ed., *The Irish World: the history and cultural achievements of the Irish people*, Thames & Hudson, London, 1977, p. 2451.

39. Dennis Clark, *Erin's heirs*, The University Press of Kentucky, Lexington, 1991, on Identity, pp. 7–49, on the Friendly Sons, pp. 22–36. See also Clark's Research Note, pp. 196–201. Clark tackles (p. 34–5) the problems posed to the essentially conservative Society of the Friendly Sons by the present day conflicts in Northern Ireland. Such problems are not, of course, unique to Irish communities – see John Shotter and Kenneth J. Gergen, eds, *Texts of Identity*, Sage, London & Newbury Park, 1989, a useful collection, built around recent developments of the Berger and Luckman 'social construction' approach to systems of intelligibility. Of particular interest is the chapter by diaspora scholar Khachig Tölölyan, Narrative Culture and the Motivation of the Terrorist. Tölölyan quotes 'the most Armenian of William Butler Yeat's poems, "Easter 1916" ', and finally suggests that 'the true audience of Armenian terrorism remains the Armenian Diaspora, whose fraying culture is constituted to a remarkable degree by old stories . . .' (pp. 115, 117).

40. John Whyte, *Interpreting Northern Ireland*, Clarendon Press, Oxford, 1991, the discussion of Tajfel is on p. 97, the formal discussion runs from 97–100, but, as Whyte's index shows, the theme of 'identity' runs right through many of the ways of understanding the Northern Ireland conflicts.

41. Henri Tajfel and John Turner, 'An integrative theory of inter-group conflict', in William G. Austin and Stephen Worchel, *The social psychology of intergroup relations*, Wadsworth, Belmont, 1979, pp. 33–47.

42. T. C. Barnard, 'Crises of identity among Irish Protestants, 1641–1685', *Past and Present*, Number 127, pp. 39, 40, 80.

43. Stephen Gwynn. *Experiences of a Literary Man*, Thornton Butterworth, London, 1926, p. 11.

44. J. C. Beckett, *The Anglo-Irish Tradition*, Faber & Faber, London, 1976, pp, 10–11.

45. One of the few such appearances is that of the 'Irish Hunt Contingent', the 13th Battalion of the Imperial Yeomanry, in the Boer War. The Battalion, the social and political showpiece of the new volunteer army, included a company of Masters of the Hounds, two companies of Ulster Protestant Unionists (including the future Lord Craigavon), and a company of men about town raised by Lord Donaghmore. The commander, Lieutenant-Colonel Basil Spragge, led his men into a stupid engagement – after some 80 casualties, 530 men surrendered to Piet de Wet. There was merriment in Irish nationalist circles. See Thomas Pakenham, *The Boer War*, Weidenfeld & Nicolson, London, 1979, p. 436.

46. Henry Boylan, *A Dictionary of Irish biography*, Gill & MacMillan, Dublin, 1978, p. 4.

47. Patrick O'Farrell, Writing the history of Irish-Australia, p. 221.

48. Jenny Cheshire, ed., *English around the world sociolinguistic perspectives*, Cambridge University Press, Cambridge, 1991, has a very interesting section, three chapters, on 'Hiberno-English', Irish English – but more useful, Cheshire's collection, with its many case studies, is an excellent introduction to the ways that socio-linguists have studied and are studying, throughout the world, relationships between the English language and cultural and ethnic identities. See, for example, (p. 571 onwards) Winford's brief discussion of Le Page's 'acts of identity' model in the Caribbean – the model does not take concepts such as 'a language' or 'a community' as givens but explores the ways through which such concepts come into being through 'acts of identity' which people make within themselves and between each other.

Let me also recommend Robert McCrum, William Cran and Robert MacNeil, *The Story of English*, Faber and Faber/BBC Books, London, new and revised edition 1992 (the revised edition is a much better book than the original, rather untidy edition of 1986). As is often the case with the book of a television series, *The Story of English* brings much new information out of academic seclusion in an accessible form. In what might look like an unfortunate association of ideas the chapter on the world-wide influence of Irish English is called 'The loaded weapon' – but, in fact, in context this title looks like an unacknowledged reference to Dwight Bolinger, *Language, the loaded weapon: the use and abuse of language today*, Longman, London, 1980, a study of racist and sexist language. In their chapter title and in the chapter McCrum and his colleagues see Irish people as having a special power within the English language – p. 171: 'What is the source of our fascination with the Irish voice? Why *is* Irish literature in English so impressive?'

Richard W. Bailey, *Images of English: a cultural history of the language*, Cambridge University Press, Cambridge, 1992, is an attack on the more smug valuations of the English language.

49. J. J. Lee' *Ireland, 1912–1985*, p. 662. The section on 'Identity', pp. 658–687, is the last section in the book.

50. J. J. Lee *Ireland, 1912–1985* p. 666.

24   *Introduction*

51. J. J. Lee *Ireland, 1912–1985* pp. 664–5.
52. J. J. Lee *Ireland, 1912–1985* p. 667.
53. J. J. Lee *Ireland, 1912–1985* p. 666.
54. In my correspondence with Karen P. Corrigan, as we planned her chapter, we actually discussed which word she should use in her second paragraph – she settled on 'usually'.
55. Lee, 'Theory of Migration', p. 56. Look back, for example, to Hanlon, Graduate emigration, Chapter 9 of *Patterns of Migration*, Volume 1 of *The Irish World Wide*, Leicester University Press 1992.
56. Lee, 'Theory of migration', p. 56. Lee adds, however, that where minus factors are overwhelming for entire population groups there may be no selection at all. He gives as one of his examples Irish famine refugees, one of his two references to the Irish Famine. We will need, in *The Meaning of the Famine*, Volume 6 of *The Irish World Wide*, Leicester University Press: forthcoming, to look critically at Lee's assumptions.
57. Lee, 'Theory of migration', p. 56. Again, there are themes here that we will want to explore further, in *The Creative Migrant* and in *Irish Women and Irish Migration*, Volumes 3 and 4 of *The Irish World Wide*, Leicester University Press: forthcoming.
58. Lee, 'Theory of migration', p. 56. The rest of this 'Characterists of Migrants' section of Lee's little article is also relevant. But I will leave you to see for yourself how well his other hypotheses are testable by our data.
59. And not all that easy to create from present day statistical material – the methodological problem is one of 'disaggregation'. See, for example, the discussion in Frank P. Forsythe and Vani K. Borooah, 'The nature of migration between Northern Ireland and Great Britain: a preliminary analysis based on the Labour Force Surveys, 1968–88', *The Economic and Social Review*, Dublin, Volume 23, No. 2, January 1992, pp.105–127. Forsythe and Borooah do embrace both wings of the U – they conclude (p. 125) that their LFS data 'suggests that during periods of relative prosperity in the national economy [that is, the economy of Great Britain] the Northern Ireland migrant population is strongly *bi-modal* [emphasis added], involving the movement not only of those exhibiting relatively high human capital potential (in terms of age, qualifications and occupational grouping), but also those who possess little in the way of formal training and qualifications, and with limited or no prospects of employment in the local labour market.' They also find evidence of what Everett S. Lee would call 'counterstream', movement by migrants back into Northern Ireland.
60. J. J. Lee, *Ireland, 1912–1922*, p. 563, 638. This section of Lee's book, Intelligence, pp. 562–643, is a wide-ranging discussion of twentieth century Ireland's intellectual life, looking at economic theory, the social sciences, history (an interesting line on the 'traditional/revisionist' debate, pp. 587–597). 'The removal of potential threats to social stability through emigration removed the main likely incentive for enhanced self-knowledge. In that sense, emigration provides a key not only to the political stability but to the intellectual derivativeness of independent Ireland' (p. 609). 'In small countries, even more than in big ones, almost everything hinges on the contribution of individuals.' (p. 620).
61. John McEldowney and Paul O'Higgins, eds, *The Common Law Tradition; essays in Irish legal history*, Irish Academic Press, Dublin, 1990. See also Chapter 5 by Gordon Forth of this volume.
62. For example, Ruth-Ann Harris, Seasonal migration between Ireland and England prior to the Famine, *Occasional papers in rural history*, edited by Donald H. Akenson, Vol. VII, pp. 363–386; Brenda Collins, Proto-industrialization and

pre-Famine emigration, *Social History*, 7, 2 (1982) pp. 127–46; also relevant is Cormac Ó Gráda, Seasonal migration and post-Famine adjustment in the West of Ireland, *Studia Hibernica*, Vol. 13 (1973), pp. 48–76. Ruth-Ann Harris, p. 383, believes that 'the experience of temporary migration taught Irish people how to take their fate into their own hands . . .' – in preparation for the great Famine.

63. Jan Lucassen, *Migrant Labour in Europe, 1600–1900: the drift to the North Sea*, translated by Donald A. Bloch, Croom Helm, London, 1987, Foreword.

64. Lucassen, pp. 108–110, 113–116, 264–266. Lucassen cites that 'excellent article', Ó Gráda, 1973 , as one of his sources here – and comments (p. 309, *n* 82) how ignorant of each others work seem the historians of the various seasonal movements by Irish, Welsh, Scottish and northern English workers.

65. Lucassen, p. 131, 125–7.

66. Lydia Potts, *The world labour market: a history of migration*, translated by Terry Bond, Zed Books, London & New Jersey, 1990, p. 133.

67. Peter Berresford Ellis, *Hell or Connaught! the Cromwellian colonisation of Ireland, 1650–1660*, Hamish Hamilton, London, p. 1975, pp. 148–154. Berresford Ellis estimates (p. 154) that 'in the region of 50,000' Irish people were 'Barbadosed'.

68. Joseph J. Williams, S. J., *Whence the 'Black Irish' of Jamaica*, Lincoln Mac Veagh/Dial Press, New York, 1932.

69. Potts, p. 199.

70. Dudley McCarthy, *The Fate of O'Loughlin*, Macdonald General Books, London, 1980, p. 67.

71. McCarthy p. 68.

72. McCarthy p. 2.

73. E. Fuller Torrey, *Schizophrenia and civilization*, Jason Aronson, New York, 1980, p. 131.

74. Torrey, p. 125.

75. See, 'A literary difficulty in explaining Ireland: Tom Moore and Captain Rock, 1824', in Roger Swift and Sheridan Gilley, eds., *The Irish in Britain, 1815–1939*, Pinter Publishers, London, 1989, p. 271, *n*75, p. 273, *n*107. See also, 'The Irish Joke', my own contribution to *The creative migrant*, Volume 3 of *The Irish World Wide*, Leicester University Press: forthcoming.

76. See, for example, the case studies in 'Colonial War and mental disorders', in Franz Fanon, *The wretched of the Earth*, preface by Jean-Paul Sartre, translated by Constance Farrington, Penguin, Harmondsworth, 1967.

77. Dennis Clark, 'Irish America: change or decline', *Irish Edition*, April 1992. The origins of *Irish Edition*, Philadelphia's Irish newspaper, are recounted in Clark, *Erin's heirs*, pp. 112–113.

1 The myth and reality of Irish migrants in mid-nineteenth-century Manchester: a preliminary study

Mervyn A. Busteed, Robert I. Hodgson and Thomas F. Kennedy

The Irish community in the city of Manchester has long been one of the most significant in Great Britain, not only numerically but also because it was one of the first to be widely discussed by early observers of the nineteenth-century urban scene. For better or worse, their reactions set a tone, and provided stereotypical images, for much subsequent analysis of, and comment upon, the Irish in urban Britain down to recent times. Investigations of the past three decades or so, focusing upon urban areas of varying size, history and socio-economic structure, have considerably refined this original picture; yet, somewhat surprisingly, very little detailed study has appeared on the Irish in Manchester,[1] the city where most of the stereotypes originated or gained credence. As a first step towards correcting this deficiency, this chapter reviews the nature, impact and reliability of the evidence assembled by these early observers before examining data from the 1851 census enumerators' returns in order to take a more detailed look at the experience of one of the best known areas of Irish settlement in Manchester.

The Irish in Manchester up to 1851

The first clear indication of a sizable Irish population in Manchester came in the late eighteenth century, when their numbers were put at over 5,000[2] (perhaps 10 per cent of the town's population). Just over 30,000 Irish Catholics were said to be in Manchester *c.* 1832,[3] while the 1841 census, providing perhaps the first reasonably reliable figure, recorded 30,304 people who had been born in Ireland.[4] By 1851, 52,801 (or 13·1 per cent) of Manchester's population were recorded as Irish-born.[5] After London (108,548), Liverpool (83,813) and Glasgow (59,801), this number represented, in absolute terms, the largest Irish community in any British town or city. The primary cause of this, by far the largest decadal influx of Irish into nineteenth-century Manchester, is, of course, well known: the destruction by blight of the Irish potato crop, the basis of the rural diet, in the years 1846–8, resulted in many deaths from starvation and led to the large-scale migration of about one million people, many to the New World, others to the expanding industrial towns of mainland Britain, including those of north-west England. Less well known and understood are the factors accounting for the growth of a substantial Irish population in and around Manchester prior to the Famine.

Of fundamental importance in encouraging early migration from rural Ireland were the better employment opportunities, anticipated if not always encountered, in British agriculture. Towards the end of the eighteenth century, however, there is evidence that Irish harvesters were forsaking in increasing numbers their long tradition of seasonal migration in favour of permanent settlement in the manufacturing towns and villages of Lancashire.[6] After 1815 their numbers were boosted when some of the Irish vagrants who had fled the depression in Irish arable farming took advantage of a relaxation of the settlement laws in England. The lack of employment opportunities in Irish industry was also an encouragement to migration; the eventual removal of protective tariffs after the 1801 Act of Union exposed embryonic Irish enterprises to competition from the more sophisticated English industries, so that both woollen and cotton manufacturing experienced a rapid decline.[7] The availability of cheap passage on the new, regular steamships of the 1830s also facilitated larger-scale movement than previously.[8] It has also been suggested that some people, chiefly Protestants, may have fled Ireland for Britain after the tensions of the 1790s which led to the unsuccessful rising of 1798 and subsequent uncertainties.[9] A final element in the Irish population in the Manchester region before the Famine influx was provided by British army personnel, many of whom were recruited in Ireland and chose on retirement to settle in Britain.[10]

To most Irish migrants, then, it must have been, above all, opportunities for employment which they sought and which Manchester, as the world's first modern industrial centre and birthplace of what is universally referred to as the 'industrial revolution', was expected to provide in abundance. In 1728 Manchester was already being acclaimed as 'famous for its Wollens, Llinens and Cotton Manufactories, whereby its immensely enriched and many 100 poor families employed from several counties',[11] but it was only in the second half of the eighteenth century that the settlement really began to break away from its medieval core at the confluence of the rivers Irk and Irwell, where its development had long been overshadowed by that of neighbouring Salford. As a town where the control of the local lord of the manor was weak Manchester was free to develop and expand when economic opportunities were opened by the beginnings of mechanization of the long established textile industry in the late eighteenth century.[12] The growing output of cloth demanded more and more water for fulling, dyeing and bleaching, and here the rivers of the Manchester area were ideal. Meanwhile, coal to power the new steam-driven machinery was readily brought from surrounding mines via the rivers and canals, which could be

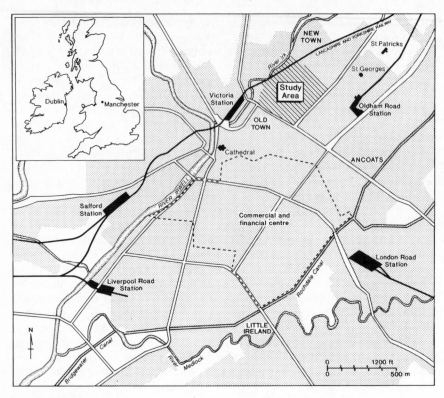

Figure 1.1 Location map

easily built thanks to low-lying relief. The construction of canals, roads, warehouses, foundries, mills and factories, residential areas and finally railways and their associated stations, goods yards and warehouses generated a demand for unskilled and semi-skilled labour which was drawn from a wide area, including Ireland. Existing Irish elements within the Manchester population were soon providing a social network of information on job prospects for family and friends back home.[13]

Thus even before the Famine of 1846–8, which is often viewed as the chief cause of nineteenth-century Irish movement to Britain, substantial Irish communities had formed in Manchester as in several other towns and cities. By *c.*1830, at the latest, they were to be found concentrated in three particular areas of Manchester (Fig. 1.1): the district on the south-western side of the urban area just off Oxford Road known, significantly, as 'Little Ireland'; the Ancoats district on the eastern side of town; and, finally, the district to the north-east of the medieval core known variously as 'New Town' or 'Irish Town', where a street called Irish Row had existed by 1794.[14] A part of the 'Irish Town' district, focusing upon a locality known as Angel Meadow, forms the case study area examined in the second part of this chapter. These, then, were the districts into which contemporary observers ventured in the 1830s and '40s, and from which they emerged with some of the earliest and most enduring images of the Irish in Britain: images which were to colour both popular and academic outlooks for many decades to come.

The symbolic significance of the Irish in Manchester

The earliest, and by far the most influential, commentator was Dr J. P. Kay (later Sir James Kay-Shuttleworth), who, as honorary physician to the dispensary of the Ardwick and Ancoats districts, had responsibility for most of the densely populated areas of Manchester. In 1832 he published a pamphlet describing conditions among the cotton employees of the city,[15] and while his concern was for the population in general the Irish came in for frequent adverse comment. Irish areas, he reported, were notable for their high levels of dirt, disease and overcrowding, the very worst of housing and sanitation; their 'habitations' were the 'most destitute'[16] for want of bedding, food, clothing and fuel, and not infrequently they were shared with pigs and other animals. Moreover, these conditions, he suggested, were in part at least the fault of the Irish themselves; indeed, by their very presence the members of this 'uncivilised race' had infected the native working classes with their fecklessness.[17] By their acceptance of lower than average wages, he contended, they soon dissipated 'wealth which they did not accumulate' and became in a few years 'burdens to a community whose morals and physical power they have depressed'.[18] Whilst conscious of the evils which he believed resulted from the immigration of the Irish, he did not think, however, that either the application of the English Poor Law or the passage of legislation would redress the situation; 'much less could the habits of the Irish be corrected by a parliamentary enactment: and to attempt the removal of their misery, by a constant supply of their wants, would be to offer direct encouragement to idleness, improvidence, and dissipation'.[19] It was a viewpoint which many contemporary believers in totally free trade and the uninhibited operation of the market, including the supply of labour, would have applied to any element in the population, but to Kay it seemed that the Irish had something inherent in their nature which made them a particularly destitute and threatening element in the population.

Kay's opinions of the Manchester Irish were soon being corroborated and embellished. Gaulter, in his study of the 1832 cholera outbreak in the town, judged the Irish 'remarkable for their love of tumult and violence and their filthy habits'.[20] Similarly uncomplimentary were the views of Manchester witnesses who, early in 1834, gave evidence to the commission investigating the condition of the Irish poor in Great Britain. Mr Thomas Armitt, Directing Overseer of the Township of Manchester, was in no doubt that when it came to deceiving the Poor Law system the Irish were pastmasters; their 'pilfering, making of smuggled whiskey, living by sleight of hand, and begging' accustomed them to such dishonesty.[21] In vast numbers the Irish exploited the public and private charities of the town. Their artfulness did not, apparently, end at death, since 'the township gives away coffins; and the Irish get more than others; we bury nearly all the Irish'.[22] Mr John Butler, Visiting Overseer of the Township of Manchester, similarly detected a 'kind of natural ingenuity to deceive, about them'.[23] Mr John Redman of Newtown, 'often called Irishtown',[24] believed the Irish had 'no sense of independence, shame or propriety'.[25] Peter Ewart, cotton spinner and manufacturer, maintained that they 'lowered the English by their association and their bad example, by accustoming them to inferior means of subsistence, including provisions, clothing and lodging',[26] while John Potter, cotton spinner, revealed that he had sacked all but two or three of his Irish weavers 'because they did their work in a slovenly and untidy manner, on account of their mutinous disposition. They seem to have an antipathy to mental exertion of any kind.'[27]

Ten years later, Léon Faucher, though much impressed by the impact on the Irish of a recent visit by the renowned temperance reformer, Father Matthew, recorded that for several years the Irish labourers had

> formed the most abject portion of the population, their dwellings were the most dirty and unhealthy, and their children the most neglected. It was in the cellars occupied by them that the illicit distillation of spirits was carried on. Misery of every description, fever, roguery, debauchery, and theft, were rife amongst them; their neighbourhood was the chosen retreat of vagabonds and criminals.[28]

Even more illuminating is the note which, appended to the 1844 translation of Faucher's work by 'a member of the Manchester Athenaeum' (he was, in fact, the barrister J. P. Culverwell), provides a window on what by then was probably common middle-class prejudice. For this commentator the Irish were not merely a people of congenitally flawed character who lowered the native working populace in every sense, they also, quite literally,

> inflicted a deadly blow upon the health and comfort of the working classes in Manchester. They congregate together, and form in the town a number of distinct communities, each of which is a nucleus for the generation and diffusion of fever and human miasma . . . Forethought, comfort, and economy, are things they have little or no idea of . . . Indolence of disposition, and instability of character, prevent them aspiring to a higher standard of living . . . Although not destitute of natural talent, they do not possess the secret of making it available for the purpose of life . . . their labour is of the lowest description; and but few Irish Catholics are to be found in the ranks of skilled labourers.[29]

One of the best known of all commentators who visited Manchester in the 1840s, one who did as much as Dr Kay to make the unfavourable view of the Irish character and circumstances common currency, was Friedrich Engels, scion of a middle-class family which owned cotton mills in the town. Though greatly shocked by what he found, and seeing them to some extent as the most unfortunate of all victims of the industrial system, he nonetheless followed Kay in both opinions and phraseology when attributing much of the blame for the situation to their own native character: 'these folk have grown up in a virtually uncivilized condition. They are uncouth, improvident and addicted to drink. They introduce their brutal behaviour into a section of English society by no means noted for civilized habits or moral principles.'[30] Noting that they were concentrated in the less skilled occupations, he suggested that the reason was that 'the dissolute, volatile and drunken Irish are unfitted for tasks which demand either a regular apprenticeship or that degree of skill which can only be secured by a long period of unremitting application to one's job'.[31] While he argued that the good-natured Irish might well temper the unduly stolid English character with some warmth, the immediate economic results of the influx, he was sure, was a lowering of wages and living standards for native workers.[32]

The result of these and similar such observations on Manchester, and their constant repetition,[33] were to give the stereotype of uniform Irish squalor in urban Britain an unconscionably long life and to infer that in large part the Irish themselves were to blame. They were seen as overwhelmingly urban, Catholic and concentrated in certain tracts of large cities; they exhibited high levels of poverty, lack of skills, poor housing conditions and crime, and displayed a propensity to drink and to live in squalor and to lower the wages and corrupt the behaviour and health of native workers. In short, both spatially and culturally they exhibited all the characteristics of what some twentieth-century writers have described as 'ghetto' communities.[34]

Reasons for adverse reactions to Irish migrants

It is possible that some of the lurid and sometimes almost voyeuristic pictures of the Irish were originally inspired by quite lofty motives. In the case of both Kay, an early pioneer of the sanitary reform movement in Britain, and Engels, with his overt concern for the conditions of the working classes in general, it is evident that an argument in favour of remedial action was, quite naturally, being built upon an examination of the worst cases, and these just happened to involve the Irish. Equally, both these influential commentators appear to have been afflicted by a crude form of racist thinking which was becoming widespread in Britain[35] and which all too readily transformed the association between the Irish and deprivation into cause and effect. Celtic peoples, including the Irish, were thought to lack the intelligence of the 'Anglo-Saxon' race (by which were meant the inhabitants of northern and western Europe) and physical characteristics, especially facial features, were the most obvious outward expression of this inadequacy. Engels, while rebuking Carlyle for his description of the Irish as an inferior race prone to all the vices, nevertheless came close to echoing his sentiment: 'one may depend upon seeing many Celtic faces, if ever one penetrates into a district which is particularly noted for its filth and decay. These faces are quite different from those of the Anglo-Saxon population and are easily recognisable.'[36] A racist view of the Irish was to persist well into the twentieth century, especially when the more militant elements of the Irish nationalist movement carried their campaigns to the British mainland through terrorism and assassination.

Cartoons periodically appeared depicting the Irish as subhuman creatures with coarse simian features.[37]

The anti-Irish feelings provoked by these early commentators on Manchester were also part of a wider reaction of fear among the established classes of Britain over what was happening in this crucible of the industrial revolution. The rapid growth of Manchester's economy, population and built-up area astounded observers; its social and political ethos – the absence of any of the traditional social controls such as gentry and clergy, the gross inadequacy of traditional policing arrangements and the nascent radicalism of its overwhelmingly proletarian population as shown in their support for early trade unions, parliamentary reform and the Peterloo riot of 1819 – simultaneously terrified and fascinated them.[38] No wonder the city had so many distinguished chroniclers. The great fear in establishment circles was of a whole series of Manchesters which would become seedbeds of the sort of violent political and social revolution seen not so long before in France in 1789 and erupting once more in parts of Europe in 1830 and 1848. The convergence of heavy Irish immigration with growing awareness of the living conditions in urban England and a dread of revolution was to lead some to conclude that the Irish were to blame for many of the social ills and political threats of early nineteenth-century England.[39]

Although these racial, political and social fears were strongly represented among the upper and middle classes, there was, too, working-class popular prejudice against the Irish. In some instances it may have been simple xenophobia of the sort which was directed against most newcomers, and was certainly expressed against the Welsh, Scots, Jews and non-European immigrants.[40] Some of it, however, had a much more materialistic basis in that many believed that the influx of the Irish depressed the wages of the working population at large. 'By coming over in such hordes,' Mr Redman explained in 1834 to the commission inquiring into the state of the Irish poor,

> the Irish take away the labour of the English by working at prices for which the English will not work; then the English are ultimately compelled to take the wages. I have no doubt that the Irish have lowered wages in all departments of common labour in Manchester.[41]

Whatever the objective facts may have been (and some modern writers have suggested that at worst the Irish presence may only have prevented wages rising),[42] what was important was the widespread belief, among the English working classes as well as among middle-class observers, that the Irish did, indeed, depress wages.

The influx of large numbers of Irish also helped to rekindle the flames of anti-Catholicism, which, since the Reformation, had smouldered in establishment circles and English popular nationalism. The first Orange lodge outside Ireland was formed in Manchester in 1798 and the first recorded anti-Irish riot in Britain was also in the town in 1807. In the wake of the Catholic Emancipation Act of 1829, which removed the last legal impediment to the entry of Catholics to the political life of the British state, there were further outbreaks of violence in 1830, 1834 and 1835,[43] but by this time Liverpool had also become a scene of conflict, together with Glasgow;[44] and there were to be conflicts and skirmishes on varying scales in some parts of Britain for the rest of the nineteenth century and into the early years of the twentieth. The 1851 general election was the last on the British mainland to be fought on the 'No Popery' ticket, but it left a legacy of popular prejudice which took deep root in certain areas. In Merseyside, and some parts of Lancashire and Clydeside, there evolved a form of popular Toryism which mobilized significant elements of the working-class electorate with an appeal to save Church, Crown and Constitution from the Roman threat.[45] Whatever their impact on local politics, they helped to perpetuate local prejudice and the adverse view of the Irish, and made many people only too ready to blame them for the ills of the country as a whole and certainly for the conditions in which the Irish in Britain lived.

Modifications of the stereotype

A careful reading of contemporary sources suggests that even from the outset there was a certain ambiguity in attitudes towards the Irish. Several observers admitted that the Irish were capable of hard work and might live in a 'tolerably comfortable way',[46] and that in some respects – as, for instance, with regard to personal virtues and domestic loyalties – they might even be judged superior to the English.[47] The Catholic Church came in for particular mention as playing a major supportive role in the community, supplying the faithful with a multiplicity of services, mutual aid societies and sick clubs, and organizing children's Sunday parades that were notable for their neatness and decency. Catholic clergy were especially energetic in caring for their flock in times of distress, as when epidemics occurred.[48] In addition, while social and spatial segregation was clearly demonstrable to some contemporary observers,[49] it was also acknowledged that the 'lowest classes' of English society did mix with the Irish, if only to be corrupted by them, and that the English working classes had to live alongside and compete with the uncivilized Irish.[50]

A more far-reaching reassessment of the traditional picture of the Irish in nineteenth-century Britain has come in recent times from scholarly investigations which, *inter alia*, have drawn upon the evidence of the census enumerators' returns – a source providing an abundance of statistical data not accessible to most contemporary observers. These show that at mid-century the Irish had a widespread distribution, with many still in rural areas, and with the urban Irish living in towns and cities of varying size and economic structure, ranging from London, Liverpool and Manchester to smaller centres such as Cardiff, Bristol, Bradford (and nearby towns), York, Lancaster, Stafford and Greenock.[51] Also under scrutiny has been the degree of spatial and social isolation experienced by the Irish. Finnegan, for instance, has argued that the Irish community in York conformed to the ghetto model in so far as they represented a group united by ethnic origin and low social class and living apart from their English social equivalents. Other studies, however, suggest that this was not typical: particular concentrations of Irish households, occupying contiguous streets, did occur but they were seldom 'wholly isolated from the host community . . . the Irish lived cheek by jowl beside the natives of the same social class'.[52] Moreover, some Irish families, especially those who had arrived before the Famine decade, had, with the passage of time, broadened their range of skills and showed signs of spatial and upward social mobility, with the result that, at mid-century, Irish people were to be found in most parts of towns and cities regardless of their size. A study of two very different urban areas, Liverpool and Lancaster, concluded that the Irish were 'both clustered and dispersed throughout the urban structure', depending on their social class, and that 'white-collar migrants tended to live in front streets with non-Irish from the same class, whereas the unskilled lived in adjacent back streets and courts'.[53]

What, then, can be learned of the spatial and social segregation, physical conditions (housing and sanitation) and economic resources of the Manchester Irish at mid-century? While the following discussion, based on an examination of the 1851 census enumerators' returns[54] and other contemporary sources, does not provide the kind of survey that would enable us to achieve a thoroughgoing and more balanced view of the entire Irish population of the city, it is intended as a first contribution towards that end.

The study area

The area lies to the north-east of central Manchester, at the heart of one of three areas long known as districts of heavy Irish working-class settlement. In 1851 it was part of the Anglican parish of St George's which stood on the south-eastern side of Rochdale Road (Fig. 1.1). The boundaries of the study area, those to the north and east in particular, were chosen to provide a manageable area for study within the resources of time and labour available rather than because they were thought to represent any significant socio-cultural divide. Nevertheless, with Miller Street as its southern and Gould Street as its northern boundary, this is the area of quite sharply rising ground 'between the River Irk and St George's Road' (later called Rochdale Road; Fig. 1.2) which Engels gloomily described in the mid-1840s as 'composed of single rows of houses and groups of streets which might be small villages, lying on bare clayey soil which does not produce even a blade of grass' and with the houses

> in a disgraceful state because they are never repaired. They are filthy and beneath them are to be found damp, dirty cellar dwellings; the unpaved alleys lack any form of drainage . . . The lanes in this district are so filthy that it is only in very dry weather that one can reach it without sinking ankle deep at every step.[55]

To Angus Reach in 1847 this was 'the lowest, most filthy, and most wicked locality in Manchester . . . inhabited by prostitutes, their bullies, thieves, cadgers, vagrants, tramps, and, in the very worst sties of filth and darkness, by those unhappy wretches, the "low Irish" '.[56] In fact, as will be demonstrated in due course, this was not quite an area of uniform squalor.

The district was one of the first to be built on when the economy of

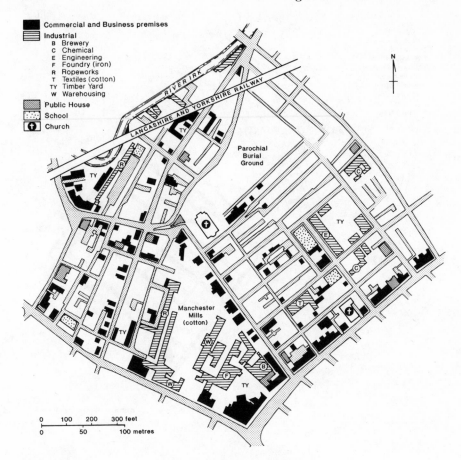

Commercial and Business premises
Industrial
  B Brewery
  C Chemical
  E Engineering
  F Foundry (iron)
  R Ropeworks
  T Textiles (cotton)
  TY Timber Yard
  W Warehousing
Public House
School
Church

Figure 1.2   The study area: non-residential land use, 1851

Manchester took off in the late eighteenth century, as a series of detailed maps makes clear. In the middle of the eighteenth century the district was still markedly rural, with a few buildings along a small part of 'Mill Gate' and at the junction of what later became Rochdale Road and Miller Street (Fig. 1.3). However, Laurent's map[57] suggests that by 1793 the transformation was well under way. Much of the western part had now been built upon, including the front of Miller Street, the west side of Angel Street, large areas south of Ashley Lane and part of Dyche Street. St Michael's Anglican church (located at the centre of the study area) had been built in 1789 to serve an area of hitherto quite large, fashionable houses. Green's more authoritative map of 1794[58] reveals how the new growth consisted of a dense mixture of both residential and industrial buildings, especially between Miller Street and Angel Street, and names such as 'Factory Lane' and 'Factory Court' appear. By 1820[59] development had engulfed all of Angel Street and was impinging on land to the north. Banks's map[60] of

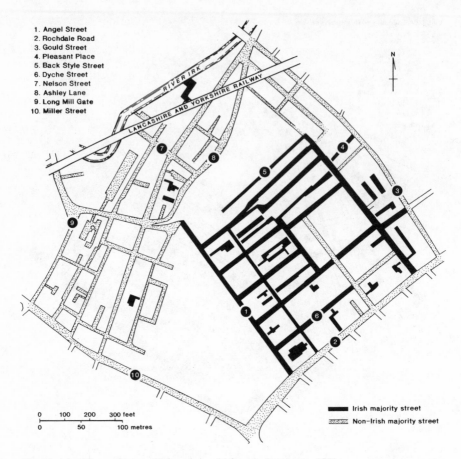

1. Angel Street
2. Rochdale Road
3. Gould Street
4. Pleasant Place
5. Back Style Street
6. Dyche Street
7. Nelson Street
8. Ashley Lane
9. Long Mill Gate
10. Miller Street

RIVER IRK

LANCASHIRE AND YORKSHIRE RAILWAY

N

0   100   200   300 feet
0   50   100 metres

■■■ Irish majority street
▨▨ Non-Irish majority street

Figure 1.3   The study area: Irish and non-Irish majority streets, 1851

1831 shows almost the entire study area covered by a dense complex of both residential and industrial buildings, a picture borne out by Davies's map of 1833,[61] which also shows for the first time the significantly named St Patrick's 'Catholic Chapel' on Livesey Street, just north-east of the study area (Fig. 1.1). The final element in the pattern was the construction of the Manchester & Leeds (later Lancashire & Yorkshire) railway line, which crossed the north-western side of the study area (Fig. 1.2). This involved the demolition of some houses and helped fix the character of the district as an inherent part of newly industrialized, working-class Manchester.

The Irish in the study area

Most scholars who have used the census enumerators' returns to study them have simply defined the Irish as those adults recorded as born in Ireland, or in some cases only those heads of households so described. For the purposes of this study, however, 'Irish' is defined as all those born in Ireland regardless of age or status within the household. In addition, also considered 'Irish' are those persons who were born outside Ireland but were returned as having two Irish-born parents. This may seem to inflate the totals, but it seems illogical to omit such people or to class them as anything other than Irish. Excluded from the category, therefore, are offspring born outside Ireland if only one parent is recorded as Irish-born, though in the case of a widow or widower, of course, the deceased spouse might for all we know have been Irish – as indeed might a parent who was omitted from the census owing to the remarriage of the recorded spouse. Finally, given the likely existence of a significant Irish population in and around the study area for at least a quarter and possibly half a century prior to 1851, it is highly likely that at least some of those returned in the census as born outside Ireland were of Irish descent and still considered themselves Irish. Unfortunately, there is no totally reliable way of tracing second and third-generation Irish through the census. Strictly, therefore, this is a study of Irish migrants and their offspring in the study area, and any efforts to generalize beyond the definitional and spatial boundaries set out above are beset with pitfalls.

The study area covers just over 12 ha (thirty acres), of which 50 per cent was in non-residential land use in 1851 (Fig. 1.2; Table 1.1). A total of 10,995 people can be identified from the enumerators' returns as living there when the census was taken on 31 March. Of these, 4,645 (42·2 per cent) had been born in Ireland, but when the definition outlined above is applied – as it will be henceforth – the figure rises by 807 (those persons born outside Ireland to two Irish parents) to give 5,452 people who may be classified as Irish (50·4 per cent of the total population). There were eighty-nine 'streets' (including courts, roads, lanes, etc.) mentioned in the census which are traceable on the Ordnance Survey's 5 ft plans (i.e. maps at a scale of 1:1056). Of these, forty-one had an Irish majority. Only six streets were entirely devoid of Irish people, only two were exclusively Irish. Irish people appear to have lived at a greater density than the non-Irish. Thus, while the census enumerators identified 1,209 inhabited houses or separate dwellings in the area, only 458 (37·9 per cent) of these were Irish houses in the sense that they were either exclusively Irish or contained a majority of Irish residents. Using this definition, only fifteen streets had no Irish houses.

The spatial patterns of these Irish and non-Irish streets are most intriguing. Streets with a simple majority of Irish people (Fig. 1.3) were strikingly concentrated in the eastern half of the study area. Indeed, of the forty-one streets with an Irish majority, thirty-seven were found within the area bounded by Angel Street, part of Rochdale Road, Gould Street, Pleasant Place, the bottom part of Gould Street and Back Style Street. Moreover, 4,595, or 82·9 per cent, of the Irish in the study area were to be found within the sub-district bounded by these streets. Inside it only four streets did not have a majority of Irish people.

The streets can also be categorized by their *degree* of 'Irishness' (Fig. 1.4). The most strongly Irish streets were to be found in the core of the sub-

Table 1.1 Land use in the study area, 1851

Premises		No.
Inhabited houses		1,209
Commercial and business premises		200
Industrial premises:		11
Brewery	1	
Chemical works	2	
Engineering works	1	
Iron foundry	1	
Ropeworks	2	
Textile mills (cotton)	2	
Warehouse complexes	2	
Public houses		12
Churches		2
Schools		4
Public baths and wash houses		1

Sources. J. Adshead, Twenty-four illustrated maps of the township of Manchester divided into municipal wards, 1851; at a scale of 80 inches to one mile, sheet 13; I. Slater, *General and Classified Directory and Street Register of Manchester and Salford and their vicinities*, 1851; Ordnance Survey plans, 1850–1, at a scale of 60 inches to one mile, sheets 18, 23, 24. Where these sources differed, Adshead's map was taken as the more reliable for land use, and the Ordnance Survey preferred for location, area and place names. See G. H. Dymond, 'A Comparative Study of the Large-scale Mapping of mid-Victorian Manchester', B.A. dissertation, Department of Geography, University of Manchester, 1991, pp. 56–62.

district already outlined. Here there was a concentration of streets where over 75 per cent of the residents were Irish. Outside this area there was a notable clustering of those streets which were non-Irish. They were to be found in the western and north-western part of the study area (Fig. 1.3), bounded by Angel Street, Miller Street, Long Millgate, the river Irk and the lower end of Gould Street (otherwise known as Back Irk Street). Within this western sub-district only four streets had an Irish majority, all four were small and only one was over 75 per cent Irish. Otherwise the sub-district was in many ways the mirror image of the eastern one, with fewer than 10 per cent of the residents Irish and fifteen streets having no Irish houses at all.

The overall impression, therefore, is of an Irish population segregated from the non-Irish population of the area. This view is only partially modified when one looks at the household level. Of the Irish population, 4,882 (88·0 per cent) were to be found in Irish houses, implying a significant degree of segregation at the household level, too. This is to some extent confirmed when one sees that the corresponding figure for the non-Irish population was almost as high, namely 4,636 (85·2 per cent). The impression that the non-Irish may have been slightly less segregated is borne out when one looks at the number of Irish and non-Irish in the different types of streets. Of the total Irish in the area, 4,682 (84·4 per cent) were

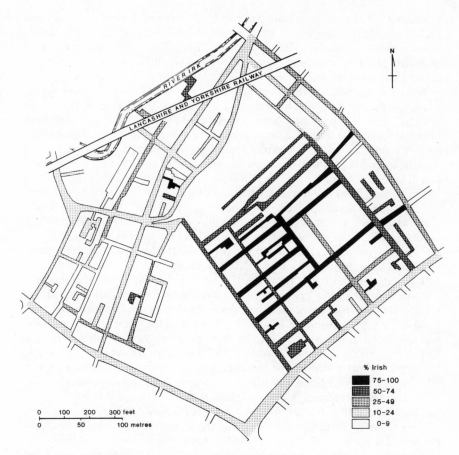

Figure 1.4   The study area: proportion of Irish residents by street, 1851

living in Irish streets, whilst, of the non-Irish, 3,696 (67·8 per cent) were in non-Irish streets. The implication is that the non-Irish were rather more dispersed than the Irish. How is this pattern of residential segregation to be explained?

Explanation and interpretation

Swift has recently argued that the pattern of Irish settlement in urban Britain was largely determined by economic considerations,[62] while Pooley, more expansively, has concluded that in Liverpool the Irish were to be found in the poorest accommodation, in the courts and alleys, and in the highest densities because they had the fewest economic resources and could buy themselves into the accommodation market only at this level.[63] Certainly the Irish, most of whom had a background in peasant subsistence agriculture, and little previous experience of urban life, were generally less literate than their English social equivalents and, overall, had little in the way of skills to offer the labour market. It has been well said that, of all migrants in nineteenth-century urban Britain, the Irish were least equipped to succeed in the new environment.[64]

To what extent, therefore, can patterns of residential differentiation found in the study area be attributed to economic factors? Is there any evidence that the Irish had fewer economic resources than the non-Irish population? This would certainly seem to have been the case, judging from contemporary observers' descriptions of the sparseness of living quarters in Irish households.[65] There is additional persuasive, circumstantial evidence. It will be noted from Figs 1.3–4 that Irish people were underrepresented on streets which 'fronted' the district, i.e. along Long Millgate, Miller Street and Rochdale Road. Indeed, all three were less than 25 per cent Irish. Coincidentally, all three were dominated by commercial and business premises. The implication is that the Irish were poorly represented in the retail and wholesale trades and were presumably therefore excluded from the small (but important) business class in the area. In this regard the situation in Angel Street is particularly illuminating. The street was the only one in the heart of the Irish–dominated sub–district which had a significant number of business premises, the remainder being overwhelmingly residential. In a population of 848, 412 (48·6 per cent) were Irish-born, and when account is taken of persons born elsewhere to two Irish parents are added the Irish proportion rises to 56·5 per cent. However, when one examines the place of birth of the fifteen proprietors of business premises who appear in both *Slater's* (trade) *Directory* of 1851 and the census of the same year for this street, only two are recorded as Irish (Table 1.2).

This leads to the conclusion that the Irish migrants may well have been overrepresented in the less skilled and therefore less remunerative occupations. To test this, the occupational structure of Dyche Street (Fig. 1.3) was examined. The street resembles Angel Street in that the Irish-born were a minority here: of the 438 residents, 215 (48·9 per cent) were Irish-born, but when offspring of Irish parents are allowed for there was an Irish majority of 56·6 per cent. Of those Irish who were economically active, seventy-one (42·0 per cent) were found to be in the least skilled jobs as opposed to thirty-nine (32·5 per cent) of the non-Irish (Table 1.3), a small but possibly significant difference in terms of resources which came into the households concerned. However, there is also a little evidence to show that not all the working Irish were mere employees in poorly paid jobs. Four were returned as employers of more than two people; three of them were located in Back Style Street, and all of them are designated as 'master' of their trade, i.e. they had completed their apprenticeship training and could engage employees. Their level of economic well–being may not have been very high, of course: two of them were cotton weavers, who, if still using hand looms, would probably have been little in demand by this date; while the remaining two were in tailoring and shoemaking, both 'sweated trades' of low status and pay.[66]

How then did the Irish cope with the situation of possibly having fewer

Table 1.2   Place of birth of Angel Street shopkeepers and traders as recorded in Slater's 1851 directory and the 1851 census enumerators' returns

Street no.	Name and occupation	Place of birth (if stated in census)
3	Wilkinson, Wm., brace manufacturer	Manchester
11	Lightowler, Wm., butcher	?
17	Isaacs, Isaac, quill dresser	Liverpool
23	Brooks, Maria, butcher	?
25	Morton, Wm., marine stone dealer	Manchester
33	Balmer, Elizabeth, beer retailer	?
35	Jenkins, Henry, frame maker	Liverpool
37	Metcalf, Maria, baker	Manchester
41	Johnson, Roger, beer retailer	?
49	Bentley, Susan, [?] dealer	Manchester
51	Chaloner, Thomas, shopkeeper	Manchester
53	Roberts, Thomas, shopkeeper	Salop
61 and 63	Roberts, Wm., shopkeeper	Manchester
69 and 71	Cliff, John, pawnbroker	Blackley
4	Connor, Andrew, hardwareman	?
6	Bianchi, John, 'Weaver's Arms'	Italy
8	Sunglie?, James, shopkeeper	Ireland
20	Wild, Charles, marine store dealer	Salford
32	Ogden, Abraham, umbrella maker	?
46	Hayes, Michael, shopkeeper	Ireland
54	Whalley, James, beer retailer	Manchester
58	Lawton, Mary, nail maker	?

economic resources to buy their way into the housing market? In comparison with the non-Irish population one might expect them to have occupied the worst housing, but this is not borne out by the evidence. Housing conditions were appalling throughout the study area, as Kay first in 1832 and a stream of visitors thereafter made plain, but it was in the western, non-Irish–dominated sub-district of older housing that they continued to deteriorate most rapidly over the next two decades. Here were the worst back-to-back houses, built in the first major surge of industrialization 'with a total neglect of order'[67] and without yards or privies, and streets that were without proper paving and sewers, so that they became filled with mud, water, offal and ordure. The problems created by the juxtaposition of industrial premises and residential housing close to the Irk were probably at their worst in the cellar in Nelson Street (Fig. 1.3). Gaulter's case notes on the 1832 cholera outbreak recorded that:

> the Irk runs under the cellar, [and there is a] door in a passage close to the river up which foetor is intolerable from a cess-poll and a skinner's yard, [the] street [is] open, but a sewer runs down it above ground. A bone boiler has his place a little higher up, and it was said that he had just thrown several tons of rotten salmon into the river.[68]

A similarly depressing situation existed in 1853 when, following a further cholera outbreak in 1849, the Manchester and Salford Sanitary Association

Table 1.3 Recorded number of Irish and non-Irish residents in least skilled occupations, Dyche Street, 1851

Occupation	Irish	Non-Irish
Labourer	39	17
Rag sorter	5	–
Servant	4	2
Hawker	6	4
Wool sorter	2	–
Cotton picker	2	1
Charwoman	2	1
Silk picker	1	–
Brick maker	1	1
Porter	1	2
Office/errand boy	1	1
Old clothes dealer	1	–
Washerwoman	1	1
Rag gatherer	1	1
Factory worker	1	3
Rag dealer	1	–
Paper sorter	1	–
Warehouse worker	1	2
Laundress	–	1
Banker's[?] boy	–	1
Beggar	–	1
Total	71	39
(As percentage of economically active in all occupations)	(42)	(32·5)

Source. 1851 census enumerators' returns.

was reporting that 'the proximity of the River Irk, which in summer weather sends forth a most pestilential effluvia, adds considerably to the prospect of contagion'.[69]

Meanwhile, in the Irish-dominated eastern sub-district near St George's Road (Rochdale Road), where in the mid-1840s Engels reported the houses to be 'built closer together' in a maze of 'lanes, blind alleys . . . back passages and courts', recent reform measures aimed at paving and draining the streets had had their greatest and most beneficial impact.[70] This could still leave the conditions of individual houses in a bad state, however, thanks to the negligence of landlords such as the owner of houses in Back Simpson Street who admitted in 1853 that his overcrowded, damp and dirty properties had not cost him 'one penny in 30 years'.[71] The whole district suffered from severe drainage problems because it had been built on impermeable, clayey ground[72] – a not uncommon occurrence in Manchester, as in other towns where working-class housing had to be built near early industries which needed a river valley location. Adding to the difficulty of natural water flow were the inadequacies of a primitive sewage system which particularly afflicted houses in streets built at right angles to the slope, as many were in the south-west–north-east-trending streets in the predominantly Irish sub-district, but which had their most devastating impact at the foot of the slope near the river Irk where non-Irish streets and households dominated. It was in this area that in addition to 'excrementious matters from some sewers' the river Irk, 'black with the refuse of Dye-works erected on its banks, receives . . . the drainage from the gas-works, and filth of the most pernicious character from the bone-works, tanneries, size manufactures and . . . tripe houses'.[73] No human habitations suffered more from the inadequacies of drainage and waste disposal than cellar dwellings which were frequently flooded and where 'influenza, cholera or fever prevailed in succession the year round'.[74] However, in contradiction of Reach's view that in 1847 most were inhabited by Irish people,[75] the 1851 census suggests that eighteen of twenty-five identified cellars had a non-Irish majority and that 62·5 per cent of all cellar dwellers were non-Irish. Clearly, living in poor housing was far from an exclusively Irish phenomenon. Yet the 1851 census and other contemporary sources do seem to indicate a significant difference between the Irish and non-Irish with regard to the way in which the space within individual houses was used, and, in some instances at least, this must have reflected differences in economic resources, or led to differences in the quality of life enjoyed by the inhabitants.

Multiple occupation

For the area as a whole there were, on average, 10·0 persons per Irish house, compared with only 6·5 persons per non-Irish house. This higher density among the Irish did not apparently result from a lack of suitable housing. The census recorded uninhabited houses in several Irish-dominated streets; for example, there were four in Angel Street alone if one includes the case where the cellar was occupied but the rest of the house was empty. Among contemporary observers, Kohl offered perhaps the most succinct explanation for multiple occupation in the older working-class areas:

> Whole rows of houses stand empty, while the remainder are overcrowded; for in some places the inmates have been expelled by the owners for non-payment of rent, while in others they have voluntarily given up their dwellings in order to live cheaper, by sharing that of another family.[76]

Three years later the *Manchester Guardian* noted the same tendency in the course of its observations on the impact of living conditions on the diffusion of infectious diseases:

> The population of the district [St George's] is, to a great extent, composed of the lower of the Irish, who live and lodge together in great numbers in the same house. In one part of the district, called Angel Meadow, it is not uncommon to find 20 or 30 persons living in one house, when there is not accommodation for one-third of that number.[77]

In examining the evidence on multiple occupation a distinction must be drawn between, on the one hand, lodging houses, which are often identifiable in the census from the description of the head of household as 'lodging house keeper', and, on the other, domestic dwellings which were in multiple occupation by a number of family groups and had no or very few lodgers. In the case of lodging houses, beds seem to have been rented at times on a nightly basis and, like the houses themselves, were in multiple occupation. Reach described the situation in one of the lodging houses in Angel Meadow thus: 'The landlady stoutly asserted that only two were to sleep in each bed, but as to the sexes she was "noways particular – lodgers was lodgers, whether they was men or women".' He also found that, in addition, it was quite common to make 'shake-downs' on the floor with 'threes and fours crammed into the same bed'. As for the cost, 'the nominal price of fourpence for a bed I found to be everywhere the same'.[78] Such arrangements clearly persisted in some of the houses inspected by the Sanitary Association in 1853, and the phraseology used implies that they were lodging houses. Thus at 9 Ludgate Street the inspectors reported 'a cellar about 14 feet square: 5 bedsteads, with Beds or a substitute for Beds, no ventilation, the Heat quite oppressive and conclude all the beds are full at night'. In Simpson Street they found 'from 5 to 13 cellars, very close and confined, from 8 to 10 sleeping lodgers', while in Baptist Street 'Cellar under No. 20 very dirty, no ventilation, no water, average 12 persons sleeping nightly. Cellar No. 22 nearly as above. Cellar under 24, 2 apartments, in other respects the same, tenants all very poor & ignorant Irish.' In a court in New Mount Street, they reported, 'the want of sufficient accommodation complained of, the houses in this locality are filled at night with casual lodgers and tenants, beyond all conception'.[79]

It is also evident that there could be a mixture of both family groups and lodgers in the same house. Thus in a small court in Simpson Street the Sanitary Association visitors found three small two-room houses, '2 families in each house, besides casual sleepers'.[80] However, this arrangement appears to have been unusual among both the Irish and the non-Irish element of the population of the study area. Among the Irish, 85 per cent were related to someone else in the house in which they lived, while the figure for the non-Irish was 87·1 per cent. The strength of family ties is also borne out by the evidence of one over-zealous enumerator who, contrary to the expectations of his brief, provided extra details on living arrangements at No. 6 Nelson Street. 'No. 1 Room' was said to contain a widow and her son, while 'No. 2 Room' held a family of three. All five had been born in Ireland. The clear implication is that efforts were being made to preserve some sort of privacy and family life, even under adverse conditions, thus bearing out the tributes paid by even hostile contemporary commentators to the chastity of the Irish and the strength of their family loyalties, and lending weight to Lees's assertion that, if anything, migration and the urban experience made family life all the more important.[81]

Family ties and kinship links were undoubtedly important as a means of informing migrants and would-be migrants about the 'Irishness', cheapness and availability of accommodation in particular streets of this and other working-class residential areas of Manchester, though the transmission of information must also have been greatly helped by the close proximity of housing areas to the main entry points for new arrivals (major roads and, later, railways) and industrial sites where work, or news of work, was to be had. Family links were demonstrably strong at times of famine. Thus in the winter of 1847 a report on a meeting to discuss the establishment of a soup kitchen in order to relieve distress among the lower classes, whose numbers had been swollen by 'a very large influx of Irish families within the last few weeks', cited the particular case of 'a poor Irishman, who had been here some time, living in a cellar' and 'had his son, son's wife, and four children come over from Ireland and place themselves upon the old man'.[82] Not all migration routes were as straightforward as this, however. At 13 Ludgate Hill (parallel to and west of Gould Street), the 1851 census records, there lived two Irish-born parents with daughters aged eleven and thirteen years who had been born in Bolton, and a son of four years born in Liverpool.

We can but speculate on the elements of choice and chance, the ties of ethnicity and friendship, which lay behind these moves. What seems clear is that, once established, patterns of segregation of working-class Irish from the working-class English became in some measure self-perpetuating in that existing groups attracted others by their kinship links and ethnic compatibility. And it has also been convincingly argued that such separation was maintained, partly by the anti-Catholic sentiments of the host population discussed above and partly by the institutions which became established in the Irish-dominated areas. The Catholic Church and parish-based schools, charitable organizations, fraternities and social clubs[83] provided the infrastructure to support a life which meant that for many migrants the Irish community was *part* of such working-class areas but not quite *of* them. Later involvement in the Irish nationalist movement could also help sustain this sense of apartness.

Conclusions

Recent attempts to move away from the purely negative images of Irish communities in nineteenth-century Britain highlight the need for a full and detailed investigation of Manchester's Irish community so that the appropriateness of these images to the place which gave them birth can be properly assessed. Meanwhile it might be thought that, by taking a case study of an area of Manchester long regarded as one of the worst for Irish settlement, the foregoing discussion has merely afforded an opportunity to reinforce rather than repudiate the stereotypical images. Significantly, this is only partly borne out by the study. The evidence so far examined would suggest that in several important ways our understanding of the nineteenth-century Irish migrant in British urban areas is incomplete or defective and certainly in need of revision in this, the city where myths about the Irish were nurtured.

It has been shown that in an overwhelmingly working-class area of poor housing there was a marked spatial concentration of Irish, with some streets notable for their high levels of residential segregation. Moreover, it was discovered that the Irish lived at higher density than the non-Irish, implying both the pressures of economic necessity and the drawing power of a combination of family ties and common ethnic compatability, reinforced by the institutions of church-based community life. The strength of the economic factor in forcing the Irish into both lodging houses and multi-family occupation of private houses is borne out by their relative poverty as shown in their undue concentration in occupations low in status, skill and remuneration. The skills they did have were more relevant to intensive peasant agriculture or the domestic stage of cotton weaving, neither of which were thriving in urban Manchester. Yet it was discovered that, even here, in what was long known as the heart of working-class Manchester, there could be no such thing as total segregation and uniform poverty. Very few streets were exclusively Irish or non-Irish, and obviously the two groups mixed and encountered people of other backgrounds as they moved about in the conduct of their daily lives. Equally, although the Irish were overwhelmingly poor and less skilled, even in this area there are traces of a few who were employers, if on a very modest scale.

The condition of the housing in the study area was undoubtedly poor, but here the traditional picture if anything requires even more rethinking. It is certainly not true to suggest that the worst housing was invariably inhabited by the Irish. In Manchester, as was often the case in other towns affected by early industrialization, the first working-class housing to be built was almost always the poorest in terms of site, materials, layout and facilities; in the study area this was to be found down by the railway and up to the line of Ashley Lane and the western side of Angel Street. With the sole exception of the last-mentioned street, this part of the district was almost devoid of Irish people (Figs. 1.3–4). This is not, of course, to deny the appalling conditions under which some of the Irish lived in some of the Irish-dominated streets. The huge influx of the 1840s must have placed an extraordinary strain on the fabric of houses and available space, on the infrastructure of drainage, sewage relief and refuse disposal. But, here again, it has also been shown from the evidence of the census that, contrary to accepted opinion, the cellar dwellings, possibly the worst afflicted of all accommodation, were markedly non-Irish in their population. Finally, the area as a whole was badly hit by the cholera outbreaks of 1832 and 1849; households were afflicted regardless of the origin of the inhabitants, showing once again that deprivation was shared, even if residential space was not.

There is ample scope for further work on the Irish in Manchester and a particular need to give yet further consideration to the statistical data contained in the census enumerators' returns, because, as this study has shown, such information can be at variance with the evidence found in the accounts of contemporary observers. The allure of statistical certainty should not, however, lead us to conclude that it was the census that was always right. Only by checking it for errors, omissions and internal consistencies and drawing comparisons with all other types of contemporary evidence can a thorough and worthwhile reappraisal of the Irish in nineteenth-century Manchester be achieved. For the case study area, and for other districts, fuller analyses are under way to discover household and occupation structures, marital linkages, age and gender, and the economic roles of Irish and non-Irish people. Furthermore the investigation needs to be extended in both spatial and temporal terms. For purposes of comparison, it will be interesting to use the 1841 census to reconstruct the situation prior to the Famine influx. Equally, it will be instructive to examine such aspects as settlement patterns, socio-economic structure, household arrangements and living conditions after 1851, to discover what features persisted or were eroded as the Irish settled into their new environment.

Such questions can be answered only by detailed study, because, as the present work has, hopefully, shown, while an individual city or portion of it many conform to the broad pattern established by work elsewhere, there are always specifically local factors which must be taken into account. Already the more detailed studies have shown that the degree to which, and the processes whereby, the Irish adapted to life in the industrial urban areas of the nineteenth century were more varied and complex than a reading of the comments of the early observers and the myths to which, often unwittingly, they contributed would lead one to suppose.

Notes

1. Of the limited work which has been done, two of the most useful pieces are I. Boocock, 'Angel Meadow,' 1980, and S. Farebrothers, 'Charter Street: a Working Class Community in Victorian Manchester', 1982, B. A. dissertations, Manchester Polytechnic. There is also useful mention of the Irish in J. H. Smith, 'Ten acres of Deansgate in 1851', *Transactions, Lancashire and Cheshire Antiquarian Society*, 80, 1979, p. 49.
2. A. Redford, *Labour Migration in England, 1800–50*, 1924; revised edition, Manchester University Press, 1964, p. 134.
3. *Report on the State of the Irish Poor in Great Britain*, 1836, Appendix III, p. 43 in *Royal Commission on the Condition of the Poorer Classes in Ireland*, Appendix G.
4. Census of England and Wales, 1841.
5. Census of England and Wales, 1851. The figure is for Manchester with Salford.
6. Redford, *Labour Migration*, pp. 133–4, 141–9; R. Lawton, 'Irish immigration to England and Wales in the mid-nineteenth century', *Irish Geography*, 4, 1959–63, p. 40; H. J. Johnson, 'Harvest migration from nineteenth-century Ireland', *Transactions, Institute of British Geographers*, 41, 1967, pp. 97–112.
7. T. P. O'Neill, 'A bad year in the Liberties', in E. Gillespie, ed., *The Liberties of Dublin: its History, People and Future*, third edition, O'Brien Press, Dublin, 1977; Redford, *Labour migration*, pp. 152–3.
8. R. Swift, *The Irish in Britain, 1815–1914: Perspectives and Sources*, Historical Association, London, 1990, p. 7.
9. F. Neal, 'Manchester origins of the English Orange Order', *Manchester Region History Review*, 4, 2, 1990–91, p. 13.
10. Swift, *The Irish in Britain*, p. 7.
11 S. & N. Buck, South-west prospect of Manchester in the Country Palatine of Lancaster . . . as delineated and sculpted, 1728.
12. N. J. Frangopoulo, *Tradition in Action: the Historical Evolution of the Greater Manchester County*, E. P. Publishing, Wakefield, 1977, p. 17.
13. *Report on the Irish Poor*, Appendix III, pp. 36–7, evidence of Mr Taylor.
14. W. Green, A plan of Manchester and Salford, 1794.
15. J. P. Kay, *The Moral and Physical Conditions of the Working Classes employed in the*

Cotton Manufacture in Manchester, London, 1833, reprinted E. J. Morten, Didsbury, Manchester 1969.

16. Kay, *The Moral and Physical Conditions*, p. 32.
17. Kay, *The Moral and Physical Conditions*, p. 27.
18. Kay, *The Moral and Physical Conditions*, p. 83.
19. Kay, *The Moral and Physical Conditions*, p. 83.
20. H. Gaulter, *The Origins and Progress of the Malignant Cholera in Manchester considered chiefly in their Bearing on the Contagiousness and the Secondary Causes of the Disease*, London, 1833, p. 36.
21. *Report on the Irish Poor*, Appendix III, p. 522.
22. *Report on the Irish Poor*, p. 522.
23. *Report on the Irish Poor*, p. 522.
24. *Report on the Irish Poor*, p. 522.
25. *Report on the Irish Poor*, p. 523.
26. *Report on the Irish Poor*, p. 537.
27. *Report on the Irish Poor*, p. 538.
28. L. Faucher, *Manchester in 1844: its Present Condition and Future Prospects*, trans. from the French, with copious notes appended, by a member of the Manchester Athenaeum, Simpkin Marshall, London, 1844; reprinted Cass, London, 1969, p. 28.
29. Faucher, *Manchester in 1844*, pp. 28–9, n. 10.
30. F. Engels *The Condition of the Working Class in England*, 1845; trans. W. O. Henderson and W. H. Chaloner, Blackwell, Oxford, 1971, p. 105.
31. Engels, *The Condition of the Working Class*, p. 107.
32. Engels, *The Condition of the Working Class*, p. 107.
33. As in J. M. Werly, 'The Irish in Manchester, 1832–49', *Irish Historical Studies*, XVIII, 1973, pp. 345–58. For the most part this consists of a collection of the more adverse comments on the Irish as given to official boards of inquiry into social and economic distress in the 1830s and '40s, with very little critical evaluation. See also E. and R. Frow, *Essays on the Irish in Manchester*, Working Class Movement Library, Salford, 1991.
34. See, for instance, Werly, 'The Irish in Manchester', for his acceptance of the concept. A more sceptical appraisal of the ghetto model has recently been proffered in P. Laxton, 'Neighbourhoods or Ghettoes? Some Considerations of the Irish Districts of English Cities in the Nineteenth Century' paper, delivered to a joint meeting of the British Academy and the Royal Academy, London, September 1986. We should like to express our sincere thanks to Paul Laxton for allowing us to read this unpublished paper.
35. S. Gilley, 'The Irish', *History Today*, 35 June 1985, p. 19
36. Engels, *The Condition of the Working Class*, p. 105.
37. L. P. Curtis, *Anglo-Saxons and Celts: a Study of anti-Irish Prejudice in Victorian England*, David & Charles, Newton Abbot, 1971.
38. A. Briggs, *Victorian Cities*, chapter 3, Pelican, Harmondsworth, 1968; G. S. Messinger, *Manchester in the Victorian Age: the Half-known City*, Manchester University Press, Manchester, 1985.
39. G. Davis, 'Little Irelands', in R. Swift, and S. Gilley, eds., *The Irish in Britain, 1815–1939*, Pinter, London, 1989, p. 104.
40. F. Neal, 'English–Irish conflict in the north-west of England: economics, racism, anti-Catholicism or xenophobia?', *North West Labour History*, 16, 1991–2, pp. 14–25.
41. *Report on the Irish Poor*, p. 523.
42. J. Williamson, 'The impact of the Irish on British labour markets during the

industrial revolution', in Swift and Gilley, *The Irish in Britain*, Neal, 'English–Irish conflict,' p. 24.

43. Neal, 'English–Irish conflict', p. 19.
44. F. Neal, *Sectarian Violence: the Liverpool Experience, 1819–1914: an Aspect of Anglo-Irish History*, Manchester University Press, Manchester, 1988; T. Gallagher. *Glasgow: the Uneasy Peace: Religious Tensions in Modern Scotland*, Manchester University Press, Manchester,1987.
45. N. Kirk, 'Ethnicity, class and popular Toryism, 1850–1870', in K. Lunn, ed., *Hosts, Immigrants and Minorities: Historical Responses to Newcomers in British Society, 1870–1914*, Dawson, London, 1980, pp. 64–106.
46. Kay, *The Moral and Physical Condition*, pp. 27, 44; *Report on the Irish Poor*, p. 536
47. Faucher, *Manchester in 1844*, p. 31.
48. Faucher, *Manchester in 1844*, p. 33.
49. Faucher, *Manchester in 1844*, p. 28, n. 10.
50. *Report on the Irish Poor*, p. 523, evidence of Mr Redman.
51. L. H. Lees, *Exiles of Erin: Irish Migrants in Victorian London*, Manchester University Press, Manchester, 1979; 'Patterns of lower-class life: Irish slum communities in nineteenth-century London', in S. Thernstrom, and R. Sennett, eds. *Nineteenth Century Cities: Essays in the new Urban History*, Yale University Press, 1969; C. G. Pooley, 'The residential segregation of migrant communities in mid-Victorian Liverpool', *Transactions, Institute of British Geographers*, new series, 2, 1977, pp. 364–82; 'Segregation or integration? The residential experience of the Irish in mid-Victorian Britain', in R. Swift and S. Gilley, eds., *The Irish in Britain, 1815–1939*, Pinter, London, 1989; C. R. Lewis 'The Irish in Cardiff in the mid-nineteenth century', *Cambria*, 7, 1980, pp. 13–41; D. Large, 'The Irish in Bristol in 1851: a census enumeration', in R. Swift and S. Gilley, (eds.), *The Irish in the Victorian City*, Croom Helm, London, 1985; C. Richardson, 'Irish settlement in mid-nineteenth century Bradford', *Yorkshire Bulletin of Economic and Social Research*, 20, 1, 1968, pp. 40–57; F. Finnegan, 'The Irish in York', in Swift and Gilley, *The Irish in the Victorian City*; J. Herson, 'Irish migration and settlement in Victorian England: a small–town perspective', in Swift and Gilley, *The Irish in Britain*; R. D. Lobban, 'The Irish community in Greenock in the nineteenth century', *Irish Geography*, 6, 3, 1971, pp. 270–81. Of course, a great deal depends upon the size and socio–economic structure of the urban area under investigation, the dimensions, rate and timing of the Irish influx, the spatial scale of the study and the quality and manipulation of the data (Pooley, 'Segregation or intergration?').
52. Swift, *The Irish in Britain*, p. 14.
53. Pooley, 'Segregation or intergration?', p. 75.
54. In common with other localities in England and Wales, the census enumerators' returns for the study area contain sins of both omission and commission. In overcoming interpretative difficulties we have been guided by the warnings and advice of other researchers, which are most usefully, though not exhaustively, covered in: E. Higgs, *Making Sense of the Census: the Manuscript Returns for England and Wales, 1801–1901*, HSMO, London, 1989; R. Lawton, ed., *The Census and the Social Structure*, Frank Cass, London, 1978; E. A. Wrigley, ed., *Nineteenth-century Society*, Cambridge University Press, Cambridge, 1972. A particular difficulty exists for some parts of Manchester in 1851: surviving enumerators' returns are damaged and incomplete so that a full reconstruction of the population throughout the city at mid–century may never be possible. The relative unimportance of this problem in the study area was one reason for choosing it.

55. Engels, *The Condition of the Working Class*, p. 65.
56. A. B. Reach, *Manchester and the Textile Districts in 1849*, Helmshore Local History Society edition, ed. C. Aspin, Helmshore, Lancs., 1972, p. 53.
57. C. Laurent (engineer), A topographical plan of the towns of Manchester and Salford and the adjacent parts, 1793.
58. W. Green, A plan of Manchester and Salford, 1794.
59. W. Johnson, Plan of the parish of Manchester in the county of Lancaster in the years 1818 and 1819, 1820.
60. Bancks and Company's plan of Manchester and Salford with their environs, etc., 1831 (1832).
61. B. R. Davies, [Plan of] Manchester, Salford and their environs, in E. Baines, *History of the County Palatine and Duchy of Lancaster*, Manchester, 1836.
62. Swift, *The Irish in Britain*, p. 14.
63. Pooley, 'The residential segregation', pp. 377–8.
64. Swift, *The Irish in Britain*, p. 16.
65. Engels, *The Condition of the Working Class*, p. 106.
66. Swift *The Irish in Britain*, p. 16.
67. Kay, *The Moral and Physical Conditions*, p. 41. Housing in a nearby and very similar area is discussed in J. Roberts, *Working-class Housing in Nineteenth-century Manchester: the Example of John Street, Irk Town, 1826–1936*, Richardson, Manchester, 1979.
68. Gaulter, *The Origins and Progress*, p. 185.
69. *Report of the Manchester and Salford Sanitary Association*, 1853, p. 10.
70. The first by-laws to regulate building in Manchester had been passed in 1792 but no really effective legislation was obtained until the new borough council (set up in 1838) obtained a Police Act in 1844 and activated its clauses to take responsibility for the whitewashing, cleansing and purifying of dwellings in May 1847. See *Manchester Guardian*, 5 May 1847, p. 5.
71. *Report of Sanitary Association*, p. 3. For evidence that such neglect by landlords was by no means confined to Angel Meadow or, indeed, Manchester see Davies, 'Little Irelands', pp. 110–11.
72. A feature noted in both Engels, *The Condition of the Working Class*, p. 67, and J. Leigh and N. E. R. Gardiner, *History of the Cholera in Manchester in 1849*, Simpkin Marshall, London, 1850, p. 6.
73. Kay, *The Moral and Physical Conditions*, p. 38.
74. *Report of the Royal Commission on the Sanitary Conditions of large towns and populous Districts, 1844: Lancashire*, pp. 4–5, evidence of Howard and Leigh.
75. Reach, *Manchester and the Textile Districts*, p. 55.
76. J. G. Kohl, *England and Wales*,1844, reprinted, Cass, London, 1968.
77. *Manchester Guardian*, 6 February 1847, p. 9.
78. Reach, *Manchester and the Textile Districts*, pp. 54–5.
79. *Report of Sanitary Association*, p. 3 (for all quotations).
80. Report *of Sanitary Association*, p. 3.
81. Lees, *Exiles of Erin*, p. 377.
82. *Manchester Guardian*, 27 March 1847, p. 7.
83. W. J. Lowe, 'The Lancashire Irish and the Catholic Church, 1846–71', *Irish Historical Studies*, 20, 1976, pp. 129–55; 'Social agencies among the Irish in Lancashire during the mid-nineteenth century', *Saothar*, 3, 1977, pp. 15–20; S. Gilley, 'The Irish', *History Today*, 35, June 1985, pp. 17–23.

Acknowledgements

We should like to express our sincere thanks to the staff of Chetham's Library and of the Local Studies section of Manchester Central Reference Library for help in tracing, and making available, contemporary sources; the Manchester and Lancashire Family History Society for assistance with the 1851 census enumerators' returns; Manchester Geographical Society and the Research Committee of the Department of Geography, University of Manchester, for financial assistance; Graeme Bowden, of the Department of Geography, for drawing and photographing our maps; and Gill Callander, Isobel Chaplain and Edward Hall for help with the survey of contemporary sources. The authors alone are responsible for the views and opinions expressed in the text.

2 The historiography of the Irish in nineteenth-century Britain

Roger Swift

Irish migration to Britain has a long and chequered history, yet only in recent years have historians examined the subject in depth, through a growing body of local, regional and national studies which have supplemented the earlier pioneering research of J. E. Handley and J. A. Jackson.[1] These studies have focused largely on the Irish emigrant experience during the nineteenth century, when Irish settlement in Britain was most pronounced. The Irish people who migrated to Britain during that period were by no means a homogenous group, for their ranks contained both rich and poor, skilled and unskilled, Catholics and Protestants (and unbelievers), nationalists and loyalists, and men and women from a variety of distinctive provincial cultures in Ireland. But poor Irish Catholics were the largest and most visible group of emigrants, and their experience has bulked large in the story of Irish migration to Britain. Yet the whole process of mass migration from Ireland and the development of Irish communities in nineteenth-century Britain continues to excite debate among historians. Indeed, three broad issues have dominated the debate thus far. First, why did Irish people leave their homeland and settle in particular districts in Britain, and what were the consequences of this process? Second, how were these migrants variously perceived by British society and how far did attitudes towards them change during the period? Third, how far did Irish emigrants integrate into British society or preserve a distinctive identity? This chapter presents a short summary of the historical debate on these and related issues. It examines, with reference to the historiography of the Irish in Britain between 1815 and 1914, the causes of Irish emigration, the patterns of Irish settlement and employment, and the extent to which Irish communities were segregated from, or assimilated into British society, with particular reference to the themes of Irish poverty, nationalism, ethnicity and religion during the period. It also indicates that, although much has been achieved in extending our understanding of the Irish immigrant experience during the nineteenth century, several fruitful areas for further historical research remain.

The causes of Irish emigration

As Roy Foster has observed, 'emigration is the great fact of Irish social history from the early nineteenth century'.[2] Indeed, between 1820 and 1910 nearly 5 million people left Ireland for destinations in Britain, Canada, Australia, New Zealand and, overwhelmingly, the United States.

The causes of this mass migration have been a source of debate among historians. The classic explanation, voiced by many British commentators during the early nineteenth century, held that Irish emigration was largely the consequence of a mounting Irish economic crisis of Malthusian dimensions, whereby a backward Irish agrarian economy was increasingly unable to support a population which had virtually doubled between 1760 and 1840. Central to this argument was the belief that Ireland's agrarian problems were the product of feudal tenurial arrangements and an abundance of discontented labourers and petty farmers, who kept wages low and prevented Irish landlords and British investors from modernizing agriculture and making it profitable. Similarly, overpopulation was regarded as the product of Catholic improvidence. Hence poverty, dearth and distress, which reached their peak during the Great Famine of 1845–52, were regarded as the inevitable outcome of Ireland's backwardness and mass emigration was seen as the only escape from famine and destitution.[3]

This classic Malthusian explanation appears increasingly inadequate in the light of recent research. Indeed, Joel Mokyr and Cormac Ó Grada have shed doubt on the whole concept of a mounting Irish economic crisis.[4] In general, whilst most historians, and particularly Irish historians, accept that British domination and exploitation lay at the root of Ireland's problems, they have also conceded that the complex causes of Irish emigration are perhaps best explained in terms of the interaction of a combination of social and economic factors, some 'pushing' the Irish out of Ireland, others 'pulling' them from Ireland. Indeed, David Fitzpatrick has observed that both 'push' and 'pull' factors were prerequisite to every individual decision to leave Ireland, and has suggested that 'push' factors tended to predominate in the pre-Famine period, and 'pull' factors thereafter.[5] Clearly, several major strains put pressure on Ireland's economy during the early nineteenth century, pushing some sectors of society towards emigration. They included the growth of population, the decline of domestic industry, the commercialization of agriculture, and proto–industrialization. In particular, the commercialization of agriculture witnessed the increasing conversion of arable land to pasture, which led to growing dependence on the potato for subsistence; an increased rate of farm consolidation, which added many smallholders and cotters to the ranks of landless labourers; and the application of new farming techniques, which made agriculture less labour-intensive and contributed to underemployment and unemployment. Poverty thus became the norm for many smallholders and labourers, largely Roman Catholic and some Gaelic-speaking, particularly in the rural west of Ireland. For many, faced with growing inequality between rich and poor, and prospects of a marginal existence at home, there was little choice other than to emigrate.

Yet emigration was also an increasingly rational alternative to the hardships of life in Ireland. Indeed, Kerby Miller has denoted a gradual change in Irish attitudes towards emigration during the pre-Famine period, whereby many Irish men and women – particularly, although not exclusively, Ulster Protestants and Anglo-Catholics – were increasingly defining their goals in materialist terms by seeking 'independence' and upward social mobility in the free-market economy. For these people, life in Ireland offered limited rewards, whereas emigration to Britain or the British colonies provided them with the opportunity to achieve levels of expectation and standards of living which were far higher than the actual possibilities at home.[6]

Moreover, emigration was also an increasingly feasible proposition during the pre-Famine period, thanks largely to the improvement in communications between Ireland and Britain. In 1818 the first steam packet (the *Rob Roy*) linked Belfast with Glasgow, and by the 1820s ferry services were also operating from Dublin and Cork, principally to Liverpool, the main port for transatlantic embarkation. Moreover, competition between ferry companies reduced fares on the Irish Sea routes to as low as 10*d*, in steerage, and 3*d*, on deck. Thus, for those who could afford it, emigration was becoming relatively easy and inexpensive. However, there were also a range of 'pull' factors which made emigration from Ireland an increasingly attractive proposition. Much Irish emigration resulted from the prospect of relatively well paid employment in the industrialized economies of Britain and America. Moreover, for many, America had the additional attraction of being free from British rule. The material aspirations of many Irish people were further fuelled by letters from Irish emigrants and by the incessant propaganda of shipping companies. Of course, in the last resort, as Colin Holmes has observed, people had to want to leave Ireland, and during the pre-Famine period it was essentially those with 'the resources, the will, the information and the aspiration to move' who sought a new life abroad.[7]

In many respects the Great Famine served as a catalyst for these processes. First, although estimates vary, Ireland's net population loss between 1845 and 1852 was about 2·5 million, of whom 1 million died and 1·5 million emigrated, and Miller has argued that these losses, coupled with the evictions which accompanied the Famine, greatly accelerated the commercialization of Irish agriculture, the decline of domestic industry and the anglicization of Irish culture.[8] Second, there is some evidence that the Famine confirmed the already established patterns of pre-Famine emigration. The highest rates of emigration, as before, were from south Ulster, east Connaught and mid-Leinster: here people were poor but not absolutely destitute, since they had the means to leave. In contrast, emigration was least in areas where pauperism was either negligible, in which case people lacked the incentive to leave, or very high, in which case they lacked the means. The abject poor and destitute, many of whom resided in west Connaught and Munster, died during the Famine. Third, the Famine affected different groups in different ways, and this was reflected in the nature of the Famine exodus. Miller and Fitzpatrick have suggested, for example, that it was the largely Catholic, Gaelic-speaking smallholders, cottiers and labourers, dependent as they were on the potato crop, who were driven from Ireland by the imminent threat of destitution or death. Of these, the majority fled to America, via Liverpool, bitterly blaming Britain for what they perceived to be *forced* exile, as epitomised in the verse 'Poor Pat *must* emigrate'. In contrast, the poorest emigrants, who could not afford the passage to America, tended to migrate to England, Scotland and Wales. Yet the Famine exodus also included formerly wealthy farmers who saw the Famine as proof of the futility of living in Ireland and who decided to cut their losses and emigrate to Britain or America. Finally, the Famine reinforced the process of 'chain migration', whereby the selection of future emigrants – Roman Catholics and Ulster Protestants alike – lay with their predecessors. Thus familial and communal ties were reforged abroad. However, there is some evidence to suggest that in Britain this process was also accompanied by 'stepwise' migration, whereby some Irish migrants established temporary residence in different localities until they could afford their passage to America or Australasia.[9]

Thus a variety of causal factors underlay Irish emigration during the nineteenth century. That said, the nature and pattern of Irish emigration to Britain differed in several respects from the migrations to North America and Australasia.

First, migration to Britain never quite had the permanent qualities of migration to the New World, owing to the short distance involved and the social, economic, political and cultural links between Britain and Ireland. Second, there was a long-standing tradition of migration from Ireland to Britain which can be traced back to the Middle Ages, and even by the early eighteenth century there were notable Irish settlements in several English towns, including London, Bristol, Canterbury and Norwich, and in garrison towns such as York. Indeed, many Irish soldiers in the British army took up permanent residence in Britain following their discharge from military duties, notably after the conclusion of the Napoleonic Wars in 1815.

Moreover, the demand for Irish labour during the industrial revolution witnessed the emergence of significant Irish communities in the industrial districts of south Lancashire and the central lowlands of Scotland, notably in Liverpool, Manchester and Glasgow, by the end of the eighteenth century. Third, there was also a long-standing tradition of seasonal migration from Ireland to Britain, whereby smallholders, principally from Connaught and Munster, sought casual employment in Britain during the harvest season in order to supplement the family income and support their domestic holdings in Ireland. Seasonal employment also encompassed casual work in mines, docks and construction industries. Fourth, although some seasonal migration led ultimately to permanent residence in Britain, it was not until the nineteenth century that large-scale Irish settlement became a permanent feature of urban life in Britain and, even then, Irish communities contained a well recognised transient population. Finally, a large but unknown proportion of the Irish who initially settled in Britain in the aftermath of the Great Famine, or who were born there of emigrating parents, eventually re-emigrated, largely to the United States. Thus 'stepwise' migration was sometimes characteristic of the Irish experience in nineteenth-century

Britain.[10] Remittances from friends and relatives abroad sometimes played an important role in this process, as the *Illustrated London News* observed in 1850:

> The great tide of emigration flows steadily westward. The principal emigrants are Irish peasants and labourers [but] it would appear that very few out of the vast army of Irish and other emigrants that proceed to the United States or the British Colonies go out as mere adventurers, without some knowledge of the country, or their chances of doing well, when they get there. The sums received by them before they leave this country are sufficient proof that they have prosperous friends upon the other side; and it is to be presumed that the friends who send them the money do not avoid sending them advice, and giving them full information, to the best of their means, as to their movements upon arrival.[11]

Irish settlement in Britain

The early decades of the nineteenth century witnessed a substantial increase in the pace and scale of Irish migration to Britain. In 1841 the Irish-born population of England, Wales and Scotland totalled 415,725, and by 1851, in consequence of the massive Famine exodus, the figure had risen to 727,326. In 1861 the Irish-born population peaked at 805,717, when it comprised 3·5 per cent of the total population. Thereafter, as migration from Ireland to Britain declined, the number of Irish-born immigrants in Britain also progressively fell, declining to 523,767 in 1921, reviving only later in the twentieth century. These figures do not, however, include the children of Irish migrants born in Britain; thus the actual size of ethnic Irish communities was undoubtedly much higher than contemporary census records suggest. Indeed, in 1872 the *Nation*, a Dublin newspaper, argued that the number of Irish-born indicated in official statistics should be doubled in order to obtain a more realistic enumeratation of the true size of the ethnic Irish community in Britain.[12]

In general, the vast majority of these migrants travelled from Ireland to Britain by one of three well established emigrant routes, each distinguished by place of origin and destination. Thus migrants from Ulster and north Connaught took the northern route, via Londonderry and Belfast, to Scotland, via Glasgow; emigrants from Connaught and most of Leinster took the midland route, via Dublin, to Holyhead and Liverpool; whilst migrants from south Leinster and Munster took the southern route, via Cork, to Bristol and thence to London.[13] However, the extent to which the ultimate destinations of Irish migrants in British towns and cities were determined by economic and cultural criteria related to their regional origins in Ireland or by the ports of embarkation and arrival is still a matter for academic enquiry. The census enumerators recorded only the country, and not the county, of birth where it lay outside England and Wales; thus the regional origins of the urban Irish in nineteenth-century Britain some-times remain as obscure as their motives for settling in one town as opposed to another. Moreover, there is some evidence to suggest that migrants from specific localities in Ireland *clustered* within British towns rather than *in* specific towns, thereby establishing differentiated 'Irish' communities on a local level.[14]

The majority of Irish immigrants were young single people. Males slightly outnumbered females in both England and Scotland until the end of the century, when, in England at least, the ratio was reversed. Once disembarked, most of these newcomers became urban dwellers in the ports of entry, notably Glasgow and Liverpool, in London, in the industrial towns of South Wales, the Midlands, south Lancashire and the north-east, and in Scotland, where there were notable concentrations in Edinburgh and Dundee. These settlement patterns antedated the Irish Famine and were confirmed by the 1851 census. This indicated that Irish settlement was most pronounced in the Scottish counties of Renfrew (14·8 per cent), Lanark (14·6 per cent) and Wigtown (12·3 per cent) and in the English counties of Lancashire (8·9 per cent), Cheshire (5·7 per cent), Durham (5·4 per cent) and Cumberland (5·1 per cent). Similarly, the four towns with the largest Irish-born population were London (108,548, or 4·6 per cent of the population) Liverpool (83,813, or 22·3 per cent), Glasgow (59,801,or 18·1 per cent) and Manchester (52,504,or 13·1 per cent), although almost two-thirds of all Irish-born immigrants were scattered in towns and cities outside these four great centres. These settlement patterns subsequently remained remarkably constant throughout the period 1851–1921, despite the overall decline in the size of the Irish-born population in Britain.[15]

It is difficult to strike a proper mean between the lighter and darker sides of the Irish urban experience, which differed from one settlement to another. Studies of the Irish presence in Bradford, Leeds, Manchester, Stockport and Wolverhampton – all of which have drawn heavily on qualitative evidence – have suggested that during the early and mid-Victorian periods in particular the newcomers were located in socially immobile and unintegrated ghettoes, 'Little Irelands' which were isolated in particular streets and courts from the surrounding population.[16] However, some historians, including E. P. Thompson, have completely rejected the concept of Irish 'ghettoization' as little more than a myth, suggesting that the Irish did not congregate in 'ghettoes' to the exclusion of other ethnic groups.[17]

Yet the whole question of Irish 'ghettoization' requires the most careful consideration. Indeed, the quantitative analysis of contemporary census data by social geographers and historical demographers has recently engendered a lively debate on the subject. For example, Colin Pooley's study of Irish settlement in Liverpool, Blackburn and Bolton suggests that, while there were areas of concentrated Irish settlement, they were not wholly isolated from the host community, and even where Irish immigrants dominated particular streets, courts and squares they were seldom shut off from the native population.[18] John Papworth has noted that even in Liverpool almost half the Irish lived in enumeration districts with low or medium concentrations of Irish population.[19] Indeed, the research of both Pooley and Papworth confirms the earlier work of Lynn Lees, on London[20] and Frances Finnegan, on York[21] which suggested that the Irish lived cheek-by-jowl beside natives of the same social class. In short, the poor Irish lived among the English poor, and the upwardly mobile among the English upper working or middle class. This also appears to have been the case in smaller English towns: John Herson has shown that the Irish were geographically dispersed in the market town of Stafford, where they lacked a common economic interest and where the formation of a community was inhibited by a high level of out-migration.[22] Thus the pattern of Irish settlement appears to have been determined largely by economic considerations, and if there was an 'Irish community' it did not rest on a pattern of rigid residential segregation. Clearly, this whole question warrants further study, in part through the continued application of quantitative analysis to the diachronic study of census returns on a local level. That said, statistical studies can take the subject only so far, in that they deal with populations in the abstract rather than with 'flesh and blood' individuals and, as Graham Davis has illustrated in his recent study of 'Little Irelands',[23] perhaps need to be placed in a broader context.

Of course, this does not altogether dispose of the ghetto. There were predominantly poor Irish streets and courts. Moreover, recent studies of Bermondsey by Alan Bartlett[24] and of Manchester by Steven Fielding[25] bear testimony to the existence of the larger Irish Catholic urban neighbourhoods with their own kind of flourishing political and religious life. Again, the *Nation* survey of the Irish in Britain in 1872, recently edited by Alan O'Day,[26] indicates the existence of Irish Catholic communities like that of St Helens which were wholly working-class and poor. But the ghetto at its strictest was not completely sealed, and the term may well be inappropriate to describe the living conditions of most of the Irish population, particularly during the second half of the nineteenth century.

Irish employment

Although most immigrants came from rural Ireland, subsistence agriculture in Ireland did not provide them with the skills for commercial agriculture in Britain. Moreover, they had little capital to invest in the British rural economy, and British landlords rarely needed or wanted them as tenants in the villages. In consequence, relatively few Irish immigrants worked on the land. There was seldom a rural labour shortage and when, on occasion, Irish migrants did find more permanent employment as agricultural workers, as in the chicory fields near York, they actually had to tramp to their workplace from their urban slum.[27] Hence Irish rural employment in Britain continued to be largely confined to seasonal harvest labour, and Irish men and women were a familiar ingredient of the British rural landscape until the early twentieth century, variously harvesting corn, digging potatoes, collecting turnips and picking hops. On the whole, relatively little is known of the nature and patterns of Irish rural employment in nineteenth-century Britain, and the whole subject is deserving of further research. That said, it appears that, as mechanization increased, there was a slight overall decline in the annual number of Irish harvesters who travelled to England, Wales and Scotland between 1841 and 1900, yet there were still 30,000 Irish people engaged in seasonal rural labour at the turn of the century. Moreover, the flow paths of Irish harvesters also changed during the period, influenced by certainty of work rather than harvest rates. Thus, whereas Irish harvesters had been generally dispersed throughout the agricultural districts during the 1840s and 1850s, by the 1880s they were increasingly active in the northern counties of Northumberland, Yorkshire and Cheshire, the Midland counties of Gloucestershire, Worcestershire, Warwickshire and Shropshire (where they worked with Welsh reapers), and in Scotland.[28] In contrast, despite the annual pilgrimage of many London Irish to the hopfields of Kent, relatively few harvesters operated in the southern England, although Flora Thompson observed them in Oxfordshire in the 1880s:

> Here comes they jabberin' old Irish, the country people would say, and some of the women pretended to be afraid of them. They could not have been serious, for the Irishmen showed no disposition to harm anyone. All they desired was to earn as much money as possible to send home to their wives, to have enough left for themselves to get drunk on a Saturday night, and to be in time for Mass on a Sunday morning. All these aims were fulfilled; for, as the other men confessed, they were 'gluttons for work' and more work meant more money at that season; there was an excellent inn handy; and a Catholic church within three miles.[29]

In contrast, the great majority of Irish, largely illiterate and unskilled, entered the lowliest and least healthy of urban occupations, unless they enlisted in the army, which was 30 per cent Irish in the mid-Victorian period. Whilst a minority of skilled workers entered sweated industries like cobbling and tailoring in the East End of London – so graphically described by Henry Mayhew[30] – those with limited or no skills were concentrated in unskilled occupations in mines and ironworks, textile mills, manufactories, in building work, in casual dock labour and street selling. These were occupations for which a highly sophisticated city like London, with a highly specialized labour force, held very few rewards and, as Lynn Lees has shown, the Irish could enter the metropolitan economy only with difficulty.[31] Tom Gallagher has shown that in Liverpool, which was a trading and commercial rather than an industrial centre, employment opportunities, housing and sanitation were overwhelmed by the sheer magnitude of Irish immigration during the 1840s, and the demand for labour lay largely in unskilled occupations for which Catholics and Protestants were in active competition. Similarly, although the Glasgow Irish were able to find employment in mills and mines, they were excluded from engineering by their lack of skill, from shipbuilding by the Orange Order and from skilled trades by the craft unions.[32] Bernard Aspinwall and John McCaffrey have shown that in Edinburgh, a city of legal, literary and ecclesiastical institutions, the Irish were confined to such menial occupations as general labouring in building, domestic service, portering, street cleaning and street lighting.[33] In contrast, Brenda Collins has suggested, the expansion of the linen and jute industry in Dundee provided the greatest possibility of advancement to Irish migrants, and Irish immigration had a considerable impact on the subsequent development of this industry through the retention of hand-loom weaving by local manufacturers.[34]

Overall, among the country immigrants to British towns and cities, the Irish were generally the least prepared to succeed in their new environment. Indeed, the *Report on the State of the Irish Poor in Great Britain* concluded in 1836 that Irish immigration 'is an example of a less civilized population spreading themselves, as a kind of substratum, beneath a more civilized community, and, without excelling in any branch of industry obtaining possession of all the lowest departments of manual labour'.[35] More recently, E. H. Hunt has suggested that a variety of factors helped to consign the Irish to the lowest occupations, including their lack of skill, capital and education; their low expectations and high leisure preferences, including a propensity to drink; the perceived impermanence of their residence in Britain, coupled with their contempt for authority, especially British authority; and the discrimination they faced from British employers and workers.[36]

Yet it is both easy and dangerous to generalize. In the first place, not all Irish immigrants, whether Catholic or Protestant, were poor: even by mid-century there was a small middle-class world of professional men, doctors, lawyers, soldiers, shopkeepers, merchants and journalists.[37] Moreover, there is some evidence to suggest that the economic position of the Irish was far less static than many contemporaries believed and that there was a degree of differentiation in Irish occupational patterns. This was certainly one of the implications of a survey of the Irish in Britain conducted in 1872 by the *Nation*, a Dublin weekly newspaper, which argued that in relative terms the economic position of the Irish depended less on the structure of the Irish community in a given locality than on the economic infrastructure of the area where they worked. In developing this argument, the *Nation* pointed to the emergence of a substantial Irish middle class in London, to the presence of skilled workers in the Midlands, and to the variable experience of the Irish in south Lancashire, where an Irish middle class had emerged in both Liverpool and Manchester, whilst in neighbouring Wigan and St Helens the Irish were almost wholly labourers of one description or another.[38] John Denvir, an Irish nationalist, pointed to similar contrasts in 1892, noting that in Liverpool:

> There has been, however, a vast change for the better in the surroundings of our people and, indeed, in every other way, so that there is no town in the country in which we have made greater progress than in Liverpool. Irishmen are gradually emerging from the ranks of unskilled labour and becoming more numerous among the artisans, shopkeepers, merchants and professional classes . . . Irish intellect and Irish courage have, in thousands of cases, brought our people to their proper place in the social scale . . . It is often noted that where an Irishman is steady and has got a good wife, he is frequently able to save enough from his earnings to open a marine store – a business our people seem partial to throughout the country – a coal yard, or a small shop. By degrees, he gets on, for, as a rule, our people are more quick-witted in bargaining than even the Jews – the difference being that Moses sticks to all he gets, whilst Pat's often too-generous nature frequently lets go easily what he has won so hardly. There are, however, hard-headed Irishmen too, men who know how to keep what they have earned. So by degrees they get into the higher circles of the commercial world, and of these there are to be seen, among the merchant princes on 'Change, men who

either themselves or whose fathers before them commenced life in Liverpool as corn or cotton porters, or even in some humbler or more precarious occupation.[39]

Clearly, the question of Irish economic mobility awaits further detailed investigation: Lynn Lees and Frances Finnegan have shown, in their respective studies of mid-Victorian London and York, that the quantitative analysis of census returns can broaden our perspectives on this subject, and there is a need for similar local and provincial studies to be conducted for the late Victorian period if we are to acquire a deeper understanding of Irish employment patterns and social mobility. Such studies might also encompass the economic role of Irish women, who, in the long term, made notable contributions to a range of low-paid professional occupations, including social work and nursing, but whose nineteenth-century role appears to have been largely restricted to employment in textile mills, laundry work, street selling and, most notably, domestic service.[40]

Discussion of the nature and patterns of Irish immigrant employment has obvious implications for the broader, controversial and much debated question of the impact of Irish immigration on the British economy during the industrial revolution.

The classic view is perhaps best exemplified in the *Report on the State of the Irish Poor* of 1836, which concluded:

> We ought not, however, to overlook the advantage of the demand for labour in England and Scotland being amply and adequately supplied, and at a cheap rate and at very short notice, by Irish; it is to be remembered that these Irish have been, and are, most efficient workmen; and they came in the hour of need, and that they afforded the chief part of the animal strength by which the great works of our manufacturing districts have been executed.[41]

This view was subsequently endorsed by several historians, including Arthur Redford, J. E. Handley and J. A. Jackson, who argued that Irish immigrants provided a large pool of cheap labour at a time of rapid industrial expansion and therefore played a crucial role in retarding workers' living standards, in contributing to rising inequality, and in fostering industrialization.[42] More recently, however, this view has been challenged both qualitatively and quantitatively. E. H. Hunt has suggested that some historians have accepted too easily the partial evidence given by employers to the *Report on the State of the Irish Poor*: in practice, many of these employers actually depended on cheap Irish labour, and their evidence was designed to further their own interests. Moreover, the 'classic view' presumed a labour shortage in industrial Britain, yet increasing Irish immigration occurred against the background of fears of the Malthusian 'trap', increased emigration from Britain, and native hostility to the importation of Irish labour, which, it was feared, would reduce workers' living standards by taking work, reducing wages and weakening trade unions. Hunt also argues that much of the heavy work on turnpikes, canals, docks, harbours and, to a lesser extent, railways was achieved by native labour before Irish immigration was of much consequence, concluding that 'the effect of Irish immigration upon the pace of British industrialization was therefore not great'.[43]

However, the classic view has only recently been submitted to rigorous quantitative study, in a thoroughly revisionist article by Jeffrey G. Williamson, which concludes that Irish labour did not play a significant role in accounting for rising inequality, lagging real wages or rapid industrialization. Indeed, Williamson suggests that Irish labour was, in general, 'simply not crucial to the British Standard-of-Living Debate' and that, although the Irish-born comprised 8·8 per cent of the British labour force by 1861, their impact as a predominantly unskilled minority of workers on the British economy was 'very small.[44] Clearly, the debate remains inconclusive, involving complex issues arising as much from the historian's method as from the conflicting nature of the evidence itself. Indeed, it may well be of greater historical significance, particularly in the examination of contemporary attitudes towards Irish immigrants, that the Irish were believed to have reduced the living standards of the British working class than that they actually did so.

The same might be said in the context of the supposed threat posed by Irish immigrants to the development of the British labour movement during the nineteenth century. During the 1830s and 1840s many English workers believed, rightly or wrongly, that Irish immigrants helped to undermine working-class trade union activity through their use by employers as strike breakers, a belief which in part underpinned Friedrich Engels's claim that the English working classes were 'degraded' by Irish competition.[45]

Yet the attitudes of Irish immigrants to industrial relations were in many respects ambivalent. On the one hand, Irish labourers were sometimes used as strike breakers: thus in 1844 Lord Londonderry tried to break the Durham colliers by importing men from his Irish estates, whilst in 1854 the cotton manufacturers used blackleg Irish labour to defeat the Preston cotton strike, which subsequently formed the backcloth for Charles Dickens's *Hard Times*. Moreover, as James Treble has shown,[46] the Roman Catholic Church in England strongly discouraged Irish immigrant involvement in trade union activity. On the other hand, some Irish immigrants, notably from Dublin and Cork, possessed previous trade union experience which they put to good use in Britain. Individual Irishmen emerged as prominent trade unionists during the period, notably in the hand-loom weaving and cotton textile districts of south Lancashire and the west of Scotland, and were often active in the organization of strikes. Indeed, John Doherty, founder of the National Association for the Protection of Labour in 1829, editor of the visionary *Voice of the People*, and one of the greatest trade union pioneers, was born and bred in Donegal.[47] Moreover, first and second-generation Irish immigrants played a prominent role in the unionization of unskilled workers in the 1880s and 1890s: Will Thorne, a member of the Social Democratic Federation, became leader of the Gasworkers' and General Labourers' Union; P. J. King organized the alkali workers in 1889; Ben Tillett, led the London dockers, including many Irish stevedores, to victory in the famous London dock strike of 1889, whilst James Connolly and James Larkin, both brought up in Irish communities in Britain, were also influential figures.[48]

Integration or separation?

Life in nineteenth-century Britain was for the Irish an often harsh and disorientating experience, and, because they were concentrated in towns and cities, the Irish stood out from the host population by their poverty, nationality, race and religion. Indeed, as David Fitzpatrick has recently suggested;

> to alien eyes and ears it often mattered little whether an Irish emigrant was from Dublin or Mayo, a Protestant or a Catholic, a labourer or an artisan, a parent or on the loose. To their great indignation, the Irish overseas tended to be lumped together as ignorant, dirty and primitive Paddies or Biddies.[49]

This raises the broader question, itself the subject of an ongoing debate among historians, of the extent to which the Irish constituted either an 'outcast' group, locked together in defensive communities in the face of British prejudice, or an ethnic minority which, although retaining a clearly defined sense of Irish identity, was nevertheless gradually and successfully assimilated into British society. In addressing this important question it is necessary to examine more closely those issues relating to Irish poverty, nationalism, ethnicity and religion which are central to the historical debate.

Poverty

Poverty, the most obvious of the immigrant's disadvantages, was the driving force of Irish emigration to Britain, and in many respects the Irish experience was unique, for in their flight from poverty and misery in Ireland they found themselves in the towns and cities of the very country many blamed for their misfortune.

Many of the emigrants suffered privation and exploitation during their passage from Irish ports, particularly during the Famine.[50] Once disembarked, a majority of the new arrivals crowded into slum tenements, lodging houses and cellar dwellings in the long-established and already overcrowded districts of Irish settlement in Lancashire and London, and even in the smaller centres their poverty and destitution tended to consign them to the filthiest and foulest of neighbourhoods. Geroid O'Tuathaigh, in a magisterial survey of the problems of integration which Irish immigrants faced, has written:

> their living conditions were generally the very worst which the Victorian industrial slum could offer. The Little Ireland ghetto in Manchester, the London courts and rookeries, the Glasgow tenements, the Liverpool cellars – all displayed the full spectrum of social evils: appalling overcrowding, little or no sanitation, open sewers and cesspools, unhealthy diet, inadequate clothing, vagrancy, disease, alcoholism and general squalor, a high quota of unemployed paupers or of underemployed casual labourers, and a high incidence of casual violence.[51]

These were the conditions which prompted Thomas Carlyle's comment of 1839 – several years before the massive Famine exodus – that 'crowds of miserable Irish darken all our towns'[52] and which subsequently attracted the attention of mid-Victorian social investigators and commentators. Indeed, for some, the influx of poverty-stricken Irish men, women and children was regarded as little short of a social disaster which, it was held, exacerbated urban squalor, constituted a health hazard, and increased the burden on the poor rates, whilst Irish fertility rates aroused fears of racial deterioration.[53]

Such fears, rooted as they were in the poverty of Irish immigrants, need to be understood in the context of the many contemporary issues – urban squalor, disease, disorder, vagrancy and unemployment – with which they became entangled, and in a sense it was a tragic coincidence that the growing awareness of acute urban problems during the 1830s and 1840s, reflected in the 'Condition of England' question, occurred at the same time as the rising tide of Irish immigration. Moreover, it was the sheer scale of Irish immigration during the Famine which compounded the social condition of British cities. In five months during 1847 some 300,000 pauper Irish landed in Liverpool alone, swamping a town with a native population of 250,000, whilst it was reported from South Wales that 'the principal cause of the excessive overcrowding found to prevail in Cardiff is the vast influx of destitute Irish from Cork and Waterford, who have been partly attracted in the hope of obtaining employment on the public works'.[54] Indeed, there were attempts by the local authorities in some towns, including Glasgow, Liverpool and Cardiff, to repatriate Irish paupers to Ireland under the removal clauses of the Poor Law. Against this background, the Irish became an easy target, and the *poor* Irish, who were the only *visible* Irish, became convenient scapegoats for environmental deterioration. Yet the plethora of urban social problems was clearly not the product of Irish immigration: these conditions had existed long before the Famine influx, which in practice served only to magnify and exacerbate them.

Nevertheless the Irish were widely perceived to be a burden on the poor rates, although this relationship still awaits detailed quantitative analysis. The dependence of Famine settlers upon parish relief, coupled with the pauper deportations of 1847–8 (when 10,000 Irish removals were authorized in Scotland alone), undoubtedly helped to entrench this view in the public mind. Yet recent studies of Irish employment patterns in Bristol[55] and York[56] have shed doubt on this popular view by showing that, at least before 1860 and the relaxation of the settlement provisions of the 1834 Poor Law, the Irish made a much smaller demand on public and private charity than their poverty and English prejudice might lead one to suppose. Moreover, after 1860 relatively few of those Irish applicants for English relief who could not prove their permanent residence in the chargeable union for a period of one year were removed to Ireland, although they were technically subject to removal. In Scotland both Poor Law legislation and practice were more rigorous, and 7,000 paupers were removed to Ireland between 1875 and 1910. But here too the number of removals was progressively declining, whilst the persistent excess of Irish paupers was largely attributable to an ageing population of Irish inmates in Scottish work-houses.[57]

It was also widely held that Irish immigrants were harbingers of crime and disorder, the ancilliaries of urban poverty and environmental deterioration. Indeed, whilst crime and disorder had long been regarded as Irish traits, it was also held that the Irish were more criminal than other sections of British society and, as such, represented a challenge on the part of 'the dangerous classes', in which the Irish bulked large, to authority and order in nineteenth-century Britain. In this context even the derivation of the term 'hooligan', first coined by the popular press to describe the behaviour of gangs of rowdy youths in London during the August Bank Holiday celebrations of 1898, is not without significance and has prompted Geoffrey Pearson to comment that 'it was most ingenious of late Victorian England to disown the British hooligan by giving him an Irish name'.[58]

Although relatively little research has been conducted into the relationship between Irish immigration and crime during the period, statistical evidence suggests that the Irish-born were almost three times more likely to face prosecution than their English neighbours and more than five times as likely to be convicted and imprisoned. Yet even here some important qualifications are called for. First, there is a wealth of evidence to suggest that Irish criminality was overwhelmingly concentrated in less serious or petty categories. In general, the Irish were not noted for crimes of great violence. Second, the evidence suggests that the Irish were not over-represented in all categories of petty crime but that Irish criminality was highly concentrated in the often interrelated categories of drunkenness, disorderly behaviour and assault (including assaults on the police) and, to a lesser extent, petty theft and vagrancy. Moreover, many of the so-called 'Irish disorders' which so concerned contemporary opinion were in practice 'anti-Irish disorders', where Irish involvement was defensive rather than offensive.[59]

Clearly, a variety of factors need to be considered in any attempt to explain the overrepresentation of the Irish in certain categories of criminal behaviour. For example, when contemporaries spoke of the Irish they broadly distinguished between the honest and the dishonest, the latter being commonly referred to as 'the lowest Irish'; thus it was in fact the very poorest Irish who were associated in the public mind with crime and disorder, and in a sense this mirrors the more negative attitudes of the period towards the poorest sections of the English working class. Moreover, much Irish criminality was clearly the by-product of a poverty-ridden and brutalizing urban slum environment, and studies of Irish criminality in Bradford and Leeds have illustrated the relationship between crime and environmental deterioration. It is also important to recognize that the moral character of Irish communities varied enormously: those of the north-east appear to have been remarkably quiescent; in contrast, the St Giles district of London, which attracted the least desirable Irish who were subsequently absorbed into a rookery of thieves and beggars, was the exception rather than the norm but, in the public mind, it was perceived as the norm, typical of all 'Little Irelands'. There is also the charge that the overrepresentation of the Irish in the statistics of crime was the result of anti-Irish prejudice. This may have been so, but it is important to recognize that the stereotype of the brutalized 'Paddy' was well entrenched in the public mind even before the large-scale immigration of the 1840s and 1850s, hence Irish districts were expected to be hotbeds of crime and disorder; as Frances Finnegan has observed, anti-social behaviour by the Irish merely confirmed preconceived notions regarding the irresponsibility and criminality of the Celt.[60] It also, of course, influenced the attitudes of police and magistrates in their attempts to combat urban crime and disorder.

Indeed, the overrepresentation of the Irish in the statistics of crime has to be seen, in part, in the context of the growth and development of provincial policing during the period. The essential targets of the 'New Police' forces which emerged from 1829 onwards were varieties of street crime – drunkenness, disorderly behaviour, petty theft, vagrancy and unruly forms of popular leisure and recreation: in short, the very offences for which the Irish had acquired a legendary reputation. The Irish were, therefore, particularly vulnerable to police surveillance, and this was subsequently reflected in the level of Irish-born prosecutions in these petty criminal categories. Of course, this raises the further question of the extent to which the police themselves were prejudiced against the Irish, and here the evidence is less clear. Indeed, several chief constables and a substantial minority of Victorian policemen were themselves Irish, so perhaps police 'prejudice' might be better explained in terms of a general discrimination against the 'dangerous' or 'criminal sections' of working-class society as a whole.

Yet, in a recent article based on an exclusive study of the Liverpool Irish, Frank Neal has added further fuel to the debate on Irish criminality by suggesting that whilst Irish poverty may well have contributed to the overrepresentation of the Irish in the statistics of crime it is also possible that there was something in the nature of Roman Catholicism that caused Catholics (and therefore many Irish) to turn to certain types of deviant behaviour. In other words, a failure of the predominant religion of the Irish in Britain was a possible reason for their overrepresentation in the prison population during the period.[61]

Nationalism

A second criterion of Irish 'outcastness' was Irish nationalism. Here again there were grounds for British conservative prejudice, in the tradition of Irish agrarian outrage, and of the 'physical force' resort to street violence and armed rebellion, or, more impressively, the recourse to mass defiance. This defiance was an attraction rather than a deterrent to some English political radicals, and all radical historians are aware of such distinctively Irish gifts to Chartism as Feargus O'Connor and Bronterre O'Brien. Yet the Irish provided more than these well known Chartist leaders, and ordinary Irish Catholics were often an integral part of British proletarian culture, in which English radicals actively championed the Irish cause and sought and gained Irish Catholic support. That said, the degree to which the

Irish were involved in Chartism has been a source of debate among historians. James Treble has suggested that the pressures acting upon Irish immigrants, including those from the Catholic Church, caused them to remain relatively aloof from the movement.[62] In contrast, Dorothy Thompson has more recently and persuasively argued that the Irish made a vital contribution to Chartism.[63] Indeed, John Belchem's study of this co-operation before 1848 and the distinctive Irish contribution to the last phase of Chartism concludes that the failure of the movement had a decided effect on the increasing social and political isolation of the Irish in Britain by mid-century.[64] There was, therefore, an Irish Chartist echo in England of the rising of the Young Irelanders in 1848, and in the 1860s the revolutionary tradition returned to England with the activities of the Irish Republican Brotherhood. Indeed, the abortive Fenian rising of 1867 and the agrarian violence of the Land War from 1879 point to the survival of a popular view of the right to rebel unique in its intensity and continuity in British political life, surviving underground to erupt in Dublin in 1916.

Yet this revolutionary tradition is deserving of greater attention from historians, for there have been few recent studies of Irish revolutionary activity in Britain during the period, most notably Lowe's study of Lancashire Fenianism,[65] Quinlivan and Rose's work on the Chester raid, the 'Manchester Martyrs', and the Clerkenwell explosion of 1867,[66] and K. R. M. Short's study of Irish-American bombers in Victorian Britain.[67] Certainly the majority of Irish immigrants had the broad political objective of redefining in some way Ireland's constitutional relationship with Britain, a broadly nationalist objective which lay outside the range of objectives accepted as legitimate by British public opinion. This deviance was resented, particularly when it impinged on the British domestic scene – witness, for example, the native outrage which greeted Fenian activities in 1867.

Yet the whole conception of the Irish as offering the 'outcast' alternative in English radical politics requires the most sensitive statement. Certainly the Irish nationalist Members of Parliament after 1829 formed an often discordant element in English political life, and different aspects of the Irish question helped to defeat the Tory party in 1846 and to destroy the Liberal party in 1886. And Irish agitation for the repeal of the Act of Union during the 1840s and for Home Rule after 1880 did seem to many Englishmen to threaten the destruction of the empire at its very heart. Yet there is evidence to suggest that the actual Irish threat to the empire was greatly exaggerated. John Belchem has argued that the Irish element in Chartism lent itself to the conservative exploitation which was one cause of its defeat.[68] Tom Gallagher[69] and P. J. Waller[70] have shown that the very strength of Irish Nationalism and Catholicism in Liverpool gave popular Orange Toryism a century of almost uninterrupted ascendancy in local politics, whilst Neville Kirk has observed that some Tory politicians were often quick to play the Irish card in the industrial towns of south Lancashire during the 1850s and 1860s.[71] In contrast, the Irish communities in York and Edinburgh appear to have been largely politically apathetic, an apoliticism which reflected the marginal position of the Irish in the economies of those cities as well as the leadership of a conservative Catholic Church. Clearly, the character of Irish political activity varied enormously from one community to another, although there is considerable room for further research into these local and provincial contrasts.

Arguably, the greatest successes of Irish political activity came only in the 1880s when the Irish parliamentary party created a mass organization harnessed to constitutional nationalism which gained a measure of respectability through Gladstone's conversion to Home Rule. Even so, the Irish remained a much constrained and limited political element: the pauper Irish often proved difficult to register as voters and were sufficiently numerous to return a nationalist Member of Parliament in only one constituency – T. P. O'Connor, for Liverpool, in 1885. [72] Irish political influence was also limited because no constituencies were sufficiently marginal to allow the Irish to hold the balance of power and, as Alan O'Day has shown, they had little influence on the Liberals whom they often helped to elect. [73] Indeed, despite the development of nationalist organizations such as the Home Rule Confederation of Great Britain (1875) and the Irish National League of Great Britain (1885) only a tiny fraction of the Irish in Britain were moved to translate their sense of identity into active political ethnicity: few were exceptionally politicized beyond a superficially nationalist sense, and for most nationalism was a limited weapon. [74] Nevertheless, the limited evidence we have suggests that late Victorian Irish communities were gradually becoming an increasingly well integrated element in British political democracy. Lynn Lees has suggested, for example, that the London Irish, though holding strongly to a commitment to Irish independence, found themselves working within the confines of the British political system, noting that 'the forms, force and style of Celtic politics in London adapted to the English political environment which had itself been partially opened to the Irish'. [75] Steven Fielding's recent study of the careers of Dan Boyle and Dan McCabe, who led Manchester's Irish nationalists at the turn of the century, has suggested that local nationalist politics paved the way for significant Irish support for radical Liberalism and then Labour before 1914. [76] Of course, if the Irish were, by 1914, increasingly a part of mainstream British political culture rather than isolated from it, the general view of the Irish as an alien and isolated group is questionable. [77] Yet, as David Fitzpatrick has observed, many Irish immigrants still retained a sentimental attachment to the Fenian vision, which was stimulated by the Gaelic revival. Romantic Ireland was particularly appealing to better-educated expatriates and their children, providing an attractive image of the Irish past, in sharp contrast with the realities of the Irish present. [78]

There was, then, a considerable complexity to the Irish political experience in Victorian Britain, a complexity which was to some extent masked by Fenian activities. The vast majority of Irish Catholic immigrants and their children were not the potential revolutionaries which contemporary opinion was often quick to imply and behaved as loyal if not always enthusiastic subjects of the Crown in England, Scotland and Wales, as in Canada, Australasia and Ireland itself. Yet we still need to know much more about Irish participation in contemporary politics, particularly at the local government level. How far, for example, did local Irish communities seek and achieve representation on borough councils, school boards and other elective bodies ? These are important questions which have some bearing on the broader question of Irish integration into British society during the period.

Ethnicity

A third criterion of 'apartness' embraces hostility towards the Irish as a separate race. E. D. Steele has suggested that 'nowhere else, save in Orange Canada, did the Irish abroad meet with such sustained antagonism' as in nineteenth-century Britain.[79] Clearly, anti-Irish attitudes in British society have a long and complex history, and their roots are a matter of some controversy. That this antagonism was an odd compound of religious, social and political elements, both rational and irrational, is not in dispute. However, some historians, including Professor Perry Curtis, have detected the emergence of a firm set of anti-Irish prejudices during the mid-Victorian period, articulated by sectors of the Victorian intelligentsia, which were based on the assumption that the native Irish were inferior in culture and alien in race to the Anglo-Saxons.[80]

There is, of course, much evidence to corroborate this view, and those guilty include figures from such diverse backgrounds as Carlyle, Engels, Disraeli, Froude and Arnold. Witness, for example, Disraeli's statement of 1836 that 'this wild, reckless, indolent, uncertain and superstitious race have no sympathy with the English character. Their fair ideal of human felicity is an alternation of clannish broils and coarse idolatry. Their history describes an unbroken circle of bigotry and blood.' Or Froude's comment of 1841 that 'the inhabitants, except when they had been taken in hand and meta-morphosed into police, seemed more like tribes of squalid apes than human beings'.[81] Or the *Punch* comment of 1862 that 'a creature manifestly be-tween the gorilla and the negro is to be met with in some of the lowest districts of London and Liverpool . . . It belongs to a tribe of Irish savages . . . When conversing with its kind it talks a sort of gibberish. It is, moreover, a climbing animal and may sometimes be seen ascending a ladder laden with a hod of bricks'[82].

However, the Curtis thesis has been challenged by several historians, most notably Sheridan Gilley, who has argued that the British stereotype of 'Paddy' had a benign as well as a menacing face and was as much an Irish creation as a British one. Hence, whilst the Irish were held, on the one hand, to be feckless, stupid, violent, unreliable and drunken, they were also perceived, on the other, as chaste, hospitable, witty, kindly and generous. Moreover, Dr Gilley has suggested that it was only on specific religious and political issues that anti-Irish attitudes became dominant among the British and, furthermore, that there were understandable social and economic reasons for much of the hostility, reasons which do not in themselves justify the term 'racial prejudice'.[83]

Clearly, the anti-Celtic stereotype was a complex one. Victorian racial theory took the form of the claim that the English were superior as a 'mixed race', not as a pure one, to the Celts; hence the best mongrel English had the good Celtic qualities as well as the good Anglo-Saxon ones, and one wonders how far Anglo-Saxonism, a product of the Victorian intelligentsia, actually percolated down to, and influenced the motives of, anti-Irish mobs. Moreover, anti-Celtism does not appear to have impeded the advancement of the small Irish Catholic middle class in Victorian Britain, and one wonders whether the prejudice which undoubtedly manifested itself was essentially focused on Irish paupers, as a parallel with the more negative attitudes towards the English poor. On the other hand, as O'Tuathaigh has pointed out, there was an almost universal tendency from the 1840s onwards to describe the immigrant Irish in distinctly racial terms, terms which have retained their use into more recent times – 'No Irish need apply here'.[84]

Thus we are left with a problem. Was anti-Irish prejudice essentially racial, was it rooted in contemporary class attitudes, or did it rest upon a combination of social, economic, political and religious factors whose impact on the fomentation of anti-Irish attitudes varied in time and place? This said, it is clear that a deep-rooted set of anti-Irish prejudices pervaded British society during the nineteenth century, which may have increased the isolation of the Irish poor in particular, who were variously perceived as a nuisance, a threat or a contagion. On the other hand, there is some evidence to suggest that sectarian and ethnic rivalries in many British towns – with the notable exception of Liverpool[85] – had been diluted by the end of the period, and were increasingly being expressed through local politics rather than through riots and window-smashing. Similarly, rivalries within Irish communities themselves were being subsumed into politics and games, notably through the Gaelic Association.[86]

Catholicism

Last, there is the claim that the Irish were outcast because they were Catholic. The English, Scots and Welsh were overwhelmingly Protestant by tradition, and after 1790 the strength of popular Protestantism was greatly reinforced by the Evangelical Revival. Protestant 'No Popery' also gained an increasing ascendancy over the established Church of Ireland, and Ulster immigrants of the Orange Order introduced their fratricidal strife with Irish Catholics into a number of British cities, notably Liverpool, where sectarian competition for jobs in a weakly unionized economy polarized local politics between the Orange and the Green.

Religion was, indeed, a vital ingredient in determining Anglo-Irish relations on a local level, particularly during the mid-Victorian period. The terms 'Irish' and 'Catholic' were virtually synonymous in British eyes and although anti-Irish sentiment was, as we have seen, more diffuse than anti-Catholicism, it is evident that the resurgence of popular Protestantism in the wake of the Tractarian controversy and the re-establishment of the Roman Catholic hierarchy in 1850 provided an additional cutting edge to Anglo-

Irish tensions. Indeed, anti–Catholic sentiment contributed to the most serious clashes between the English and the Irish during the period, notably at Stockport in 1852, Oldham in 1861, London in 1862 and during the more widespread Murphy riots of 1867–71.[87]

Some of the difficulties of interpreting this sectarian violence have been illustrated by Pauline Millward's study of the Stockport riots of 1852. The disorders may have arisen from the underlying antagonism between the masses of new immigrants and the hard-pressed English cotton workers who resented the incursion of cheap Irish labour into the mills, but the evidence is difficult to interpret and the antagonism was insufficient by itself to cause the riots, the actual occasion being the restoration of the Catholic hierarchy, fanned to a flame by the 'respectable' anti–Catholicism of local Anglican clergymen and electorally vulnerable Tory politicians who played the Irish card in a bid for political power.[88] Similar themes recur in Wolverhampton, where anti–Catholic disturbances in 1858 and 1867, in which Irish Catholics stood firm against the advent of anti–Catholic lectures, reflected a new self-confidence in the Irish Catholic community and its organization, which invoked a new and bitter Protestant response.[89]

What is clear from these and other disorders which were superficially the product of religious tensions is that more often than not they were, at root, the reflection of deeper strains and stresses within the local community. Indeed, it is important to remember that whilst the Catholicism of the Irish may well have contributed to their isolation, they were no more 'outcast' as Catholics than English or foreign Catholics on the ground of their Catholicism alone. Catholicism was unpopular as a living ideological force, and conversion to it was often regarded as an unmitigated disaster. Victorian 'No Popery' was much more than anti–Irishness: Catholicism was regarded by Victorian liberals as foreign, exotic and dangerous, the religion of Britain's traditional enemies, France and Spain, the ally of reactionary governments and the creed of superstitious peasants everywhere. Hence if we are to look to the roots of the outcastness of the Irish it is necessary to consider other things beside Catholicism.

Yet the degree of survival of Irish Catholic loyalties to faith and fatherland is also still a matter for academic enquiry. At least half the pre–Famine and Famine emigrants from Ireland were not, David Miller has argued, regular churchgoers in their homeland.[90] The Irish were loyal Catholics, but in many Irish country areas their religion was built not so much around the church and the priest as around prayer in the home and a local pattern of pilgrimage; these religious practices did not emphasize attendance at Mass every Sunday, especially in western Ireland, where there was a shortage of chapels and priests. Hence many Irish immigrants had to acquire the habit of regular attendance at Mass if they were going to remain good Catholics in England.

Gerard Connolly has recently queried the simple identification of 'Irish' with 'Catholic', suggesting that Irish Catholic rates of Sunday church attendance in London and south Lancashire were often below those for English Protestants, if higher than those for the English working class. Certainly, Irish Catholics were less inclined to formal worship than English

Catholics, and there is evidence to suggest that they were regarded as an embarrassment to the English Catholic mission rather than a reinforcement of it. Moreover, Connolly has suggested that the challenge of the unchurched Irish to clerical idealism and corporate self-interest played a vital role in bringing the English Catholic Church, with its lay traditions, under clerical control and in reinvigorating the priesthood as a profession.[91] Indeed, Sheridan Gilley has shown on a local pastoral level how the new religion was defined for the immigrant community, arguing that the Oratorian version of Christianity enhanced its attractiveness to those who had little hope of improving their lot in this world.[92] Similarly, the popular foundations of priestly authority in Irish Catholic communities have been well delineated by Raphael Samuel, though it is possible that local factors may have differentiated the Irish Catholic immigrant experience more sharply than Samuel suggests.[93]

Thus the Roman Catholic Church may not have been quite as powerful a force for Irish segregation as some historians have suggested. Moreover, the Catholic Church did not reinforce the nationalist aspirations of the Irish in Britain, which may also have minimized the extent of Irish apartness: as David Fitzpatrick has suggested, 'so long as Irishness signified nothing more sinister than saints and shamrocks it could be treated with benevolence by British Catholics, Protestants and unbelievers alike'.[94] Of course, this is not to deny that, in so far as it was successful, the creation of an expatriate Irish church-related culture was also the creation of a low-profile community founded in family relationships and in many ways invisible to outsiders. And the effects of this were sometimes double-edged, creating, as Lynn Lees has succinctly stated, 'a resilient, tenacious subculture that not only sheltered but bound its members, not only strengthened but limited their ability to adapt to urban life'.[95]

Summary

Thus it appears that, during the mid-Victorian period in particular, the pauper Irish Catholic immigrants look like the outcasts of Victorian society. Outcast from British capitalism as the poorest of the poor, from mainstream British politics as separatist nationalists and republicans, from the 'Anglo-Saxon' race as 'Celts', and as Catholics from the dominant forms of British Protestantism, the Irish were the outcasts of Victorian Britain on the basis of class, nationality, race and religion, with an accumulated body of disadvantages possessed by no other group of similar size until the Eastern European, largely Jewish immigration of the late Victorian period. It was on all these grounds taken together that the Irish could be regarded as the largest unassimilated section of their society, a people set apart, rejected and despised. Indeed, their perceived exile, nationalism, closeness to Ireland, disadvantages in British life and historic distrust of British institutions all served to consign them to the margins of British life. Moreover, the various aspects of the 'apartness' of the pauper Catholic Irish Celt tended to reinforce one another, as in the effect of the church-related Irish culture on

Irish poverty, as the resulting social segregation inhibited the development of closer personal contacts with, and therefore of wider economic opportunity in, the British Protestant-owned and run economy. Of course, it could be argued that the role of Catholic education and charity encouraged social mobility by providing schooling and communal self-help in deprived and poverty-ridden neighbourhoods, but the full measure of this revolution occurred only in the twentieth century.

Indeed, Lynn Lees has suggested that 'throughout the process of adapting to London life, most migrants held resolutely to their ethnic identity. Although a certain amount of cultural diffusion took place over time, the Irish resisted assimilation and the third and fourth generations still clung to the symbols of their ancestors' past. The Irish reworked their cultural heritage to fit the demands of life in an urbanising industrial country.'[96] There were, of course, many explanations for this conservatism among Irish migrants: familiar faces and accents, familiar landscapes such as pubs and shops, all helped in creating a sense of cohesion within the immigrant community, reinforcing its social and occupational conservatism.

Yet it is almost impossible actually to measure the extent to which Irish immigrants and their descendants actually identified with Irish culture, belief and traditions. Whilst the survival in Britain of many popular Irish cultural traditions indicates that many Irish-born and their descendants retained an Irish identity, there were undoubtedly others who did not, and who adopted the cultural *mores* of British society. Unfortunately, as Colin Pooley has observed, birthplace data in the census returns reveal little of the diversity or coherence which existed within Irish communities in Britain.[97] Indeed, some historians have argued that the experience of successive generations of Irish migrants in nineteenth-century Britain offers an illustration of massive assimilation rather than integration. Of course, the assimilation of the Irish into British society was one of the great fears voiced by Irish nationalists during the nineteenth century. Thus in 1872, urging the Irish in Britain to maintain 'close and constant union with Ireland in all things', the *Nation* claimed that 'Everything good which the Irish in England have preserved is their own; their vices in nine cases out of ten are acquired. A closer conformity to English life would destroy the former and extend the latter.'[98] Yet the *Nation* also acknowledged that it was almost impossible for the Irish in Britain to live in complete isolation. Indeed, in his recent study of the Irish in seven mid-Victorian Lancashire towns (Liverpool, Manchester, Oldham, Preston, St Helens, Salford and Widnes), W. J. Lowe has concluded that by the 1870s the Lancashire Irish had already achieved a level of community confidence and accomplishment which made it possible for them to use their community life and institutions as 'a bridge to modern industrial culture'. Moreover, in concluding that the experience of the Lancashire Irish during the period was hardly one of static isolation and failure, Lowe notes that by the 1870s the Lancashire Irish community was becoming progressively less distinct and more difficult to portray: 'members of the Irish community, more and more of whom were English-born, generally looked and behaved more like the population in general, which is at least incipient assimilation'.[99] James Walvin has suggested that by 1900 the Irish had, in many respects, bettered themselves, concluding that 'successive generations simply merged into the anonymous background of English and Scottish urban life . . . they had their own religion and their politics, but they were otherwise indistinguishable'.[100] A similar, if more detailed analysis has been provided by Colin Holmes, in an excellent survey of immigration in Britain between 1871 and 1971, which suggests that by 1914 the Irish had managed to effect a transition from a rural society to one of the most advanced industrial nations in the world. Holmes emphasizes that this transition was not a painless or effortless process, but it had at least proceeded more smoothly than at one stage had seemed possible. Moreover, he acknowledges that the Irish did not reject their origins and, like other immigrants, their internal sense of cohesion continued to be reinforced by the hostility they encountered in Britain.[101] In contrast, David Fitzpatrick has questioned the whole concept of developing Irish communities in Victorian Britain and has argued that despite their low social status Irish migrants adopted patterns of residence, religious practice, political participation and criminality which are not indicative of a segregated population locked together in defensive ethnicity.[102]

Clearly, there is much evidence to suggest that the Irish were in many respects 'outcasts' in nineteenth-century Britain. But there is also some evidence to suggest that by 1914 they had won a measure of acceptance in British society, although the process had been a slow one and anti-Irish attitudes were only gradually and partly abandoned, subsequently resurfacing at times of public excitement.

Thus the debate remains open. Were Irish migrants segregated from, or integrated into, British society during the period? Or did the Irish immigrant experience reflect a curious combination of achieved Irish integration and acceptance with a surviving Irish apartness, a view first advocated by Gearoid O'Tuathaigh and subsequently endorsed by some local studies? Clearly the study of the subject involves complex issues to which there are no easy answers, and much remains to be achieved in terms of historical research.

First, there are still relatively few comprehensive studies of the Irish experience in individual towns and cities during the period. Finnegan's *Poverty and Prejudice* and Lees's *Exiles of Erin* are exceptions, for most local studies have tended to concentrate on specific dimensions of the Irish experience such as poverty, crime, public health, housing, education or religion rather than on an holistic approach. Even then, micro-studies can, at best, tell only part of the story and there is clearly room for further comparative intra-regional studies of Irish communities on the lines of Lowe's *The Irish in mid-Victorian Lancashire*. For example, whilst the Irish experience in Lancashire and London has been reasonably well charted, studies of the Irish in the Midlands, Yorkshire and the north-east have been relatively sparse. Similarly, whilst there have been a number of useful studies of the Irish in South Wales, the Irish experience in North Wales remains relatively obscure. Arguably, until further regional studies are undertaken there will always be the danger that the experience of the Irish in south Lancashire – especially Liverpool – will continue to unduly colour, if not dominate, our understanding of the Irish in Britain during the period.

Second, as this chapter perhaps illustrates, the bulk of scholarly research on the Irish in Britain has overwhelmingly focused on the early and mid-Victorian periods – the period of maximum Irish immigration – where source materials are more accessible. In contrast, we know relatively little of the experiences of second and third-generation Irish during the late nineteenth and early twentieth centuries, and until this is achieved it remains difficult to assess just how far the Irish integrated into British society in the long term and the degree of differentiation in the Irish experience in both time and place.

Third, the study of the Irish in nineteenth-century Britain has tended to focus, in broad terms, on social and religious themes rather than on economic and political issues. We need to know much more about Irish settlement and demography, in and out migration, social mobility, employment patterns and mixed marriages. Until this is achieved, in part through the diachronic analysis of census data, it is difficult to assess how static or dynamic Irish communities were. Indeed, in many towns the 'Little Irelands' of the 1840s and 1850s had disappeared by the end of the century in the wake of slum clearance programmes, yet the districts where the Irish resettled still await detailed investigation. We also need to know much more about the internal dynamics of Irish communities in terms of leadership, both clerical and lay, community organizations, and cultural and recreational provisions. Indeed, the full spectrum of associations dedicated to the cultivation – and protection – of Irish music and song, Irish debating and literary societies, Gaelic League branches and Irish sporting clubs – all of which constituted manifestations of group identity – await serious research. Equally, studies of Irish political and trade union activity are particularly thin on the ground. We know, for example, that there was a significant Irish ingredient in the 'new unionism' in the East End of London during the 1880s, yet the Irish contribution elsewhere remains obscure. We also need to learn much more about the political, social, economic and cultural roles and experiences of Irish women, Irish Protestants and the Irish middle class. Our knowledge of Orangeism beyond Lancashire and Clydeside is at best patchy. Finally, and somewhat surprisingly, the experience of Irish rural workers in nineteenth-century Britain remains largely uncharted territory, despite a wealth of primary source material. Here, surely, lies a potential gold mine for an aspiring doctoral student?

Clearly, although much has been achieved in recent years, we are to a certain extent still scratching at the surface, and even then it is important to acknowledge that much of the surviving qualitative evidence of the Irish in nineteenth-century Britain is non-Irish in character, providing limited and at times highly coloured external perceptions of Irish migrant culture.[103]

Thus, in relative terms, the study of the Irish in nineteenth-century Britain remains retarded in comparison with the nature and parameters of research on the Irish in North America and Australia during the same period. Arguably, if historians are to penetrate the opaque society of the Irish in Britain, there is much to be gleaned from Irish studies world-wide, not least because the loyalty of Irish men and women was not simply a communal one to the Catholic Church and nationalist society, but to these entities in their widest manifestations. Religious, national and ethnic identity came together in the international consciousness of the Irish Catholic emigrant who, aware through newspapers, parochial organizations and political parties of events in Ireland and throughout the Irish diaspora, was part of an international community pervaded by the nationalist movements and the Roman Catholic Church.

Notes

1. See, for example. J. E. Handley, *The Irish in Scotland, 1798–1845*, Cork University Press, Cork, 1943, and *The Irish in Modern Scotland*, Cork University Press, Cork, 1947; J. A. Jackson, *The Irish in Britain*, Routledge, London, 1963. For a comprehensive bibliography of more recent studies see Maureen Hartigan and Mary Hickman, eds., *The History of the Irish in Britain: a Bibliography* Irish in Britain History Centre, London, 1986; see also the select bibliographies in Roger Swift and Sheridan Gilley, eds., *The Irish in Britain, 1815–1939*, Pinter, London, 1989, and Graham Davis, *The Irish in Britain, 1815–1914*, Gill & Macmillan, Dublin, 1991.
2. R. F. Foster, *Modern Ireland, 1600–1972*, Allen Lane, London, 1988, p. 345.
3. See, for example, Jackson, *Irish in Britain*, pp. 1–5.
4. See especially J. Mokyr, *Why Ireland Starved: a Quantitative and Analytical History of the Irish Economy, 1800–50*, Macmillan, London, 1983; C. Ó. Grada, 'Some aspects of nineteenth-century Irish emigration', in L. M. Cullen and T. C. Smout, eds., *Comparative Aspects of Scottish and Irish Economic and Social History, 1600–1900*, Donald, Edinburgh, 1977.
5. David Fitzpatrick, *Irish Emigration, 1801–1921*, Studies in Irish Economic and Social History 1, Economic and Social History Society of Ireland, Dublin, 1984, pp. 26–9.
6. Kerby A. Miller, *Emigrants and Exiles: Ireland and the Irish Exodus to North America*, Oxford University Press, Oxford, 1985, pp. 267–80.
7. Colin Holmes, *John Bull's Island: Immigration and British Society, 1871–1971*, Macmillan, London, 1988, p. 22.
8. Miller, *Emigrants and Exiles*, pp. 131–2.
9. Foster, *Modern Ireland*, p. 350. For migration to Australia see especially Patrick O'Farrell, *The Irish in Australia*, New South Wales University Press, Sydney and Belfast, 1987, chapters 1 and 2; see also R. Reid, 'Green threads of kinship! Aspects of Irish chain-migration to New South Wales, 1820–86', *Familia (Ulster Genealogical Review)*, 2, 3, 1987, pp. 47–56; T. Parkhill, 'That infant colony: aspects of Ulster emigration to Australia, 1790–1860', *Familia*, 2, 3, 1987, pp. 57–72.
10. Fitzpatrick, *Irish Emigration*, pp. 33–4.
11. *Illustrated London News*, 6 July 1850.
12. See especially Alan O'Day, ed., *A Survey of the Irish in England, 1872*, reprinted Hambledon Press, London, 1990, p. xxii.
13. Arthur Redford, *Labour Migration in England, 1800–50*, London, 1926; revised edition Manchester University Press, Manchester, 1964, pp. 132–49.
14. See, for example, Colin Pooley, 'Segregation or integration? The residential experience of the Irish in mid-Victorian Britain', in Swift and Gilley, *The Irish in Britain*, pp. 71–110.

15. See, for example, David Fitzpatrick 'A curious middle place?, The Irish in Britain, 1871–1921', in Swift and Gilley, *The Irish in Britain*, pp. 19–70.
16. See, for example, Clem Richardson, 'The Irish in Victorian Bradford', *Bradford Antiquary*, IX, 1976, pp. 294–316; T. Dillon, 'The Irish in Leeds, 1851–61', *Thoresby Miscellany*, XVI, 1979, pp.1–29; J. M. Werly, 'The Irish in Manchester, 1832-49', *Irish Historical Studies*, xviii, 71, 1973, pp. 345–58.
17. E. P. Thompson, *The Making of the English Working Class*, Gollancz, London, 1963, pp. 469–81.
18. Pooley, 'Segregation or integration?', pp. 71–110.
19. For further details see J. D. Papworth, 'The Irish in Liverpool, 1835–71: Family Structure and Residential Mobility', Ph.D. thesis, University of Liverpool, 1982.
20. Lynn Lees, *Exiles of Erin: Irish Migrants in Victorian London*, Manchester University Press, Manchester, 1979, pp. 55–87.
21. Frances Finnegan, *Poverty and Prejudice: Irish Immigrants in York, 1840–75*, Cork University Press, Cork, 1982, pp. 16–68.
22. John Herson, 'Irish migration and settlement in Victorian England: a small-town perspective', in Swift and Gilley, *The Irish in Britain*, pp. 111–37.
23. Graham Davis, 'Little Irelands', in Swift and Gilley, *The Irish in Britain*, pp. 138–86.
24. Alan Bartlett, 'The Churches in Bermondsey, 1880–1939', Ph.D. thesis, University of Birmingham, 1987.
25. Steven J. Fielding, 'The Irish Catholics of Manchester and Salford: Aspects of their Religious and Political History, 1890–1939', Ph.D. thesis, University of Warwick, 1988.
26. Alan O'Day, ed., *A Survey of the Irish in England*, 1872, reprinted The Hambledon Press, London, 1990.
27. B. S. Rowntree, *Poverty: a Study of Town Life* Nelson, London, 1903, p. 10.
28. For further details see especially D. Morgan, *Harvesters and Harvesting, 1840–1900*, Croom Helm, London, 1982, chapter 5, pp. 76–87; J. H. Johnson, 'Harvest migration from nineteenth-century Ireland', *Institute of British Geographers*, 41, 1967, pp. 97–112; E. J. T. Collins, 'Harvest technology and labour supply in Britain, 1790–1870', *Economic History Review*, XXII, 1969, pp. 453–73.
29. Flora Thompson, *Lark Rise to Candleford*, Oxford University Press, London, 1939, pp. 257–8.
30. See especially E. P. Thompson and Eileen Yeo, eds., *The Unknown Mayhew: Selections from the Morning Chronicle, 1849–50*, Merlin Press, London, 1971, pp. 217–73.
31. Lees, *Exiles of Erin*, pp. 88–122.
32. Tom Gallagher, 'A Tale of Two Cities: communal strife in Glasgow and Liverpool before 1914', in Roger Swift and Sheridan Gilley, eds., *The Irish in the Victorian City*, Croom Helm, London, 1985, pp. 106–29.
33. Bernard Aspinwall and John McCaffrey, 'A comparative view of the Irish in Edinburgh in the nineteenth century', in Swift and Gilley, *The Irish in the Victorian City*, pp. 130–57.
34. Brenda Collins, 'Irish emigration to Dundee and Paisley during the first half of the nineteenth century', in J. M. Goldstrom and L. A. Clarkson, eds., *Irish Population, Economy and Society*, Clarendon Press, Oxford, 1981, pp. 195–212. For an interesting analysis of the positive contribution of Irish immigrants to textile industries, see F. J. Williams, 'The Irish in the East Cheshire Silk Industry, 1851–61', *Transactions of the Historic Society of Lancashire and Cheshire*,

136, 1986, pp. 99–126.

35. *Report on the State of the Irish Poor in Great Britain*, Parliamentary Papers, 1836, 34, xxxiv, 456–7.

36. E. H. Hunt, *British Labour History, 1815–1914*, Longman, London, 1981, pp. 158–79.

37. See, for example, Owen Dudley Edwards and Patricia Storey, 'The Irish Press in Victorian Britain', in Swift and Gilley, *The Irish in the Victorian City*, pp. 158–78.

38. Alan O'Day, *A Survey of the Irish*, p. 153.

39. John Denvir, *The Irish in Britain*, Kegan Paul, London, 1892, pp. 435–7.

40. The potential for research in this area is reflected in M. Lennon, M. McAdam and J. O'Brien, *Across the Water: Irish Women's Lives in Britain*, Virago, London, 1988.

41. *Report on the State of the Irish Poor*, P.P. 1836, xxiv–xxvii.

42. Redford, *Labour Migration*, pp. 159–64.

43. Hunt, *British Labour History*, pp. 158–79.

44. Jeffrey G. Williamson, 'The impact of the Irish on British labour markets during the industrial revolution', *Journal of Economic History*, XLVI, 1986, pp. 693–720.

45. F. Engels, *The Condition of the Working Class in England*, 1844, reprinted Penguin, London, 1987, pp. 123–6.

46. James Treble, 'The attitude of the Roman Catholic Church towards trade unionism in the north of England, 1833–42', *Northern History*, V, 1970, pp. 227–47.

47. See especially R. G. Kirby and A. E. Musson, *The Voice of the People: John Doherty, 1798–1854, Trade Unionist, Radical and Factory Reformer*, Manchester University Press, Manchester, 1975, pp. 85–117.

48. For the career of Tillett see John Saville and A. J. Topham, 'Ben Tillett', in J. Bellamy and J. Saville, *Dictionary of Labour Biography*, 4, Macmillan, London, 1977, pp. 177–85; for John Wheatley see Sheridan Gilley's biography, *Dictionary of Labour Biography* 7, 1984, pp. 251–5; see also Dr Gilley's 'Catholics and socialists in Scotland', in Swift and Gilley, *The Irish in Britain*, pp. 280–323; for James Larkin see E. Larkin, *James Larkin: Irish Labour Leader, 1876–1946*, Routledge and Kegan Paul, London, 1965; for Connolly see C. D. Greaves, *The Life and Times of James Connolly*, Lawrence & Wishart, London, 1961.

49. Fitzpatrick, *Irish Emigration*, p. 13.

50. Frank Neal, 'Liverpool, the Irish steamship companies and the Famine Irish', *Immigrants and Minorities*, v, 1986, pp. 28–61.

51. M. A. G. O'Tuathaigh, 'The Irish in nineteenth-century Britain: problems of integration', *Transactions of the Royal Historical Society*, xxxi, 1981, pp. 149–74.

52. Thomas Carlyle, *Chartism*, 1839; Everyman edition, London, 1972, p. 183.

53. Hunt, *British Labour History*, pp. 161–2. For a useful local study of the perceived link between low standards of public health and the Irish presence see Audrey Coney, 'Mid-nineteenth-century Ormskirk: disease, overcrowding and the Irish in a Lancashire market town', *Transactions of the Historic Society of Lancashire and Cheshire*, 139, 1990, pp. 83–111. The extent to which Irish living conditions influenced both the contemporary social policy debate and contemporary social reforms are discussed by Catherine Jones, *Immigration and Social Policy in Britain*, Tavistock, London, 1977, pp. 43–65.

54. *Report of the Select Committee on Poor Removal*, P.P., 1854, 396, xvii, Minutes of Evidence, pp. 474–6.

55. David Large, 'The Irish in Bristol in 1851: a census enumeration', in Swift and Gilley, *The Irish in the Victorian City*, pp. 37–58.
56. Finnegan, *Poverty and Prejudice*, pp. 110–18.
57. Fitzpatrick, 'A curious middle place', in Swift and Gilley, *The Irish in Britain*, pp. 19–70.
58. Geoffrey Pearson, *Hooligan: a History of Respectable Fears*, Macmillan, London, 1981, p. 74.
59. See, for example, Roger Swift, 'Another Stafford Street row: law, order and the Irish presence in mid-Victorian Wolverhampton', *Immigrants and Minorities*, 3, 1, March 1984, pp. 5–29.
60. Finnegan, *Poverty and Prejudice*, p. 153.
61. Frank Neal, 'A criminal profile of the Liverpool Irish', *Transactions of the Historic Society of Lancashire and Cheshire*, 140, 1991, pp. 161–99. For other aspects of Irish criminality in Liverpool see also Norman Murdoch, 'Salvation Army disturbances in Liverpool, England, 1879–1887', *Journal of Social History*, 25, 8, 1992, pp. 575–93; John Bohstedt, 'More than one working class: Protestant–Catholic riots in Edwardian Liverpool', in John Belchem, ed., *Popular Politics, Riot and Labour: Essays in Liverpool History*, Liverpool University Press, Liverpool, 1992, pp. 173–216. For a full discussion of the relationship between Irish immigration and crime see Roger Swift, 'Crime and the Irish in nineteenth-century Britain', in Swift and Gilley, *The Irish in Britain*, pp. 217–33.
62. Treble, 'The attitude', pp. 227–47.
63. Dorothy Thompson, 'Ireland and the Irish in English radicalism before 1850', in James Epstein and Dorothy Thompson, eds., *The Chartist Experience*, Macmillan, London, 1982, pp. 120–51.
64. John Belchem, 'English working-class radicalism and the Irish, 1815–50', in Swift and Gilley, *The Irish in the Victorian City*, pp. 85–97; see also Dr Belchem's analysis, 'Liverpool in the year of revolution: the political and associational culture of the Irish immigrant community in 1848', in J. Belchem, ed., *Popular Politics, Riot and Labour*, Liverpool University Press, Liverpool, 1992, pp. 68–97.
65. W. J. Lowe, 'Lancashire Fenianism, 1864–71', *Transactions of the Historic Society of Lancashire and Cheshire*, CXXI, 1977, pp. 156–85.
66. Patrick Quinlivan and Paul Rose, *The Fenians in England, 1865–72* Calder, London, 1982.
67. K. R. M. Short, *The Dynamite War: Irish-American bombers in Victorian Britain*, Gill & Macmillan, Dublin, 1979.
68. Swift and Gilley, *The Irish in the Victorian City*, pp. 85–97.
69. Gallagher, 'A Tale of Two Cities', pp. 106–29.
70. P. J. Waller, *Democracy and Sectarianism: a Political and Social History of Liverpool, 1863–1939*, Liverpool University Press, Liverpool, 1981.
71. Neville Kirk, 'Ethnicity, class and popular Toryism, 1850–1890', in Kenneth Lunn, ed., *Hosts, Immigrants and Minorities: Historical Responses to Newcomers in British Society, 1870–1914*, Folkestone, 1980, pp. 64–105.
72. See especially L. W. Brady, *T. P. O'Connor and the Liverpool Irish*, Royal Historical Society, 1983.
73. Alan O'Day, 'Irish influences on parliamentary elections in London, 1885–1914', in Swift and Gilley, *The Irish in the Victorian City*, pp. 98–105.
74. Alan O'Day, 'The political organisation of the Irish in Britain, 1867–1890', in Swift and Gilley, *The Irish in Britain*, pp. 234–79.
75. Lees, *Exiles of Erin*, p. 242.

76. Steven J. Fielding, 'Irish politics in Manchester, 1890–1914', *International Review of Social History*, XXXIII, 1988, pp. 261–84.
77. See, for example, Fitzpatrick, 'A curious middle place?'
78. Fitzpatrick, 'A curious middle place?', p. 32.
79. E. D. Steele, 'The Irish presence in the north of England, 1850–1914', *Northern History*, XII, 1976, pp. 220–41.
80. L. P. Curtis, *Apes and Angels: the Irishman in Victorian Caricature*, David & Charles, Newton Abbot, 1971.
81. Curtis, *Apes and Angels*, p. 100.
82. *Punch*, 18 October 1862.
83. Sheridan Gilley, 'English attitudes to the Irish in England, 1780–1900', in Colin Holmes, ed., *Immigrants and Minorities in British Society*, Allen & Unwin, London, 1978, pp. 81–110.
84. O'Tuathaigh, 'The Irish'.
85. See especially Frank Neal, *Sectarian Violence: the Liverpool Experience, 1819–1914*, Manchester University Press, Manchester, 1987.
86. Fitzpatrick, 'A curious middle place?', p. 34.
87. For further details of these disturbances see especially Pauline Millward, 'The Stockport riots of 1852: a study of anti-Catholic and anti-Irish sentiment', in Swift and Gilley, *The Irish in the Victorian City*, pp. 207–24; J. Foster, *Class Struggle and the Industrial Revolution*, University Paperbacks, London, 1974, pp. 243–6; Frank Neal, 'The Birkenhead Garibaldi riots of 1862', *Transactions of the Historic Society of Lancashire and Cheshire*, 131, 1982, pp. 87–111; Sheridan Gilley, 'The Garibaldi riots of 1862, *Historical Journal*, XVI, 4, 1973, pp. 697–732; W. J. Arnstein, 'The Murphy riots: a Victorian dilemma', *Victorian Studies*, XIX, 1975, pp. 51–71.
88. Millward, 'The Stockport riots', pp. 207–24.
89. Roger Swift, 'Anti-Catholicism and Irish disturbances: public order in mid-Victorian Wolverhampton', *Midland History*, IX, 1984, pp. 87–108.
90. D. W. Miller, 'Irish Catholicism and the Great Famine', *Journal of Social History*, IX, 1975, pp. 81–98.
91. Gerard Connolly, 'Irish and Catholic: myth or reality?', in Swift and Gilley, *The Irish in the Victorian City*, pp. 225–54.
92. Sheridan Gilley, 'The Catholic faith of the Irish slums: London, 1840–70', in H. J. Dyos and M. Wolff, eds., *The Victorian City: Images and Realities*, II, Routledge, London, 1973, pp. 837–53; see also Dr Gilley's 'Vulgar piety and the Brompton Oratory, 1850–60', in Swift and Gilley, *The Irish in the Victorian City*, pp. 255–66.
93. Raphael Samuel, 'The Roman Catholic Church and the Irish poor', in Swift and Gilley, *The Irish in the Victorian City*, pp. 267–300. For the response of the Catholic Church to the Irish presence in Wales see especially Paul O'Leary, 'Irish immigration and the Catholic Welsh district, 1840–50', in G. H. Jenkins and J. B. Smith, eds., *Politics and Society in Wales, 1840–1922: Essays in Honour of Ieuan Gwynedd Jones*, University of Wales Press, Cardiff, 1988, pp. 29–45.
94. Fitzpatrick, 'A curious middle place?', p. 38.
95. Lees, *Exiles of Erin*, p. 250.
96. Lees, *Exiles of Erin*, p. 249.
97. Pooley, 'Segregation or integration?', pp. 71–110.
98. *The Nation*, 29 October, 1872, cited in O'Day, *A Survey of the Irish*, p. 129.
99. W. J. Lowe, *The Irish in mid-Victorian Lancashire: the Shaping of a Working Class Community*, Lang, New York, 1989, pp. 211–12.
100. James Walvin, *Passage to Britain: Immigration in British History and Politics*,

Penguin, London, 1984, pp. 58–9.
101. Holmes, *John Bull's Island*, pp. 20–2, 36–42.
102. Fitzpatrick, 'A curious middle place?', pp. 50–1.
103. For an analysis of some of the major primary sources for the study of the Irish in nineteenth-century Britain see Roger Swift, *The Irish in Britain, 1815–1914: Perspectives and Sources*, Historical Association H93, London, 1990, pp. 33–7.

3 Faction fights: the Irish worlds of Butte, Montana, 1875–1917

David M. Emmons

In 1917 Father Patrick Brosnan, recently arrived at his new assignment at St Mary's parish in the copper-mining town of Butte, Montana, wrote a letter to his father in Limerick. His words were encouraging. 'Butte,' said the young priest, 'is a great city. We have seven fine Catholic parishes, all Irish.' Later in the letter he elaborated on what he meant by 'all Irish'. 'Everyone here,' he said, 'is from Castletownbere.' His reference was to a small township in West County Cork, and in making it he lent his own impressionistic authority to two enduring and defining truths and half-truths of Butte and its history: it was a town with a large and important Irish enclave, and many of those Irish were from West Cork.[1]

The reality was different from these perceptions – but not by much. Butte in 1917, as it had been in 1900, was the most Irish town in the United States. In 1900 first and second-generation Irish numbered over 8,000 in a total population of just over 30,000. Thus 26 per cent of the residents of the city, 2,500 miles from the nearest eastern port, were either Irish-born or the children of the Irish-born. Brosnan made more of this than the facts warranted; only five of its seven Catholic parishes, including his own St Mary's, were all – or even nearly all – Irish. Given the population figures, however, Brosnan may be forgiven his slight exaggeration of Irish ecclesiastical influence.[2]

Brosnan's Castletownbere reference is more troublesome. In Butte, Castletownbere was a generic label, used to identify those from the town as well as from its largest neighbouring villages in West Cork, including particularly Allihies, Eyeries and Bere Island. Obviously, everyone from Ireland was not from West Cork, but just how many were and what the full effect of this regional concentration may have been are not easily known. The US Bureau of the Census did not enquire about Irish counties of origin; neither, until 1906, did the US Immigration and Naturalization Service. Evidence of a mass chain migration, at whatever moment prior to 1906, when the West Cork connection was fixed in the public mind, can be had only by an investigation of the surnames of Butte's Irish and the counties with which those names were usually associated.

For any other immigrant group this would be impossible, but for the Irish, tied to their place of birth by powerful cultural and historical bonds, tentative conclusions as to county of origin are possible. The most common surnames in West Cork were Sullivan, Shea, Lynch, McCarthy, Harrington and O'Neill. These are offered in no order, although a strong case can be made for Sullivan as the name most likely to be encountered in or near Castletownbere. It was also the name most likely to be encountered in Butte, outnumbering Smith and everything else by many dozens of entries in the city directories. The other West Cork names were equally well represented.[3]

The membership records of the largest Irish-American associations in Butte tell the same story. The Ancient Order of Hibernians (AOH) and the Robert Emmet Literary Association (RELA) – the Butte chapter of the Clan-na-Gael – both formed in 1881, and both enrolling thousands of Irish over the years, were dominated by men whose names suggest West Cork origins. This was particularly the case in the early years when Butte's reputation as a place where 'everyone was from Castletownbere' was being formed. There were natives of other Irish counties in this early Irish blend, but the AOH enrolment records for 1885–8 make a clear point. Of eighty-seven men admitted to membership, twenty-eight bore one of the six names listed above. There were doubtless many others among the eighty-seven from West Cork, but let any error be on the side of caution.[4]

Recently published genealogies complete the picture of this Castletownbere supply line. Riobard O'Dwyer, a native of the area, traced the family histories of over 14,000 men and women from Castletownbere, Eyeries, Allihies, and Bere Island. From Eyeries alone over 1,700 people emigrated to the United States between 1870 and 1915; of that total, 1,138 went to Butte. The predominance of Sullivan among Butte surnames is no mystery; O'Dwyer lists members of seventy-seven different Sullivan (or O'Sullivan) families who left Eyeries for Butte. Harringtons and Sheas were close behind.[5]

A final check on the accuracy of name/place association was provided after 1906 when the US Immigration and Naturalization Service began to list county or village of origin on petitions for naturalization. Of eighty-two Sullivans, Harringtons and Sheas who filed that document in Butte, eighty-one were from a West Cork village. It is more than just unlikely, it is very nearly unthinkable that more than a tiny handful of Butte's thousands of Sullivans, Harringtons or Sheas were from any other part of Ireland.[6]

This remarkable concentration of West Corkmen was no historical accident. Butte was a copper-mining town, by 1895 the largest and most productive in the world. West Cork had had the only copper mines in Ireland, at Hungry Hill, near Allihies. Some of its sons went direct to Butte's mines, part of a chain migration that would last for fifty years and nearly depopulate Hungry Hill. Others made intermediate stops in the copper mines of the upper peninsula of Michigan or in the hard rock mines of California, Nevada and Colorado, participants in a slightly different chain migration. The point is the same in either event. Many West Corkmen knew how to mine; Butte had need of their skills.[7]

One of the first to recognize this happy pairing was Marcus Daly, one of Butte's legendary copper kings. Father Brosnan acknowledged Daly's importance when he wrote to his father that it was Daly who 'made Butte an Irish town. . . . He did not care for any man but an Irishman and . . . did not give a job to anyone else.' As before, Brosnan exaggerated – but, also as before, only slightly. Of the 5,369 working Irishmen in Butte in 1900, just under 4,800, a remarkable 90 per cent, worked in one of its mines. Of 5,534 miners working in Daly's Anaconda Mine in 1894, 1,251 were Irish-born; at least another 1,000 second-generation Irish joined them.[8]

Daly's preference for Irish miners came naturally to him. He was himself a native of Ballyjamesduff in the Ulster county of Cavan. He was also an active Irish-American nationalist, host to Michael Davitt during the latter's 1886 visit to Butte, a member of the AOH and proposed for membership in the RELA. Daly, like many others of considerably less wealth and influence, wore his Irishness like a badge. As the founder and chief executive of the Anaconda Copper Mining Company he was in a position to make Butte an Irish town. His hiring officers were almost always Irish; job notices were often in Gaelic Irish; he closed his mines on St Patrick's Day and other Irish holidays; he routinely met with Irish associational 'hiring committees', groups of influential Emmets or Hibernians formed to insure jobs at ACM mines for recently arrived Irish. As John J. McCarthy, mine foreman, union and AOH officer, and native of Castletownbere, once told the Hibernians, Irishmen not in the AOH were no loss to the association. 'Let them join the Birds' and Animals' organizations and see how many jobs they will secure for them.' The AOH secured the jobs because Daly favoured its members.[9]

The anti-Irish and anti-Catholic American Protective Association charged that this meant that ' "NO ENGLISH NEED APPLY" was virtually posted on the doors of the Anaconda mines', and that 'Pope Marcus', the 'boss Irishman', was establishing a personal Irish fiefdom in Butte. All of this may have been true; perhaps that is what Brosnan meant when he called Butte a 'great city'. But national loyalties were not conspicuous in the managerial style of American capitalists, and Marcus Daly was no blind sentimentalist. It bears repeating: most of the men from West Cork knew how to mine. Under their tutelage other Irishmen could learn. Daly, a veteran of the Comstock and Utah mines, knew that. And so he filled his mines and his corporate boardroom with his countrymen, in the process making the Anaconda company one of the more important of the Irish organizations in Butte.[10]

Daly died in 1900 and his successors as head of ACM were less accommodating. Each of them from 1900 to 1956 – William Scallon, John Ryan and Con Kelley – was Irish and each was a member of the AOH, the RELA or both. The Irishness of the ACM had not changed, but its hiring practices had. In part this was owing to changes in corporate organization that denied Scallon, Ryan and Kelley the freedom that Daly had had. In larger part it arose from technological changes. New mining machinery and techniques reduced ACM's dependence on experienced miners, of whatever nationality. From 1876 to 1900, however, while Daly was still in charge and Irish mining skills were still in demand, the Irish and the company forged a close and mutually beneficial partnership. And Butte began to take on a West Cork character it would never lose.[11]

An estimate is here in order. The evidence is unscientific but compelling. By 1900 at least half and probably nearer to 60 per cent of Butte's 5,300 Irishmen were from Castletownbere or some place very near it or were the sons of parents from that part of West Cork. The result was an enclave within an enclave, a world of skilled miners from West Cork living at the heart of a larger Irish mining community. It was an exclusive club, this informal fraternity of West Cork miners. Irishmen could enter the ethno-occupational enclave almost anywhere, but only those with the right credentials could penetrate its core.

There are two features of the Irish immigration generally that set the Irish apart from other non-British immigrant groups. The first of these is its duration. Significant numbers of Irish began to arrive in the United States in the 1830s; they continued to arrive in significant numbers until the 1920s. Only the German-Americans had a comparable experience with long-running immigration. For almost a century, spanning five generations, the people of Catholic Ireland came of age knowing that emigration was a part of the social calculus of their lives. For that same century, Irish in America grew up knowing that every year would bring new boatloads of impoverished Irish to America. But the calculus changed as Ireland and America changed. The emigrant of 1841 left for different reasons and retained different memories from the emigrant of 1881 or 1911. Early arriving Irish had both problems and opportunities unknown to those who came after and on account of them. They encountered an often hostile host society, but they also entered an Irish-American world at the moment of its creation; they would become its senior partners. The transition of later arriving Irish was smoothed by the pioneering of those who had come first, but the short cuts to power within that community were gone, taken either by the pioneers or by their sons. The result was a divided Irish-American world.[12]

The other distinguishing feature of the Irish immigration is that Ireland was an 'enslaved nation' and that this contradiction in terms conditioned and defined the Irish-American response to everything from social organization to worker protest to political decision-making. Ireland had to be made free; English control had to end. Ireland's exiled children were as answerable on that score as those who remained 'at home'. There were, to be sure, different ways to achieve freedom, and different ways to define and order a free Ireland once it had been achieved. It is also true that wealthier Irish tended to be more cautious in their selection of means, more conservative in defining the ultimate ends. America had made them wealthy; Ireland, they believed, should become America writ small. Conversely, those whom America had not favoured were less likely to describe their new home as heaven descended and more reluctant to see Ireland pattern itself after it. In general, however, a devotion to Ireland's welfare and to its 'exultation among the nations' cut across class lines and united the Irish as no other issue could have.[13]

There is no contradiction between these two facets of the Irish immigration. Its duration, the successive waves of Irish coming to America, had a centrifugal force, creating socially fragmented ethnic communities. The commitment to some kind of independent Ireland, shared by each of the immigrant generations, was centripetal, providing a cause around which all in the community could gather. Both could and did operate at the same time within the same community. They often took turns in the dominant role, depending on events in Ireland, America or the community itself. Each feature, however, was always present and each was always influenced by the other.

There may be no place in America where these patterns were revealed more clearly than Butte, Montana. Irish began arriving in the 1870s; they continued to arrive until the 1920s. This, in itself, does not set Butte apart. But the fact that the first Irish to arrive were the first of any nation to arrive meant a quick Irish ascension to positions of power. There was no host society to obstruct them, and the early Irish formed Butte far more than Butte formed them. Their associations were socially determinative, not ethnically segregant.

Those associations also gave voice to the causes of Ireland. The most important of them were the AOH and the RELA. In no other town did either association enrol a higher percentage of the eligible Irish than they did in Butte. There was some rivalry between the two groups, though not enough to interfere with their joint ownership and operation of Hibernia Hall. Both were Irish nationalist associations dedicated to Irish independence in one form or another. They were both overwhelmingly working-class miner in membership – however divided this working class might be on the basis of age, skill, Irish county of origin, marital status, residence and, for want of better terms, certainty of livelihood. But both associations also and quite intentionally worked to remain inter-class in outlook and agenda. There were social classes in Ireland and in Irish-America. Bloodletting between them, however, had to be postponed until Ireland was free. On this, AOH and RELA were in total accord.[14]

The results were strikingly at variance with what conventional class analysis would yield. Marcus Daly was proposed for RELA membership by Joseph Norris; a year later Norris was elected president of the Butte Miners' Union (BMU). Walter Breen, a miner, union officer and physical force nationalist, proposed Con Kelley's name for AOH membership. John J. O'Meara, a brewing company executive, served on a joint RELA–AOH memorial committee with Daly, Anthony Shovlin, a BMU officer, and James Maher, secretary of the Western Federation of Miners (WFM), an organization with advanced radical ideas.[15]

The close relationship between the Irish associations and the Butte Miners' Union warrants particular attention. The BMU was formed in 1878. Potentially, it could have been one of the most radical unions in America. It begat the Western Federation of Miners, which begat the Western and American Labor Unions which begat the Industrial Workers of the World (IWW). Butte was known as the Gibraltar of American unionism, and the BMU was the rock upon which Butte's house of labour was built. It seemed to be an industrial rather than a trade union; it appeared to be democratically run and inclusionist (except for Asians) in its membership policies. It insisted upon and got a closed shop agreement from the mining companies; it stood guard over the best paid work force in America; and it became the largest local association of working men anywhere in the world.[16]

This putative radicalism, however, was at best superficial, at worst a delusion. For the BMU also bought company stock; negotiated time contracts in violation of WFM rules; acquiesced in hiring practices that discriminated on the basis of ethnicity; made firm distinctions between miners and mine workers; allowed – nay, encouraged – a system that favoured contract over salaried miners; and never in its entire thirty-six year history engaged in a strike, work slow-down or job action of any sort. Little wonder that contemporaries called it 'the most conservative labor organization in the West', even 'the means of preventing serious strikes by other organizations . . .'. Less wonder still that in 1902 Ed Boyce, the genuinely radical, County Donegal-born president of the WFM, moved the federation's headquarters from Butte to Denver to escape the influence of the BMU, which, for Boyce at least, 'was in control of M's Daily [sic]', and did not 'speak its own interests'.[17]

The BMU, however, was not just conservative; it was also Irish-run. From 1885 to 1914, 180 BMU officers were listed in the Butte city directories; 145 of them, a remarkable 80 per cent, were Irish, many of them of West Cork origin. As important as their Irishness was the fact that most of these officers were also active members of the AOH and/or the RELA. The names of the ninety-four different Irishmen who held those 145 offices were checked against the Irish associations' membership ledgers between 1882 and 1915; sixty-four of the ninety-four were members of one or both.[18]

Obviously, questions arise from all this. Was the BMU's conservatism in any way a function of its Irishness? The answer can only be yes. But that begs the next question: why would Irish miners in a town like Butte be this protective of corporate privilege? One possible answer might be that in this instance the corporation was itself protective of workers' privileges, or at least of the privileges of those workers whose Irishness matched that of the corporation's chief officers and managers. For the ideologically pure – if not rigid – this suggests class collaborationism, worker false consciousness. This was what Boyce meant when he said that the BMU did not speak its own interests. To Boyce, himself a member of the RELA, the Butte union was little more than an extension of Hibernia Hall.[19]

All of this, of course, assumes that class allegiance was more natural than ethnic, that the Irish *should* have behaved differently, been more inclusionary, less protective of their own job security. In an imaginary world, in an impossible place, all this might be so. But of all the world's people, the Irish of the second half of the nineteenth century were arguably the most unsettled and insecure. Battered by social and economic forces they could not control and did not understand, they were unlikely candidates for immigrant fast tracks, whether of upward mobility or worker radicalism. They were driven by a need to find steady work and fix themselves to a place, and to build in that place an Irish enclave capable of recreating some of the social and cultural patterns of a land suddenly old in more ways than one. That enclave had also to be able to protect the jobs that alone could give it meaning and permanence.[20]

The jobs 'reserved' for the Irish were not sinecures. The work was hard and dangerous. More to the immediate point, it was only as steady as the wild cyclical swings of industrial capitalism could make it. The extended shutdowns of 1893, 1903 and 1907–8 demonstrated that that was not always as steady as an Irish miner might wish. Note then, in this context, how many of the Irish-led BMU's 'sins' against the working class involved the embrace of union policies calculated to ensure a measure of job security for its members, institutional security for itself: the purchase at a discount of blue-chip stock in the fourth largest corporation in the United States; the negotiation of time contracts that tied wages to the price of copper; support for a hiring system that gave job preference to the steady men – of whatever nation; hostility to the excesses of some of its 'offspring', the WFM and the IWW. The Irish may have led the BMU on a conservative and exclusionary course, but no one can say that it was not a job-conscious one.[21]

The English historian of labour Eric Hobsbawm has argued that 'the power to exclude' was fundamental to the working class's ability to protect its job security by controlling the size of the work force. Ideally, men were excluded from a labour force because they lacked the requisite skills, the simple ability to do the work. The result of this exclusion was a natural aristocracy of labour. Skill, however, was a useful criterion for exclusion only as long as the skills themselves were useful. But well-honed skills – with hammer and drill in deep hard-rock mines, for example – began losing their economic relevance around the turn of the century. Machines – in this case pneumatic drills in the hands of men with little experience underground – began to do work once thought a craft. Air drills increased the number of men who could extract copper ore by a factor of many hundreds. Company executives were elated. They had worked closely with the Irish associations during the Daly years. They had, after all, been dependent upon Irish goodwill in assembling a skilled work force. Now they could ignore the old Irish. The number of places where men could be found to work in the mines grew to include every place where strong men were unemployed: Finland, Italy, Serbia, Montenegro – and all parts of Ireland.[22]

This deskilling process presented established miners with a genuine crisis. The Irish among them had once been able to count on their skills and on ACM hiring preference; by 1907 the former were useless and the latter did not survive Daly. As a result, they faced the loss of the jobs that had made possible the enclave which made sense of the world. BMU conservatism must be interpreted in this context. Non-Irish miners, understandably, were not sympathetic, but neither were many of the Irish miners who had migrated to Butte after the shutdown of 1907–8. The non-Irish are known to historians as 'new' immigrants. The older Butte Irish called them 'Bohunks', 'European Chinamen'; they were only slightly kinder to the new men who came from Ireland.[23]

By whatever name, and from whatever place, the new immigrants laid siege to the Irish aristocracy. The Irish-run BMU would lead the counter-attack. In 1912 the union supported – may even have initiated – a hiring system known as the rustling card that self-styled insurgents in the union called a system of blacklisting. That same year the BMU refused to strike or take any other action to protest the firing of 500 Finnish socialists from the Butte hill. Union rebels knew why. As one of them explained, 'the great majority of the members are conservatives, . . . the Catholic Irish have been the leading factions among the conservatives'. Two years later, in 1914, insurgents blew up Miners' Union Hall and destroyed the Gibraltar of unionism. An IWW leader by the name of Arturo Giovannitti gave a speech in Butte in which he congratulated the rebels for having ended the reign of the BMU, 'an obsolete union'. Pointing to the rubble of what had been Union Hall, Giovannitti told his listeners that ' "Here Lies the Remains of 36 Years of Peace and Prosperity." The working men of Butte should be ashamed of those thirty-six years.' Whether ashamed or not, they never recaptured them. From 1914 to 1921 Butte was rocked by four strikes, occupied and policed by the US Army, terrorized by ACM gunmen and IWW agitators, and generally split apart by violent class war.[24]

The dynamiters of Miners' Union Hall were identified as 'Austrians, Finns and Montenegrins'. Giovanitti was an Italian. So far the story reads like any standard chapter on the ethnic diversity and fragmentation of the American working class. Indeed, had the BMU been an AFL local (certainly it acted like one), the story would fit perfectly Gwendolyn Mink's division of the American working class into 'old labor and new immigrants', with the latter the victims of the nativism of the former. The difference in Butte was that many of the radical leaders – Muckie McDonald, Ed Keenan, Pat Wallace, Joe Shannon, Joe Kennedy, P. W. Flynn, Dan Shovlin, Maurice Ferriter, James Treanor, John Lennon, Bill Dunn, and there were many, many more – were themselves Irish. The warfare that destroyed the BMU was intra- as well as inter-ethnic. The Irish were both the old labour and the new immigrants.[25]

Other researchers will have to comment on whether this pattern was repeated in other American-Irish towns, but at least in Butte there was a first first generation of Irish and a second first generation, and the two evinced very different values. This distinction is not intended literally, any more than any reference to generations can be. No fixed date marks the end of one and the beginning of another. The fact, however, is that those Irish who arrived in Butte after about 1907 behaved differently from those who arrived between 1880 and 1907. Much of this is altogether to be expected. The later arrivals – the second first generation – were younger than the Irish-born who had been in Butte for a decade or more. As a consequence, late arriving Irish immigrants tended to associate more with the sons of the first first generation than with their 'fellow immigrants' and to take on some of the attitudes of these American-born, including perhaps what Charles Fanning calls the 'archetypal second generation's genteel rejection of the old country'. In Butte that meant as well a rejection – though it was seldom genteel – of the old associations, the protectors of the old country's interests.[26]

But there was much more to this disaffection with the established associations than just changing attitudes toward Ireland and its various and conflicted fights for freedom. The AOH and the RELA were more than nationalists' clubs. They had been, and to a certain though lesser extent still were, central partners in what the non-Irish and many new Irish thought were collusive sweetheart deals with the BMU and ACM. Those deals guaranteed a certain job security; they may even have involved the assignment of associational Irishmen to safer and cooler levels in the mines.

Safe and steady work was less important to these later arriving Irish than it had been to immigrants who came before them. The new Irish, for example, were markedly slower to take out naturalization papers than the first first generation had been. But, more important than what this may indicate about their settled habits, they objected to the fact that safer and more stable jobs had been purchased at such cost to worker solidarity. As one old Irishmen said by way of explaining why new arrivals had rejected membership of the AOH, the younger Irish were afraid that what was being said 'at meetings [was] being reported on the 6th floor', a reference to the Hennessy Building, where ACM had its corporate headquarters. Another veteran Hibernian had worse news. Young 'contumelious' Irishmen, it seemed, 'ridiculously scorned' the AOH; they thought of it as tired and dottering, little more than the Irish branch of the Knights of Columbus.[27]

As the AOH and the RELA fell from favour, the younger Irish put together an association of their own. They called it the Pearse–Connolly Irish Independence Club, and, though no membership records survive, it had an obvious appeal to younger and more ideologically adventurous Irish. Named after the two leaders of the 1916 Rising, Patrick Pearse, mystic poet, and James Connolly, Marxist ideologue, it was formed at the urging of the Irish socialist Con Lehane, who visited Butte in 1916, and inspired by the overheated rhetoric of another Irish radical, Jim Larkin, who visited three times between 1915 and 1917. It kept a not very respectful distance from the established Irish. It did not meet in Hibernia Hall but in Finlanders' Hall, where it shared space with the striking Metal Mine Workers' Union, the Finnish Workers' Club and the Industrial Workers of the World. From this address it joined in strikes in 1917, 1918, 1919 and 1920; this after thirty-six years of BMU and Irish-sponsored peace and prosperity! Only the 1917 strike had any support from older Irish, undoubtedly because the issues in 1917 included America's entry into the war on the side of Britain, the nation that had 'riveted the chains of slavery around Ireland'.[28]

Obviously, the Pearse–Connollys did not march with, or to the tune of, the ethnic exclusionists in the BMU and the ACM as, it was charged, had the older Irish associations. Rather, it lined itself up with the ethnic inclusionists in the IWW. It mourned Frank Little, the martyred Wobbly, lynched in Butte in 1917. Robert Emmet, the martyred patriot, was too distant and abstract. In 1917 Judge Jeremiah Lynch, forty-six years old, a West Cork native, and the best known Irishman in Butte, told a newspaper man that he knew nothing of the Pearse–Connolly Club's plans for the first anniversary of the 1916 Rising, because 'I have no influence with them.' Neither did the AOH. When asked by the Pearse–Connollys to march on St Patrick's Day the Hibernians 'turned down the invitation of Peirce and Connelly Club to parade', announcing instead that 'we are going to Mass'. The misspellings of the two names were *probably* unintentional.[29]

None of this should occasion great surprise. The young men of 1907–20 left an Ireland vastly different from that of 1880. Mink refers to the 'workers' rebellion' in Britain in the early twentieth century, and certainly some of that impassioned worker radicalism had to have influenced Britain's Irish subjects. But even those remote from or unmoved by workers' rebellions lived through politically relevant changes. The early emigrants' sense of grievance was formed by their family's landless status and by the exploitation of that fact by the Land Leagues. They thought of their emigration as coerced and tragic. Those who stayed in Ireland were the lucky ones. The later emigrants, on the other hand, grew up in an Ireland where much of the land had been restored to Irishmen, though seldom of the poorest class, and where the messages of class-conscious workers, however indistinct, were part of the ideological mix. Their emigration was not thought coerced but rather the result of a purposeful decision. It was not a tragic event but very nearly a blessed one. A proletarianization of sorts had taken place in Ireland between 1880 and 1905, and with it came a loss of moderation and a far greater willingness on the part of the Irish poor to acknowledge that their class enemies were as often clad in coats of Irish green as of Protestant orange or English red.[30]

Clearly, the latter immigrants came from a different Ireland, but they also came from different parts of the country. Here is where that minor change in bureaucratic record keeping becomes important. In 1906 the Immigration and Naturalization Service was placed under the Department of Labor – itself a matter of historical significance – and began to enquire about an immigrant's town and/or county of origin. It is possible to know with certainty from which counties the second first generation of Irish immigrants to Butte came. The problem with this method is that it can be used only to trace those Irish who declared their intention of becoming an American citizen or who actually petitioned for naturalization. This excludes those who did not seek citizenship or had taken out their papers somewhere else. The sample, in other words, is of those who were – or thought they might one day be – settled. A fair number of Butte's new Irish fitted neither category. They wandered into Butte as they had wandered into other American industrial towns, stayed a few months or years, then wandered out. These types could not be tracked. Those who could were typical of the whole *only for Irish county of origin.*

Data were collected for 846 wage-earning men who petitioned for naturalization in Butte between 1906 and 1928, the years when ACM was assembling its 'new' immigrant work force. It was a different group of Irishmen from that which came before it. The 846 came from all thirty-two of Ireland's counties. County Cork still topped the list, but with only 233 or 27 per cent of the whole, a percentage less than half that of the earlier years. Of those Corkonians, moreover, a considerable number were from Macroom, Ardgroom, Cork city and Bantry, and did not bear the old surnames. Many still came from 'Castletown', and Eyeries, but few were recorded from Allihies and, on balance, the West Cork share of the county's immigration seems as diminished as the county's share of Ireland's. Another salient feature of this second Irish immigration was its distinct northern flavour. There were 100 men from Mayo, forty-two from Galway and thirty-seven from Sligo, all in Connaught; there were 113 from Donegal and fifty-six from Down in Ulster. Ulster counties, in fact, supplied 230 of the men in the survey.[31]

All of this reflects national trends. Beginning in the 1890s, the sources of Irish immigration generally were moving from south to north. But as the immigration 'virus' moved north it mutated. The Ulster connection, for example, may provide a part of the explanation for the different habits and attitudes of the new Irish immigrants in Butte. First, Ulstermen would certainly have been more aware than most Irish of the depth of Irish Protestant hostility to an independent Ireland. Second, they would likely have been more familiar with the socialist messages of James Connolly and Jim Larkin.[32]

It is difficult to learn anything of where these men lived between the time they left Ireland and their arrival in Butte. The only query that is helpful concerned the birthplace of children, and that, of course, is definitive only for the mothers. Two hundred and eleven men of the total had children and, assuming they were with their wives at birth, of that number 179 were in Butte at the birth of at least one. But, of the others, thirteen listed Glasgow, Paisley, Kelty or simply Scotland as birthplaces; another eight cited Liverpool, Charly, Blackburn or England. All of these twenty-one with previous residence in Britain were either from Ulster counties or from neighbouring Mayo. Assuming that a comparable number of those without families had also sojourned in industrial Britain, the case that a significant number of these north county Irish had encountered Larkin or Connolly – and in one of their more radical moments – is strengthened. This is not to say that these Irish should be counted among the immigrants pre-radicalized by their European experiences; it is to say that their perspectives on both Irish and worker rights would not have been the same as those of the average Kerryman – or Corkonian.[33]

Based, then, on county of origin, the new Irish immigration was appreciably different from the old. For the non-Irish in Butte this would have been of no importance. Irish, they reasoned, were Irish – or, in the language of the time, flannelmouths, savages, man-eaters, cannibals and harps. For the Irishman, however, these regional distinctions may have been very important indeed. One Butte Hibernian referred to 'countyism', another to 'factional prejudice', as Ireland's great curse, the modern expression of the intertribal warfare of ancient Gaelic chieftains and faction fighters. If everyone really had been from Castletownbere, intense localism would have been a powerful source of community. But not everyone was from Castletownbere, and the number of those who were not increased dramatically after 1907.[34]

The extent of these county rivalries and how deeply they cut cannot be known. It was not as simple as West Cork versus the rest of Ireland. The men and women from Tipperary and Donegal, from Mayo and Kerry, were themselves self-consciously of their county and distinct in important ways from those Irish from other and less favoured ones. It is more difficult to judge the depth of Irish provincialism. Intense localism was thought the near exclusive property of the rural Irish. The new Irish, however, like the old, were not necessarily from rural Ireland. Being from County Down, for example, almost always meant from the town of Rostrevor; Sligo meant Charlestown; Mayo meant Westport. Those were hardly cosmopolitan centres but neither were they places that would have bred a particularly intense form of 'countyism'. The urban nature of this second immigration would also suggest that most of Butte's new Irish were the sons of artisans, labourers and shopkeepers rather than farmers. This would not have made them freethinkers but it should have made it easier for them to understand the earlier Irish response to Butte. The fact is, it did not. There was countyism. The point is that it cannot have sprung from the usual sources.[35]

It arose, rather, because county distinctions were indirectly involved in the older Irishmen's efforts to control the work force. It is not that West Corkmen discriminated against other Irish; countyism and factionalism did not extend that far. But older West Corkmen, by virtue of their years in Butte and, in some cases, the special skills they had brought with them, had risen to higher rank than the younger Irish of whatever county. Their skills had lost much of their usefulness, but their desire to protect the jobs that allowed them to cling to their place in Butte had lost none of its potency. Old Irish hostility to new Irish would exhibit a strong county bias simply because of the sequence of Irish settlement in Butte.

As a result the old Irish viewed the later arrivals as only slightly less obnoxious than the other 'new' immigrants. The new Irish were not like the Finns, or 'Bohunks', or Italians: they spoke English; they were Catholic – though their faith, like their manners, needed improvement; their names had a familiar and resonant sound. But, like all the other new men, they were too young, too untrained, too dangerous to work around, too willing to work for low wages, and too ready to listen to the mindless radicalism of BMU insurgents. Some of this is simply the grumbling of old men, but more of it is the class-conscious wail of settled workers, aware that their wages and their job security were imperilled by what amounted to a new and disposable labour force. Father Brosnan wrote home in 1917 that 'some 2,000 Irish boys had come to Butte in the last month. Hundreds who were raised decent now stand and beg for ten cents to get a drink.' The Irishness of those '2,000' would not have counted for much; their effect on the work force would be no different from that of 2,000 young and transient from any other nation.[36]

For their part, the 2,000 can have felt no friendlier toward the old Irish. The latter would have been approximately the age of the fathers the young men had left behind. They would have been seen as examples of what twenty-five years in America did to a man. Some of the young men – not necessarily those whose names do not appear on petitions of naturalization – may have envied the security of their elders, but very few can have envied the way the old men got that security. The debate over whether Ireland should try to be a smaller United States or something very different would have taken on a new generational dimension. Worker consciousness would not have been passed down from 'father' to 'son', from one Irish generation to the next. But neither would it likely have passed up from 'son' to 'father'.

The two generations of Irish immigrants would have viewed one another from across a deep and widening cultural divide.

This cultural division could easily have been overlooked. Of the second first generation for whom data exist, outward behaviour was remarkably like that of the first first generation. They still toiled underground: 669 of the 846 (79 per cent) worked as miners. They were no more assimilationist: 750 of them were accompanied by two other Irishmen when they petitioned for naturalization. Residential patterns remained the same: the new Irish opted to live in old Irish neighbourhoods. Chain migration was still the rule. You could see it at work in the naturalization records. From Donegal came the Harkins, the Rodgerses, the Thorntons and the Bonners; from Mayo came the McGinns and the Loftuses.[37]

But these were superficial similarities, for two reasons. The first has been noted: the new Irish whose behaviour was most unlike that of the settled men were the younger, unmarried transients who had little interest in American citizenship and hence do not show up in the sample. The second involves a number of selective points. The new Irish, however temporary their sojourn in Butte, may have preferred Irish companionship, but it was the companionship of younger Irish, first and second-generation, that they sought. The new men moved into old Irish neighbourhoods, but partly because many of the old Irish had moved out. Younger brothers/cousins/ nephews/friends – including Sullivans and Harringtons from West Cork – still followed older Irishmen to Butte, but not necessarily into Butte's older Irish associations, and seldom for the same reasons the Irish had once come. What the Irish experience in Butte showed is that migration chains work only if those at the receiving end can promise jobs. If the ability to provide work is lost, the old chain breaks; the new one does not function in the same way.[38]

The most important differences followed from this last. Irish work patterns and worker consciousness were altered; the balance between the centrifugal and centripetal forces of Irish-American life was inverted. The first first generation was drawn to skilled mining jobs; the second first generation to industrial jobs that involved taking heavy equipment underground. There were literally worlds of difference between the two. The differences were at least as great as those between the lives of the Irish-American capitalist or would-be capitalist and the new Irish working class. The fragmentation in Irish Butte was far more advanced in 1908 than it had been in 1890. Some of the old Irish were wealthy beyond the imagining of the young men; some were mired in a poverty as deep as that they had left in Ireland. But it must also be kept in mind that the Pearse–Connolly was an *Irish independence* club; that Pearse had identified himself as 'an old fashioned Catholic nationalist', and that Connolly, as he reminded his non-Irish socialist comrades, was also 'an Irishman'. The new Irish did not abandon the patriot game; they just redefined it.[39]

This last point was a key one, largely because it was Larkin himself who provided Butte's renegade young Irishmen with their new definitions. Larkin's visits to Butte came just as the second immigrant generation of Irish was beginning to challenge the first. His speeches were filled with tangled messages. Larkin argued, as Connolly had, that the cause of Ireland was the cause of the working class, that loyalty to the first demanded loyalty to the second. He minced no words. 'I am an Irishman,' he began. 'I love my native land and I love my race, but when I see some of the Irish . . . you have in Butte, my face crimsons with shame.' He mentioned specifically the 'clean-faced gentlemen (with black hearts) – the so-called labour leaders'. 'I tell you, the Irish champions of freedom . . . would spit in the faces of these shoneen Irish of Butte.' Shoneen meant, depending on the context, traitor to the Irish cause, someone who fancied himself British and aped British ways, or simply an 'ass licker'. Larkin meant all three. Their 'parish pump form of patriotism' was hypocritical cant. They were guilty of 'brutalizing and searing the bodies and souls of their race, over whose overworked and ill-fed and ill-clothed bodies' they had made their fortunes. He reminded his listeners of 'the Ryans, the Walshes, the Farrells, the Crimmonses, the Dalys', shoneens all, who 'ground out their wealth from their oppressed and overworked Irish slaves'. Larkin challenged these 'malignant beasts in human form' to match their devotion to Ireland with a comparable compassion for the Irish poor – wherever they were found.[40]

There were, in other words, green-suited class enemies in Butte as surely as in Ireland. Obviously, this lesson made more sense to a young man from County Down, striving to dismantle a closed ethnic/corporate/union world, than it did to an old man from West Cork, striving as hard and with greater resources to keep even a small part of that world alive. The Pearse–Connollys challenged that old Irish accommodation at every point: they rejected the AOH and the RELA, declared unremitting class warfare against the ACM, and shared a hall and office space with the three organizations most responsible for the destruction of the BMU. Larkinism was a central element in the politics of Butte; it took life through the young Irishmen of the Pearse–Connolly Club.

Of all the elements of the American working class, only the Irish were bombarded by such contradictory messages, or so riven by age, skill level, social status, political commitment or county of origin. By 1910 some Irish immigrant workers had been in Butte for thirty years; others for thirty days. To assume that they shared either ethnic or class interests is folly. They arose from and occupied different and mutually hostile worlds. Larkin and Larkinism are wholly unimaginable in any other ethnic working-class culture. He spoke only to the Irish; he persuaded only the youngest of them. Larkin did not create the splits in Butte's Irish enclave, but he did put them on public view, and in the process he deepened them and made them even more intractable. The Irish centre could not hold. No one needed it any more, and Larkinism – the latest form of Irish faction fighting – together with the powerful centrifugal forces of a long-running immigration sundered the ethnic community.

Notes

1. Brosnan to his father, 18 February 1917, Brosnan letters. I am indebted to Professor Kerby Miller for sending me a copy of these letters. For evidence that others thought of Butte as Brosnan did see Works Projects Administration, *Copper Camp: Stories of the World's Greatest Mining Town, Butte, Montana*, Hastings House, New York, 1943, p. 173.
2. Bureau of the Census, *Twelfth Census of the United States: 1900, Population*, Part I, Government. Printing Office, Washington D.C., 1901, pp. clxxvi–clxxix, 768, 798, 875. For St Mary's see Fr. Michael Hannan, *Father English and St Mary's Parish, Butte, Montana: the Miners' Catholic Church*, privately printed, Butte, 1911, copy in St Mary's Parish File, Diocese of Helena Office.
3. For Irish fixed in place see Kerby Miller, *Emigrants and Exiles: Ireland and the Irish Exodus to North America*, Oxford University Press, New York, 1985, pp. 9–130, *passim*. On name/place association see Edward McLysaght, *Irish Families: their Names, Arms, and Origins*, Crown Publishers, New York, 1972, pp. 16–17, 28–37. R. L. Polk, *Butte City Directory, 1887–1915*, Polk, St Paul and Butte, 1888–1916.
4. AOH, Membership and Dues Ledgers, 1882–1939; RELA, Financial Records, 1883–1946. Irish Collection, University of Montana, microfilm copy. Hereafter cited as IC.
5. R. O'Dwyer, *Who were my Ancestors? A Genealogy of Eyeries Parish, County Cork*, Stevens, Astoria, Ill., 1976. The other O'Dwyer volumes bear the same general title and publisher. The Allihies volume was published in 1988, the Castletownbere and Bere Island volumes in 1989.
6. Department of Commerce and Labor, *Naturalization Service, Petition and Record* 1–16. Second District Court, Silver Bow County, Butte, Montana.
7. Butte Chamber of Commerce, *Resources of Butte: its Mines and Smelters*, Intermountain Printers, Butte, 1895, pp. 7–10. For the Irish mines at Hungry Hill see Daphne du Maurier, *Hungry Hill*, 1943, reprinted Bentley, Cambridge, 1971. For the routes from Ireland to Butte see David M. Emmons, *The Butte Irish: Class and Ethnicity in an American Mining Town, 1875–1925*, University of Illinois Press, Urbana and Chicago, Ill., 1989, pp. 16–19.
8. Brosnan to father, 17 February 1918, Brosnan Letters. Bureau of the Census, *Manuscript Census, Population Schedules*, 1900, Silver Bow County, microfilm copy. ACM, 'General Office Records', Subject File 522, ACM Papers, Montana Historical Society, Helena.
9. For Daly see Emmons, *Butte Irish*, pp. 19–21, 139–41, 199–201. The reference to job notices in Gaelic is from Fr Sarsfield O'Sullivan, interview, 19 November 1984. McCarthy's remark is from AOH, Div. 3, Minute Books, 19 April 1913, IC.
10. For the APA see its newspaper, *The Examiner*, 18 May, 1, 15 June 1895; 27 February, 19 March, 19 April, 3 September, 3 October 1896. The 'boss Irishman' quote is from Committee on Privileges and Elections, *Report relative to the Right and Title of Wm. A. Clark to a Seat as Senator*, Senate Report 1052, 56th Cong., 1st sess., 1900, Government Printing Office, Washington D.C., 1901, p. 1402.
11. For Daly's successors, and the corporate and technological changes, see Emmons, *Butte Irish*, pp. 107–8, 223, 237–9, 244–8. See too Michael Malone, *The Battle for Butte: Mining and Politics on the Northern Frontier*, University of Washington Press, Seattle, 1981.
12. Immigration data from *The Statistical History of the United States from Colonial Times to the Present*, Fairfield, Stamford, Conn., 1956, pp. 56–9.

13. On class splits within Irish-American nationalism see Emmons, *Butte Irish*, pp. 45–54, 322–8. The reference to 'exultation among the nations' is, of course, from Padraic Pearse's 1916 proclamation of the Irish Republic. That a free Ireland elevated the social status of Irish-Americans is a theme of Thomas Brown, *Irish American Nationalism, 1870–90*, Lippincott, Philadelphia, Pa., 1966, pp. 23–8.

14. For working-class dominance of the memberships nationally, Eric Foner, 'Class, ethnicity, and radicalism in the Gilded Age: the Land League and Irish America', in *Politics and Ideology in the Age of the Civil War*, Oxford University Press, New York, 1980, pp. 150–200. For membership figures see AOH, Membership and Dues Ledgers; RELA, Membership Ledgers, IC. For the inter-class 'harmony' of the two see Emmons, *Butte Irish*, pp. 191–8, 203–5.

15. Emmons, *Butte Irish*, pp. 191, 202–3.

16. On the BMU see Norma Smith, 'The Rise and Fall of the Butte Miners' Union, 1878–1914', M.A. thesis, Montana State University, 1961; Emmons, *Butte Irish*, pp. 221–34, 276–7. On Asian exclusionist policies see Stacy Flaherty, 'Boycott, in Butte: organized labor and the Chinese community, 1896–7', *Montana: the Magazine of Western History*, 37, 1, 1987, pp. 34–47.

17. For a general discussion of BMU conservatism see Emmons, *Butte Irish*, pp. 187–8, 206–8, 222–4, 228–36, 264–75. The most conservative reference is from C. P. Connolly, 'The story of Montana', *McClure's Magazine*, 27, 1906, pp. 459–60. That the BMU blocked other strikes is from testimony to the Industrial Commission, *Mining Conditions and Industrial Relations at Butte Montana*, Senate Doc. 415, 64th Cong., 1st sess., *Final Report and Testimony*, 4, 1915, Government Printing Office, Washington, D.C., 1916, p. 3757. For Boyce's comments, see 'Travel Diary', 24 May 1897, in Ed Boyce papers, Eastern Washington State Historical Society, Spokane, and *Miners Magazine*, June 1902.

18. Polk, *Butte City Directory*, 1885–1915; AOH, Membership and Dues Ledgers; RELA, Membership Ledgers, IC.

19. On the general point of worker co-operation with those more powerful, John Bodnar, *Workers' World: Kinship, Community, and Protest in an Industrial Society, 1900–40*, Johns Hopkins University Press, Baltimore, Md, 1982 p. 4–9, 65.

20. Aileen Kraditor, *The Radical Persuasion: Aspects of the Intellectual History and Historiography of Three American Radical Organizations*, Louisiana State University Press, Baton Rouge, La., 1981, pp. 1–34, 43–5, 55–85. On Irish 'insecurity' see Miller, *Emigrants*, pp. 427–35, 441–4, 556–8. For the role of the enclave see Emmons, *Butte Irish*, pp. 61–93.

21. On job hazards see David Emmons, 'Immigrant workers and industrial hazards: the Irish miners of Butte, 1880–1919', *Journal of American Ethnic History*, 5, 1985, pp. 41–64; Emmons, *Butte Irish*, pp. 147–59.

22. On the importance of exclusion see Eric Hobsbawm, 'The aristocracy of labour reconsidered', 1978, in *Workers: Worlds of Work*, Pantheon, New York, 1984, pp. 227–52, particularly p. 234. On drills see Mark Wyman, *Hardrock Epic: Western Miners and the Industrial Revolution*, University of California Press, Berkeley, Cal., 1979, pp. 12, 84, 88–90, Industrial Commission, *Mining at Butte*, 1915, p. 3857.

23. The 'Bohunk' references are from the *Butte Evening News*, 18, 23 July 23 1910.

24. Emmons, *Butte Irish*, pp. 268–75. The Irish as conservatives comment is from WFM, *Proceedings, twentieth Annual Convention*, Victor, Colo. 1912, WFM, Victor, 1912, p. 260. Giovannitti's comments were quoted in *Miners Magazine*, 9 July 1914.

25. The *Montana Socialist*, 28 June 1914; WFM, *Proceedings Twenty-first convention*, 1

biennial, Denver, 1914, WFM, Denver, 1914, p. 193. Gwendolyn Mink, *Old Labor and New Immigrants in American Political Development: Union. Party and State, 1875–1925*, Cornell University Press, Ithaca, N.Y., 1986. Mink argues that by 1896 the Irish were definitely thought of as 'old labor', pp. 125–7. On the Irishness of some of the rebellious 'new' immigrants see Emmons, *Butte Irish*, pp. 230–4, 263–5, 277–84, 359–73.

26. C. Fanning, *The Irish Voice in America: Irish-American Fiction from the 1760s to the 1980s*, University Press of Kentucky, Lexington, Ky, 1990, pp. 3–4, 205–6, 238–56; the quote is from p. 205.

27. Naturalization Service, *Petition and Record*, Silver Bow Co. AOH, Div. 3, Minute Books, 30 October 1915; John D. Sullivan to Patrick Kenny, 17 September 1911, Correspondence, IC.

28. For Lehane see *Montana Socialist*, 23 December 1916. The move to Finlander Hall is from the *Anaconda Standard*, 5 June 1917. For later strikes see Emmons, *Butte Irish*, pp. 398–9. The 'riveting chains' reference was in a typed bulletin, undated and without attribution, included in the file of the *Joint Strike Bulletin* and *Strike Bulletin*, 1917–20, microfilm copy.

29. The Pearse-Connollys, wearing green sashes, joined the IWW, wearing red, in leading Little's cortege. *Strike Bulletin*, 6, 17 August 1917. Lynch made his comment to the *Anaconda Standard*, 9 April 1917. AOH, Div. 3, Minute Books, March 10, 1917, IC.

30. Mink, *Old Labor*, pp. 253–4; Miller, *Emigrants*, pp. 429–33, 499–503, 551–4; Joseph Lee, *The Modernization of Irish Society, 1848–1918*, Gill & Macmillan, Dublin, 1973; Patrick Blessing, 'Irish emigration to the United States, 1800–1920: an overview', in P. J. Drudy, ed., *The Irish in America: Emigration, Assimilation, and Impact*, Cambridge University Press, Cambridge, 1985, pp. 19–21.

31. Naturalization Service, *Petition and Record* 1–16.

32. Miller, *Emigrants*, tables, pp. 569–82. For Larkin's career see Emmet Larkin, *James Larkin, Irish Labour Leader, 1876–1947*, MIT Press, Cambridge, Mass., 1965.

33. Naturalization Service, *Petition and Record* 1–16.

34. Emmons, *Butte Irish*, p. 14; AOH, Div. 3, Minute Books, 15 July 1907; John Sullivan to M. J. McDonough, 2 April 1923, Correspondence, IC.

35. Miller, *Emigrants*, pp. 364–426. Naturalization Service, *Petition and Record* 1–16.

36. For examples of old Irish criticism of young see AOH, Div. 3, Minute Books, 17, 24 June 1907; 22 June, 6 July 1908; AOH, County Board, Minute Books, 28 September, 6, 11, 31 October 1909, IC. Brosnan to mother, 11 April 1917, n.d., 1917, Brosnan letters.

37. Naturalization Service, *Petition and Record* 1–16.

38. Naturalization Service, *Petition and Record* 1–16.

39. The Pearse and Connolly quotes are both from F. S. L. Lyons, *Culture and Anarchy in Ireland, 1890–1939* Clarendon Press, Oxford 1979, pp. 94, 97.

40. Only the *Montana Socialist* carried the full text of Larkin's remarks; 25 September, 2, 9 October 1915; 22 July, 7 October, 23 December 1916; 27 January 1917. See also Larkin, *James Larkin*, p. 204.

4 The historiography of the Irish in the United States of America

Donald Harman Akenson

I

Denial. It is the behaviour that most clearly characterizes the second half of the twentieth century. Instead of dealing with their own fundamental problems (and those that they have caused in the Second and Third Worlds), Western cultures have simply willed them away. Denial, far from being indicative of weak volition, requires strong will but, like most other exercises, becomes easier each time it is practised. The historiography of the Irish in the United States is typical of our age, for it is based on a systematic denial of the most central facts of the historical record. Indeed, I can think of no cultural or ethnic group in the modernized, industrialized world whose accepted historical literature is as far divorced from historical reality as is that of the Irish in the United States.

Of course, that is a generalization, and like all such has to be qualified. There are some quite wonderful books on the field of Irish–US studies – especially local and regional studies[1] – but the overall picture is disheartening. As Patrick O'Sullivan, editor of this series of volumes, has observed, Irish culture has 'mystified' migration. This mystification has been particularly acute in Irish–US historiography, because of a predilection for psychological explanations of various facts. This is doubly bad, because as O'Sullivan points out, the historians who practise this rhetoric are not trained in the discipline[2] – and also because the pseudo-psychological explanations involve a presumption of certain 'facts' which are anything but factual. Thus arises the necessity of denial.

II

Denial of what? First, of the almost universally ignored fact that *the bulk of the Irish ethnic group in the United States at present is, and probably always has been, Protestant*. The historical literature of the last fifty years deals almost entirely with Roman Catholics and in many cases explicitly states that the Irish in the United States are, and were, entirely Catholic.[3]

In order to deal with this peculiar historiography, a simple matter of method and vocabulary must be underscored, namely that the migrant generation and the entire ethnic group in any country are quite different entities. The migrants are sometimes referred to as the *Irish-born* or as the *first generation*.[4] In contemporary historical accounts these persons are called 'emigrants' or 'immigrants'. (Because these two usages are confusing, they are not here employed.) All of these terms apply to a single generation.

In contrast, the ethnic group is a *multi-generational* phenomenon and in historical discussion it includes not only the migrant generation but their direct offspring and, often, subsequent generations of descendants. Exactly what the borders of any ethnic group are is a matter of great argument (for how long does a sense of ethnicity last?) and certainly cannot be decided here. The effective point is that when an historian refers to 'the Irish' in the United States (or in Great Britain, or in any new homeland) he or she should make it clear whether the reference is to the migrant generation or to the multi-generational ethnic group. Assertions that hold true for the migrant generation are frequently not true for the entire ethnic group, and too often conclusions about 'the Irish' as a multi-generational group have been drawn from data that really concern only the Irish-born. Therefore, in this chapter, 'the Irish' means the entire ethnic group. When the migrant generation is meant, that will be clearly indicated by such terms as 'Irish-born' or 'migrant generation' or 'first generation'.

The data which indicate that 'the Irish' – that is, the entire multi-generational group – in the United States are predominantly Protestant come from three independent sources. The first of these is a set of studies done in the 1970s by the National Opinion Research Center of the University of Chicago[5] and the second in the 1980s by the Gallup polling organization.[6] These revealed that most Americans who said that their primary ethnic group was Irish were Protestants – 56 per cent in the NORC survey and 54 per cent in the Gallup study. These were sophisticated and technically expert studies, but they have been dwarfed by the material that is at present being published as a result of 'The National Survey of Religious Identification, 1989–90', being conducted under the directorship of Professor Barry A. Kosmin by the Graduate Center of the City University of New York. This study involves the random survey of 113,000 American households (a massive number for a random survey) and deals with religion, ethnicity, race and a number of demographic variables. The religious affiliations of persons who identified themselves as being of Irish ethnic origin are shown in Table 4.1.

Within Irish demographic studies a standard (if perhaps unintentionally sectarian) mode of expressing religious identity is a ratio of Catholics to 'non- Catholics'. In the United States in 1989–90 the Catholic/non-Catholic ratio of persons of Irish ancestry was 33/67. I think, however, that this ratio overemphasizes the degree of Protestantism, for it is only in the Irish homeland that a person who is non-Catholic can with reasonable accuracy be assumed to be a Protestant. I would suggest that the most accurate reading would be to lump the 'undefined Christian' category with the Protestants. This would yield the following conclusion: that the ratio of

Table 4.1 Religious affiliation of Americans identifying themselves as being of Irish origin, 1989–90

Religious affiliation	%
Christian ('so stated')	3
Roman Catholic	33
Jewish	0
Protestant	51
No religion, or non-Christian other than Jewish	13
Total	100

Source: Barry Kosmin *et al.*, *Research Report: the National Survey of Religious Identification, 1989–90*, selected Tabulations, New York, CUNY Graduate Center, 1991, p. 14

Protestants to Catholics among persons who professed a Christian religion was 54 to 33. That is to say, the Protestant proportion of Irish persons in the United States was 58·6 per cent of those professing Christianity.

The import of these studies cannot be rationally denied: they were conducted independently of each other, at an acceptable level of professional competence, and they produced similar results. One naturally asks, how far back in the history of the United States does the predominantly Protestant character of the Irish as an ethnic group hold?

For reasons that I will explain in the next section, one cannot cite any direct data in answer to that question, because the United States government never collected any information on the matter. Nevertheless, a strong logic tree exists. It works as follows. Given that the bulk of persons who lived in the United States in the second half of the twentieth century were Protestants, then this situation held throughout US history *unless* either (1) at some time in earlier US history there was a massive apostasy whereby a predominantly Catholic group of Irish persons switched to Protestantism, or (2) the Irish as a group in some period early in their history in the United States (in the colonial period, or, in any case, prior to the Great Famine) were overwhelmingly Roman Catholic and these numbers were later swamped by great hordes of migrating Irish-born Protestants.

Neither of these alternatives holds. Nowhere in the vast literature of American religion history is there any serious documentation of large-scale Irish Catholic apostasy.[7] Indeed, the success of the Catholic Church in holding the faithful (and in reindoctrinating those who had become virtually irreligious) is one of its proudest claims.

Further, virtually the entire historiography of Irish migration to the United States, and the documentation which surrounds that writing, indicate that the great flood of post-Famine century migration was Roman Catholic in character. Even if the degree of Catholicism of the post-Famine migrants is overemphasized (as I suspect it is), it is clear that overwhelmingly the migrants were Catholics. Therefore, condition '2' does hold any more than does condition '1'. Hence the unavoidable conclusion is that the

Irish as an ethnic group in the United States always have been mostly Protestant.

Here we enter a minefield. Some of the more politically 'progressive' attacks on racism (as, for example, the Human Rights Code of Ontario) have defined racism as appertaining not merely to skin colour but to ethnicity, religion and national origin. Anything that demeans, derogates or devalues an individual or group unjustly on any of these matters is seen as racism. And rightly so. With very rare exceptions, the history of the Irish in the United States (and, especially, almost all of the general surveys) have either been written so as to make the Irish Protestants in the United States non–existent, or have made them appear as historical anachronisms, odd groups that arrived before the 1840s and faded into inconsequence thereafter. This would be morally wrong (for racism is a moral, more than a merely intellectual, failing), even if the Protestants were merely a slim minority of the Irish ethnic group. Considering that they were the majority, one is encountering an historiographical omission of astounding proportions.[8]

A variety of ingenious methods of excusing this racism have been (and I think will continue to be) employed. The crudest of them is simply to argue that no Protestant can be 'truly' Irish. This viewpoint has a considerable resonance in Irish nationalist thought, and at present is used by extremists to justify acts of violence against Protestants within Ireland. There is little one can say in response to such a viewpoint, since it is based upon a faith equivalent to that of religious belief and so is not capable of examination in the present world. Within the United States it has its counterparts in persons who say that Jews, blacks, Buddhists or gays cannot be real Americans.

Sometimes it is suggested that the Protestants from Ireland were almost entirely Presbyterians (Ulster Scots) and that they called themselves 'Scotch-Irish' and refused to identify themselves as Irish, in the United States, so they can be ignored. There is just enough accuracy in these beliefs to be misleading. It is true that, when the Famine floods arrived, the Irish Protestants in the inland rural areas were willing to escape nativist prejudice against the Irish Catholics. But in fact the adoption of a separate sobriquet was not necessitated by American events, but rather was a function of something that happened in the homeland in the first half of the nineteenth century. Daniel O'Connell, the Great Liberator, was not merely one of the greatest persons in modern Irish history but one of the shrewdest. He understood that, to be successful, he had to unite in one crucible Irish nationalism, Irish cultural identity and Roman Catholicism. In this he succeeded. As D. G. Boyce has pointed out, by 1840 when a person in Ireland talked of 'Ireland for the Irish' everyone knew he meant the Catholics; and when someone talked about the Irish people he meant the Catholics; and when someone talked of the faith of the Irish people he meant Roman Catholicism.[9] This nominalist by-play is a standard technique of the propagandist, but no less successful for being that. The result was that the Protestants of Ireland, while thinking of themselves as being 'Irish and a bit more', when talking to a wider audience were forced to make it clear that they were not Irish in O'Connell's sense. In the United States, since the name they had once used for themselves was now pre-empted by the Catholic migrants, they had to develop a new terminology. Among themselves they kept alive a sense of their Irish background (however else would they have been evident in the NORC, Gallup and CUNY surveys?) but, to uninformed outsiders who told them that they were not Irish, they merely shrugged and walked away.

For an historian who does not wish to become stained by the sectarianism that runs through so much Irish historical writing (however unconsciously), there are only two parameters for encompassing an accurate historical discussion of the Irish in the United States. The first is that any permanent resident of Ireland who migrated from Ireland to the United States – whatever his or her religious or political background – should be counted as an Irish migrant. That is methodologically simple. It includes everyone who grew up in the social system that was Ireland. And, secondly, anyone who says that his or her ethnicity is Irish should be credited with being Irish. Once those two parameters are accepted, more subtle matters can be dealt with.

In almost all the instances when Protestants have been included in the historiography of the Irish in the United States they have been mislabelled and chronologically segregated. Segregated? In the sense that it is held that there was no significant Irish Protestant migration after the Famine. This is almost certainly untrue, although it is difficult to ascertain directly. And mislabelled? This has occurred because of the assumption that the Irish Protestants were overwhelmingly Presbyterian – that is, Ulster Scots – in background. Actually there is no solid proof that the Presbyterians predominated. It is probable that the other major Protestant group – the 'Anglo-Irish', consisting of 'Anglicans', to use an anachronistic term, or, properly, adherents of the Church of Ireland – sent as many migrants. This can be inferred (although not directly proved) by examining the Irish census data. The first Irish religious census was taken in 1834 and the second in 1861. They yielded the results shown in Table 4.2.[10]

That is, although within Ireland the Anglican or Presbyterian proportions of the total Irish population rose, they experienced a considerable decrease in their absolute numbers. Moreover, if one adds to the statistical series the data for the remainder of the nineteenth century, the results are striking (Table 4.3). Of course, there is a myriad of possible hypotheses that would explain these trends in census data,[11] but certainly there is a *prima facie* case for social historians investigating these two: that in the second half of the nineteenth century the Irish Protestants in general emigrated in large numbers and that this Protestant emigration was not solely from among the Ulster Scots but even more from among the Anglican population (which, for convenience, if not with perfect accuracy, we may identify as the 'Anglo-Irish').

Unlike the Anglicans, who were distributed, at least patchily, around the entire country, the Presbyterians were concentrated in Ulster. Thus the data on post-Famine emigration from Ulster are illuminating, if somewhat sketchy.[12] They reveal that the historical province of Ulster (nine counties)

Table 4.2 Proportions of different denominations revealed by the Irish religious censuses of 1834 and 1861

Year	No. of Catholics	% of Population	No. of Anglicans	% of Population	No. of Presbyterians	% of Population
1834	6,427,712	80·9	852,064	10·7	642,356	8·1
1861	4,505,265	77·7	693,357	12·0	523,291	9 0

Note. The residual population in each year's figures consists of 'Other Protestant Dissenters (especially Methodists)', 'Jews', 'Atheists' and 'Unknown'.

Source. Derived from *First Report of the Commissioners of Public Instruction, Ireland*, pp. 9–45 [45], H.C. 1835, XXXII, and from *Report and Tables relating to the Religious Profession, Education and Occupations of the People*, p. 28 [3204–III], H.C. 1863, LIX. The 1834 data were later 'corrected' by various governmental authorities, not always convincingly, yet not to such an extent as to change by more than a few tenths of a percentage point the figures taken from the primary document.

Table 4.3 Proportions of different denominations in Ireland, decennial intervals, 1871–1901

Year	No. of Catholics	% of Population	No. of Anglicans	% of Population	No. of Presbyterians	% of Population
1871	4,150,867	76·7	667,998	12·3	497,648	9·2
1881	3,960,891	76·5	639,574	12·4	470,734	9·1
1891	3,547,307	75·4	600,103	12·8	444,974	9·5
1901	3,308,661	74·2	581,089	13·0	443,276	9·9

Source. Census of Ireland, 1901, Part II, *General Report*, p. 50 [Cd 1190], H.C. 1902, CXXIX.

was the second major provincial source of emigrants (Table 4.4). And, to take a mid-point in this period, 1871, the religious composition of Ulster was as shown in Table 4.5.

Granted, this does not prove that Protestants of whatever stripe migrated in large numbers, but note two facts: first, that 70·0 per cent of the emigrants from Ulster in the period 1851–1900 came from the six counties, that is, from the predominantly Protestant part of Ireland,[13] and, second, that, within the historical nine counties of Ulster, the largest outflow in absolute terms came from the most Protestant counties, Antrim and Down.[14] No one would suggest that this proves that there was a major Protestant exodus from Ulster: a cynic might suggest that conceivably all the migrants were Catholics who were shrewd enough to leave at the first opportunity. But, cynicism aside, the hypothesis that large numbers of Ulster Scots and Anglo-Irish left Ireland in the second half of the nineteenth century seems reasonable, given the available Irish data. And one can reasonably suggest that a significant number migrated to the United States, the recipient of the largest number of Irish migrants in the nineteenth century.

The most promising way of making sense of the religious pattern of Irish

Table 4.4   Source of Irish emigrants, by province, 1851–1900

Province	No.	%
Munster	1,346,889	36·8
Ulster	1,015,737	27·7
Leinster	683,209	18·7
Connaught	616,439	16·8
Total on whom information available	3,662,274	100·0

Note. The table does not include 110,668 emigrants of unspecified origin belonging mostly to the years 1851–2, before the improvement in record keeping introduced in 1853.

Source. Derived from data in Commission on Emigration and other Population Problems. 1948–54, *Reports* [Pr 2541], Dublin Stationery Office, Dublin, 1954, pp. 315–16 and 325. The figures have to be derived indirectly, as the republic's governmental commission that produced this study apparently did not wish to highlight the high proportion of overseas emigration that came from what is now Northern Ireland.

Table 4.5   Religious composition of Ulster in 1871

Religion	%
Catholic	47·8
Anglican	21·8
Presbyterian	25·9
Other	4·5
Total	100·0

Source. W. E. Vaughan and A. J. Fitzpatrick, eds, *Irish Historical Studies, Population 1821– 1971*, Royal Irish Academy, Dublin, 1978, p. 59.

migration to the United States and of the subsequent religio–ethnic history is to recall the basic distinction between migrants and the multi-generational ethnic cohort – and then to introduce the variable of *time of arrival*, which is a crucial determinate of the overall character of any ethnic group. By taking into account the differential time of arrival of the two major religious strands among Irish migrants, one can see a simple pattern. (1) At some period in the pre-Famine migration to the United States (precisely what years is in doubt) the Protestant Irish migrants (both Anglo-Irish and Ulster Scots) significantly outnumbered the Catholic migrants. (2) Nevertheless, it is almost certainly true that, over the entire history of Irish migration to the United States, more individual Catholics than Protestants arrived. The Catholics, however, in general came later. That pre-Famine (or, at least, pre–1815) migration was tilted towards Protestant groups means that a multiplier existed. To use a simple example: although a Catholic migrant from Munster in 1930 and an Ulster Protestant in 1830 were both single dots on the graph of migration flow, by 1930 the Ulster migrant had scores of descendants within the Irish-descended group, but the Munster migrant only one: him or herself. That there was a significant difference along these lines is indicated by the NORC General Social Survey, which found that in its sample 41 per cent of Irish Catholics (as of the 1970s) were fourth-generation in the United States, while 83 per cent of the Irish Protestants were.[15] (3) It is thus easy to accommodate within this framework the fact that significant Protestant migration continued after the Great Famine. It was much smaller than the Catholic migration, but far from inconsequential. And (4) it is also easy to accept within this framework the suggestion that the Protestant migration to the United States was not an Ulster Scots migration but was broadly representative of the entire spectrum of Irish Protestantism, which included two major denominations (Presbyterian and Church of Ireland) and several minor ones. Protestant migration had a wide geographical range, and did not stem merely from Ulster. Nor indeed did origin in Ulster imply that the Protestant migrant was Presbyterian, for a considerable portion of the Ulster plantation was formed by Anglicans. Therefore (5) one can accept the corollary of Protestant variation in the homeland, namely that the Protestant Irish in the United States took many forms. Any serious non-racist history of the Irish in the United States should spend as much time upon the Baptists (especially the Southern Baptists), Methodists, Anglicans and Presbyterians as upon the history of the Catholic Church. Only when the life of William Bell Riley (the founding father of twentieth-century American fundamentalism) is as well known as, say, that of Cardinal Spellman will the historiography of the Irish in the United States have come of age.

III

Denial – again, of what? Secondly, of the awkward fact that *there is not and never has been accurate systematic demographic data on several of the most fundamental characteristics of the Irish in the United States.* Yet there are hundreds of books that generalize about the Irish as an ethnic group, and even the most careful of local and community studies usually take for granted an assumed national context that in fact is unrelated to any verifiable data base.

'Demography' is a word that scares some historians, but it need not. What it refers to is simply the counting of people. If one wishes to draw accurate generalizations concerning the Irish in the United States, what one requires is either (1) a professionally conducted random study, such as was done in the case of the NORC, Gallup and CUNY studies that were cited earlier, or (2) a direct count of all the people in a certain jurisdiction (such as a state or an entire nation). The governments of most modern nations conduct periodic 'enumerations' or 'censuses' of population. In each instance, random survey or full census, the group's most important characteristics – economic, religious, etc. – are ascertained. Each person studied by either type of demographic investigation is a dot on a great social map, and taken together these dots potentially permit a set of accurate generalizations about the Irish or whatever group one wishes to study. But without the existence of either of these two forms of basic demographic data – accurate direct censuses or reliable surveys – generalizations about any ethnic or social group are mere fancy or, worse, prejudice.

Thus it comes as an unpleasant recognition to note this fact: there exists *no* body of basic demographic data on the Irish (or any other group) as an ethnic group in the United States. None. Until 1969–70 none of the decennial censuses of the United States asked a question concerning the ethnicity of the individuals whom they were enumerating, and the census is the only potential source of such data. Granted, in the late 1920s the American Council of Learned Societies tried to rework the 1790 census data to give an indication of ethnicity at the end of the colonial period, but this effort failed miserably.[16] No further comprehensive attempt at dealing with ethnicity was made until 1969–70, when the Census Bureau asked an ethnicity question. Unhappily, the collection of the data was bungled and no firm conclusions came from it.[17] In 1980, and again in 1990, the ethnicity question was again asked, and again it was mishandled, so as to be virtually useless.[18]

Even more extraordinary is that *never* have the United States census authorities collected information on the religious affiliation of specific individuals. The Census Bureau once, in 1957, asked a religion question of a voluntary sample group, but it met with so much opposition that the attempt was never repeated.[19] This refusal to deal with religious persuasion, except by querying the various denominational authorities for their alleged total number of adherents, seems so perverse to non-American historians as to be almost pathological. But whatever the reasons for this refusal to enumerate individuals by religion,[20] it precludes the formulation by historians of any general statement based on official census information of the relationship of religion and of Irish ethnicity.

Given that there are no comprehensive data either on Irish ethnicity or upon the religious persuasion of individuals of Irish background in the United States, it follows, *mutatis mutandis*, that there are no cross-tabulations extant which relate either the ethnicity or the religious persuasion of persons of Irish background to such fundamental characteristics as their place of residence and occupation. Granted, there are several – indeed, dozens – of valuable studies of the Irish in various cities of America, but in none of them is the matter of ethnicity or of religion defined for the entire population of the town or city with which the authors deal, and for none of them is it established where in the total context of the Irish in America their study group fits. This is not the authors' fault; the census data are lacking. But, unfortunately, because of the lack of data defining the entire Irish profile, ethnically or religiously, historians have studied the sub-groups on which data come most easily to hand – Catholics in large cities – and have given the impression that the characteristics of these easily researched Irish persons were universal in America.

But, surely, there must be some pieces of comprehensive data about the Irish? There are. Beginning with the *1850* census of the United States, we know, at decennial intervals, the birthplace of everyone in the population.[21] This is useful indeed, as long as one remembers three points: first, that the data on the foreign-born in general, and on the Irish in particular, are information only on migrants, not on the bulk of the ethnic group; second, that the data on the Irish include both Catholics and Protestants, with no effort having been made to distinguish the respective proportions of each denomination; and, third, that the earliest data we have on the Irish reflect the situation *after* the extraordinary migration induced by the Great Famine had been several years in full spate. In other words, we have *no* demographic baseline which allows us to determine what the character and extent of Irish migration to the United States were before the Famine. This is especially crippling because, although it is quite clear that there was heavy Irish migration to the United States before the Famine, the US immigration statistics before 1855 are not trustworthy.

Manifestly, the material available on the number of Irish-born persons among the American population from 1850 onwards is much better than no information at all, but it is not until 1860 that one finds even rudimentary printed cross-tabulations of the data on Irish-born persons with residence in various cities, and not until the 1870 census are data on occupation and on place of birth cross-tabulated.

In 1870 the census authorities asked each individual whether or not he had foreign-born parents, but the information was elicited only in the form of a yes–or–no answer, not what country the parents were from. The next census, that of 1880, asked the specific origin of those natives of the United States who had foreign-born parents and cross-tabulated this material in a refreshingly useful fashion. This quasi-ethnicity item was as close as the Census Bureau ever came in the last century to dealing with ethnicity in the true sense. As one authoritative study conducted in the early 1920s lamented, 'The foreign stock can be traced back only one generation . . . Beyond this the population must, in most cases, be treated as an undifferentiated body of native stock.'[22]

There are ways out of the evidentiary black hole into which the history of the Irish in the United States threatens to disappear, but they will take time and money. Many of the original manuscript census records still exist, and these give data on specific individuals which can be linked to various other pieces of information – assessment records, vital statistics, etc. – and then retabulated to produce results that the nineteenth and early twentieth-century authorities did not elicit. It is immaterial whether a sampling technique on these original census data is employed or a complete retabulation essayed.

The promise of this sort of restudy of census data is that, from 1850 onwards, it would be possible to determine where persons of Irish birth lived in the United States and, potentially, this could be linked to socioeconomic data from other sources. From 1880 onwards it would be possible to determine the place of residence both of the Irish-born and of persons who had Irish parents, and perhaps to link this to socio-economic data.

But one must accept the limits of even such a mega-cost project. For instance, the 1890 census schedules were burned in 1921,[23] and US policy about releasing personal records makes it unlikely that historians will be given full access to material even up to the First World War. And, whatever such a large project learnt, it would not be able to break through the two great barriers of Irish–US historiography, namely that in the historical records religious data simply do not exist and neither do real ethnic data.

IV

Denial? Yes, again, in a third instance. Perversely, framers of the US historiography of the Irish have refused to look to the one source of information that would help them out of many of their difficulties, namely the Canadian material. This is based on the denial of the fact that *there is no history of the Irish in the United States: the history is of the Irish in North America*, and that is something very different indeed.

The necessity of dealing with North America as a unit is simply put. Until very recently (until roughly the middle of the twentieth century) the US–Canadian border was a very permeable membrane. Despite ideological differences between the two nations, individuals and families moved across the border with relative ease. It was not at all uncommon for a person to spend part of his or her working life in, say, Toronto and then move on to Buffalo, later to Minneapolis, and then on to Winnipeg. Branches of various Irish families spanned the border, half in Seattle, say, half in Vancouver. The Eastern Townships of Quebec contained many Irish families who had branches in Vermont. The border between Maine and Canada was in many places a figment, and the axis of movement between the Maritimes and the 'Boston States' was a virtual highway. To segregate the Irish in Canada is to trepan the history of the Irish in North America, the largest of the New Worlds to which the Irish migrated. It is similar to someone truncating the history of Ireland by removing from the story the life histories of everyone, say, from Connaught.

Secondly, in arguing the absolute necessity of dealing with the Irish in the United States within the context of North America, one should note that there are certain sources of crucial historical data for the Irish migrants and for the Irish ethnic group that are not found any place else in North America. For instance, some Canadian provinces conducted censuses of population well before the Great Famine. These allow the historian to establish a baseline and thus permit the drawing of accurate generalizations about the nature of Famine migration, which is impossible if one is limited to US sources.

Part of the American problem is that, until 1855, US immigration statistics are much less help than one would expect. The Immigration Act of 1819, effective in 1820, required that all ships bringing migrants to the United States should prepare passenger lists or manifests giving the sex, age, occupation and the 'country to which they severally belong' of all their passengers. The data thereby collected suffered by virtue of incomplete

Table 4.6   Foreign-born persons arriving in
the United States via Canada

Decade	No.
1815–20	12,157
1820–30	26,524
1830–40	56, 364
1840–50	90,718

Source. Edward Jarvis, 'Immigration',
Atlantic Monthly, 29, 1872, p. 456, quoted in
E. P. Hutchinson, 'Notes on immigration
statistics of the United States', *American
Statistical Association Journal*, 53, 1958, pp.
968–79, at p. 976.

enforcement of the law (and, thus, undercounting) and by an ambiguity in
the definition of nativity: it was not made clear whether it meant the
country of birth, of citizenship or of last long-term residence. These matters
were corrected by the Immigration Act of 1855, but that is too late to throw
light on the crucial dark ages of the Irish migration into America, the period
from the end of the Napoleonic Wars to the census of 1850.[24]

But even if the pre-1850 US immigration data had been trustworthy, one
would still need to adopt a wider, North American perspective. Why?
Because before the mid-1840s, when changes in the navigation laws
removed the price advantage of sailing to St John's, Newfoundland, St
John, New Brunswick, or to Quebec city, the cheapest way to get to the
United States was by way of Canada. Hence, even had they been accurate,
US port-arrival data would have seriously underestimated the actual number of Irish-born persons who eventually fetched up in the States. One mid-
nineteenth century authority estimated that in the 1820s (when most migrants from the British Isles to Canada were Irish) 67,993 immigrants came
to the United States through Canada and that in the 1830s the number was
199,130 (again, at a time when most migrants from the British Isles to
Canada were Irish).[25] This same authority estimated that US immigration
totals should have been increased by 50 per cent to allow for arrivals from
Canada. A rather more conservative estimate was made in the early 1870s
and suggested that the number of foreign-born persons coming to the
United States via Canada was as shown in Table 4.6. Given that from 1825
onwards (when data become available) the Irish migrants comprised considerably more than half the migrants from the British Isles to Canada, it is
highly likely that most of the persons in the above estimate were Irish-
born.[26]

Were not these individuals recorded in US immigration statistics? No.
Efforts at recording land-border crossings into the United States began and
then fitfully – only in 1853 and were completely abandoned during the
American civil war. The practice was reintroduced in 1865, but abandoned
as being unsatisfactory and without a legal basis in 1885. The counting of

migrants from Canada and Mexico to the United States did not begin again until the fiscal year 1908.[27] An indication of the data thus lost is found in a study showing that for the years 1879–85 the very incompletely recorded immigration from Canada and Mexico together totalled more than one-seventh (almost 14·6 per cent) of all recorded immigration into the United States (99·4 per cent of this Canadian and Mexican total was Canadian). And, since the Irish were a larger proportion of the immigrant population in Canada than they were in the United States,[28] one can reasonably guess that more than one-seventh of the Irish immigrant flow was entering the United States unrecorded, and that at a very late date. Early in the process, before 1845, the proportion of the flow from Canada must have been considerably higher, the Canadian flow comprising perhaps as much as one-quarter of the total Irish-born influx into the States.

Thus, if one is to make any headway in understanding the fundamental mysteries of pre-1850 Irish migration to the United States, one must think in terms of a *North American* pool of migrants from Ireland, some of whom sailed to Canada and stayed, others of whom migrated direct to the United States and settled, but others of whom arrived in the United States and moved to Canada and many more of whom disembarked in Canada and subsequently moved on to the States.

There are two statistical series which try to define the primary dimensions of this North American pool of Irish migrants. Both of these series were put together during the late 1940s and early 1950s, and they are far from being in agreement. Unfortunately, having been compiled roughly contermi-nously, each was published in isolation from the other, with the result that neither addresses its disagreements with the other. The first appeared in 1953 and was done on behalf of the General Register Office of the United Kingdom by N. H. Carrier and J. R. Jeffery. In its approach it was comprehensive, being a complete study of all the available statistics on external migration from the British Isles from 1815 to 1950. The Irish data, which began in 1825, were one sub-set of the larger British Isles infor-mation base. The compilers were scrupulous in discussing the limits on the reliability of their data. In particular, however, it must be emphasized that the direct data on emigrants given in Table 4.7–8 (ultimately based on ships' muster rolls, whatever the intermediate source) dealt only with migrants from Irish ports.

But of course Irish emigration was not limited to Irish ports. Many Irish persons left for the New World from Liverpool and from Greenock and from a few other British ports. Until 1853, however, precise data on Irishmen on British-originating ships are not available, so some compen-sation has to be allowed for. This is done in the second major emigration series, published in 1954 by the Republic of Ireland's Commission on Emigration and other Population Problems. This body added to the Irish total two-thirds of the number of persons who sailed overseas from Liverpool in the period 1825–40, and for 1840 onwards made some con-siderable augmentations in the Irish estimates, but did not tell us on what they were based. (The statistics based on the sources, the reports of the Colonial Land and Emigration Commissioners, contain elements of esti-

Table 4.7 UK estimates of migration from Irish ports to North America, 1825–50

Year	To US	To Canada	Total
1825	4,387	6,841	11,228
1826	4,383	10,484	14,867
1827	4,014	9,134	13,148
1828	2,877	6,695	9,572
1829	4,133	7,710	11,843
1830	2,981	19,340	22,321
1825–30	22,775	60,204	82,979
1831	3,583	40,977	44,560
1832	4,172	37,068	41,240
1833	4,764	17,431	22,195
1834	4,213	28,586	32,799
1835	2,684	9,458	12,142
1836	3,654	19,388	23,042
1837	3,871	22,463	26,334
1838	1,169	2,284	3,453
1839	2,843	8,989	11,832
1840	4,087	23,935	28,022
1831–40	35,040	210,579	245,619
1841	3,893	24,089	27,982
1842	6,199	33,410	39,609
1843	1,617	10,898	12,515
1844	2,993	12,396	15,389
1845	3,708	19,947	23,655
1846	7,070	31,738	38,808
1847	24,502	71,253	95,755
1848	38,843	20,852	59,695
1849	43,673	26,568	70,241
1850	31,297	19,784	51,081
1841–50	163,795	270,935	434,730
Grand total 1825–50	221,610	541,718	763,328

Source. Compiled from General Register Office, *Studies on medical and Population Subjects* 6, *External Migration: a Study of the available statistics, 1815–1950*, by N. H. Carrier and J. R. Jeffery, London, HMSO, 1953, p. 95. For a discerning discussion of the limits of the date see pp. 137–9.

mation, the basis of which varied from time to time.) The resulting series purported to be a complete estimate of Irish emigration to the New World.

The main troubles with the republic's series were, first, that unnecessarily large gaps were left in the estimate for the 1830s (the data, as the UK series indicated, were available) and, second, that the procedures by which the compilers corrected the raw data for the 1840s were not recorded.

In any case, for the 1825–30 period, it is virtually certain that even the republic's augmented estimates of migration to the New World were low, because the compilers corrected only for the probable Irish emigration from Liverpool. In fact in addition to the Liverpool route (which was used almost exclusively for the US trade from the south of Ireland) there was in many

Table 4.8 Number of overseas emigrants from Ireland (thirty-two counties),
classified by destination, 1825–50

Year	US	Canada	Total
1825	4,387	7,031	11,418
1826	5,447	10,669	16,116
1827	10,372	9,229	19,601
1828	7,573	6,816	14,389
1829	9,583	7,935	17,518
1830	12,467	19,877	32,344
1825–30	49,829	61,557	111,386
1831	13,240	42,221	55,461
1832	14,675	39,184	53,859
1833			n.a.
1834			n.a.
1835	13,039	9,818	22,857
1836			n.a.
1837	21,702	23,856	45,558
1838			n.a.
1839			n.a.
1840			n.a.
1831–40	62,656	115,079	n.a.
1841	3,893	24,089	21,982
1842	6,199	33,410	39,609
1843	23,421	13,578	36,999
1844	37,269	16,485	53,754
1845	50,207	24,713	74,920
1846	68,023	37,889	105,912
1847	118,120	98,485	216,605
1848	151,003	23,543	174,546
1849	180,189	31,865	212,054
1850	184,351	25,264	209,615
1841–50	822,675	329,321	1,151,996

Source. Compiled from Commission on Emigration and other Population
Problems, 1948–54, *Reports* [Pr 2541], Dublin Stationery Office, Dublin, 1954,
pp. 314–16.

years a greater number of migrants from Greenock and Glasgow who went
mostly but not exclusively to Canada. (That the republic's commission
ignored this trade from the north of Ireland is culturally diagnostic.)
Second, children were undercounted, sometimes not being kept on ships'
muster rolls, sometimes being counted as equal to one-third an adult,
sometimes as equal to one-half. The under-enumeration varied from year to
year, but in general was much greater for ships going to Canada than for
ships going to the United States. Therefore the figures both for the United
States and for Canada need further augmentation, but those for Canada
need proportionally greater adjustment. Further, especially in the case of the
Canadian trade, over-packed ships often off-loaded illegal passengers in
Newfoundland or in the Maritimes before proceeding up the St Lawrence
river.

This is not the place to try to resolve these problems, save to call attention to the work of William Forbes Adams, which, despite its having been done more than half a century ago, still stands as the only somewhat successful attempt at grappling directly with the fundamental problems concerning the data on the Irish migrants to North America. The field desperately requires someone with Adams's sense of proportion and scepticism concerning data and who is willing to work once again step by step through the primary sources.[29]

In arguing that one can discuss sensibly the size and nature of the Irish migration to the United States in the nineteenth century (and, most especially, in the years before the first census of the foreign-born in 1850) only by adopting a North American context, I am of course discussing only the migrants, the so-called first generation. There is more to the point than that, however. Ultimately historians of the Irish in America would like to be able to deal not only with immigrants but with the entire ethnic group. Hence it is worth noting that, in all probability, of these second and third-generation Irish in America a significant component were the children and grand-children of migrants who had settled not in the United States but in Canada. In the absence of direct studies on this matter, the point has to be drawn inferentially from the facts that (1) the Canadian-born were a large element in the US population (for reference, comparative figures for the Irish-born are provided), and (2) persons of Irish ethnicity composed the largest non-French ethnic group in Canada until the late 1880s or 1890s.[30] Hence, unless one wishes to postulate a much lower propensity to migrate on the part of Canadians of native Irish ethnicity than for other groups, one has to infer that a significant proportion of the Irish-American ethnic cohort actually came, most recently, from Canada, and was of Canadian nativity.

Obviously, what the US census data say about the Canadian-born and what they mean in terms of the Irish in America are two different things. Although the Canadian-born were tallied as foreign-born (and thus as first-generation Americans), the fact is that they were at least second, and sometimes third or fourth, generation *North* Americans. Thus they should be plugged into any explanation of the total ethnic pattern of the Irish in the United States, not in the immigrant generation, but in the second and subsequent generations. Just as the path of the Irish migrants to the United States can be understood only as a forked one, some coming direct, others via Canada, so that of the second, third and fourth generations can be understood only if one accepts their duality of nativity, Canadian and US. Manifestly, once one recognizes these facts the permutations of immigration patterns and of ethnic mobility multiply and the accepted picture of the Irish in the United States as having stemmed from a simple, if cruelly uncomfortable, transatlantic passage to New York or Philadelphia, or Boston, disappears.

In arguing the absolute necessity of dealing with the Irish in the United States (both the migrant generation and the entire ethnic group) within the overall context of North America I have pointed out that there are certain pre-Famine censuses of Canadian provinces that were conducted before the Famine. Crucially, from the early 1840s onward, various Canadian enume-

Table 4.9 Proportion of Canadian-born in the US population, decennial intervals, 1850–1930

Year	Canadian-born			Irish-born	
	No. in US	% of US population	% of foreign-born	% of US population	% of foreign-born
1850	147,711	0·64	6·6	4·15	42·8
1860	249,970	0·79	6·0	5·12	38·9
1870	493,464	1·28	8·9	4·81	33·3
1880	717,157	1·43	10·7	3·70	27·8
1890	980,938	1·56	10·6	2·80	20·2
1900	1,179,922	1·55	11·4	2·13	15·6
1910	1,204,637	1·31	8·9	1·47	10·0
1930	1,286,389	1·05	9·1	0·75	6·5

Source. Compiled from Leon E. Truesdell, *The Canadian Born in the United States: an Analysis of the Statistics of the Canadian Element in the Population of the United States, 1850 to 1930*, Yale, University Press, New Haven, Conn., 1943, tables 2 and 7, pp. 10 and 19; Niles Carpenter, *Immigrants and their children*, 1927, p. 79; Arnold Schrier, 'Ireland and the American Emigration, 1850–1900', Ph.D. thesis, Northwestern University, 1956, p. 231. Despite the author's wide reading, Marcus Lee Hansen's posthumous volume *The Mingling of the Canadian and American Peoples*, Yale University Press, New Haven, Conn., 1940, has very little in the way of statistical evidence.

rations enquired not only into nativity but also into religion, something that never was done in the United States. And, most important, from 1871 onwards the Dominion of Canada census authorities recorded not only each persons's religion and place of birth but also his or her primary ethnicity, something that, again, has never been done in the United States.

Clearly, if one wishes to draw any valid generalizations about the Irish as an ethnic group – What, for example was their rate of social mobility? What occupational patterns emerged? In what sort of environment did they settle? How geographically mobile were they? How upwardly mobile economically were they? And how did religion affect these matters? – one would do well to use the Canadian information. Of course the situation in, say, Ontario in 1880 was not identical to that of, say, Illinois in the same year. No two social situations are ever identical. But careful experimental design can produce reliable results that are transportable across state and provincial borders.

The fact is, the historian of the Irish in any part of the United States who does not the Canadian data know, knows not the Irish in the United States.

V

Denial? The final form of denial that characterizes the historiography of the Irish in the United States is a refusal to see that *much of the literature is based on a derogatory (and inaccurate) interpretation of the cultural background of the nineteenth-century Irish Catholic migrants.* Simply put, the general view has been (and still is) that the cultural characteristics associated with Roman Catholicism in Ireland were an impediment to the migrants' adaptation to the New World.

Potentially, being Catholic could have been a handicap to Irish migrants to the United States in two ways. One was that the existing American society treated Catholics with prejudice. Certainly this happened in the nineteenth century, on a widespread basis, and to a lesser degree in the early twentieth century. To note such an occurrence is in no way potentially misleading, nor in any way derogatory of the nineteenth-century migrants.

The second potentiality, however, can be harmful: the idea that the culture of Roman Catholicism as it was imported from Ireland in some way made the Irish migrants and their offspring backward and not fully able to cope with modernizing America. Usually this view has been put forward by persons who themselves are of Irish Catholic background, so no conscious racism is involved. And, when put forward by professional historians who are non-Catholic, the intent of these ideas has been to understand, not to defame. It is indeed possible that the Irish Catholic culture as imported from the homeland was in some ways a handicap to the migrants, a shackle that made them relatively backward as compared with other migrant groups in the United States. However, if one is articulating such a potentially derogatory conclusion about any ethnic group, even though no conscious racism is involved, one owes it to everyone concerned to operate at a high standard of proof.

Fortunately, we possess an excellent test case of that conclusion, one that saves us from the tedious necessity of having to provide portmanteau citations. This is the *ne plus ultra* of the historiography of the Irish in the United States, Kerby Miller's monumental *Emigrants and exiles.* The volume captured both the Merle Curti Award in American Social History and the Saloutas Memorial Book Award in American Immigration History. The study is at once an encapsulation of almost the entire body of literature on the Irish in the United States (up to the time of its writing) and the most forceful and expert articulation of what US historians of the Irish believed they knew (again, at the time of its writing). The volume, therefore, is an appropriate and fair place to focus upon the historians' view of the Catholic culture of the nineteenth-century migrants, for it is the strongest statement available of the conventional wisdom.

Miller's volume is in most ways an advance over anything done by his predecessors. Not least among these are his attempts to include the Protestant migrants and their descendants in history. That in fact he leaves them on the periphery and does not include them in his main set of hypotheses is unfortunate, but at least he granted their existence as part of the Irish migrant stream, something few of his predecessors did. And, unlike almost all of his predecessors, Miller attempts to write about the Irish in North America, not merely about the Irish in the United States. This means that he understands that his assertions and theories can legitimately be examined by reference to the appropriate Canadian data as well as to whatever one finds available in the US demographic sources.

The heart of the book, on which it must be judged, concerns the years 1815–1921, the era of the great Irish diaspora. Miller writes gracefully, and it is with an apologetic philistinism that one must wrench his argument from his prose and coldly outline his logic. To begin with, he has a phenomenon that he wishes to explain. This is his observed fact that nineteenth-century Irish emigrants were predisposed to perceive or at least justify themselves not as voluntary, ambitious emigrants but as involuntary, non-responsible 'exiles' compelled to leave home by forces beyond individual control, particularly by British and landlord oppression.[31] Note that this observation involves only Irish Catholic emigrants, not Protestant ones. Miller pays considerable attention to Protestants, but his primary observation and his explanation of it concern only Roman Catholics.

To explain this primary phenomenon he introduces several causal factors. First, that, beginning in the late 1820s, *relatively* (italics Miller's) poor Catholics from the three southern provinces constituted a major proportion of the movement overseas.[32] Second, the increasingly Catholic stream of emigrants was a river of reluctant exiles. According to Miller, much evidence indicates that Catholics throughout Ireland, not just in remote Irish-speaking areas, were much more reluctant to leave home than were their Protestant countrymen.[33] Third, for Catholics emigration posed severe social, cultural and even psychological problems.[34]

As a link between his primary observed phenomenon and these causal factors Miller presents an intervening variable. He does not give it a name, but it can be denominated the 'Gaelic-Catholic Disability'. He says, concerning 'traditionalist rural Catholics', that, among those who emigrated, 'their outlook on life . . . was fatalistic and dependent, and their religious faith was usually neither generalized nor internalized, but instead was almost inseparable from archaic customs and landmarks rooted in particular locales now thousands of miles behind them'.[35] He postulates 'a Catholic Irish propensity to avoid individual responsibility for innovative actions such as emigration and to fall back on communally acceptable explanations embedded in archaic historic and literary traditions and reinforced by modern Irish political rhetoric'.[36] Even the Irish language is fitted into this variable: the semantic structure of the Irish language itself reflected and reinforced an Irish world view which emphasized dependence and passivity.[37] Thus, 'armed with a world view so shaped, the Irish experienced the socioeconomic changes associated with the modern commercial and industrial revolutions with certain psychological, as well as political and economic, disadvantages'.[38] Such people perceived their movement into the then modern world of nineteenth-century North America as banishment. As the century progressed, and as a higher and higher proportion of emigrants came from western districts with a strong Gaelic-Catholic culture, the pervasive sense of exile increased.

The potential importance of Miller's Gaelic-Catholic Disability in the study of Irish history is prodigious. This is because the alleged phenomenon is not just a matter that relates to the Irish in the United States. It represents a theory of the Irish Catholic culture at home. And that culture was eventually taken not only to the United States but around the world.

Therefore his Gaelic-Catholic Disability is nothing less than a theory of Irish Catholic culture world-wide.

How does one examine such a world-encircling thesis? One could test for accuracy the hundreds of quotations from the collections of roughly 5,000 emigrant letters and memoirs that are found in Miller's text, but this is just short of impossible: Miller's publisher has allowed him only one endnote for each paragraph and, since there are usually multiple quotations within each paragraph as well as statements of fact, it is difficult, if not impossible, to identify the source of any given statement. Alternatively, one could collect still more emigrant letters and thus try to ascertain whether the attitudes that Miller purports to find are indeed representative. Suffice it to say that at this point no one has checked Miller's quotations for accuracy and representativeness and that the only scholar to work through material similar to his concerning North American emigrants does not find the passivity, or the other characteristics that lead Miller to create his Gaelic-Catholic Disability variable.[39] Nor do studies conducted of emigrant letters from non-US migrants find anything like the backwardness-inducing attitudes that Miller posits. However, I think that it would be a mistake to make too much of these contradictions, since there are technical differences in the various collections of emigrant letters that make it difficult to compare them with Miller's.[40] For the moment, one should assume the accuracy of Miller's data collection, transcription and selection of material as far as migrant attitudes are concerned.[41]

If we make that assumption, the next logical step is to ask: what are the implications of what I have called Miller's 'Gaelic-Catholic Disability Variable'? If that intervening variable is accurate and apposite, not only will it explain why the Irish Catholics wrote all those mournful exile songs and sent those tear-stained letters home, it will permit us to form hypotheses about the Irish Catholics in North America that can be empirically tested. If the hypotheses are confirmed, the probability that Miller's Gaelic-Catholic Disability variable is valid will be greatly heightened. If, on the other hand, the hypotheses are disproved, the validity of Miller's argument will have been shown to be so improbable as to be worthless.

Fortunately, the elegant simplicity of Miller's model permits a series of simple and effective tests. Since his position is that the Irish Catholic culture was both singular and a liability, then if it were found that the Irish Catholics (either in the migrant generation or among their immediate descendants) and Irish Protestants (who certainly did not share the Gaelic-Catholic culture) were fundamentally similar in behaviour, it would have been proved that the Gaelic-Catholic Disability was a chimera and that this interpretation of the Irish Catholic culture should not be adopted as part of the explanation of the history of the Irish Catholics world-wide.

It seems fair to suggest that from Miller's model of Gaelic-Catholic culture, and from his contrasts, both explicit and implicit, between Irish Protestants and Irish Catholics, one would predict of nineteenth-century North America, first, that, because of the communal and familial nature of their culture, as described by Miller, Irish Catholics would be much less successful than Irish Protestants in operating in the isolated world of nineteenth-century North American agriculture, and thus one would expect the Irish Catholics necessarily to huddle together in cities and to avoid the solitariness of rural life; second, that Irish Catholics would have a significantly lower occupational profile than would Irish Protestants; third, that Irish Catholics would show less rapid upward social mobility over time than would Irish Protestants.

Fortunately, there are three separate sets of studies, each of which includes wide-scale observations of the behaviour of Irish migrants or of the entire ethnic group. Each set deals with behaviour, not psychological presumptions, and each set is capable of being replicated. The first set, and the most important, is the extraordinary work of Gordon Darroch and Michael Ornstein.[42] This work, is by far the most sophisticated research design yet adopted in North American ethnic historiography, and it should serve as a model for what eventually must be done with the US manuscript census data. What Darroch and Ornstein did in substance was virtually to retabulate from original manuscript sources the 1871 Dominion of Canada censuses. This was done so as to permit the framing and answering of many questions that did not occur to the nineteenth-century enumeration officials. In particular, the nineteenth-century Canadian censuses are notoriously frustrating in that they contain data on several important variables but do not provide cross-tabulations of those variables. To overcome such difficulties, Darroch and Ornstein drew from the 1871 dominion census a random group of 10,000 male heads of household, on each of whom there were data on several dozen characteristics. They followed up this massive sampling by linking a large body of their 1871 data to other records on individuals who lived in central Canada during the third quarter of the nineteenth century. This allowed the tracing of several thousand randomly selected life patterns.

What Darroch and Ornstein's studies revealed was, first, that Irish Roman Catholics were not disabled by their cultural background from entering the most important entrepreneurial occupation of the time, farming, either on the frontier or in already settled areas. Indeed, farming was the most common Irish Catholic occupation, as it was of the Irish Protestants. The Irish Catholics were only slightly less likely to go into farming – less than 10 per cent below the national average – than were the average run of Canadians. The Irish were not ineluctably urban.

Further, Darroch and Ornstein show that, contrary to the hypothesis, Irish Catholics in Canada did not have a markedly lower economic profile than did persons of Irish Protestant ethnicity. The proportions of Irish Catholics and Irish Protestants among manufacturers, white-collar workers and artisans were virtually identical in Canada in 1871. Catholics were underrepresented in the professional class – only 3 per cent of the total population, in any case – and were more likely than other groups to have labouring occupations, but *not* markedly so. Put simply, persons of Irish Catholic ethnicity did slightly less well than did persons of Irish Protestant ethnicity, but not enough to lend credence to the idea that Catholics were heavily handicapped by their cultural background. Strikingly, in rural areas it was found that the Irish Catholics has slightly greater proportions in the bourgeois occupations than did the Scots or Germans.[43]

Moreover the data show that, contrary to the hypothesis, Irish Catholics did not evince significantly less upward mobility over time than did Irish Protestants. Among Irish-born persons – that is, Irish migrants – linked by Darroch and Ornstein between 1861 and 1871 there was no dramatic difference either in occupational distribution or in occupational mobility between Irish Catholics and Irish Protestants. Irish Catholic immigrants started out somewhat overrepresented in labouring occupations, but their rate of mobility out of labouring into more desirable occupations – and especially into the nation's most desired way of earning a living, farm ownership – *exceeded* that of the Irish-born Protestants.[44]

What this adds up to is a crushing disproof of the validity of Miller's main explanatory concept, the idea that the Gaelic-Catholic culture was a heavy disability for individuals dealing with the modern world of nineteenth-century North America. Admittedly, one could suggest that, somehow, the Irish Catholics who settled in Canada were more able than those who settled in the United States, but, if anything, the opposite is true. From the beginning of the Famine onwards, US regulations were more strict than Canadian regulations, and Canada, not the United States, was most apt to be the repository of the most tired, hungry and worn.

A second set of studies which permit an evaluation of the validity of interpreting the Gaelic-Catholic background as a cultural disability is my own work. Found in five recent books that deal with New Zealand, Australia, South Africa, as well as with Canada and the United States, these studies present several million datum points, each systematically generated by the census authorities in most of the jurisdictions where the Irish settled in large numbers.[45] The student of the Irish diaspora will necessarily encounter those books directly: here suffice it to say that in no jurisdiction in which there are comprehensive and reliable data is there any indication of the Gaelic-Catholic culture being a disabling factor. More important, in those jurisdictions in which there is information upon the religious persuasion of the Irish migrants there is compelling evidence of close similarities as between Irish Catholic and Irish Protestant matters of residence, occupation, family structure and economic mobility. And where multi-generational data are available there is strong positive evidence of close similarities between the Catholic portion and the Protestant portion of the Irish ethnic group. The concept of the Gaelic-Catholic culture being linked to backwardness and inability to take advantage of the various New Worlds is fully disproved.

A third set of studies conducted in the 1970s and 1980s serves as confirmation of the previous two. These are the results yielded by data collected by the National Opinion Research Center of the University of Chicago. (Because these data were generated quite late in the history of the Irish diaspora they are not as compelling as the nineteenth and early twentieth-century data, but they are revealing nonetheless.) The NORC studies found that the Irish group in the United States was polarized between two groups: Catholics, 70 per cent of whom lived in the north-east and north central United States, and Protestants, over half of whom lived in the American south. The Catholics of Irish ethnicity were less likely to be working-class than were the Protestants. As a group the Catholics were twice as likely to be university graduates as were Protestants. As a group the Catholics were twice as likely as to be university graduates as were Protestants of Irish ethnicity, and the Catholic Irish had family incomes significantly higher than those of the Protestant Irish.[46]

The intriguing questions that follow from this information are: when did the Irish Catholics cross the US demographic line to the side of privileged status? And when did the Irish Protestants slide below it, on their way to becoming the most disadvantaged of major groups? Andrew Greeley's estimate, based on his employment of survey data to reconstruct earlier group cohorts, is that this socio-economic watershed was crossed by the Irish Catholics during the decade of the First World War, 1910–19.[47] Irish Protestants, on their collective way downward, crossed by later, probably in the 1930s.

These data are very spiky indeed. The association for most of the present century of Irish Catholicism with relative privilege and of Irish Protestantism with relative disadvantage makes it very hard to present the Irish Catholic culture as a disabling force in US society.

Does this mean that one is rejecting the concept of a Gaelic-Catholic cultural background as part of the heritage common to many of the migrants from Ireland to the United States? Or that one is rejecting the picture whereby the wider society discriminated strongly against the Irish Catholics on the basis of their religion? No. What is rejected is the idea that their cultural background was in itself a handicap for the Irish Catholics as they coped with the New World.

VI

Denial. In this assessment of the historiography of the Irish in the United States I have used 'denial' to describe four specific behaviours practised by historians. At no time have I imputed motive to persons exhibiting those behaviours, or engaged in a 'psychological' explanation of such behaviour. The historiography of the Irish in the United States has gotten itself in deep trouble because of its predilection for pop psychology, as Patrick O'Sullivan has made clear.

The wonderful thing about behaviour is that it can be changed. Accurate scholarly work is a behaviour that is rewarding in itself. And it is the best homage that one can pay to the Irish migrants and their descendants.

Notes

1. For example, R. A. Burchell, *The San Francisco Irish, 1848–1880*, University of California Press, Berkeley, Col., 1980; Dennis Clark, *Hibernia America: the Irish and Regional Cultures*, Greenwood Press, Westport, Conn., 1985; David M. Emmons, *The Butte Irish: Class and Ethnicity in an American Mining Town, 1875–1925*, University of Illinois Press, Urbana, Ill., 1989.

2. Patrick O'Sullivan, Introduction to this volume, p. 7.
3. For entry into the literature see R. A. Burchell, 'The historiography of the American-Irish', *Immigrants and Minorities*, 1, 3, 1982, pp. 281–305; David Noel Doyle, 'The regional bibliography of Irish America, 1800–1930: a review and addendum', *Irish Historical Studies*, 23, 91, 1983, pp. 254–83; Seamus P. Metress, *The Irish-American Experience: a Guide to the Literature*, University Press of America, Washington, D.C., 1981.
4. This is North American usage. British Isles usage sometimes employs 'first generation' to mean the first generation born in the new homeland. Here North American usage is adopted.
5. Andrew M. Greeley, 'The American Irish: a Report from Great Ireland', *International Journal of Comparative Sociology*, 29, 1979, pp. 67–81; 'Ethnic minorities in the United States: demographic perspectives', *International Journal of Group Tensions*, 7, 1977, pp. 84–97; *Ethnicity in the United States: a Preliminary Reconnaissance*, Wiley, New York, 1974, pp. 35–89; 'The success and assimilation of Irish Protestants and Irish Catholics in the United States', *S.S.R.*, 72, 4, 1988, pp. 229–36; Fred Boal, 'Who are the "Irish Americans"?', *Fortnight*, 155, 1977, pp. 4–5.
6. George Gallup, Jr, and Jim Castelli, *The People's Religion: American Faith in the '90s*, Macmillan, New York, 1989, pp. 119–22.
7. The closest anyone with historical evidence has come to suggesting such an apostasy is Michael O'Brien. He was a late nineteenth and early twentieth-century antiquarian, of prodigious devotion, and not a fool. He attacked the idea that the only colonial Irish settlers were Ulster Scots, and on that point he was certainly correct. He also believed that both Anglo-Irish and Ulster Scots were Irish, and on this one must concur (for certainly they saw themselves as Irish). What is doubtful is O'Brien's view that many Irish Catholics abandoned their faith in colonial New England and other colonies. O'Brien cites numerous Irish names in baptismal records of Protestant churches. In future writing I shall attempt to assess in some detail O'Brien's work on the 'appostasy' issue. See Michael J. O'Brien, *Irish Settlers in America: a Consolidation of Articles from the Journal of the American-Irish Historical Society*, Gencological Publicity Co., Baltimore, Md, 1979, *passim*.
8. When one leaves the historical literature of the 'Irish-Americans' (a code phrase for Roman Catholics of Irish background), and enters that of the so-called 'Scotch-Irish', one enters a strange underwater kingdom. The two classic books on the subject which set the framework for the continuing emphasis on the eighteenth century and upon a virtually racialist view of the differences between the Ulster Scots and the Irish Catholics are: Charles A. Hanna, *The Scotch-Irish, or, The Scot in North Britain, North Ireland, and North America*, Nickerbocker Press, New York, 1902, and Henry Ford Jones, *The Scotch-Irish in America*, Princeton University Press, Princeton, N.J., 1915.

   In a summary of his own book, written for a popular audience, James G. Leyburn states categorically that 'There was almost no further influx from northern Ireland after the Revolutionary war' ('The Scotch-Irish', *American Heritage*, 22, December 1970, p. 99.) See also James G. Leyburn, *The Scotch-Irish: a Social History*, University of North Carolina Press, Chapel Hill, N.C., 1962. For a revisionist view concerning the eighteenth century see David Noel Doyle, *Ireland, Irishmen, and Revolutionary America, 1760–1820*, published for the Cultural Relations Committee of Ireland by the Mercier Press, Dublin, 1981.

   The substance of R. J. Dickson's *Ulster Emigration to Colonial America 1718–75*, Routledge, London, 1966, is a dispassionate, thorough and convincing monograph. The author's introduction, however, repeats the assertion that there were two distinct groups of people who emigrated from Ireland to the United States: 'The hundreds of thousands of Irish emigrants to colonial America who have been overshadowed by the millions who emigrated from Ireland in the second half of the nineteenth century' (p. ix). One of the more engaging discussions of the Ulster Scot as a rural phenomenon was provided by the late Estyn Evans, Ireland's pioneering historical geographer, in the 'The Scotch-Irish in the New World: an Atlantic heritage', *Journal of the Royal Society of Antiquaries of Ireland*, 95, 1965, pp. 39–49. Rather broader recent interpretations of the same agreed phenomenon are Forrest McDonald and Grady McWhiney, 'The antebellum southern herdsman: a reinterpretation', *Journal of Southern History*, 41, 1975, pp. 147–66; Forrest McDonald, 'The ethnic factor in Alabama history: a neglected dimension', *Alabama Review*, 32, 1978, pp. 256–65; Forrest McDonald and Grady McWhiney, 'The Celtic south', *History Today*, 30, July 1980, pp. 11–15.

9. D. G. Boyce, 'Sense and Sensibility', *Irish Literary Supplement*, fall, 1990, p. 28.

10. This use of census data, admittedly quite crude, is loaded *against* suggesting that the Irish Protestants emigrated quite frequently: presumably the Catholics, being over-represented in the pauper class, more frequently starved or died of Famine-related disease than did the Protestants; therefore, much of their population loss was from those causes, not solely from emigration. Religious percentages in Ireland before 1834 are highly problematical. For a sensible, although not definitive, attempt to deal with the earlier situation see Appendix B, 'Statistics of religious affiliation in Ireland in the eighteenth and nineteenth centuries', in S. J. Connolly, *Priests and People in Pre-Famine Ireland, 1780–1845*, Gill & Macmillan, Dublin, 1982, pp. 281–3.

11. For example, one might hypothesize that the drop in the Protestant population came from a lowering of family size (and thus of religious-specific fertility) while the Catholic drop in population came chiefly from emigration. Actually, however, the opposite is more likely to have happened. That is, the brunt of the Famine having fallen on the Catholic poor, the limits on marriage that developed in the post-Famine era (described, for example, in Conrad M. Arensberg and Solon T. Kimball, *Family and Community in Ireland*, Harvard University Press, second edition, Cambridge, Mass., 1968), probably fell more severely on the Catholics. Again, I am presenting the census data in such a way as to minimize the possibility of our having to accept the idea of large-scale Protestant emigration; even so, that hypothesis emerges as one most needful of being tested.

12. As David Fitzpatrick points out in 'Irish emigration in the later nineteenth century', *Irish Historical Studies*, 22, September 1980, pp. 127–8, from 1851 to 1876 the data are wobbly but not without worth. In 1876 the method of making the count was revamped to abolish local anomalies in the collection method.

13. Derived from the same source as Table 4.4

14. See W. E. Vaughan and A. J. Fitzpatrick, eds., *Irish Historical Statistics, population, 1821–1971*, Royal Irish Academy, 1978, pp. 311–32.

15. Andrew M. Greeley, 'The success and assimiliation of Irish Protestants and Irish Catholics in the United States', *S.S.R.*, 72, 4, 1988, p. 229.

16. See Donald H. Akenson, 'Why the accepted estimates of the ethnicity of the American people, 1790, are unacceptable', *William and Mary Quarterly*, third series, 41, 1984, pp. 102–19.

17. The problem was that persons returning more than one ethnic origin were lumped into an 'other' category which embraced roughly half the population!

See Charles A. Price, 'Methods of estimating the size of groups', in Stephen Thernstrom, ed., *Harvard Encyclopedia of American Ethnic Groups*, Harvard University Press, Cambridge, Mass., 1980, pp. 1033–4.

18. Once again, individuals were allowed to list multiple ancestries rather than a single dominant one, so that 55 per cent listed two or more in the 1980 census. Thus the data on ethnicity cannot be related to any other variable, nor, in fact, can they serve as the basis of anything but the crudest guessing about what the real ethnic composition of the country actually is.

19. Price, 'Methods of estimating', p. 1040.

20. For a fascinating discussion of this fear of collecting religious data, and especially of the trouble which arose when it was proposed to include religion on the 1960 census, see William Petersen, 'Religious statistics in the United States', *Journal for the Scientific Study of Religion*, 1, 1965, pp. 165–78. This article also discusses the Census Bureau's suppression (!) of the data it had collected in the 1957 voluntary-sample study.

21. A very useful version of that census was compiled by J. D. B. Debow, superintendent of the US census, *A Statistical View of the United States . . .*, Beverley Tucker, Senate Printer, Washington, D.C., 1854.

22. Niles Carpenter, *Immigrants and their Children: a Study based on Census Statistics relative to the Foreign-born and the Native Whites of Foreign or Mixed Parentage*, Census Monographs VII, Government Printing Office, Washington, D.C., 1927, p. 2. Although the US Census Bureau's collections of ethnic data went no further than the migrants and their offspring, it is of course possible to do extrapolations of the gross number of persons in the third generation. This was attempted by the Census Bureau for the 1920 census (see Carpenter, p. 92) and, further, amateur demographers were always willing to try to establish the total strength of the Irish ethnic group from the limited knowledge available concerning the first two generations in the United States. Michael J. O'Brien, historiographer of the American-Irish Historical Society, surveyed some of the early attempts and shrewdly, if tiredly, remarked that 'to form any reliable estimate of the numerical strength of the Irish and their descendants in the United States, I believe, would be a hopeless task and while several have attempted to do so, I am of the opinion that all such estimates should be discarded as mere conjecture', 'The Irish in the United States', in Joseph Dunn and P. J. Lennox, eds., *The Glories of Ireland*, Phoenix, Washington, D.C., 1914, p. 208.

23. Burchell, 'The historiography', p. 281. A 'public use sample' for 1900 is available.

24. E. P. Hutchinson, 'Notes on immigration statistics of the United States', *American Statistical Association Journal*, 53, 1958, pp. 968–79. I am here leaving aside entirely the problem involved with the counter-flow from the United States to various foreign countries. Net migration data are what one requires, but in the absence of records on alien departures from the United States there is no way of measuring net immigration before 1908. (Carpenter, *Immigrants and their children*, p. 3).

25. Estimate found in J. D. B. DeBow, *The Industrial Resources Statistics, etc., of the United States*, third edition, Appleton, New York, 1854, 3, pp. 396, 424, cited in Hutchinson, 'Notes on immigration statistics', p. 975.

26. I am here avoiding the virtually insoluble question of how great was the counter-flow of British Isles-born persons who shipped to the United States and came from thence to Canada. Undoubtedly it was much less than the flow from Canada into the United States, but whether it was 2 per cent or 20·3 per cent or

30 per cent no one really knows (see Hutchinson, 'Notes on immigration statistics', p. 976).

27. Hutchinson, 'Notes on immigration statistics', pp. 974–81.
28. Computed from Hutchinson, 'Notes on immigration statistics', p. 981. For instance, the Irish-born constituted 4·81 per cent of the US population in 1870, while in 1871 the Irish-born constituted 6·2 per cent of the Canadian population. Compare the text above with *Seventh Census of Canada, 1931*, King's Printer, Ottawa, 1936, I, p. 517.
29. William Forbes Adams, *Ireland and the Irish Emigration to the New World from 1815 to the Famine*, Yale University Press, New Haven, Conn., 1932. See especially his appendix, 'Statistics of Irish emigration, 1815–45', on which my comments in the text are largely based. Adams's work is often paid lip service but its substance is generally ignored, largely, one conjectures, because it runs against the grain of the present consensus among historians of the Irish in the United States. That is, Adams's work implicitly affirms three points: first, that the central episode in the history of the Irish in the New World begins not with the Famine but in 1815; second, that one must deal with all of North America if one is to come to terms with the Irish in the United States, and, third, that, no matter how difficult the task, one must work with the available demographic data and in particular, have an explicit understanding of the limits of that data. That, sixty years after Adams's work, I am having to argue explicitly what Adams accepted implicitly is not entirely heartening.
30. The precise date is problematical. The Irish were the largest Canadian ethnic group in 1881, but the English had surpassed them by 1901. Unfortunately, the 1891 census did not yield ethnicity data in a form comparable to that provided by the censuses of 1881 and 1901, so one must necessarily be vague. For the data see *Seventh Census of Canada, 1931*, I, p. 710.
31. Kerby A. Miller, *Emigrants and Exiles: Ireland and the Irish Exodus to North America*, Oxford University Press, New York, 1985, p. 556.
32. Miller, *Emigrants and Exiles*, p. 198.
33. Miller, *Emigrants and Exiles*, p. 238.
34. Miller, *Emigrants and Exiles*, p. 240.
35. Miller, *Emigrants and Exiles*, p. 259.
36. Miller, *Emigrants and Exiles*, p. 277.
37. Miller, *Emigrants and Exiles*, p. 119.
38. Miller, *Emigrants and Exiles*, p. 8.
39. Ruth-Ann Harris, 'America Imagined, America Realized: new Perspectives on the American Letter', unpublished paper, American conference for Irish Studies, April 1990; Ruth-Ann Harris to author, 22 May 1990.
40. See D. H. Akenson, 'Reading the texts of rural immigrants: letters from the Irish in Australia, New Zealand, and North America', *Canadian Papers in Rural History*, 7, 1990, pp. 387–406, reprinted in *Migration and New Zealand Society*, Stout Research Centre, Victoria University, Wellington, New Zealand, 1990, pp. 1–17; David Fitzpatrick, ' "An ocean of consolation": letters and Irish immigration to Australia', in Eric Richards, Richard Reid and David Fitzpatrick, eds., *Visible Immigrants: Neglected Sources for the History of Australian Immigration*, Research School of Social Sciences, Australian National University, Canberra, 1989, pp. 47–86; E. R. R. Green, 'Ulster emigrants' letters', in E. R. R. Green, ed., *Essays in Scotch-Irish History*, Routledge, London, 1969, pp. 87–103; Cecil J. Houston and William J. Smyth, *Irish Emigration and Canadian Settlement: Patterns, Links and Settlers*, University of Toronto Press, Toronto, 1990, pp. 241–333; Patrick O'Farrell, *Letters from Irish Australia, 1825–1929*,

126   *Donald Harman Akenson*

New South Wales University Press, Sydney, and Ulster Historical Foundation, Belfast, 1984. The chief problem of comparability is the over-representation of Protestants in most of the studies mentioned above, in comparison with Miller's sample. This is particularly true of the Green, O'Farrell, and Houston and Smyth items.

41. The fundamental difficulty in using emigrant letters as the basis for any study of the Irish diaspora is that there are so few letters in relation to the huge population of migrants, and this is doubly true of the Catholics. The really troublesome question is why are there so very few surviving emigrant letters sent back from Irish Catholic migrants. This holds not only for the United States but for Australia, New Zealand and Canada. This despite the fact that the Irish Catholic emigrants were mostly literate and despite the fact that Irish Catholic families in the homeland have shown themselves very good at maintaining family artefacts and heirlooms – and one would have thought they would have kept letters and that they would have found their way, after 1922, into the museums and archives of newly independent Ireland. Miller has done the best collecting job yet, but even he has only 5,000 letters drawn from a migrant population of millions and (one assumes) from a flow of migrant letters home that numbered in the several millions. Such a sample size just might be large enough to produce meaningful results if it were drawn (1) with a knowledge of the context within which each letter was written or (2) if it were part of a competently designed random survey (always assuming that the message of each letter is not misrepresented by its being gutted to fit an historical argument). In fact the context of the letters Miller cites is hardly ever known, and the actual letters themselves cannot be taken as anything approaching random. Thus any conclusions that one could draw from them in all probability are not representative of the reference group (Irish migrants) to which they are believed to refer.

42. Gordon Darroch, 'Class in nineteenth-century central Ontario: a reassessment of the crisis and demise of small producers during early industrialization, 1861–71', in Gregory S. Kealey, ed., *Class, Gender, and Region: Essays in Canadian Historical Sociology*, Committee on Canadian Labour History, St John's, Nfld., 1988, pp. 49–72; A. Gordon Darroch and Michael Ornstein, 'Ethnicity and class: Transitions over a decade: Ontario, 1861–71', Canadian Historical Association, Ottawa, *History Papers, 1984*, pp. 111–37; 'Ethnicity and occupational structure in Canada in 1871: the vertical mosaic in historical perspective', *Canadian Historical Review*, 61, 1980, pp. 305–33.

43. Darroch and Ornstein, 'Ethnicity and occupational structure', pp. 320–5.

44. Compare the table in Darroch and Ornstein, 'Ethnicity and class', pp. 121–2.

45. *Occasional Papers on the Irish in South Africa*, Institute of Social and Economic Research, Rhodes University, Grahamstown, 1991; *Half the World from Home: Perspectives on the Irish in New Zealand*, Victoria University Press, Wellington, 1990; *Small Differences: Irish Catholics and Irish Protestants, 1815–1921: an International Perspective*, McGill–Queen's University Press, Kingston and Montreal, 1988, and Gill & Macmillan, Dublin, 1990; *Being Had: Historians, Evidence and the Irish in North America*, Meany, Toronto, 1985; *The Irish in Ontario: a Study in Rural History*, McGill–Queen's University Press, Kingston and Montreal, 1984.

46. Andrew Greeley, 'The success and assimilation of Irish Protestants and Irish Catholics in the United States', *S.S.R.*, 72, 4, July 1988, pp. 231–2.

47. Greeley, 'The success and assimilation', p. 231.

Acknowledgement

I am grateful to my friend and publisher Pat Meany (of P. D. Meany Publishers, Ontario) for his kind permission to reprint some material from my book *Being Had: Historians, Evidence and the Irish in North America*, Meany, Toronto, 1985.

5 'No petty people': the Anglo-Irish identity in colonial Australia

Gordon Forth

In December 1840, on a visit to the recently founded settlement of Port Phillip, George Winter clashed bitterly with a fellow Ascendancy colonist, Augustine Barton, in the presence of another member of the 'Irish cousin-age', the diarist Charles Griffith. In the course of an 'unpleasant altercation' Winter denounced Barton's conduct as 'very colonial', a statement which Griffith considered 'expresses what we call at home going very close to the wind'.[1] Some months later, Griffith and no doubt other Port Phillip gentlemen were struck by the appearance of George Winter's younger brother Samuel as he rode through the settlement. A confident and experienced bushman of twenty-five, full-bearded, tall and strikingly handsome, the younger Winter reminded Griffith of 'one of the knight errants in the days of chivalry'.[2] On such occasions it was apparently Winter's custom to have an aboriginal page in livery mounted up behind him and to be escorted by several retainers on foot. In attempting to play the eighteenth-century-style *grand seigneur* Winter was undoubtedly influenced by romantic images from his Irish Ascendancy background. In a modified colonial fashion he seemed to be striving to emulate those grand Irish magnates who a century earlier had received official guests resplendent in brilliant feudal regalia and attended by mounted retainers. Representative of a separate British national sub-group, Anglo-Irish colonists such as Winter brought with them to Australia distinctive and commonly held attitudes and customs. Both consciously and unconsciously this Anglo-Irish tradition influenced the responses of these migrants to their new and changing circumstances in the Australian colonies.

Before discussing how the Old World tradition found expression in the form of Anglo-Irish identity in colonial Australia, it is first necessary to establish just who the Anglo or Ascendancy Irish actually were. For it is due largely to confusion over their national identity that the Anglo-Irish as a group have been so neglected in the writing of Australian history. Evidence of a distinctive Anglo-Irish presence in Australia was most apparent during the period 1820–50. Australia's Anglo-Irish population before 1820 consisted of a few transported convicts and officials, mainly serving military officers, involved in the establishment of penal settlements in New South Wales and Van Diemen's Land. On the whole efficient and humane administrators, most left the colonies when their term expired or their regiment received a new posting. A few, such as Captain Francis Allman, a native of County Clare who served as convict commandant at Port Macquarie, chose to resign their commission and remain to take advantage of the land grant system to establish themselves as colonial gentry. Before 1815 there was little to attract Anglo-Irish gentlemen migrants to the remote Australian colonies. The wars with France resulted in high prices for Irish agricultural products, and provided opportunities for 'younger sons' of Ascendancy families to obtain commissions in the expanded British forces. This situation changed drastically after 1815, with a sharp downturn in the Irish economy and the forced retirement of large numbers of Anglo-Irish officers on half pay. Fortunately for the Ascendancy, these changes coincided with the introduction of policies by the British government designed to encourage private capital investment in Australia's newly established pastoral industry.

A sustained period of economic depression and high unemployment in Ireland coincided with the creation of investment and employment opportunities in Australia which resulted in significant Anglo-Irish migration to all the Australian colonies between 1820 and 1850. As senior and middle-level administrators, founding members of the newly established professions and pioneering pastoralists, the Anglo-Irish were a distinctive presence in pre-gold rush colonial society. After 1850 the genteel, pastoral society of which the Anglo-Irish were an influential part was swept aside by changes which accompanied the Australian gold rushes. Though Anglo-Ireland continued to provide post-gold rush Australia with energetic, able administrators and talented professional men, the collective influence of the Anglo-Irish soon declined. Less sure of their Irishness, and blending easily into the local Protestant establishment, evidence of a distinctive Anglo-Irish identity becomes increasingly difficult to find. With their imperialist outlook, patrician manner and conservative views the Anglo-Irish were increasingly out of place in late nineteenth-century Australia. While a few continued to arrive to take advantage of employment opportunities not available in Ireland, the prospect of permanent settlement in an essentially democratic and increasingly urbanized and industrialized Australia had little appeal to most prospective Ascendancy migrants. By the early twentieth century the Anglo-Irish presence in Australia was so reduced as to be of historic interest only. Yet even here the role of the Anglo-Irish as a formative influence in Australian colonial society has often been ignored or misrepresented.

This century, Ireland's long suppressed Catholic Gaelic majority has been extremely successful in having its claims to be the Irish nation recognized. Certain English writers have joined extreme Irish nationalists in refusing to recognize Protestants of English descent but Irish birth as Irish. In the introduction to his 1934 biography of Wellington, *The Duke*, Philip Guedalla comments that 'Castes mark their children deeply and as a caste the resident gentry in Ireland were most pronounced'.[3] Hearing themselves referred to as *English* would certainly have puzzled most of Wellington's fellow Ascendancy, who never doubted for a moment that they were Irish without qualification. Indeed, in both early nineteenth-century Ireland and Australia it was Protestant Irish gentlemen rather than the native Catholic peasantry who were regarded, and regarded themselves, as the true Irish.

With the demise of the Protestant Ascendancy in Ireland, the term 'Irish' has come to be used almost exclusively to refer to those of the Catholic faith and Gaelic tradition. As a result, historians writing in the Ascendancy period have been required to use 'Anglo-Irish' to differentiate those of Irish birth but predominantly English origin and Episcopalian faith from both their Catholic Gaelic and their Ulster Presbyterian countrymen. Clearly the use of the term 'Anglo-Irish', which not all historians accept, has contributed to the view that these descendants of Protestant settlers were not really Irish but English, foreigners who just happened to have been born in Ireland.

Essentially a modern historian's invention, the term 'Anglo-Irish' is not to be found in Australia's early historical records. This may help explain why, until recently, Anglo-Irish colonists as a group have been largely ignored by Australian historians. Due also to the small size and scattered nature of Australia's Anglo-Irish population, the omission also reflects the ease and rapidity with which these Irish Anglicans were absorbed into the local Protestant establishment. Basically, this neglect stems from the assumption on the part of historians that the Anglo-Irish in Australia were English rather than Irish. While the two nationalities obviously had a great deal in common, the Anglo-Irish *were* Irish and brought with them to Australia their own quite distinctive attitudes and values. J. C. Beckett's *The Anglo-Irish Tradition, 1602–1921*[4] is the best known recently published work which explains how these distinctive attitudes and modes of behaviour evolved as a result of the Ascendancy's particular situation in post-Cromwellian Ireland.

Even less valid is the assumption that the Irish in Australia were simply Irish – that the Anglo-Irish or Irish Anglicans differed no more from their Catholic countrymen than did, say, English or Scottish Protestants from theirs. The Ulster or Scotch Irish aside, the Irish in Australia obviously represented two nations, one the privileged Protestant minority, the other the Catholic Gaelic majority. The divisions were by no means clear-cut, with class and education rather than religion and ethnic background determining to which nation one belonged. In colonial Australia, as in Ireland, representatives of the surviving 'Old English' Catholic aristocracy obviously had more in common with Protestant gentlemen than with their co-religionists of peasant background. Prominent Irish Catholic colonists such as the Trinity-educated lawyers Sir Roger Therry and Sir John Hubert Plunkett can quite properly be regarded as Anglo-Irish.

The tendency to regard Australia's Anglo-Irish as English may also have contributed to the their lack of recognition by historians. In his study of gentlemen migrants on the Canadian frontier, Patrick Dunae points out that '. . . until recently the English have not been regarded as a distinct ethnic group . . . but as a kind of core community around which other ethnic communities developed'.[5] The fact that the Anglo-Irish were so closely identified with Australia's ruling class also helps explain why they have been overlooked. Reflecting changing preoccupations and ideological concerns, Australia's current generation of academic historians have concentrated on groups which were inadequately represented in 'elite' histories of the past. As a result, while aborigines, women, ethnic minorities and sections of the working class have been substantially rescued from the shadows, the history of gentry migration to Australia, Anglo-Irish or otherwise, has hardly been a fashionable topic for research. The actual number of Anglo-Irish in colonial Australia at any one time is difficult to gauge, as most came as private or cabin passengers, and shipping records provide only the barest details. The Anglo-Irish population in Australia probably never amounted to more than a few hundred at any one time and would not have exceeded 5 per cent of all Irish migration to Australia before 1900. As a demographically insignificant, scattered and rapidly assimilated population it is hardly surprising that Australia's other Irish have received so little recognition. Yet in pre-gold rush New South Wales and Tasmania they were, in Patrick O'Farrell's estimation, 'a neglected but crucial factor in the colonising process'.[6] As well as being significantly over-represented among the colonial administrative, professional and gentry class, their influence reflected the Ascendancy's perception of themselves as civilising colonists with an important historic role to play within the British empire. As government officials of high and low degree, pioneering squatters and leaders in the professions, their contribution was distinctive and considerable. Influenced by their Old World Ascendancy tradition as well as by the circumstances in which they found themselves as colonists, most strove enthusiastically and with a fair degree of success to improve Australian society.

The Old World tradition which so influenced the behaviour of these colonists had its origins in the situation of Ireland's newly established Protestant landed class following Cromwell's defeat of the Catholic rebel armies. Officers and adventurers who had helped finance Cromwell's campaign were entitled to apply for grants of land from the defeated Catholics' forfeited estates. On the basis of his analysis of Burke's *Landed Gentry of Ireland* Curtis concludes that the overwhelming majority of Ascendancy families settled in Ireland at this time.[7] During the late seventeenth and eighteenth centuries the descendants of these military conquerors developed a life style and attitudes which came to be recognized as typical of their class. Though having much in common with the English gentry, whom they strove to emulate, their situation as an alienated ruling class, exposure to Gaelic culture and the difficulties of life in rural Ireland resulted in significant differences. As well as certain unconsciously held beliefs, representatives of the Irish Ascendancy brought with them to Australia a conscious awareness of themselves as the descendants of a conquering military caste. British occupation of Australia, however, provided these Anglo-Irish with little opportunity to distinguish themselves through military action, with distance and the harsh environment rather than armed resistance by the native population the main obstacles to European settlement. However, the crude frontier society of pre-gold rush Australia provided the individual Anglo-Irish with ample scope to take on the role of civilizing colonists.

Ireland's newly established Protestant gentry possessed the typical colonists' contempt for the native population. Regarding themselves superior on account of their proven military prowess, religious orthodoxy, English blood and more advanced culture, few Protestants mixed freely with the Catholic Celtic population. With most Catholic gentry having either fled abroad or been confined to Ireland's barren west, the Protestants presided over a leaderless and submissive native population. Yet not until the comprehensive Williamite victory over resurgent Catholic forces at the Boyne in 1791 were Ireland's Protestant gentry really free from the threat of dispossession by military or legal means. The Protestant Ascendancy's dominance was now reinforced by the introduction of harsh penal laws designed to prevent further Catholic uprisings. Well armed and organized into local militia, Ireland's Protestant community continued to rely on English military support to maintain their position. Unable or unwilling to assimilate with the native Irish, these Protestants remained psychologically dependent on English culture, institutions and military force. Loyal monarchists and staunch defenders of empire, yet distrusting the English, the Anglo-Irish remained ambivalent regarding their national allegiance.

Their situation as an imposed and hated ruling class resulted in the adoption of a garrison mentality among Ireland's resident gentry class – an attitude which persisted long after the reasons for it had ceased to be important. Above all, it was the fierce desire to maintain their privileges and property which united Ireland's Protestants into a particularly close-knit and resilient community. In pre-gold rush Australia there was a tendency among Ascendancy migrants to form temporary enclaves based on Old World friendship or kinship associations. The formation of such enclaves was part of the process of chain migration as more established settlers sponsored personal and family friends or relatives from Ireland. These close-knit, temporary associations provided a basis from which newly arrived migrants could gain experience and acquire local knowledge before branching out on their own. In north-eastern Tasmania during the 1820s and 1830s representatives of the Bryan, Fenton, Talbot and Winter families were closely associated as neighbouring landholders. During the late 1830s an offshoot of this group consisting of Samuel and John Bryan and Samuel, Trevor and George Winter were among the first to establish pastoral runs in the Wannon River area of the Portland Bay district of New South Wales. The best known example of an Ascendancy enclave in Australia was Port Phillip's 'Irish cousinage' of the 1840s. This group, which was extremely influential in setting the tone of Port Phillip society, consisted mainly of Anglo-Irish squatters and lawyers and included among its membership Redmond Barry, Augustine Barton, James Croke, James Moore, William Stawell and William Talbot.

Given the Ascendancy background, it is hardly surprising that the most distinctive feature of Anglo-Irish identity in Australia was the extent to which the attitudes and values of these colonists were those of a landed, gentry class. Even well into the nineteenth century, Ireland remained basically a backward agrarian society with little by way of a separate middle or commercial class to challenge the landed interest. Lacking alternative areas of investment and employment, the Irish Ascendancy looked to landed estates not only as their major source of income but as the basis of a family's social standing. As well as actual landlords (perpetual tenants and landowners) the Irish gentry included many propertyless younger sons whose income and status came mainly from landed estates. While some profited from their role as middlemen, subdividing and sub-letting leased land, others were employed as salaried estate managers. Owing to substantially lower costs, in Ireland it was possible for such individuals to maintain a basic gentry life style on a fairly modest income. It was, of course, the idle habits and dissolute ways of these petty squireens and the ruthless manner in which they treated their tenants which attracted so much criticism from Arthur Young[8] and other visitors to Ireland.

A proportion of Anglo-Irish migrants in Australia were either practising members of a profession or came from middle-class professional rather than resident gentry backgrounds. Yet to make too much of the landed/middle-class division in Anglo-Irish society is to underestimate the extent to which Ascendancy Ireland was a landed society. Town dwellers engaged in commerce or the professions were frequently members of or at least closely linked with gentry families. As well as being related through birth or marriage to several landed families, a Trinity-educated lawyer or medical practitioner living in Dublin was likely to derive a substantial part of his income from landed estates and belong to the same gentlemen's clubs and learned societies as members of the gentry class. Take for example the case of Redmond Barry, a Trinity College graduate who became a founding judge in the Supreme Court of Victoria. It appears to have been normal practice for male members of Barry's family to spend only their childhood, holidays and retirement on the family's Cork estates. This was certainly the case with Barry's father, who rose to the rank of major-general in the British army, and with two of his four brothers who also pursued a military career. Prior to migrating to New South Wales in 1839, Barry spent several years in Dublin attending university and trying unsuccessfully to establish himself as a barrister. Yet it would be incorrect to regard Barry as a member of an urban professional class, as he was and clearly saw himself as gentry. It was significant that, like many other Ascendancy lawyers in Port Phillip, Barry briefly dabbled in squatting before heeding his mother's advice 'to pursue a profession as country pursuits are too expensive'.[9]

Apart from its sharp division on religious lines, the most striking feature of Irish society at the beginning of the eighteenth century was just how successful the Protestants had been in the struggle for land and power. As well as dividing most of Ireland's agricultural land between themselves, the Protestants monopolized public offices, higher education and the professions. Little restrained by the law or social convention, the power of many Protestant landlords over their Catholic tenantry was absolute. Following his tours of Ireland in the 1770s Arthur Young claimed that 'a landlord in Ireland can scarcely invent an order which a servant, cotter or labourer dares to refuse to execute. Nothing satisfies him but unlimited submission.'[10]

In the more remote pastoral districts of pre-gold rush Australia also, Anglo-Irish colonists found themselves subject to little legal restraint or direct government control. Yet, as certain individuals were to discover, Irish gentlemen in colonial Australia were certainly not as free to behave as they wished as most Protestant gentry in Ireland. For a start, the law in the Australian colonies, being centrally administered, was more equitable in its application than in Anglo-Ireland. In the penal colonies of New South Wales and Tasmania, Irish gentlemen found themselves subject to military-style regulations designed for the efficient administration of penal settlements. Anglo-Irish colonists who assumed immunity from the law on account of their status as Irish gentlemen, and openly flouted such regulations, risked public censure and even prosecution.

The Bryan case, or the 'Bryan Imbroglio', as one writer refers to it,[11] illustrates the basic incompatibility of this aspect of Anglo-Irish identity with the British government's view of Tasmania as a penal colony. Though not as well connected as he claimed to be, William Bryan, the younger son of a Church of Ireland clergyman, was related to the much respected Talbot and Butler families. In 1824 William responded to his elder brother Samuel's invitation to join him in Van Diemen's Land, and shortly after his arrival received an initial land grant of 1,000 acres in the Westbury district, south of Launceston.[12] By November 1831 Bryan had been appointed a magistrate, could claim title to over 11,000 acres and had a large force of convict labourers to work for him. Regarding himself as above the law, in August 1833 Bryan sought to establish his own pastoral tenantry by entering into an illegal agreement with two of his convict servants. More seriously, Bryan apparently condoned the regular cattle-stealing activities of two new tenants who helped themselves to his neighbours' unbranded cattle to stock their leased land. Unfortunately for Bryan, one of the neighbours involved was Tasmania's influential Chief Magistrate, a Captain William Lyttleton, who complained to the Lieutenant Governor, Sir George Arthur. When Arthur decided to make an example of Bryan by depriving him of his magistracy and assigned convict servants, the fiery Irishman reacted by challenging Lyttleton, a senior government official and his social superior, to a duel and by placing a number of highly inflammatory notices in the local press. Though he certainly made the situation worse by his intemperate behaviour, Bryan had reason to believe that he had been singled out because he was an Irish gentleman. Faced with prosecution, he fled to London, where he spent most of 1834 unsuccessfully pursuing his case for compensation with such fervour that the Colonial Secretary expressed doubt about his sanity.[13]

Ascendancy settlers in Australia who oppressed or ill-treated their farm servants in the worst traditions of Irish landlordism risked creating serious difficulties for themselves. For, while chronic unemployment and widespread poverty produced a large and servile work force in Ireland, labour remained scarce and independently-minded in the Australian colonies.

Given the one-sided provisions of the Masters and Servants Act, employers in pre-gold rush Australia had little to fear should their farm or domestic servants complain to the authorities. However, harsh and overbearing employers like George Winter faced possible retaliation or, at the very least, the potentially ruinous desertion of workers. In the summer of 1845 George was unable to have his flocks shorn, as 'no men [would] stay with him owing to the way he treated them'.[14] Winter, who upset his neighbouring pastoralists when he resorted to employing escaped convicts, failed as a squatter basically because of his inability to retain a stable work force.

Yet even those Anglo-Irish colonists who treated their workers in a just and humane fashion were not generally successful as pioneering pastoralists. While those with a gentry or military background seemed reasonably well equipped to cope with life on the Australian frontier, few possessed the determination necessary to succeed as pioneering pastoralists. In contrast, the Scots, with a Calvinist-inspired commitment to hard work, frugality and perseverance, were particularly successful as squatters. As gentlemen migrants the Anglo-Irish were also always going to experience some difficulty in adapting to the lonely and often arduous life of a pioneer. Their lack of commitment and readiness to exchange the squatting life for less demanding employment can also be related to the Ascendancy's general attitude to land ownership and utilization. A deep-rooted sense of insecurity, together with the difficulties of living and travelling in Ireland, influenced the way successive generations of Protestant landlords in Ireland regarded their estates. Deeply etched in the Ascendancy psyche was the view that land was something to be exploited to support their gentry life style rather than an asset to be managed and improved.

Like many of their Ascendancy forebears, most Anglo-Irish in Australia regarded their colonial holdings as short-term, speculative ventures from which they hoped to make a quick return on capital invested. In the case of young Irish gentlemen who took up pastoral runs in pre-gold rush Australia, this view was reinforced by the hardships and general insecurity of squatting. Within a few years, most Anglo-Irish who took up squatting had given up their runs and either found alternative employment in the colonies or returned to Ireland.

Others such as Samuel Pratt Winter responded in traditional Ascendancy fashion by becoming absentee squatters. For if landlordism was the basis of Anglo-Irish society, absenteeism was one of its distinctive features. As well as the difficulties and dangers of living in Ireland, the fact that many landlords owned several estates had resulted in extensive absenteeism. Most English gentry resided on or at least regularly visited their county estates, but many Irish landlords rarely or never visited theirs, choosing instead to live abroad or in Dublin. While circumstances in Australia offered few opportunities for Anglo-Irish migrants to become landlords, their situation as pioneer pastoralists certainly encouraged absenteeism. Irish gentlemen on their isolated stations in Australia often experienced the same sense of isolation and boredom, harsh living conditions and danger of attack as had their forebears in eighteenth-century Ireland. Not surprisingly, those who could arrange it employed managers and spent the greater part of each year in the more settled areas. Melbourne's Irish cousinage in the 1840s was largely made up of 'absentee' squatters, most of whom, needless to say, were not very successful. Even Samuel Pratt Winter, one who did eventually succeed, rarely stayed on his Spring Valley run for more than a few weeks at a time.

As conditions worsened in Ireland after 1815 resident landlords became more subject to violent attacks by elements of an increasingly desperate Irish peasantry, who regarded acts of agrarian terrorism as their sole defence against evicting or otherwise oppressive landlords. Such attacks were usually carried out by members of secret Catholic societies such as the notorious Whiteboys or Steelboys. These outrages and the savage reprisals they provoked formed part of Ireland's still unresolved tradition of mutilation, murder and revenge. Captain Charles Harvey Bagot of County Clare, a successful mine owner and pastoralist in South Australia during the 1840s, was one Anglo-Irish colonist whose family had actually been the subject of such an attack.[15] Few of the Ascendancy Irish who came to Australia would have had experiences similar to Bagot's or been involved in punitive expeditions against known or suspected Catholic terrorists. Yet, as an inescapable part of their upbringing in Ireland, most inherited something of that violent, turbulent tradition which, according to Jonah Barrington, involved the Protestants' use of 'the bullet, the sabre and the bayonet, lash and halter', being met with equal ferocity by the Catholic peasantry's use of 'the pike, the scythe, the blunderbuss and the firebrand'.[16]

During the first decades of white settlement in Australia, Anglo-Irish colonists in remote locations also faced the prospect of attack by aborigines, bushrangers or even their convict servants. Given the violent tradition referred to above, Anglo-Irish might have been expected to feature as leaders of private expeditions organized to punish those thought responsible for such attacks. Yet, possibly because they were aware of the cycle of violence this type of reprisal had provoked in Ireland, there are few known instances of Irish gentlemen being involved in vigilante activities. Before his disastrous clash with the authorities William Bryan and his brother Samuel had been warmly praised by the authorities for their role in an official campaign against bushrangers in northern Tasmania. However, attempts by Ascendancy colonists to emulate Ireland's Protestant gentry by taking the law into their own hands could lead to serious consequences. In January 1841 George Winter and his men fired on a group of aboriginals, killing five, and then failed to report the matter to the authorities.[17] On receiving an official report of the incident Superintendent La Trobe ordered a full investigation and advised that Winter should be charged with murder unless he could prove he was acting in self-defence. Presumably owing to the lack of admissible evidence, George was not charged.

George Winter's attitude towards aborigines does not seem to have been typical of Anglo-Irish colonists. In a number of serious clashes between aborigines and Europeans the Anglo-Irish involved seem to have gone out of their way to ensure that the natives were treated in a just and humane fashion. During the 1840s Redmond Barry regularly acted as defence counsel without payment for aborigines charged with serious offences against white settlers. In 1839 Samuel Pratt Winter and Augustine Barton incurred the wrath of local pastoralists when they attempted to have a Wannon District station manager brought to trial who they believed had murdered aborigines by giving them poisoned flour.[18] Some years before, another group of aborigines were brutally murdered by station hands at Myall Creek in New South Wales. The extermination of aborigines was accepted by most Europeans at the time as an unfortunate yet necessary part of the pastoral occupation of eastern Australia. In the Myall Creek case, Captain Edward Denny Day, the police officer who pursued and arrested the Europeans responsible, and John Hubert Plunkett, the judge whose persistent efforts were responsible for the conviction and execution of several of them, were both Anglo-Irish.

In these and similar incidents Anglo-Irish colonists clearly saw themselves as civilizing agents with a special responsibility for maintaining proper standards of British justice on the imperial frontier. As itinerant and resident police magistrates, police officers, county court judges and other officers of the Crown, individual Anglo-Irish featured prominently in establishing, adopting, enforcing and generally administering the law in the more remote areas of the Australian colonies. In the newly settled pastoral districts, former army officers such as Edward Denny Day and Captain Foster Fyans were just two of an impressive number of energetic Anglo-Irish officials who sought to enforce the law under particularly difficult circumstances. Other Anglo-Irish made their careers as senior officers in the newly established colonial police forces. After several appointments as a county police magistrate, Edward Colburn Mayne as Chief Commissioner was responsible for remodelling the New South Wales Police Force along the lines of the Royal Irish Constabulary.

It was, however, in the legal profession itself that Anglo-Irish colonists were most influential. This was especially the case in the colony of Victoria (before 1851 the Port Phillip District of New South Wales), where even today the Supreme Court retains distinctively Irish features. In Port Phillip's newly established courts, Irish barristers included such influential figures as Edward Jones Brewster, the first Chairman of Quarter Sessions, William Jeffcott, the first Judge of the Supreme Court of New South Wales for the District of Port Phillip, and his successor, Roger Therry. From early 1839, when the first barrister arrived in Melbourne, to August 1851 40 per cent of barristers in the Port Phillip District were Anglo-Irish.[19]

As the descendants of militant Protestants, it is perhaps surprising that in the bitter sectarian debates that were a feature of Australian colonial society Anglo-Irish spokesmen usually supported greater toleration of Catholics and Nonconformists. The relatively liberal attitude of these Anglo-Irish on religious issues had to do with changes in Ascendancy society as well as with their different situation as Protestants in Australia. By the late eighteenth century, though the Church of Ireland continued to provide a focal point for scattered Protestant communities, active membership was for most an expression more of Protestant solidarity than of genuine religious commitment. During the eighteenth century the Protestant Ascendancy looked less to their Anglican orthodoxy to justify their continued domination of Ireland. Their failure to convert the Catholic masses through systematic coercion was followed by a marked softening of attitude towards Catholics. Unlike Ulster's hard-line Presbyterians, the Ascendancy's collective memory of massacre and pillage seems to have faded with the passing of the generation that experienced it. By the time the Anglo-Irish began to arrive in Australia, a majority of this class had recognized the absurdity and injustice of continuing to persecute countrymen whose sole crime consisted of maintaining a different doctrinal interpretation of Christian theology. Increased toleration of Catholics also reflected growing religious indifference among the Ascendancy, although this trend was interrupted by the Evangelical Revival, which spread to Ireland following the Act of Union. McConville is of the view that 'rakes, bucks . . . and eccentrics faded as subspecies during the first half of the nineteenth century' when 'the Anglo-Irish knuckled under to conformist respectability that flowed from Victorian England'.[29] Yet, among Australia's Anglo-Irish, ardent evanglicals seemed far less common than nominal Anglicans. Protestant zealots such as the Rev. Zachary Barry of Cork, sent to Western Australia in 1853 by the Society for the Propagation of the Gospel, and a prominent member of the Orange Order, were very much the exception. In Australia as in Ireland, Irish episcopalians obviously benefited from their membership of a privileged, though not established, Anglican Church. However, while the Ascendancy's situation in Ireland as a dominant but disliked religious minority produced an aggressive and insular Protestantism, in Australia the Anglo-Irish found themselves part of a large Protestant majority. This change in their situation, plus an awareness of the extent to which bitter sectarian feeling had been the root cause of so much misery and hatred in Ireland, helps explain their relatively liberal stance on religious issues in colonial Australia.

Though most supported the gradual repeal of anti-Catholic legislation, few among the Ascendancy seriously questioned the morality of their continued domination of Ireland. Most intuitively recognized that any substantial move towards wider political representation or a more equitable distribution of land must threaten the very basis of Ascendancy society. Because of their situation in Ireland, many of the Ascendancy who in England would have been Whigs or even liberals remained staunchly and inflexibly Tory. In Australia, Anglo-Irish colonists were obviously less threatened by moves towards a more liberal democratic society. For some a shift in political and social attitude began on the voyage out. Necessity forced them to be part of a makeshift community which helped break down the social and religious divisions of their homeland.[21] From the beginning, most leading Anglo-Irish in New South Wales such as D'Arcy Wentworth were opposed to the 'Exclusive' Tory faction over such issues as the reform and abolition of transportation and moves towards more representative forms of government.

Partly a response to their changed situation in Australia, the tendency for Anglo-Irish colonists to support liberal democratic reforms was also an outcome of their Old World tradition. In Ireland, although unwilling to enfranchise or make other significant concessions to the Catholic majority, within their own ranks the Ascendancy practised a kind of aristocratic egalitarianism. In an inherently unstable Ascendancy society, land ownership and achievement rather than lineage determined an individual's status. To enhance their prospects of survival, the Protestants needed to foster all available talent. Thus ambitious young Protestants from relatively humble backgrounds could aspire to be admitted to Trinity College, Dublin, where sizarships were available to assist the most able. Compared with the Tory backwaters of Oxford and Cambridge, Trinity, in 1793 the first British university to readmit Catholics, was a relatively liberal institution. The liberalizing effect of a Trinity education and Trinity's diverse student population is important, as something in the order of 40 per cent of Australia's adult male Anglo-Irish had been students of this University. The situation of Ireland's resident gentry, isolated on their estates and in need of agreeable company, discouraged the maintenance of rigid class distinctions among the Ascendancy. It was significant that the Ascendancy's civilian militia, the Volunteers, elected their own officers, a practice then unthinkable in the rest of Britain. Overall, the belief in a flexible social structure with the possibility of advancement on merit alone was central to Anglo-Irish identity in colonial Australia as well as in Ascendancy Ireland.

The idea of the Anglo-Irish being liberal-minded or democratically inclined hardly tallies with the generally accepted view of Ireland's Protestant Ascendancy. According to J. C. Beckett, in the traditional picture of Anglo-Ireland, the most familiar figure 'is that of a tyrannical landlord squeezing the last penny of rent out of a starving tenantry and spending the proceeds in the fashionable world of London or Bath or in riotous living at home'.[22] Uncritical acceptance of such stereotypes which depict the Irish gentry as claret-swilling, whip-wielding tyrants has contributed to a tendency to dismiss the Anglo-Irish as a class of parasitic landlords, the agents of a foreign power and apostles of a foreign culture. Other writers, seeking to entertain their readers have looked to the Anglo-Irish as a rich source of comedy. Michael McConville in his history of the Ascendancy describes in some detail the eccentric and often violent antics of such certifiable misfits as 'Fighting' Fitzgerald and 'Hairtrigger Dick' Martin. Less colourful descriptions of the life style and character of the Irish gentry are to be found in the memoirs and family histories produced by some of the more literate members of the Ascendancy. Written at a time when the Ascendancy's once impregnable world was beginning to crumble or had all but disintegrated, such accounts are usually tinged with a deeply felt sense of loss for happier times past. Genteel and witty, reminiscences such as Somerville and Ross's *Irish Memories*[23] avoid confronting the unpleasant truth that the maintenance of the Ascendancy's privileged life style necessarily involved the continued exploitation of the dispossessed native Irish population.

The truth concerning the nature of the Old World tradition the Anglo-Irish brought to Australia remains elusive and the search for it involves reconciling conflicting views of the Irish Ascendancy. Allowing that this tradition changed significantly over time, recent scholarship supports the view that Ireland's Protestant gentry were neither as unpopular nor as wicked as has been supposed.[24]

Each generation of the Ascendancy brought with it to the New World a different experience of Ireland. Though impossible to prove, it would seem that the Anglo-Irish who arrived in Australia before 1860 represented a generation that was better educated and more liberal-minded than those which preceded and succeeded it. Basically, the Anglo-Irish who arrived in pre-gold rush Australia represented a society that had peaked intellectually and culturally and was about to enter a period of stagnation and decline. During the later nineteenth century the Irish Ascendancy, confronted with the rising tide of Catholic nationalism, lost its nerve and became classbound and intellectually rigid.

Common sense and anecdotal evidence support the view that it was generally the more determined and physically robust 'younger sons' of Ascendancy families who were prepared to accept the discomforts and uncertainties that migration to the Australian colonies involved. In any case, to succeed as a colonist in pre-gold rush Australia, one had usually to be both committed and resourceful. Those who lacked such attributes tended to remain at home or to return disappointed after a brief period of colonial experience.

Because of the particularly difficult economic situation in post-Waterloo Ireland, the need for younger male members of Ascendancy families to leave Ireland in search of employment and investment opportunities extended further up the social and ability scale than in the rest of Britain. With Ireland's overcrowded professions and and little chance of obtaining a commission in a British regiment, some of the Ascendancy's most talented sons looked to the recently settled Australian colonies for employment and investment opportunities. Approximately half the adult male Anglo-Irish who arrived in Australia before 1850 had already studied, worked, or lived abroad – usually in England or in one of the British colonies. It is difficult to judge just how these colonists differed from those members of the Ascendancy who decided to leave Ireland in order to migrate to Australia. One suspects that those who had already coped with the problems of living outside Ireland would have been more independently minded and adventurous as colonists in Australia.

Anglo-Irish identity in colonial Australia, though both distinctive and historically significant, was certainly not enduring. Though local factors played a part, the lack of a continuing Anglo-Irish presence in Australia had largely to do with the Protestant Ascendancy's demise in Ireland. For even if the changes which accompanied the gold rushes of the 1850s had not so overwhelmed the genteel, pastoral society in which Irish gentlemen were such an influential element, it is doubtful whether any significant Anglo-Irish presence would have survived into the twentieth century. Faced with economic decline, a loss of vitality through migration and the inevitable triumph of Catholic nationalism, Ireland's Protestant Ascendancy gave up its claims to Irishness and chose to become British. By the late nineteenth century the trickle of Ascendancy Irish who arrived in Australia usually saw themselves and were regarded by others as British. In any case, as being Irish became synonymous with being Catholic and Gaelic and it increasingly suited Australia's Anglo-

Irish to forsake their 'Irishness' and be quietly absorbed in the Protestant mainstream.

Notes

1. Charles Griffiths, Diary 1840–41, 8 December 1840, State Library of Victoria. For a detailed account of the Winters and the Irish Cousinage of Port Phillip see G. J. Forth 'The Anglo-Irish Tradition in Australia Felix', Ph.D thesis, Monash University, 1984.
2. Griffiths, Diary, 1 February 1841.
3. Philip Guedalla, *The Duke*, Hodder & Stoughton, London, 1931, 3.
4. J. C. Beckett, *The Anglo-Irish Tradition, 1602–1921*, Faber, London, 1976, 73.
5. Patrick A. Dunae, *Gentlemen Emigrants: from the British Public School to the Canadian Fontier*, Douglas & MacIntyre, Toronto, 1985, 6.
6. Patrick O'Farrell, *The Irish in Australia*, New South Wales University Press, Sydney, N.S.W., 1986, 94.
7. E. P. Curtis 'The Anglo-Irish predicament', *Twentieth Century Studies*, 1, 1970, 40. According the Curtis's calculations, based on the 1912 editions of Burke's *Landed Gentry of Ireland*, 'Some two-thirds of the 925 families entered in the 1899 edition had settled in Ireland after 1600, the overwhelming majority of those in the seventeenth century'.
8. Arthur Young, *A Tour of Ireland in the years 1776, 1777 and 1778* 1, 24.
9. Phoebe Barry to Redmond Barry, undated letter *c.* 1840, Redmond Barry papers. State Library of Victoria.
10. Young, p. 67.
11. Marnie Bassett, *The Hentys: an Australian Colonial Tapestry*, Oxford University Press, London, 1954; see chapter 10.
12. For details relating to the Bryan case see George Arthur to E. G. Stanley, Correspondence relating to the conduct of Mr. W. Bryan, 3 November 1824, *British Parliamentary Papers relating to Australia, 1833–36*, London.
13. James Stephen to George Arthur, 16 March 1827, Arthur papers, State Library of New South Wales.
14. Thomas Murphy to Samuel Pratt Winter, 31 October 1845, Winter Cooke papers, State Library of Victoria.
15. Charles Harvey Bagot, *A Holographic Memoir*, written by Bagot in 1851 and published by the Pioneers' Association of South Australia, Adelaide, 1860.
16. Sir Jonah Barrington, *The Ireland of Sir Jonah Barrington: Selections from his 'Personal Sketches'*, ed. Hugh B. Staples, Peter Owen, London, 1968, 6.
17. For details of the case see Forth, 'The Anglo-Irish Tradition', pp. 179–82.
18. Samuel Pratt Winter's account of the incident was contained in his article 'When the blacks prepared for war', written July 1873 and published in the *Hamilton Spectator*, 7 March 1876, 3.
19. Ruth Campbell, 'Irish Lawyers in the Port Phillip District, Victoria, 1938–1860', paper given at the sixth Irish–Australia conference, Melbourne, July 1990, 2.
20. Michael McConville, *Ascendancy to Oblivion: the Story of the Anglo-Irish*, Quartet, London, 1986, 154.
21. P. O'Farrell, *Letters from Irish Australians,1825–29*,ed. by Brian Trainor, New South Wales University Press, Kensington, and Ulster Historical Foundation, Belfast, 1984, 19.
22. Beckett, *The Anglo-Irish Tradition*, 73.

23. Edith Oe Somerville and Martin Ross, *Irish Memories*, Longmans, London, 1925.
24. See, for example, W. F. Vaughan, 'An assessment of the economic performances of Irish landlords' in F. S. L. Lyons and R. A. J. Hawkins, eds., *Ireland under the Union: Essays in Honour of T. W. Moody*, Clarendon Press, Oxford, 1980.

6 'I gcuntas Dé múin Béarla do na leanbháin': eisimirce agus an Ghaeilge sa naoú aois déag'*

Karen P. Corrigan

This chapter focuses on the effects which migration to the United States had on the status of Gaelic in nineteenth-century Ireland and America. The loss of Irish during this period can be viewed as an extreme case of language contact which eventually resulted in the victorious language – namely English – ousting the dying language in all domains.[1]

This systematic replacement of an indigenous language with that of an outside, dominant group is usually[2] a consequence of both internal and external factors. Internal causes of language shift are primarily psychological – arising from a desire within the individual to integrate and conform. External causes tend, by contrast, to be community-centred – the result of economic, political, historical and socio-cultural determinants.

Since it is the dominant group that holds ultimate power within a community, the only means by which an outsider can advance is by adopting the norms and *mores* of the elite, and in certain circumstances this will entail acquiring their language. When adaptation to standard social norms results in the negation of one's own language in this way, identity conflicts and transformations are inevitable.[3]

Moreover, in cases of migration, the stereotypes and prejudices affecting the immigrant who uses a low–status minority language often encourage migrants to adopt similar attitudes to their own cultures, ethnicities and mother tongues in their efforts to assimilate.[4]

Language death at the community level is similarly due to the loss of prestige status for the language in question. This can occur for a variety of reasons, but case studies[5] in the field appear to suggest that external factors such as modernization and colonization are the root causes.

The complex, 700 year history of the English language and people in Ireland has had a marked effect on Ireland's economic, political and socio-cultural structures. Inevitably, the colonization has also been consequential for the vernacular, which began ceding to English in the seventeenth

---

* 'For God's sake, teach the children English': emigration and the Irish language in the nineteenth century.

century. It is generally held that this process originated in urban areas and other locations (such as the Pale) in which the English colonists had gained the upper hand in political and economic affairs. Thus P. L. Henry in a paper entitled 'Anglo–Irish and its Irish background' makes the following claim:

> The outcome of war in Ireland in the seventeenth century was the split society of the eighteenth in which the winner proceeded to take all. . . . It became a rule of privilege versus deprivation and disability. English became the language of politics, of public service, of commerce and education. Irish clung to the countryside remote from where the action was.[6]

It is estimated that in the final years of the eighteenth century a significant number of young people were Irish-speaking but that they had either shifted entirely to English or else had become proficient bilinguals during the course of their lifetime. As a result only 2 per cent of the succeeding generation are reported as being Irish monoglots in the census of 1861.[7]

This radical change is held to have been a consequence of various inter-related factors which affected the Irish populace throughout the eighteenth and nineteenth centuries.

1. Gaelic – a minority language in global terms – was confronted by a 'world language' spoken by an unsympathetic occupying power which had legislated against its use since 1366.[8]

2. The British (and Anglo–Irish) took a number of steps to undermine the value and status of Irish, especially among the younger generation. To this end, when the National Schools were established in 1831, it was English rather than Gaelic which was designated as the medium of instruction. This was in spite of the fact that a significant number of school-going children would have had Irish as their first language. It was for this reason that Padraig Pearse ascribed the term 'murder machine' to the educational system of the period. By various methods the National Schools performed what is commonly called 'linguacide'. The most notable of these techniques was the introduction of the *báta scóir* – a tally stick which recorded the number of times per day that its wearer spoke Gaelic (and therefore the amount of punishment which the individual would later receive).[9]

3. A number of historians and sociologists have claimed that nineteenth-century migration made a significant contribution to the loss of Irish in two respects: firstly, during the hard economic times and famines of the years 1830–50, nearly 2 million people – primarily from the gaelicized south and west – either died or emigrated. Secondly, in the words of the late Maureen Wall, 'These people were emigrating to countries which were English-speaking. It was naturally to their advantage to know the language of the land to which they were going.'[10] Thus migration launched a two-pronged attack on Gaelic: it significantly reduced the number of speakers and created a climate in which competence in English became a key to survival.

The remainder of this chapter explores some of the internal (psychological) and external (sociological) factors (especially those associated with colonization and migration) which may be seen to have promoted language shift among the Irish both at home and abroad. In order to stress the global and interconnected nature of the Irish experience in this regard, reference will be made throughout to other linguistic communities which have suffered a similar fate.

Language loss and the implications for Irish

Theoretical considerations

A review of other instances of language loss on a similar scale[11] indicates that languages are prone to decline under the following conditions.

1. In those 'unstable' bilingual communities where one language is (or becomes) more powerful than another. In such instances the recessive language allows the more prestigious to intrude upon all its domains. For instance, the use of each language may have originally been dictated by context – the prestige form confined to formal and the recessive to informal occasions. With the passage of time the prestigious form spreads at the expense of the recessive language, eventually replacing it in even the most informal contexts.

2. Language contact situations brought about either by voluntary migration or by annexation. Joshua Fishman[12] has used the following formula to describe language shift among migrants: $B \rightarrow A = A$ (where A is the majority language of the host community and B the intrusive language of the immigrant). He claims that B is lost in order for the migrant to gain technical, professional, educational and other benefits. Moreover, under such circumstances, the mastery of A gains status for the migrant within the minority language community. This, in turn, serves as a motivating factor, encouraging other migrants to acquire proficiency in A in order to accrue similar benefits, status and the like.[13]

Fishman formulates the type of language loss associated with colonization/annexation as $B \rightarrow A = B$ (where B is the language of the colonizer and A that of the indigenous population). In such cases the economic, technical and cultural superiority associated with the B group attracts those A speakers who are eager for advancement. Eventually the indigenous language becomes associated with the disadvantaged, and this consequently leads to further erosion.

3. Languages which are perceived either as being low in status or as having marginal utilitarian value are rarely maintained. Research on attitudes to minority/indigenous languages has shown that their speakers attribute negative properties to their own language and positive qualities both to majority languages and to those (like French and English) which are involved in international communication. In his study of Pennsylvania German Huffines has this to say: 'As members of a minority group become more fluent in the language of the majority, they tend to use their own language less and may even come to regard it as inferior . . .'[14] Similarly, Appel and Muysken contend that Spanish speakers in the south-west of the United States have negative feelings towards their language, which cannot hope to compete for equal status with either English or standard Spanish.

They are reported to claim, for instance, that it is 'only a dialect'/'border slang'/'not a real language'.[15]

Attitudes such as these have two consequences for low-status languages. Parents who believe that the language which they speak is 'backward' are unwilling to lumber their offspring with a similar disadvantage. Moreover, they project these attitudes to subsequent generations by delimiting the use of the inferior language. Curtailing the domains in which a language can function suggests that it is unimportant and that there is little motivation to perpetuate its use.

Allied to parents' desire for their child to advance is the mistaken belief among many speakers who have a first and a second language that maintaining the mother tongue will adversely affect their child's knowledge of the prestige language. This is primarily because second-language acquisition does not usually lead to the same kind of proficiency as first-language acquisition. Thus the second-language-speaking parent is prone to make grammatical, lexical and phonological errors which result from mother-tongue interference. Uriel Weinreich describes the phenomenon in the following way: '[the] greater the differences between the systems, i.e. the more numerous the mutually exclusive forms and patterns in each [language], the greater is the learning problem and the potential area of interference'[16] Contrary to popular opinion, this is not the case with proficient bilinguals (normally, individuals who learn the two languages simultaneously and use them in clearly defined domains).

Dorian and Huffines both report that those parents who have Scots/ Gaelic or Pennsylvania German as their first language, and are keen to ensure that their children are upwardly mobile, show signs that they are affected by misapprehensions such as these.[17]

4. The related forces of industrialization, urbanization and modernization have been responsible for many instances of language loss world-wide. Industrialization creates a demand for an expanded labour force. Consequently, majority-language speakers may migrate to a minority community in which there are greater economic opportunities. Invariably, such situations will initially result in bilingualism, but eventually, a shift towards the more prestigious majority language becomes unavoidable. Thus the migration of English-speakers to the coal-producing regions of Monmouth and Glamorgan in the 1850s is said to have undermined the use of Welsh in those areas.[18]

The migration of minority speakers to more industrialized locations often causes depopulation on such a scale that language shift ensues. If income can be generated only outwith the minority community, then an ability to speak the majority language will be an obvious advantage. Out migration after the Second World War from the rural Hungarian-speaking areas of Austria to the German-speaking industrialized cities caused a shift within these rural communities to German.[19]

The rise of the mass media is often cited as being responsible for the erosion of several minority languages. Radio and television facilitate contact between isolated rural areas and the majority (usually urban) language and culture. Dorian, for instance, describes the consequences of modern communications on the Scots-Gaelic speakers of east Sutherland: 'So long as the Gaelic speakers of East Sutherland had remained isolated within a region where the indigenous culture prevailed, they were able to resist – or more accurately to ignore – the superior prestige of English.'[20]

5. Several minority and indigenous languages have been oppressed and discriminated against by the governmental policies of the majority group which view them as a source of political, social and national instability. Thus in his discussion of the attrition of Welsh since the medieval period Adler cites a clause from the Act of Union (1536) which represents the first governmental attempt to legislate against the language: 'No person or persons that use the Welsh speech or language shall have or enjoy any manner of Office or Fees within this realm of England, Wales or other of the King's Dominion . . .'.[21]

Implications for Irish

In 1983 John Edwards published a bibliography of works on the Irish language, covering the period 1772–1982.[22] The reasons which are cited for the nineteenth-century shift to English in the majority of these publications (both early and late) are curiously uniform. Thus in 1896 Henry Dixon claimed that, since the Irish people had shown themselves to be uninterested in their language in the past, they were unlikely to become so in the future.[23] Similarly, Sydney Brooks, writing in 1907, put forward the idea that the loss of Irish resulted from the fact that the population as a whole was not 'determined to keep it alive'.[24] In 1966 Tim Pat Coogan claimed that the major reason for the decline was the growing feeling that there was little 'practical use for the language'.[25] More recently, Seán de Fréine has suggested that the movement to English was explicable only in terms of the 'collective behaviour' of a population attracted by the rewards of English and repelled by the association between Irish and poverty. Again, he proposes that 'the worst excesses were not imposed from outside'.[26]

Alongside proposals like these which name the Irish people as 'murderers' of their own language, other authors cite external factors such as those outlined above (migration, politics, modernization and so on). While such claims appear to comply with those external and internal causes of decline proposed for other languages and ethnic groups, the picture for Irish remains far from clear. In the first place, the onset of major decline can be located in the latter half of the eighteenth century – prior to the opening of the National Schools, the Great Famine and the mass migrations of the nineteenth. Perhaps, then, it may be more accurate to regard the effects of these later historical events as ensuring the continued decline of the language rather than being precipitative or causative in themselves.[27] Secondly, there is little concrete evidence in either the earlier or the later works of the internal psychological factors that have been commonly associated with language shift in other situations. It is still not clear, for instance, how negative the average citizen's or migrant's attitude to Gaelic may actually have been in nineteenth-century Ireland (or America, for that matter). For reasons such as these, much of the discussion which follows will include – where possible – comments on language taken from a range of historical documents (including personal diaries and letters, legislation, newspaper reports and so on) in an effort to make a case for internal/external causation in a way which will avoid the kind of generalization and surmizing characteristic of much of the material cited in Edwards's bibliography.

Finally, it must be emphasized that many of the factors examined below seem to form a network of interconnected causes and consequences. For instance, it is more than likely that prospective migrants who know that their mother tongue will be of little utilitarian value in the host country will view the language rather differently from a peer who never intends to leave home.[28]

Irish–English bilingualism in the eighteenth and nineteenth centuries

Hindley is the most recent substantial publication in the field of language loss in the Irish context. On the relationship between bilingualism and decline he remarks that:

> a necessary precondition of adjudging Irish unnecessary or 'useless' would be the achievement of very widespread near-universal fluency in English. . . . universal bilingualism was the essential transitional stage on the way from an Irish-speaking Ireland to an English-speaking Ireland. By 1800 bilingualism was well advanced and the ultimate fate of the native language was near to a final decision.[29]

Unfortunately for our purposes, the records relating to the state of the Irish language during the crucial period circa 1750 to 1850 are provided by barony rather than nation-wide and are estimated rather than actual figures. Nevertheless, in his paper on language loss between 1771 and 1871, Fitzgerald maintains that they are 'internally consistent' and 'provide a valid measure of the minimum level of Irish-speaking amongst successive new generations of young people'. Thus it is claimed that during the early part of the nineteenth century Irish was declining on a region-wide basis, surviving only in southern and western coastal areas. Furthermore, there is evidence to suggest that 'inroads were beginning to be made even in these regions'.[30]

The first Irish census which made reference to language was conducted in 1851. The returns indicated that out of a total population of 6,552,365 only 1,524,286 individuals were bilingual and the remainder were English monoglots. In fact these figures grossly understated the actual situation and were the result of inaccurate methods of enumeration coupled with a reluctance among the populace to admit knowing Irish, because of its lack of social prestige. In this regard the secretary of the Society for the Preservation of the Irish language commented:

> the returns [1851] do not include the entire number of people who speak Irish, since it is well known that many persons, for want of education in the vernacular [Irish] and of due appreciation of its value, do not admit their knowledge of the

language, and that many more who know it were never questioned on the subject at the census taking.[31]

Nevertheless, it is apparent even at this early stage that Irish–English bilingualism was becoming increasingly unstable. Moreover, the decennial censuses from 1861–1891 record declines of between 26 per cent and 28 per cent, with the result that in the last census of the period in question there were only 38,121 Irish monoglots in the entire population of 4,704,750 individuals.[32]

The picture which emerges from the figures themselves suggests that in the early 1800s Irish was the first language of the majority and that speakers were bilingual to the extent that they used English in public domains like commerce and politics. As the century progressed, the restrictions on the use of English in more domestic contexts were relaxed and it was Irish that became increasingly marginalized. Such a scenario would also be concomitant with the degree of underreporting evidenced in the census figures from 1851 onwards. Thus it would appear that individuals preferred to claim that they were bilingual when they were actually Irish monoglots or that they were English-speakers at a time when they clearly must have been Irish–English bilinguals.

Consequently Anderson, writing in the early 1800s is of the opinion that:

> the great majority [of those who are said to understand English] *do not*, and even with regard to those who do, to what extent are they acquainted with the English language? . . . Does it follow because a native Irishman can buy and sell, or because an Irish waiter at a country inn can reply to a traveller in English that either of them can reason in that language . . . ?[33]

Commentators writing towards the end of the period paint a rather different picture. Thus Ravenstein in his address to the Royal Statistical Society in 1879 states that 'the next census will probably show the Irish language to have become virtually extinct'.[34]

The effects of migration on Gaelic

Ireland's long tradition of both seasonal and permanent migration burgeoned in the nineteenth century as a consequence of poor socio-economic conditions and the increased opportunities for migration offered by various governmental, charitable and voluntary schemes.[35]

Few of the major works on the decline of Irish in the nineteenth century neglect to mention migration as a causative force. Canice Mooney,[36] for instance, suggests that during the period in question the vernacular was seen as a 'fatal luxury' for a people who could survive only by emigrating to the United States. Moreover, there is a general consensus that the rural depopulation caused by the migration of individuals from the predominantly Gaelic-speaking areas of the south and west was also a contributory factor.

There are, however, a number of issues which remain to be addressed regarding the effect of migration on the use of Gaelic in Ireland. Firstly, what evidence is there to suggest that a knowledge of English was indeed perceived to be an advantage to the prospective migrant? Secondly, while migration is often cited as a force precipitating language loss, the exodus from the Irish Gaeltacht did not take place until after the Famine, by which time most of the inhabitants would already have been Irish–English bilinguals.

The modernization of Ireland in the nineteenth century brought with it greater opportunities for the advancement of ordinary people in commercial, political and professional life both at home and abroad. Literacy and a knowledge of English were the key components in their struggle for an improved life style, and these skills were offered by the National School system which was established for the purpose in 1831. Several conflicting views have emerged as to the orientation and effectiveness of these schools. There are those, for instance, who claim that the Commissioners for National Education actively promoted the language, customs and values of England.[37] Others argue that their role was more passive and that they were effective simply because they responded to the perceived need for English within the community as a whole.[38]

In fact the demand for English through education antedates the National Schools, since it would also appear to have been the objective of the privately run 'hedge schools' and urban 'academies' which served Catholics during the eighteenth and early nineteenth centuries. Thus Richard McElligott, advertising his services as a teacher in the *Limerick Gazette*:

> begs leave to inform the Public, that [he] teaches to Spell, Read, and Write the English Language correctly; that [his] rules for Reading, derived from the highest authorities . . . and that [his] English Grammar is so clear as to be immediately understood. . . .[39]

Moreover, numerous contemporary and later commentators accuse the education system of actively promoting migration by equipping the pupils with the necessary skills (both vocational and linguistic) for advancement in the United States.[40] It is difficult to decide whether such accusations are spurious or not, but, even if they are true, such a strategy was inevitable (and probably laudable), given that American public opinion held that 'The ignorance of our language [English] often subjects the honest immigrant to imposition from the unprincipled marine's agent [sic] or boarding-house keeper.'[41]

The demand for an English education was greatest in isolated rural areas were there was little opportunity to communicate in English on a daily basis. Thus Patrick Keenan, a National Schools inspector, makes the following remarks in his report on the island schools of north-west Donegal:

> On Inishboffin people up to thirty years come to school. This passion may be traced to one predominant desire – the desire to speak English. They see whenever a stranger visits their islands that prosperity has its peculiar tongue as well as its fine coat and if they ever cross to the mainland for the 'law' as they call any legal process they see that the solemn words have come to them second hand through the office of an interpreter.[42]

Evidence of the utilitarian value of English is also contained in numerous letters sent from the United States by established migrants. Thus Seán Ó

Dúbhda, a respondent to the Irish Folklore Commission's emigration questionnaire, states that the American letter was instrumental in the anglicization of Ireland during the nineteenth century. He recalls his father telling him that 'nearly every letter' urged parents to teach their children English and to prolong the amount of time they spent at school in order to enhance their command of spoken and written English. He cites the following advice given in family correspondence:

> I gcuntas Dé múin Béarla do na leanbháin is ná bídis dall ar nós na n-asal a teacht anseo amac.
> For God's sake teach the children English and don't be blind like the asses [fools] who have come out here.[43]

Similarly, a member of the Anderson family, writing home to a sibling in 1842 suggested that 'the[e] learn to read and spell English well as it will be useful to the[e] if spered [spared] to come to this conterey [country]'.[44]

Letters written in Irish like that of Ó Dúbhda above are highly unusual, and this in itself provides evidence not only for the prestigious status of English during the period but also of the fact that while the majority of migrants could not write Gaelic they were clearly literate in English. Moreover, it is a well documented fact that Irish-speaking parents were frequently obliged to have the American letters of their offspring translated by the local schoolmaster or cleric.[45] Father Tadhg Ó Murchadha, for instance, testifies that the letters were 'always in the English language of course' and that they were 'listened to attentively even by old persons who didn't know English'.[46]

Evidence of this kind suggests that those who intended to advance materially (and migration was considered to be an important means of achieving this) were under quite considerable pressure from a variety of sources to acquire oral and written skills in English. In fact Patrick Blessing in a recent publication goes so far as to propose that 'Extensive movement overseas went hand-in-hand with the appearance of a new generation literate in English, the products of public schools established in Ireland during the 1820s.'[47]

It would be a gross exaggeration of the facts, however, to claim that all nineteenth-century migrants had achieved fluency in English before departing for America – despite the obvious incentives and the facilities which were made available for them to do so. Indeed, there are numerous recorded cases of migrants who were Irish-speaking monoglots. J. O'Keefe, for example, in answer to a question regarding whether it was necessary for a migrant to have a command of English in order to succeed in the United States, cites the case of William Morrissey. He is said to have emigrated in 1860 with 'no education, no English and no money' and to have died intestate in 1912 'worth thousands of pounds'.[48] Similarly, a number of commentators have reported entire shiploads of migrants unable to complain of the atrocious conditions on board during their passage because they spoke only Gaelic. There is also substantial evidence that clerics sent to minister to migrants in America were chosen not just on the basis of their 'good Constitution' but also because they 'could speak Irish'.[49]

Given the wider availability of schooling and the perceived need for English (even within the most rural of communities) why was it that large numbers of migrants still remained ignorant of English? First of all, reports such as these are especially common from the time of the Famine onwards. As such they are a reflection of the fundamental difference between the type of migrant attracted to America in the period 1800–45 and those who came after that time. In the early decades the heaviest migration is thought to have been from the predominantly English-speaking (and Protestant) regions of northern, central and eastern Ireland, while in the later period it was concentrated in the Catholic, Irish-speaking districts to the south and west.[50] While Fitzgerald has demonstrated that Irish was declining in gaelicized areas long before the Famine, it is likely that migrants from these regions retained a superior command of Irish and that this is what is reflected in the reports.[51]

Secondly, the onset of language change is a localized phenomenon which may take quite some time to spread outwards from the centre of origin. Although there was a nation-wide trend towards language loss during the period it is perfectly plausible to assume that there would also have been individuals and pockets of speakers cut off from this shift as a result of either physical (geographical) or psychological barriers to communication.[52] Thus it is not unreasonable to expect that there would have been groups of speakers even among the early non-Gaeltacht migrants who were shielded from the trend towards English and who consequently show up as Gaelic-speakers in the commentaries.

Vaughn and Fitzpatrick have produced figures for the numbers of migrants from Gaelicized areas between 1856 and 1910. These, coupled with the discussion and estimates in Ó Cuív, Cousens, Miller and MacAodha provide substance for the claim that the heaviest migration from these regions occurred in the years following the Famine.[53] Thus Miller estimates that 'a substantial proportion of those emigrating [to North America] in 1845–55 regarded Irish as their primary, if not only, language' (p. 297).

Herein lies the dilemma for those who would wish to claim that the large-scale population movement from the south and west was a causative factor in the decline of Gaelic. In the first instance – as Miller rightly attests – some of those migrants will have had Irish as their mother tongue, with English as their second language, while others will have been Irish monoglots. He makes no binding claims as to the proportions of each and is justified in not doing so, for contemporary comments on the issue are conflicting (in all probability a reflection of the arbitrary manner in which linguistic change spreads). Consequently, if there is no means by which the numbers of migrating monoglots can be calculated with any accuracy, then to pose the question 'What effect?' is a nonsense. How can cause be established if the necessary data are beyond retrieval?

Moreover, even if a substantial proportion of these individuals spoke Irish only, and had they remained *in situ* instead of migrating, it is unlikely that they would have managed to fend off the spread of English for much longer anyway, since Fitzgerald and others have argued convincingly that their cohorts were unable to do so.[54] Either way, then, the loss of these

Irish-speakers can hardly be claimed to have been significant. Those who migrated embraced the dominant language and culture – those who were left behind followed suit.

Language attitudes, migration and assimilation

Joshua Fishman in a discussion of language maintenance in contemporary America states that:

> All Americans, and speakers of non-English languages in particular, are aware of the value our society places upon cultural and linguistic unity. The desirability of such unity is explicitly or implicitly conveyed by citizenship requirements, by voting requirements, by the common public school, by the many agencies whose task it is to 'naturalize' and Americanize immigrants. . . .[55]

Haugen and Huffines[56] examine the impact of migration to the United States on Norwegian and German-speaking populations in the nineteenth and early twentieth centuries. Their conclusions as regards attitudes to ethnic groups and the languages they speak mirror those of Fishman above. Furthermore, they suggest that the pressure for conformity in order to advance is so great that migrants themselves often adopt the negative stereotypes of the majority towards their own language and culture.

This drive towards a homogeneous English-speaking America is not a twentieth-century phenomenon, in fact there is a body of opinion which suggests that it originated some 200 years ago. Thus M. L. Hansen in his account of the Atlantic migrations dates American intolerance of foreigners as far back as the late eighteenth century.[57] He cites a number of causes for the anti-foreign lobby which came into force around this time, including 'commercial and agricultural depression', which resulted in intense competition for employment, and 'the Civil War', which so divided the country that its end brought with it a resolve for unity – whatever the cost. The ethos of the period is typified by J. Hector St John de Crèvecoeur in an essay entitled 'What is an American?' in which he claims that 'Here all individuals of all nations are melted into a new race of men, whose posterity will one day cause great changes in the world.'[58]

The next century saw steady increases in the number of migrants and the positive harmonious ideals of Crèvecoeur and his ilk were transformed into negative stereotypes and prejudice. Ethnic groups came to be viewed as an unstable force in society – one that was associated with (and invariably blamed for) crime, poverty, ignorance and disease. A report in the *New York Mirror* (1855) entitled 'America for the Americans'[59] has this to say:

> Let it be looked to that foreign nationalities are rooted out; that foreign regiments and battalions are disarmed; that the public laws and schools of the country are printed and taught in the language of the land; that no more charters for foreign titled or foreign charactered associations – benevolent, social or other – are granted by our legislatures. America for the Americans! We have had enough of 'Young Irelands', 'Young Germanys' and 'Young Italys'.[59]

Given the prevailing American attitude that migrants ought to be assimilated as rapidly as possible, what consequences did this have for the Irish-speaking migrants of the nineteenth century?[60]

Recall that in the previous section it was claimed that the majority of gaelicized, post-Famine migrants originated in the impoverished, predominantly Catholic regions of the Atlantic coast. As such they were entering America already burdened by a number of disadvantages which the early Irish migrants (a large number of whom were Protestant, anglicized and literate) did not suffer.

Moreover, in the closing decades of the nineteenth century Irish-Americans had begun to establish themselves as a relatively powerful social and political group.[61] Just as the politicizing of Ireland under O'Connell was achieved through the medium of English (in spite of the fact that Gaelic was his first language) parallel developments in America took a similar course. The changing status of the Irish-American had a number of consequences. First of all, the prestige of English (as the language of political, economic and social attainment) was reinforced among the Irish minority. Secondly, Irish-American efforts to compete for employment and a say in their own government and their continued attachment to Gaeldom brought a backlash from the WASP majority which took a variety of forms[62] and resulted in the Irish language/'brogue', [63] religion and culture being subjected to considerable prejudice throughout the period.

The contempt in which the Irish were held is reflected in the comments of W. H. Gregory: 'Everywhere in the United States, the Irish-born part of the population is only tolerated by the native Americans as what has been termed a 'serviceable nuisance'; it is a population of foreigners and outcasts . . .'[64] Thus, while Gaelic enclaves are reported to have existed in several states – especially in the urban tenements of the eastern seaboard – such speakers were under considerable pressure from their peers and from the xenophobic attitudes of the community at large to cast off the low-status language with which they were afflicted.

There is substantial evidence from personal correspondence and memoirs that Gaelic-speakers shifted to English quite rapidly. Moreover, as the language was replaced most Irish-Americans adopted the same negative attitudes towards it as the dominant group.

Proof that Gaelic-speakers shifted readily to English can be seen in the comments of Daniel Guiny in a family letter: 'girls that used to be trotting on the bogs at home to hear them talk English would be of great astonishment to you'.[65] Successful second-language acquisition – especially for adults – is generally held to be affected by the learner's motivation to join the target-language community. As such, numerous empirical studies[66] have concluded that there is a positive correlation between a learner's desire for assimilation and the speed/effectiveness of the learning process. The implication therefore of remarks such as those of Guiny above is that, since the girls in question appear to have become fluent English-speakers within a relatively short period, they must have developed strong loyalties to the American speech community.[67]

It is not difficult to uncover evidence which suggests that the attitude towards Gaelic among Irish-Americans and non-Irish Americans alike was invariably prejudiced and overwhelmingly negative. Thus, in a report (dated 1848) of the Massachusetts Committee on laws relating to alien paupers the Irish migrant is held to suffer 'embarrassment from not clearly comprehending our language' while his mother tongue is described as 'an obstacle' to advancement.[68] Irish-Americans too had begun to believe that Gaelic was a liability, and their letters stress its lack of utilitarian value and its association with poverty and ignorance, thereby echoing sentiments such as 'Irish will get you nothing and nowhere'; 'even in Ireland the respectable people do not speak it', which had already become commonplace back home.[69]

It would appear, then, that the American 'melting pot' depicted in Israel Zangwill's play of the same name[70] dissolved linguistic as well as cultural, ethnic and religious variance. It is clear too that this dissolution was intended, as is evident from such policy statements as that issued by Theodore Roosevelt in 1919: 'We have room for but one language and that is the English language, for we intend to see that the crucible turns out our people as Americans . . . not as dwellers in a polyglot boarding-house.'[71]

Conclusion

Séan de Fréine has described the lack of interest shown by historians in the decline of Gaelic during the nineteenth century as 'The Great Silence'.[72] The same criticism has been levelled by Edwards at the dearth of research on the Irish language in North America, which he says is 'strange considering the many books on the Irish themselves, and the centrality of the language'.[73] Apart from MacAonghusa's chapter in *The Celtic Consciousness*,[74] the subject has been virtually ignored by linguists and historians alike. Moreover, much of the available material is either anecdotal or else couched in a sentimentality reminiscent of the Revival Movement (in Ireland and the United States) of the late nineteenth and early twentieth centuries.

This state of affairs is regrettable, given the fact that even a modest and rather generalized account such as this one can reveal a number of insights about the nature of the relationship between language, migration and assimilation. Fundamentally, the chapter challenges the notion that the decline of Gaelic was precipitated solely by a series of adverse historical events – an idea espoused by the majority of commentators on the subject. While it is true that external forces such as migration, economics and politics facilitated the spread of English it is also the case that internal pressure to adopt the norms of the dominant group played an equally vital role. Moreover, it is important to view this amalgam of external and internal factors as operating not just on individual Irish citizens or migrants but also on the society in which they chose to live. As such the contention is that Gaelic was ousted in Ireland and America by a number of interrelated sociological and psychological processes, one acting upon the other – sometimes randomly, sometimes with intent.

Thus, socio-historical accounts which cite the anti-Gaelic forces of education, and Irish and Irish-American politics along with British foreign and

American internal policies offer only partial explanations. It is evident that the decline in Gaelic during this period was also rooted in the Irish psyche, which had come to perceive the acquisition of English as a prerequisite of social and economic advancement in an expanding and increasingly urbanized world.

Notes

1. For a discussion see N. C. Dorian, 'Language loss and maintenance in language contact situations', in R. D. Lambert and B. F. Freed, eds., *The Loss of Language Skills*, Rowley, New York, 1982.
2. I employ 'usually' here since there are invariably those who will persist in the use of the mother tongue despite being pressurized to innovate. N. C. Dorian 'Grammatical change in a dying dialect', in *Language*, 49, 1973, p. 33 ff., cites one such 'resistant personality'.
3. It is generally held that this is because the language in which we receive primary socialization is intimately connected with our conception of selfhood. R. Le Page and A Tabouret-Keller make such suggestions in an article entitled 'Models and stereotypes of ethnicity and language', *Journal of Multilingual and Multicultural Development*, 3, 1982, pp. 161–92.
4. H. Kloss, 'Stable bilingualism in an alien milieu', in *Actes du 2 Colloque Canadien de Linguistique Appliquée*, Centre Educatif et Cultural Inc., Montreal, 1971, pp. 23–8, and O. Lamtzidis, 'La révivescence (l'optisme de la réminescence) chez les réfugies Grecs de Pontos et ses conséquences pour l'étude des dialectes Pontiques', in *Unterlagen des 2. Internationalen Dialectozgenkongresses*, Steiner, Wiesbaden, 1968, pp. 407–12, describe the effects on language use of homesickness and nostalgia among migrants.
5. For instance, S. Gal, *Language Shift: Social Determinants of Linguistic Change in Bilingual Austria*, Academic Press, New York, 1979, p. 3, cites 'industrialization' as the ultimate cause of the shift from Hungarian to German among a peasant community in Oberwart, Austria. The colonization of the Cherokee tribe indigenous to Oklahoma, described by W. Pulte, 'Cherokee: a flourishing or obsolescing language?', in W. C. McCormack and S. A. Wurm, eds., *Language and Society: Anthropological Issues*, Mouton, The Hague, 1979, pp. 423–32, ascribes language loss to annexation. A useful overview of these and other relevant case studies is given in R. Appel and P. Muysken, *Language Contact and Bilingualism*, Edward Arnold, London, 1987, chapter 4., pp. 32–45.
6. 'Anglo-Irish and its Irish background', in D. Ó Muirithe, ed., *The English Language in Ireland*, Dublin, Mercier Press, 1977, pp. 20–36, at pp.20–1.
7. These proportions ignore important regional differences between age cohorts. Levels of competence in Irish were markedly different in Ulster and the southeast, for instance, than was the case farther south and west. Moreover, it has been established by many recent studies that the eighteenth and nineteenth-century census figures on the language question are notoriously unreliable. For a discussion of these and allied issues see G. B. Adams, 'The validity of language census figures in Ulster, 1851–1911', *Ulster Folklife*, 25, 1979, pp. 113–22, and G. Fitzgerald, 'The decline of the Irish language', in *The Origins of Popular Literacy in Ireland*, ed., M. Daly and D. Dickson, Anna Livia, Dublin, 1990, pp. 59–72.
8. These statutes were passed at a parliament sitting in the town of Kilkenny. Although compiled in Norman French (the legalese of the day) their purpose is

thought to have been to 're-anglicize' the Anglo-Normans, who were beginning to show signs of assimilating with the native Irish. While these particular statutes were to prove ineffective they mark the first governmental attempt to formulate a language planning strategy within Ireland. See, for instance, E. Curtis, *A History of Ireland*, Methuen, London, 1936, p. 112.

9. P. H. Pearse, *The Murder Machine*, Whelan, Dublin, 1916, reprinted with other essays, Mercier, Cork, 1976. On the notion of 'linguacide', see H. Kloss, *Grundfragen der Ethnopolitik in 20 Jahrhundert*, Bad Godesburg, Vienna, 1969, p. 177.

10. M. Wall, 'The decline of the Irish language', in B. Ó Cuív, ed., *A View of the Irish Language*, Oifig an tSolatháir, Dublin, 1969, pp. 81–90, at p. 87.

11. See, for instance, N. Denison, 'Language death or language suicide?', *International Journal of the Sociology of Language*, 12, 1977, pp. 13–22; S. Gal, *Language shift*; H. and R. Kahane, 'Decline and survival of Western prestige languages', *Language*, 55, 1, 1979, pp. 183–98; N. Dorian, *Language Death: the Life Cycle of a Scottish Gaelic Dialect*, University of Pennsylvania Press, Philadelphia, Pa., 1981.

12. J. Fishman, *Language and Ethnicity in Minority Sociolinguistic Perspective*, Multilingual Matters, Philadelphia, Pa., 1989.

13. This is an established scenario for the majority of migrants to the United States. I will claim later that it was the case for the Irish in nineteenth-century America – Haugen and Huffines have both made similar remarks about other ethnic groups. See, for instance, E. Haugen, *The Norwegian Language in America*, University of Pennsylvania Press, Philadelphia, Pa., 1956, and, more recently, M. L. Huffines, 'Pennsylvania German: maintenance and shift', *International Journal of the Sociology of Language*, 25, 1980, pp. 42–58. Migrant language settings outside the United States are described by J. E. Hofman and H. Fisherman in 'Language shift and maintenance in Israel', *International Migration Review*, 5, 1971, pp. 204–26, G. E. Lewis, 'Migration and language in the USSR', *International Migration Review*, 5, 1971, pp. 147–79.

14. Huffines, 'Pennsylvania German', p. 45.

15. Appel and Muysken, *Language Contact*, p. 34. For an overview of case studies and methodological approaches in the field of language attitudes see R. Agheyisi and J. A. Fishman, 'Language attitude studies, *Anthropological Linguistics*, 12, 5, 1970, pp. 137–57.

16. U. Weinreich, *Languages in Contact: Findings and Problems*, Mouton, The Hague, 1978, p. 1. For a fuller discussion of the differences between bilingualism and second-language acquisition see Appel and Muysken, *Language Contact*, chapters 6–9.

17. Dorian, *Language Death*; Huffines, 'Pennsylvania German'.

18. R. Wardhaugh, *Languages in Competition*, Oxford, Blackwell, 1987, gives an account of the loss of Welsh and other languages as a result of in-migration.

19. Gal, *Language Shift*, has compiled a detailed study of one such community in the rural area of Oberwart, Austria.

20. Dorian, *Language Death*, p. 51.

21. M. K. Adler, *Welsh and other Dying Languages of Europe: a Sociolinguistic Study*, Helmut-Verlag, Hamburg, 1977, p. 9. Brian Weinstein discusses in some detail the nature and extent of the relationship between language and politics in *The Civic Tongue: Political Consequences of Language Choices*, Longman, London, 1983.

22. J. R. Edwards, *The Irish Language: an Annotated Bibliography of Sociolinguistic Publications*, 1772–1982, Garland, New York, 1983.

23. H. Dixon, 'Irish language', *Shan Van Vocht*, 1896, 1, pp. 67–9.

24. S. Brooks, 'The Gaelic League', *The New Ireland*, Maunsel, Dublin, 1907, pp. 19–35.
25. T. P. Coogan, 'Gaelic movement', *Ireland since the Rising*, Pall Mall, London, 1966, pp. 183–205.
26. S. De Fréine, 'The dominance of the English language in the nineteenth century'; in Ó' Muirithe, *The English Language*, pp. 71–87.
27. This notion underlies much of the discussion which follows, i.e. that migration, for example, did not cause the decline single-handed but in conjunction with a number of other external (social) and internal (psychological) forces.
28. Dorian, *Language Death*, mentions the case of two siblings in east Sutherland. One member of the pair is keen to seek employment elsewhere and consequently has become a 'semi-speaker' (shows dysfluency in her use of Scots-Gaelic). The other has no such intention and his Gaelic remains fluent.
29. R. Hindley, *The Death of the Irish Language: a Qualified Obituary*, Routledge, London, 1990, p. 12.
30. Fitzgerald, 'The decline', pp. 64–6.
31. Mr J. J. MacSweeney, quoted on p. 581 of G. Ravenstein, 'On the Celtic languages in the British Isles: a statistical survey', *Journal of the Royal Statistical Society*, 42, 1879, pp. 579–643.
32. See the census report of 1881 (Part II, General Report, 74), *Census of population: Ireland* (1841–1911), Registrar General, HMSO, London, for further confirmation of the inaccuracy of the 1851 figures. Hindley, *The Death*, Fitzgerald, 'The decline', and Adams, 'The validity', all testify to this unwillingness on the part of Irish-speakers to claim any knowledge of the language and propose that there was a significant level of underreporting during the whole of the nineteenth century. This is a familiar problem for many minority-language censuses and is examined in some detail by R. Fasold, *The Sociolinguistics of Society*, Blackwell, Oxford, 1984, pp. 113–24, 215–16.
33. This quotation is dated 1828 and is cited on pp. 608–9 of E. Cahill, 'The Irish language in the Penal Era', *Irish Eccelsiastical Record*, fifth series, 55, 1940, pp. 591–617.
34. Ravenstein, 'On the Celtic languages', p. 582.
35. This is a rather simplistic view of the situation. For a more cogent discussion see A. Schrier, *Irish and the American Emigration*, University of Minnesota Press, Minneapolis, Minn., 1958, chapter 1 and appendices; R. D. Black, *Economic Thought and the Irish Question, 1817–1870*, Cambridge University Press, Cambridge, 1960, chapter VII; J. Jackson, *The Irish in Britain*, Routledge, London, 1963, chapter 1; J. Mokyr, *Why Ireland Starved: a Quantitative and Analytical History of the Irish Economy, 1800–1850*, Allen & Unwin, London, 1985, chapter 8; C. Ó Gráda, *Ireland before and after the Famine*, Manchester University Press, Manchester, 1988.
36. C. Mooney, 'The beginnings of the Irish language revival', *Irish Ecclesiastical Record*, 64, 1944, pp. 10–18.
37. Namely Maureen Wall, 'The decline', and Séamus Ó Buachalla, 'The language in the classroom', *Crane Bag* V, 2, 1981, pp. 849–51.
38. D. H. Akenson, *The Irish Education Experiment*, Routledge, London, 1970, p. 181. For a fuller discussion of these and related issues see M. Daly, 'Literacy and language change', *The Origins of Popular Literacy in Ireland*, ed. M. Daly and D. Dickson, Anna Livia, Dublin, 1990, pp. 153–66.
39. *Limerick Gazette*, 31 January 1815. This desire to acquire English through education is also reflected in the number of elementary English as opposed to Irish textbooks which were published during the period. For a discussion see

J. R. R. Adams, *The Printed Word and the Common Man: Popular Culture in Ulster, 1700–1900*, Institute of Irish Studies, Queen's University, Belfast, 1987.

40. Patrick Callan, in an unpublished M.A. thesis for University College, Dublin, 1975, p. 105, cites a resolution issued by the Catholic Clerical Managers' Association in 1905 that 'all incentives to Emigration, through the books, copybooks or otherwise be excluded from our National Schools'.

41. This is taken from a report dated 1845 entitled 'Destitution among immigrants' cited in E. Abbott, *Historical Aspects of the Immigration Problem: Selected Documents and Case Records*, University of Chicago Press, Chicago, (also published as *The American Immigration Collection*, Arno Press, New York), 1969, p. 583.

42. *Twenty-third Report of the Commissioners for National Education in Ireland*, B.P.P. 1856, Appendix B, p. 143.

43. Irish Folklore Commission, questionnaire, 'Emigration to America', Roinn Bhéaloideas Éireann, University College, Dublin, 1955, Ms. 1407.

44. Anderson Family Letters, Public Record Office of Northern Ireland, 1842, Ms. D/1859 5.

45. On the oral nature of Gaelic cultural life during this period see L. M. Cullen, *The Emergence of Modern Ireland, 1600–1900*, Batsford, London , 1981, p. 132. Furthermore the migration correspondence housed in the institutions listed in my Acknowledgements, p. 161, is written predominantly in English.

46. Irish Folklore Commission questionnaire.

47. P. J. Blessing, 'Irish emigration to the United States, 1800–1920: an overview', in P. J. Drudy, ed., *The Irish in America: Emigration, Assimilation and Impact*, Irish Studies 4, Cambridge University Press, Cambridge, 1985, p. 16.

48. Irish Folklore Commission questionnaire.

49. Thus the Rev. Andrew Talty, in a letter to Dr Woodlock of All Hallows College, Dublin, claims that this is why he was selected. Furthermore, when describing the nature of his parishioners in Virginia, he claims that 'the Irish won't think anything [of any person] unless they know Irish.' (A copy of this letter, dated 25 January 1851 was given to me by Professor Kerby Miller.)

50. See K. Miller, *Emigrants and Exiles*, Oxford University Press, Oxford, 1985, pp. 297 ff.

51. Fitzgerald, 'The decline'.

52. For a discussion of the mechanisms of language change and diffusion see J. Aitchison, *Language Change: Progress or Decay?*, Fontana, London, 1981.

53. W. E. Vaughn and A. J. Fitzpatrick eds., *Irish Historical Statistics: Population, 1821–1971*, Royal Irish Academy, Dublin, 1978, pp. 261–353; B. Ó Cuív, *Irish Dialects and Irish-speaking Districts*, Dublin Institute for Advanced Studies, Dublin, 1951, pp. 77–93; S. H. Cousens, 'The regional pattern of emigration during the great Irish famine, 1846–51', *Transactions and Papers of the Institute of British Geographers*, 28, 1960, pp. 119–34; 'Regional variations in population changes in Ireland, 1881–91', *Transactions and Papers of the Institute of British Geographers*, 33, 1963, pp. 145–62; Miller, *Emigrants and Exiles*, pp. 296–7; B. S. MacAodha, 'Aspects of the linguistic geography of Ireland in the early nineteenth century', *Studia Celtica*, 20–1, 1985–6, pp. 205–20.

54. Fitzgerald, 'The decline'.

55. J. Fishman, *Language in Sociocultural Change*, Stanford University Press, Stanford, Cal., 1972, p. 23.

56. See note 13 above.

57. M. L. Hansen, *The Atlantic Migration, 1607–1860*, Harvard University Press, Cambridge, Mass., 1945, pp. 305–6.

58. The essay is dated 1782 and is reprinted in Abbott, *Historical Aspects*, pp. 416–22; the quotation is at p. 418.
59. Cited in Abbott, *Historical Aspects*, pp. 791–3, at p. 793.
60. The ensuing discussion – given the space available – is necessarily overgeneralized and as such takes no cognizance of the fact that individual circumstances may have been markedly different.
61. For a discussion see A. J. Ward, *Ireland and Anglo-American Relations*, Trinity Press, London, 1969, pp. 2–3; K. Miller, 'Assimilation and alienation: Irish emigrants' responses to industrial America, 1871–1921', in Drudy, *The Irish in America*, p. 112.
62. These would include the 'Know-nothing' agitation of 1852–6 during which Catholic institutions are reported to have been attacked and the Irish prevented from voting by 'native citizens'. For informative contemporary accounts see Abbott, *Historical Aspects*, pp. 466–7, 625–8.
63. Even those Irish-Americans who no longer spoke Gaelic would have had an accent and dialect which were clearly distinct from those of their American peers. In this regard, one commentator in the *Citizen* (1854) remarks that 'your brogue is unmusical to our ears'. See Abbott, *Historical Aspects*, pp. 466–7.
64. See Abbott, *Historical Aspects*, pp. 105–10, at p. 110.
65. Buffalo, 9 August 1850; 'Letters from the Quit Rent Office, the Four Courts, Dublin', *Analecta Hibernica*, 22, 1960, pp. 387–94. A copy of this letter was sent to me by Professor Kerby Miller.
66. See, for example, R. C. Gardner, A. C. Muchnik and D. E. Wolfe, 'Second-language learning: a social-psychological perspective', *Canadian Modern Language Review*, 32, 1976, pp. 198–213.
67. Interestingly, there are numerous contemporary remarks about the speed with which English-speaking migrants acquired 'Americanisms' in their efforts to conform which clearly parallel the case of the Irish monoglots. Joseph Wade, for instance, reports that 'the old maids adopted so much American English that they were nearly Greek to the people around' (Irish Folklore Commission questionnaire, Ms. 1408).
68. 'A demand for the control of foreign pauperism in Massachusetts', *Report of the Joint Special Committee of the Legislature of Massachusetts appointed to Consider the Expediency of Altering and Amending the Laws relating to Alien Passengers and Paupers*, 1848, cited in Abbott, *Historical Aspects*, pp. 584–93, at p. 591.
69. Cited in Miller, *Emigrants and Exiles*, p. 418. G. Borrow, *Lavengro*, 1851, reprinted John Murray, London, 1907, p. 59.
70. I. Zangwill, *The Melting Pot*, Macmillan, New York, 1909. For other perspectives on the question of assimilation see W. Herberg, *Protestant, Catholic, Jew*, Doubleday, New York, 1855; N. Glazer and D. P. Moynihan, *Beyond the Melting Pot*, second edition, MIT Press, Cambridge, Mass., 1970.
71. Quoted by T. Kochman, 'Black speech events and a language programme in the classroom', in C. Cazden, ed., *Child Language and Education*, Holt Rinehart & Winston, New York, 1972, p. 212.
72. S. De Fréine, *The Great Silence*, Foilseacháin Náisiúnta Teo, Dublin, 1965, pp. 2–7.
73. Edwards, *The Irish Language*, p. 134.
74. P. MacAonghusa, 'Reflections on the fortunes of the Irish language in Canada, with some reference to the fate of the language in the United States', in R. O'Driscoll, ed., *The Celtic Consciousness*, Dolmen, Dublin, and McClelland & Stewart, Toronto, 1981, pp. 615–621.

Acknowledgements

I would like to thank the keepers of manuscripts at the following institutions for access to their collections of migration records, letters and so on: National Library of Ireland, Public Record Office of Northern Ireland, Roinn Bhéaloideas Éireann, University College, Dublin. I am also grateful to Ms. J. L. Corrigan for research assistance and to Professor Kerby Miller for sending copies of emigrants' letters from his own collection and giving me permission to cite and quote from them.

7 Australia *felix*: Irish doctors in nineteenth-century Victoria

Laurence M. Geary

> Since the beginning of the eighteenth century Ireland's greatest contribution to the world has been her people. Emigration has been a continuing phenomenon of Irish history. [J. J. Auchmuty, 'The Anglo-Irish influence in the foundation of Australian institutions', *University of Melbourne Gazette*, 25, 3, 26 May 1969, p. 3]

The discovery of gold at Ballarat in August 1851 transformed the fledgling colony of Victoria. The most immediate impact was a migratory deluge, with the Victorian population exploding from less than 80,000 people in 1851 to 1,140,000 in 1891, an increase of 1,200 per cent in forty years.[1] The rise of the colony coincided with the cataclysmic changes in the political, social and demographic life of mid-nineteenth century Ireland. Haemorrhagic emigration was one of the most malevolent features and legacies of the Great Famine. While Britain and North America were the favoured destinations, more than 100,000 Irish people migrated to Australia in the 1850s, the first decade of the gold rushes.[2] The Irish in Victoria accounted for no more than 2 per cent of the total nineteenth-century Irish diaspora, but their impact on the host society was substantial. The Irish contribution to Melbourne university life, to the Victorian bar and politics, to journalism and a number of the other liberal professions has long been recognized by historians.[3] Their impress was largely due to the disproportionate numbers of Anglo-Irish who arrived in the colony from mid-century, attracted thither by one of those unaccountable accidents of history, dislocative political and social pressures in Ireland and the serendipitous discovery of gold half a world away in the British colony of Victoria.

Richard Townshend Mahony, the eponymous hero of Henry Handel Richardson's brilliant depiction of nineteenth-century Victorian life and *mores*,[4] was the archetypal Anglo-Irishman. He was ambitious and well educated, a member of the Established Church and of a socially acceptable profession. A vast social, cultural and educational gulf separated Mahony and the class he represented from the bulk of Irish migrants to Australia, Catholics mainly, from Munster, south-east Leinster and the border counties of Ulster.[5] The fictional Mahony was loosely based on the novelist's father, Walter Lindsay Richardson, who had been born into an Anglo-Irish household in Dublin in the mid-1820s. Like many an Irish medical student before him, Walter Richardson was attracted to Edinburgh, that mecca of eighteenth and early nineteenth-century medical education. He graduated MD from the University of Edinburgh in 1849 and became a licentiate of the city's highly respected college of surgeons in the same year. Richardson gained nine months' postgraduate experience in medicine, surgery and obstetrics in a number of Edinburgh institutions, after which he served as an assistant to a general practitioner in Wales and subsequently to one in Kent, remaining with the latter until he left for Australia early in 1852.[6]

Richardson let it be understood that he went in order to replenish the family coffers, which had been rifled by his half-brothers. The more likely, if less romantic, reason for his departure was his lack of career prospects in Britain. The year 1851 had been a somewhat Micawberish one for him. His miserable income of fifty guineas had barely covered his expenditure. It was all very well to console himself with the notion that he had 'spent money in acquiring knowledge and time in acquiring experience in professional matters',[7] but there was little future for a talented and ambitious man in such a subordinate role. A medical assistantship was regarded as arduous and poorly paid 'hack work', with minimal prospects. It was a career path to be avoided if at all possible.[8] Without the necessary funds to establish a practice of his own at home, Richardson and many an impecunious medical man like him may have been spurred into migrating by the publicity and euphoria that surrounded the discovery of gold in Australia.

Others left for a variety of reasons, personal and circumstantial, as well as professional. There were few opportunities for worthwhile private practice in Ireland, and public appointments were necessary to augment meagre private earnings. Those who did find employment in the expanding Irish Poor Law medical service in the post-Famine period complained of being shabbily treated. Among their many grievances were heavy and exhausting duties, inadequate pay and extensive dispensary districts. Dispensary doctors enjoyed neither holiday entitlement nor pension rights and there was little chance of promotion. In the opinion of the president of the Royal College of Surgeons in Ireland, the dispensary service was one to be shunned.[9] Yet there was fierce competition for such appointments, partly to guarantee an income, however inadequate, partly to nullify the threat from potential rivals for whatever private practice did exist. According to one journal, Irish medical men had the advantage over their English counterparts of enjoying higher social standing.[10] It may have been a consideration for some that they could meet the local gentry on terms of equality, but such a consolation buttered very few parsnips. The financial rewards were much greater on the other side of the Irish Sea, but those who went in search of them encountered extensive prejudice, particularly in England.[11] This did not stop large numbers from working there, but, as the case of Walter Richardson demonstrated, their career prospects were often circumscribed. Furthermore, there were frequent complaints of overcrowding in the profession during the second half of the nineteenth century and the various medical journals were inundated with queries from frustrated practitioners seeking an outlet for their talents and ambitions in Australasia and other outposts of the empire.

In individual cases, familial and other considerations added weight to or superseded professional ones. Walter Richardson may have migrated partly to get away from the ogrish and baneful personality of his mother. But even in Victoria he could not escape it entirely. She wrote to him constantly '. . . in tones of implacable doom, recounting with relish every personal and public disaster which came under her notice,' his daughter's biographer wrote.[12] James Joseph McEniry, son of a prosperous tenant farmer from Clonmel, County Tipperary, used the spurious offer of an assistantship in Melbourne, with the princely salary of £1,000 a year, to forestall parental objections to his decision to leave Ireland. He informed his brother that he was motivated by an overriding ambition to sever parochial ties and forage for himself.[13] Some, such as Thomas Rowan, who was threatened with tuberculosis, migrated for health reasons.[14] The toss of a coin determined the destinational fate of Richard Thomas Tracy.[15] A chance remark took George Cuscaden to the antipodes.[16] Gerald Henry Fetherston, the son of a County Roscommon medical practitioner, was on his eighth voyage to Australia as surgeon to one of the ships of the famous Black Ball line when he met Sarah Ellen Harvey, a solicitor's daughter from Nottingham. Fetherston completed the return journey and acquired extra qualifications before returning to Australia to marry his erstwhile fellow passenger and settle permanently.[17]

Walter Richardson arrived in Melbourne in July 1852 to find the colony gripped by gold fever, 'an epidemic of unrest which had swept through the country, upsetting the balance of men's reason', as his fictional *alter ego* phrased it.[18] On the Ballarat diggings of the 1850s, amidst the ubiquitous squalor, the ever present moral and physical dangers, the possibility of undreamt-of riches, Richardson met with little success either as a digger or subsequently as a shopkeeper, a calling for which the fictional Mahony – and by implication, Richardson – was both temperamentally and socially unsuited. Richardson had practised medicine sporadically during these years and returned to it on a full-time basis in March 1857. He was a competent doctor, with a particular aptitude for obstetrics.[19] He prospered, but owed his financial success more to mining speculation than to his medical practice, and in this he was probably typical of the majority of goldfield doctors. Certainly, if the experiences of George Wakefield[20] were anything to go by, conditions in the later 1850s and early 1860s were extremely difficult. Shortly after commencing practice at Ballarat in 1855, Wakefield informed his father that the miners were 'very bad payers' and that everything was 'awfully expensive'. Towards the end of 1859 he complained that it was 'impossible to obtain a living'. Ballarat was so oversupplied with doctors that fees had been reduced to a minimum. 'In the medical profession things are awful . . . There is no place in the world that the profession would not stand a better chance than here.'[21]

There were at least forty-four Irish doctors among the 380 or so medical men who have been traced to the Ballarat, Castlemaine and Bendigo goldfields.[22] There is no reason to suppose that their experiences would have differed substantially from Wakefield's or that they would have fared any better than he. At best they would have enjoyed a modest competence from the practice of their profession. If, like Richardson, they prospered, it is likely to have been as a result of dabbling in the share market, an activity that seems to have held as much fascination as the pursuit of an elusive Eldorado on the Victorian diggings. But fortunes that are speculatively made can be lost just as easily, as Richardson and countless others discovered. He spread his investments over eight companies, but tilted at the winds of fortune with his largest holding, 200 of the magnificently named Great Extended Hustlers.[23]

Irish doctors who practised on the Victorian goldfields constituted about 10 per cent of the total number of Irish medical men who registered in the colony before 1901. But, as nineteenth-century medical qualifications were an indication neither of nationality nor of place of education, it is necessary to define what is meant by the term 'an Irish doctor'. For the purposes of this chapter, I have regarded individuals with Irish qualifications as Irish doctors, on the grounds that they were likely to have received all or a substantial part of their medical training in Ireland. Few Scots qualified outside their own country and, as the Irish curriculum was at least as demanding as the English one, English students are unlikely to have obtained Irish qualifications in preference to their own unless they were educated in Ireland. There are certain difficulties with this approach, not least in some of the strange bedfellows it threw together, such as the notorious Melbourne practitioner 'Diamond Jim' Beaney[24] who obtained the licence of the King and Queen's College of Physicians of Ireland in 1878 under somewhat unusual circumstances,[25] and Stanislaus Zichy Woinarski, a graduate of Melbourne University who became a fellow of the Royal College of Surgeons in Ireland in 1892. But the numbers concerned are so small as to be insignificant. To those with Irish qualifications must be added those who were born or received their medical education in Ireland but who obtained Scottish diplomas. These two groups totalled 386 individuals, or 16 per cent of all the doctors who registered in Victoria in the nineteenth century. To this minimum figure should be added those who were born or trained in Ireland but who obtained English qualifications, a group for whom no data are available.

The total would be boosted still further if it included first-generation Irish Australians who graduated in medicine from the University of Melbourne, individuals like Patrick Moloney,[26] Charles Henry Molloy[27] and Cornelius George Crowley.[28] Moloney was the first medical student to enrol at Melbourne University and one of its first two medical graduates. Hundreds of Melbourne University medical students completed their education and obtained their qualifications in Britain, including a number of Irish Australians, like the Keogh brothers, Arthur George and Eustace Julian, sons of a Melbourne pharmacist who had left County Roscommon with his parents in 1841.[29] Arthur graduated from the University of Glasgow in 1884 and his brother from the University of Edinburgh four years later. Like the Keoghs, there were many Victorian-born Catholics, with distinctive Irish names, who were educated in Melbourne and licensed in Scotland. They included Denis Doolan,[30] John James Sylvester Healy,[31] James Patrick Kelly,[32] Thomas John Lonergan,[33] Peter Lynch,[34] Maurice

Patrick MacGillicuddy,[35] John Francis McGivern[36] and Patrick Noonan,[37] all of whom obtained the so-called triple qualification of the Scottish corporations, which was awarded for the first time in the mid-1880s.

Using Victorian census data, Oliver MacDonagh calculated that between 1851 and 1901 the Irish population of Victoria varied from a minimum of 15 per cent to a maximum of 35 per cent of the total population and he suggested a mean of 23 per cent.[38] As noted above, Irish doctors constituted at least 16 per cent of all medical men who registered in Victoria before 1901. Thus the ratio of Irish medical practitioners to the Victorian profession as a whole corresponded proportionally with the lower reaches of the general Irish population in the colony during the second half of the nineteenth century.

The vast majority of Irish doctors received their medical training, though not necessarily their qualifications, in Ireland. Until the middle of the nineteenth century, apprenticeship was probably the most common method of entering the medical profession. James Charles Gilhooley, from Ballaghaderreen, County Mayo, was indentured to Archibald Armstrong, surgeon and apothecary, on 19 July 1845 for a period of two years. He contracted to serve his master faithfully and to protect his person and property. He was also obliged to keep his secrets and obey his lawful commands. The young apprentice was expressly forbidden to gamble, fornicate or marry. He was not allowed to engage in any commercial pursuits, to haunt or use taverns, ale-houses, or play-houses, or to absent himself unlawfully from his master's service at any time. In return Armstrong pledged to teach Gilhooley the rudiments of his profession and to provide him with 'board, lodging, washing and diet' and all other necessities, 'according to the custom of the country'.[39] Eleven years later Gilhooley became a licentiate of the Royal College of Surgeons in Ireland and shortly afterwards migrated to Sydney, where he practised for the remainder of his life.

In Ireland and in England, though not in Scotland, licentiates far outnumbered university graduates. In the eighteenth and early nineteenth centuries a number of factors restricted an Irish university medical education to all but a few. For the majority, university training had to be sought elsewhere, usually in Edinburgh, where, in the words of one medical journal, they were provided with 'a first-class education and an irreproachable good name as graduates'.[40] Nearly 2,000 Irish medical students graduated from the University of Edinburgh in the two centuries following the establishment of its medical faculty in 1726.[41] But, by the middle of the nineteenth century, this migratory trend had ceased almost entirely.[42] The explanation was to be found in Ireland, rather than in Edinburgh, specifically in two developments affecting Irish university life, the modification of the University of Dublin's entrance requirements and the establishment of the Queen's University in Ireland, with constituent colleges in the three provincial capitals outside Dublin.

The two Irish universities differed fundamentally, separated one from the other by a quarter-millennium of history. The University of Dublin, or Trinity College, as it is more popularly known, with its Church of Ireland ethos and cosmopolitan nature, was the natural home of the Anglo-Irish. The Queen's University, whose establishment owed as much to contemporary politics as it did to educational necessity, was aimed at a different constituency. The Queen's Colleges at Cork and Galway were intended for Catholics from Munster and Connaught, but, as it transpired, were as likely to have attracted Protestants as Catholics. The students who attended Queen's College Belfast were Presbyterians in the main, but with a leavening of Catholics and others, from Belfast and the surrounding counties of Antrim and Down. The medical degrees offered by the two institutions and the opportunities they provided were as distinct as the students they attracted.

In the second half of the nineteenth century Trinity's medical education and qualifications were highly regarded. Only arts graduates could become candidates for its medical, surgical and obstetric degrees, a requirement shared only by the universities of London and Oxford and one which served to underline its exclusiveness. Trinity's qualifications were sought by those whose eyes were fixed on the highest professional and social prizes. According to one journal, it was axiomatic that an individual with a Trinity medical degree would enter the profession 'with all the prestige of an educated gentleman'.[43]

Not so with the Queen's University. A quarter of a century after its foundation its medical students were depicted as 'deficient in education and resources'.[44] The reputation of the Queen's University was never high and its degrees had nothing like the cachet attached to those of the University of Dublin. But it did provide a university education for those who could never have afforded Trinity's fees. Furthermore, its arts requirements were minimal and the medical curriculum was less demanding than that of Trinity College, the Royal College of Surgeons in Ireland or the King and Queen's College of Physicians of Ireland.[45] The main disadvantage was the difficulty of the final medical examination, which either discouraged students entirely or led to many failures.[46]

The curriculum for the Queen's University degree was broadly similar to that required for Scottish medical and surgical licences and, for many Irish students, Scotland provided the easiest and cheapest route to the profession.[47] The curricula and qualifications of the Irish colleges of physicians and surgeons were regarded as superior to those of the Scottish corporations and of the Queen's University.[48] As the college of surgeons was a teaching body which required two years' residence in Dublin, its licentiates tended to be students who had trained in the capital. The remaining Irish licensing body was the Apothecaries Hall, Dublin, whose main advantage was the relative cheapness of its diplomas and the perceived ease with which they could be acquired. In the early 1880s its licence cost £59, less than one-third of that for the combined arts and primary medical and surgical degrees of the University of Dublin.[49] But, as one acute observer phrased it:

No man would be got to take this diploma if he could get that of the College of Physicians for the same money. The day which beholds uniformity of fees will also see this excellent body in the throes of dissolution.[50]

Table 7.1   Qualifications of Irish doctors who registered in Victoria in the nineteenth century

(a) University graduates

University	Degree holders	Degrees held	Additional qualifications	Total qualifications
Dublin	49	95	28	123
Queen's	23	41	13	54
Royal	18	41	5	46
Scottish (various)	19	27	26	53
Others	15	27	28	55
Total	124	231	100	331

(b) Licentiates

Licensing bodies	With single qualifications	With complete qualifications	Total licentiates	Total qualifications
Irish	70	82	152	254
Irish and Scottish		29	29	68
Irish and English		21	21	48
Irish, English and Scottish		3	3	10
Scottish	10	40	50	102
Scottish and English		7	7	15
Total	80	182	262	497

Total graduates and licentiates	386
Total qualifications	828

Source: Victorian doctors in the nineteenth century – data, microfiche (see n. 52) and student records of Irish and Scottish universities and licensing bodies.

Students did not always seek the best education but, frequently, the easiest, quickest and cheapest method of acquiring a registrable qualification.

It has been calculated that some 2,500 medical practitioners, possessing almost 5,300 professional qualifications, registered in Victoria between 1834 and 1901. British and Irish institutions awarded 3,807, or 72 per cent, of these qualifications. In all, 645 Scottish, ninety-two Irish and sixty-eight English degrees were registered, as well as 1,415 Scottish, 1,188 English and 449 Irish licences.[51] But, if the Irish statistics are taken as the benchmark, the entire set of figures relating to qualifications is suspect. For instance, seventy-eight of the ninety-two Irish degrees were attributed to the University of Dublin, thirteen to the Queen's College, Ireland (*sic*), and one to the Royal College of Surgeons, Ireland. My calculations, which are based on the same data,[52] indicate that of the 124 Irish medical graduates who registered in Victoria, forty-nine obtained their degrees from the University of Dublin, twenty-three from the Queen's University in Ireland and eighteen from its successor, the Royal University of Ireland. Between them, these ninety individuals possessed at least 177 primary and post-graduate medical, surgical and obstetrical degrees. The minimum number of qualifications possessed by the 386 Irish doctors whom I have been able to identify amounted to 828.

A number of general observations can be made regarding the qualifications held by Irish practitioners in Victoria. Licentiates outnumbered degree holders by more than two to one. The vast majority of Irish doctors practised on complete qualifications, that is, they were licensed in both medicine and surgery. This had been recommended in the Medical Act of 1858 but did not become a legal requirement until 1886. Those who practised on a single qualification numbered fewer than one in four of all registered Irish doctors, and more than half of these had obtained their qualifications prior to 1858, a time when there were no prohibitions against any individual, qualified or otherwise, practising any branch of medicine or surgery and when those possessing even a single diploma were substantially in the minority. Thirty-three Irish practitioners in Victoria had obtained a higher qualification from either the King and Queen's College of Physicians of Ireland or one of the surgical licensing bodies, usually the Royal College of Surgeons in Ireland. The University of Dublin provided the largest number of degree holders, forty-nine, or 13 per cent of Irish doctors in Victoria. This was a surprisingly high number, given the cost and length of the university's medical course. Forty-one individuals were graduates of either the Queen's University or the Royal, while another thirty-four held a variety of overseas degrees. As a group Trinity graduates tended to be the most highly qualified, seven holding fellowships and fourteen higher university degrees. In sum, Irish medical practitioners in nineteenth-century Victoria were very well qualified. Their level of professional training and competence was at least on a par with that of any other ethnic group who practised in the colony.

They were recruited from every county in Ireland except Longford. There is no information on the origins of twenty-six, or 6.7 per cent, of the total number of Irish medical practitioners who registered in Victoria. Furthermore, the numbers for Dublin are artificially high. Occasionally, licentiates listed their Dublin residential address rather than their place of birth in the records of the Irish colleges of physicians and surgeons, thereby inflating the numbers for Dublin. Consequently the data in Table 7.2 should be seen as a useful indicator rather than an absolute guide. Provincially, Connaught supplied a mere sixteen practitioners, or just over 4 per cent of the whole. Munster and Ulster were virtually identical and between them accounted for slightly less than 40 per cent of all Irish doctors in Victoria. Leinster was the largest single contributor. Even if we discount the seventy-four licentiates with Dublin addresses, we are still left with eighty-four Leinster-born migrants. On a broader basis, the number of Australians with Irish qualifications was only one less than the combined British total. Thirteen of the seventeen Australians were university graduates, with the others opting for licences.

The entrance books of the University of Dublin provide detailed infor-

Table 7.2 Origins of Irish doctors who registered in Victoria in the nineteenth century

Origin	A	B	C	D	E	F	G	Total
Leinster								
Dublin	74	17	2	1	6	8	2	110
Meath	5							5
Westmeath	1	1						2
Louth	2				1	2	1	6
Kilkenny	3				1			4
Wexford	6					1		7
Queen's	1	2						3
King's	5					2	1	8
Kildare	1					2		3
Wicklow	3	3						6
Carlow	3					1		4
Munster								
Cork	10		5	1		8	1	25
Tipperary	13	1				4		18
Limerick	5	5			1	3	1	15
Waterford	2					1		3
Clare	3	2		1		2		8
Kerry	4					3		7
Ulster								
Antrim	2		4	2	2	1		11
Down	4	1	2	1		3	1	12
Derry	1				1	1	1	4
Cavan	4	1						5
Donegal	2			1				3
Armagh	5	1		1		1		8
Fermanagh	4					2		6
Monaghan	3	2						5
Tyrone	1		2	1	2	5	1	12
Belfast			3	1		3		7
Connaught								
Leitrim	1							1
Roscommon	2					2	1	5
Galway	2	3					1	6
Sligo					1			1
Mayo		1		1		1		3
England and Wales	15				1			16
Unknown	11	3	5	1	2	1		23
Australia	4	5		4	1		3	17
Scotland	1			1				2
Samoa	1							1
Jersey	1							1
France		1						1
India				1				1
Canada							1	1
Total	205	49	23	18	19	57	15	386

Key. A Irish licences, *B* University of Dublin, *C* Queen's University in Ireland, *D* Royal University of Ireland, *E* Scottish degrees, *F* Scottish licences, *G* Other degrees plus Irish licences.

Source: Student records of Irish and Scottish universities and licensing bodies.

mation on matriculating students, including the individual's religion and his father's occupation. Records were found for all but three of the doctors with Trinity qualifications and bear out the observation that the University of Dublin was fundamentally a middle-class institution.[53] Anglicanism was the predominant religion, with thirty-seven adherents. Of the remainder, five attended the minor Protestant Churches, while another five were Catholics. The main surprise is that four of the latter were Australian-born. They described their fathers' occupation as warden's clerk, gentleman, merchant and 'none'. The professions dominated the paternal occupation league. Nine of the students were the sons of clergymen, six the sons of medical practitioners, and two the sons of lawyers. Six other professions were listed. Ten students registered their fathers' occupations as manufacturers or traders of various kinds, including grocer, draper and merchant. Four were the sons of gentlemen[54] and another four the sons of administrators and clerks, while three came from a farming background. No occupations were given for the remainder.[55] Medical students attending the other Dublin schools or the provincial colleges reflected regional variations in religion and paternal occupation, but the likelihood is that they were drawn from a similar social background.

Medical practitioners were as willing as any other group to use whatever contacts and influence they possessed in order to establish themselves, both socially and professionally. Thomas Falkner Fleetwood landed in Victoria in 1874 with an introduction from Sir William Wilde to Richard Ireland, the noted lawyer and parliamentarian. Wilde described his erstwhile assistant at St Mark's Opthalmic Hospital, Dublin, to his one-time schoolfellow, as a gentleman by birth and education, a distinguished graduate of the University of Dublin and a highly qualified medical practitioner. 'If opportunity occurs give him a help and oblige,' Wilde requested.[56] Joseph Hines Wolfenden, the Tipperary-born son of the Rev. Henry Bingham Wolfenden, assisted his brother in a country practice in England after qualifying in 1873. Towards the end of the following year he migrated to Australia to act as *locum tenens* for another brother, James, who was in practice in Dunnolly. Joseph was subsequently appointed surgeon to the local hospital and practised in the area for more than forty years.[57] Samuel Connor, from County Antrim, a twenty-one-year-old graduate of the Queen's University, was the nephew of Joseph H. Connor, who represented Geelong in the Legislative Assembly of Victoria. Shortly after arriving at his uncle's house in mid-1882 Connor was informed that Dr Foster of Colac wanted an assistant, at a salary of £150 per annum. He was offered and accepted the position but, on the advice of his friend, Dr Warren of Richmond, refused to sign an undertaking that he would not practice within a twenty-five-mile radius of Colac for a period of ten years following the completion of his contract. Instead, he applied for a junior hospital position in Sydney and also met a representative of the people of Coleraine, in the Western District of Victoria, who were in urgent need of a doctor and who were prepared to provide him with certain financial guarantees. Connor was more attracted to Sydney and decided to go there to canvass personally. He called on Presbyterian ministers, medical practitioners and businessmen but, after about ten days, realized that it was useless to proceed any further, 'as so many people had their fingers in the pie'. Instead he returned to Victoria and accepted the Coleraine offer on being informed that it was still open.[58]

Thirty-eight residents of the town and its neighbourhood guaranteed Connor an income of £400 if he practised there for twelve months. If he left before that time he was subject to a penalty of £50. If he wished to leave after the contracted period he was obliged to give one month's written notice. Connor was to adopt the 'usual scale' of fees and to keep proper accounts, which were to be audited after six months and on termination of the agreement.[59]

With the exception of an eleven months' sojourn in Geelong, Connor practised in Coleraine for the remainder of his life. Paid and honorary appointments rapidly came his way. He became a Medical Officer of Health, public vaccinator and analyst. He was gazetted surgeon to the militia, acted as surgeon to the Oddfellows' Lodge and to the Sons of Temperance and was elected honorary surgeon to Hamilton Hospital. Such a career pattern was fairly typical of the majority of country doctors, hospital appointments in particular being enormously significant in establishing a successful practice. The number of social positions filled by Connor reflected the generally high esteem in which doctors in Australia were held. A deeply religious man, he was closely involved with the Presbyterian Church and Sunday school. He was also a local Justice of the Peace and was president of several educational and social organizations.[60]

There were many parallels between the general careers of Fleetwood and Connor.[61] Fleetwood was active in Anglican affairs and, like his compatriot, was a staunch temperance advocate. He was a major shareholder in a temperance hotel, the suggestively named, elaborately constructed and financially disastrous Warrnambool Ozone Coffee Palace. This venture does not seem to have dented his finances too severely. He was able to bring his wife and two young children on a ten months' trip to Ireland and England after practising at Warrnambool for four years.[62] Matrimony was undoubtedly one of the prerequisites of professional success, although some, like Edward Francis O'Sullivan, of Yarrawonga, took out a double indemnity by marrying for social advantage also.[63] Samuel Connor was secure enough financially to marry shortly after discharging his contractual obligations in Coleraine and to honeymoon in Ireland and Scotland for a total of seven months. In fact Connor's earnings over his first ten years of practice consistently outstripped the guarantee he had been given when he first came to Coleraine. For the eight years 1885–92 his average annual earnings were £723, and for the five years 1888–92 they averaged £826.[64] The medical publisher and bookseller Ludwig Bruck estimated that in the early 1890s about 90 per cent of Australasian medical practitioners earned between £350 and £1,200 a year, with the remainder grossing a maximum of £6,000, and that the average for all doctors was probably between £700 and £800. Bruck argued that such an income was not inordinate and was necessary to compensate for higher rents and wages in the colonies and for the loss of social and other advantages that were readily enjoyed 'in the more civilised regions of Europe and America'.[65] In monetary terms, therefore, Connor's practice was an 'average' one. But he was probably better circumstanced than most country doctors. Legacies from Ireland and returns on investments augmented his professional earnings substantially.[66]

Not all were as fortunate. William Harvey Jackson, from Cork, a licentiate of the Apothecaries Hall, practised at Merino in the Western District. In March 1872 he was returned for trial for the manslaughter of a stillborn infant. Eventually the Solicitor-General concluded that there was no case to answer and the charges were dropped.[67] Nonetheless, Jackson felt compelled to leave Merino. He went to Tasmania, which proved to be a disastrous move. In February 1876 a clearly overwrought Jackson appealed to the secretary of the Medical Benevolent Society of Victoria to help him to secure a post as ship's surgeon so that he and his wife could return to Ireland. He described their struggle as hopeless and he was determined to get away, irrespective of the cost.[68]

J. J. McEniry's desire for independence brought him to Victoria shortly after qualifying in 1887. Initially he was employed by an insurance company as a travelling medical referee. Insurance companies generally guaranteed their medical examiners twenty cases a month, usually at a fee of one guinea for an ordinary examination. In addition, they paid travelling expenses of two or three guineas a week.[69] McEniry tired of this work very quickly. Drink was the great temptation associated with insurance travelling, he said, and he could never save a penny. He described insurance work 'as one of the lowest grades of living which a doctor is compelled to pursue'. There was no society, no responsibility and no social standing, according to McEniry. Next he worked in Hobart as a locum, initially for one month but subsequently for twelve, at a guinea a day plus expenses.[70] On completion of the agreement he returned to Victoria and practised in Charlton. After sixteen years a decline in the local population, brought about by the consolidation of farm holdings, compelled him to transfer to Kerang. Once again McEniry built up a successful practice but, as he admitted later, lived up to it fully, 'like most Irishmen here'. In his late fifties he suffered an incapacitating stroke and died three and a half years later, having made little provision for his wife and five children, who ranged in age from ten to twenty-two. His family were reduced to hotel keeping at an outpost some thirty-two miles from Kerang, although his admirable wife, Florence, was determined to abandon the liquor trade at the earliest possible opportunity in favour of a general store, where most of her family could be employed.[71]

Like McEniry, the vast majority of nineteenth-century Australian medical practitioners were extremely mobile, as even the most cursory examination of the five Australasian medical directories produced by Ludwig Bruck in the last two decades of the nineteenth century will reveal.[72] Doctors seemed to move with ease between rural and urban centres and within and between colonies. A significant number returned overseas. Furthermore, many practitioners remained on the register of the Medical Board of Victoria long after they had ceased to practice in the colony. It is difficult to say whether these migratory tendencies were indicative of ambition, failure or social pressure, or whether they were simply a reflection on the profession itself. About 70 per cent of Irish doctors who registered in Victoria appear in one or more of Bruck's directories. As a very rough guide, about two in five were traced to at least one other colony in addition to Victoria. About one in three practised in metropolitan Melbourne. Of these, almost one-third had their consulting rooms in the city of Melbourne, generally in Collins Street or Lonsdale Street. The next highest concentrations were in Richmond and St Kilda, followed by South Melbourne and, then, by Hawthorn, Brighton and Fitzroy. Those with superior qualifications and experience tended to gravitate to the city and the more affluent suburbs, where their professional and social ambitions were given the fullest possible rein.

Irish practitioners made a significant contribution to the medical life of Melbourne, to its hospitals and to the university school of medicine. Among the earliest were Richard Eades, a graduate of the University of Dublin and Fellow of the Royal College of Surgeons in Ireland, and James B. Motherwell, from County Sligo. Both were connected with the Melbourne Hospital and the university from an early date. Eades served a term as mayor of Melbourne, while Motherwell was closely involved with medical politics.[73] As surgeons Henry Michael O'Hara and Thomas Naghten Fitzgerald were unsurpassed. Both were Dublin-trained and both were Fellows of the Royal College of Surgeons in Ireland. O'Hara was prominently identified with the Alfred Hospital for forty-three years, while Fitzgerald had an even longer association with the Melbourne Hospital as acting house surgeon, honorary surgeon and consulting surgeon. He was also consultant to a number of other Melbourne hospitals. In 1884 Fitzgerald was awarded the first clinical lectureship in surgery at the Melbourne Hospital. He was the first practitioner in Australia to receive a knighthood for his contribution to medicine and was, according to his biographer, 'the unquestioned leader of the profession in all the Australasian colonies'. At least two of his obituarists described him as a 'genius'.[74]

Irish-trained doctors were largely responsible for the introduction of ophthalmology to Victoria.[75] But it was in the field of obstetrics and gynaecology that Irish influence was most keenly felt. Richard Thomas Tracy, who co-founded Melbourne's Lying-in Hospital and Infirmary for Diseases of Women and Children in 1856, was the most eminent figure in obstetrics and gynaecology in Australia in the nineteenth century. He secured an international reputation for his pioneering work in gynaecological surgery and was honoured by a number of overseas bodies. He was appointed first lecturer in obstetric medicine and diseases of women and children at the University of Melbourne in 1864.[76] His approach was eminently practical. He informed his first students that 'no amount of book or purely theoretical knowledge' would enable them to become competent and useful practitioners. Instead he impressed upon them the necessity to learn 'the daily, practical details of hospital, medical and surgical practice'.[77] On Tracy's death his protégé, Lawrence Joseph Martin,[78] bought his Collins Street house and practice and also succeeded to his university lectureship. In turn, Martin's position at the Lying-in Hospital was filled by another Irishman, Stephen John Burke.[79] Others associated with the institution in the early period were Thomas Rowan[80] and Michael Ulick O'Sullivan, as well as successive generations of Cuscadens[81] and Fetherstons,[82] for a period of fifty-one years and forty-nine years respectively.

In the course of the 1956 R. H. Fetherston Memorial Lecture at the University of Melbourne, Colin Macdonald opined that the Irish possessed certain temperamental qualities that made them good doctors. He speculated on their fascination with obstetrics and gynaecology, suggesting that it arose from the domestic squalor and poverty of nineteenth-century Ireland, in particular the tendency of the poor to share their homes with their pigs and the equal and entirely natural propensity of the latter to propagate themselves therein. Irish doctors were recruited from an entirely different social milieu and, even if they were familiar with the domiciliary arrangements of the poor, porcine births are unlikely to have fuelled their ambitions or furthered their careers as obstetricians. Macdonald was on safer ground when he claimed that it was the training they received as students in the medical schools and hospitals of nineteenth-century Dublin that made them such useful and competent doctors.[83] By the beginning of the nineteenth century Dublin's lying-in hospitals had secured an international reputation as teaching centres and, in the half-century from the 1830s to the 1870s, the Dublin school of medicine, drawing on broad European influences and innovations, reached the pinnacle of its own considerable achievement. The skills that were assimilated there enabled Irish doctors to contribute to Victorian society in a manner as beneficial and pioneering as that of their compatriots in law, politics and higher education and to leave their own particular stamp on what one historian has termed 'that most "Irish" of Australian colonies'.[84]

Notes

1. Oliver MacDonagh, 'The Irish in Victoria', in T. Desmond Williams, ed., *Historical Studies* VIII, Gill & Macmillan, Dublin, 1971, p. 72.
2. Patrick O'Farrell, *The Irish in Australia*, New South Wales University Press, Sydney, 1986, pp. 63, 85.
3. MacDonagh, 'The Irish in Victoria', pp. 70–1; MacDonagh, 'Emigration from Ireland to Australia', in Colm Kiernan, ed., *Australia and Ireland, 1788–1988: Bicentenary Essays*, Gill and Macmillan, Dublin, 1986, pp. 128–9. See also, O'Farrell, *The Irish in Australia*, pp. 93–7, and J. J. Auchmuty, The Anglo Irish influence in the foundation of Australian institutions, *University of Melbourne Gazette*, 25, 3, 26 May 1969, pp. 2–8.
4. Henry Handel Richardson, *The Fortunes of Richard Mahony*, Heinemann, London, 1930.
5. David Fitzpatrick, 'Irish emigration to nineteenth-century Australia', in Kiernan, *Australia and Ireland*, p. 140.
6. Dorothy Green, *Ulysses Bound: Henry Handel Richardson and her Fiction*, Australian National University Press, Canberra, 1973, p. 22, n. 7.
7. Henry Handel Richardson Papers, National Library of Australia, Ms. 133/1/292.
8. *Medical Press*, 12 September 1894, p. 252.

9. Thomas Myles, 'Medical careers', *Dublin Journal of Medical Science*, third series, 112, 1901, pp. 413–16.
10. *Medical Press and Circular*, 18 September 1872, p. 241.
11. *Medical Press and Circular*, 18 September 1867, p. 262, 18 September 1872, p. 241, 22 September 1875, pp. 247–8, 22 September 1880, p. 237.
12. Green, *Ulysses Bound*, p. 341.
13. J. J. McEniry to William McEniry, 17 April 1888, McEniry Papers, xerox copies in the possession of Ms P. J. McEniry, Fitzroy, Vic.
14. Colin Macdonald, 'A Book of Remembrance: Volume 1 of Biographies of the Medical Staff of the Lying-in Hospital, Women's Hospital, Royal Women's Hospital, Melbourne', typescript, 1967, Royal Women's Hospital, Melbourne. For a discussion of Australia as a health resort, particularly for tuberculosis patients, see J. M. Powell, 'Medical promotion and the consumptive immigrant to Australia', *Geographical Review*, 63, 4, 1973, 449–76.
15. Frank M. C. Forster, 'One hundred years of obstetrical and gynaecological teaching in Victoria', *Australia and New Zealand Journal of Obstetrics and Gynaecology*, 6, 1966, p. 101.
16. *Medical Journal of Australia*, 15 April 1933, p. 476.
17. R. H. J. Fetherston, typescript autobiography, copies in Royal Women's Hospital, Melbourne, Acc/1990/5/18, State Library of Victoria, La Trobe collection, Ms. 9865, and in the library of the Australian Medical Association, Parkville, Vic, 3053. Ms. 1970.
18. Richardson, *Richard Mahony*, p. 166.
19. Frank M. C. Forster, 'Walter Lindesay Richardson, 1826–1879, as obstetrician: his casebook and midwifery practice in early Ballarat', *Festschrift for Kenneth Fitzpatrick Russell*, Queensberry Hill Press, Melbourne, 1978, pp. 140–58.
20. Born London, 1814; L.S.A., London, 1841; d. Kerang, Vic., 1888.
21. Keith Macrae Bowden, *Goldrush Doctors at Ballarat*, n.p., 1977, pp. 91–5.
22. Bowden, *Goldrush Doctors*, pp. 108–20; Bowden, *Doctors and Diggers on the Mount Alexander Goldfields*, n.p., 1977, pp. 197–209.
23. Green, *Ulysses Bound*, p. 345.
24. For Beaney see *Australian Dictionary of Biography*, Melbourne University Press, Melbourne, 1966–90, 3, pp. 124–6.
25. Minutes of the Royal College of Physicians of Ireland, Kildare Street, Dublin 2.
26. Born Camberwell, Vic., 1843; M.B., 1867; d. Ulverston, Lancs., 21 September 1904. See Leonard J. T. Murphy, Patrick Moloney, M.B. (Melbourne), 1843–1904', in Harold Attwood, Frank Forster and Bryan Gandevia, eds., *Occasional Papers on Medical History Australia*, Melbourne, 1984, pp. 1–33.
27. Born Ballarat, Vic., 11 July 1863; M.B., 1886, M.D., 1892; d., 31 January 1931. See *Medical Journal of Australia*, 28 March 1931, pp. 392–3.
28. Born Bendigo, Vic., October 1872, M.B., B.S., 1896; d. Malvern, Vic., 9 May 1936. See *Medical Journal of Australia*, 20 June 1931, p. 768.
29. H. Victor Feehan, 'Early Irish Pharmacists in Victoria: the Keoghs', State Library of Victoria, La Trobe collection, Ms. 11101.
30. Born Emerald Hill, South Melbourne, 14 April 1865; educ. Christian Brothers School, East Melbourne.
31. Born Oakleigh, Vic., 20 April 1863; educ. St Patrick's College, Melbourne.
32. Born Sandridge, Vic., 16 May 1865; educ. St Francis Xavier College, Kew.
33. Born Carlton, 8 April 1868; educ. St Patrick's College, Melbourne.
34. Born Smythesdale, Vic., 8 July 1858; educ. Grenville College, Ballarat.
35. Born Benalla, Vic., 27 August 1871; educ. St Patrick's College, Melbourne.
36. Born Abbotsford, 22 February 1866; educ. St Patrick's College, Melbourne.

37. Born Stradbroke, Vic., 5 December 1866; educ. State School 490.
38. MacDonagh, 'Emigration from Ireland to Australia', p. 128.
39. Australian Medical Association Archives, Ms. 1336.
40. *Medical Press and Circular*, 18 August 1875, p. 133.
41. *University of Edinburgh: Bicentenary of the Faculty of Medicine, 1726–1926; Records of the celebration*, Edinburgh, 1926, pp. 122–4.
42. Robert Christison, 'President's address delivered at the forty-third annual meeting of the British Medical Association, held in Edinburgh, 3–6 August 1875', *British Medical Journal*, 7 August 1875, p. 156. See also Christison, 'Graduation address to the gentlemen who obtained their medical degrees in the university of Edinburgh, 1 August 1866', *Edinburgh Medical Journal*, 12, 1, 1866. p. 198.
43. *Medical Press and Circular*, 18 September 1872, p. 242. See also the issues for 20 September 1876, p. 238; 22 September 1880, p. 238; *Medical Press*, 19 September 1888, p. 291.
44. *Medical Press and Circular*, 18 August 1875, pp. 132–4.
45. *Medical Press and Circular*, 18 September 1872, p. 242; 18 August 1875, pp. 132–4; 22 September 1880, p. 238; 19 September 1888, p. 296.
46. T. W. Moody and J. C. Beckett, *Queen's, Belfast, 1845–1949: the History of a University* I, Faber, London, 1959, pp. 268–77.
47. Moody and Beckett, *Queen's*, pp. 269–70, 276. See also *Medical Press and Circular*, 22 September 1880, p. 248.
48. *Medical Press and Circular*, 18 September 1872, p. 242; 18 August 1875, pp. 132–4.
49. *Medical Press and Circular*, 22 September 1880, p. 248; *Medical Press*, 19 September 1888, p. 291.
50. Thomas Laffan, *The Medical Profession in the Three Kingdoms in 1887*, Fannin, Dublin, 1888, p. 285.
51. Diana Dyason, 'The medical profession in colonial Victoria, 1834–1901', in Roy Macleod and Milton Lewis, eds., *Disease, Medicine and Empire: Perspectives on Western Medicine and the Experience of European Expansion*, Routledge, London and New York, 1988, pp. 195–7. For a discussion of the medical profession in Victoria between 1870 and 1933 see T. S. Pensabene, *The Rise of the Medical Practitioner in Victoria*, Australian National University Press, Canberra, 1980, chapter 4.
52. 'Victorian doctors in the nineteenth century – data', microfiche available from the Department of History and Philosophy of Science, University of Melbourne, Parkville, Vic. 3053, Australia. This database was compiled under Diana Dyason's aegis and presumably she used it for her own calculations.
53. R. B. McDowell and D. A. Watt, *Trinity College Dublin, 1592–1952*, Cambridge University Press, Cambridge, 1982, p. 508.
54. The university's historians define 'gentlemen' as 'people of independent means who do not adopt a profession or trade'; 'administrators' were 'largely civil servants of various grades', McDowell and Watt, *Trinity College*, p. 507.
55. Entrance Books, University of Dublin Archives.
56. John F. Fleetwood, 'Thomas Falkner Fleetwood (1847–1933): a paper read to the section of the history of medicine of the Royal Academy of Medicine in Ireland, 14 February 1973', privately printed, copy in author's possession, pp. 3–8. For Ireland see Tony Pagliaro, 'Irish events of the 1840s and the Victorian career of R. D. Ireland', in Oliver MacDonagh and W. F. Mandle, eds., *Irish-Australian Studies: Papers delivered at the fifth Irish-Australian Conference*, Australian National University Press, Canberra, 1989, pp. 267–83.
57. *Medical Journal of Australia*, 19 August 1922, p. 228.

58. Samuel Connor Mss, in possession of Merran Samuel, Armadale, Vic.
59. Samuel Connor papers, Australian Medical Association Archives, Ms. 619.
60. Connor Mss, in possession of Merran Samuel. There are conflicting opinions on the social status of Australian medical practitioners. See, for instance, Evan Willis, *Medical Dominance: the Division of Labour in Australian Health Care*, Allen & Unwin, Sydney, 1983, pp. 45–6.
61. Fleetwood, 'Thomas Falkner Fleetwood', pp. 9–13.
62. Fleetwood, 'Thomas Falkner Fleetwood', p. 10.
63. Mrs Samuel Fitzpatrick to her son, Dr David O'Sullivan, 3 June 1979, O'Sullivan papers, Australian Medical Association Archives, Ms. 2294.
64. Connor Mss, in possession of Merran Samuel.
65. Ludwig Bruck, 'The present state of the medical profession in Australia, Tasmania and New Zealand', *Australasian Medical Gazette*, March 1893, p. 97.
66. Connor Mss, in possession of Merran Samuel.
67. W. H. Jackson papers, Australian Medical Association Archives, Ms. 922. See also *Australian Medical Journal*, April 1872, pp. 102–3, May 1872, pp. 147–8, June 1872, p. 179, and Frank M. C. Forster, 'Mrs Howlett and Dr Jenkins: Listerism and early midwifery practice in Australia', *MJA*, 25 December 1965, p. 1051.
68. Jackson to Dr Martin, 22 February 1876, Jackson papers, Australian Medical Association Archives, Ms. 922.
69. Ludwig Bruck, ed., *The Australasian Medical Directory and Handbook*, Australasian Medical Gazette, Sydney, 1892, p. 228.
70. J. J. McEniry to William McEniry, 17 April 1888, McEniry papers.
71. J. J. McEniry to Anne McEniry, 4 July 1910, and to William McEniry, 3 February 1917; Florence McEniry to William McEniry, 10 April 1926, McEniry papers.
72. See note 67.
73. *Australian Medical Journal*, October 1867, pp. 309–12; 15 May 1886, pp. 224–5.
74. *Australian Dictionary of Biography*, 4, pp. 180–1. See also *Intercolonial Medical Journal*, 20 July 1908, pp. 379–86. For O'Hara see *Medical Journal of Australia*, 18 June 1921, pp. 512–13.
75. Ronald F. Lowe, 'William R. Wilde, Andrew S. Gray, and two eye and ear hospitals of very similar name', *Australian and New Zealand Journal of Surgery*, 51, 6, 1981, pp. 630–6. See also R. F. Lowe, 'T. Aubrey Bowen, oculist, 1837–93', *Australian Journal of ophthalmology*, 9, 1981, pp. 155–62.
76. Forster, 'One hundred years', pp. 100–1.
77. R. T. Tracy, 'Inaugural lecture of the course on obstetrics and diseases of women and children', *Australian Medical Journal*, April 1865, pp. 113–14.
78. Born Dundalk, Co. Louth, 1826; L.A.H., 1851, L.R.C.S.Ed., 1853, M.B., M.D., Mel., 1862; d. Cannes, 19 January 1879. See *Australian Medical Journal*, April 1879, pp. 186–9.
79. Born Killarney, Co. Kerry (not. Co. Roscommon, as in Macdonald, Book of remembrance), January 1836; M.R.C.S., 1856, L.K.Q.C.P.I., 1862; d. 24 November 1898; family information in possession of Burke's grandson, Antony Knowles, Clayton, Vic.
80. Born Newry, Co. Down, 1852; L. 1872, F. 1876, R.C.S.Ed.; L.R.C.P.Ed., 1872; M.B., 1876, B.S., M.D., 1882, Mel.; M.D., Syd, 1882; d. 1935. See John Atherton Young, Ann Jervie Sefton and Nina Webb, *Centenary Book of the University of Sydney Faculty of Medicine*, Sydney, Sydney University Press, 1984, p. 96.
81. Sir George and W. G.; George, b. Wexford, 1858; L.R.C.S.Ed., L.R.C.P.Ed.,

1880; d. 1933. See, *Medical Journal of Australia*, 15 April 1933, pp. 476–7.

82. Gerald Henry Fetherston, b. Roscommon, 20 October 1829; L.A.H., 1856; L.R.C.P.Ed., L.F.P.S.Glas., 1860; M.D., Mel., 1864; d. 10 September 1901. Richard Herbert Fetherston, b. 2 May 1864, Melbourne; L.R.C.S.I., 1884; L.K.Q.C.P.I., 1885; M.B., Ch.B., Edin., 1886; M.D., Edin., 1888; M.D., Mel, 1889; d. 1943. See Fetherston autobiography and *Medical Journal of Australia*, 21 August 1943, pp. 1589.

83. Colin Macdonald, The Fetherstons and their colleagues: early history of the Royal Women's Hospital, Melbourne, *Medical Journal of Australia*, 12 January 1957, pp. 25–6.

84. O'Farrell, *The Irish in Australia*, p. 148.

Acknowledgement

I would like to acknowledge my indebtedness to the Wellcome Trust, whose generous support in the form of a fellowship made possible the research on which this chapter is based.

8 'We can't all live on a small island': the political economy of Irish migration

Ellen Hazelkorn

The 1980s witnessed a dramatic and rapid return to mass migration from Ireland.[1] Reflecting the significant structural changes within Irish society since the 1950s, the estimated 210,000 people who left the country between 1982 and 1991 reveal a more complex class structure than previous generations. For Irish migrants with few or no qualifications, their place in the secondary labour market has been confirmed; their work is casual, non-unionized, often subcontract, giving the impression that a specific kind of Irish migrant labour is entrenched. This group has been strongly represented among contemporary Irish migrants to the UK, constituting a migrating underclass of labour. Education, health, clerical, catering and cleaning for women, and construction and metal processing for men, remain the largest employment sectors. But the 1980s have also seen the growing presence of skilled and graduate migrants in the professional, managerial and administrative fields, thus illustrating that the migration experience is strongly influenced by the class structure of the indigenous society.

The complexity presented by this picture challenges the dominant interpretations offered by migration literature about Ireland. The conventional view advocated by 'discrimination literature' studies, community/welfare agencies and anecdotal accounts describes the Irish migrant experience as primarily distressing, exploitative and typified by unskilled cheap labour, employed below skill or educational level.[2] With occasional reference to Marx's *Capital* and Engel's *Condition of the Working Class in England* – both of which highlight the Irish case – migrants are depicted as a 'reserve army of labour', willing to work for wages and conditions unacceptable to indigenous workers and promoting internecine conflict among a homogeneous working class to the applause of the bourgeoisie.[3] O'Connor[4] uses a 'functionalist analysis of the relationship between racism and migration' to compare the Irish in Britain with the Afro-Caribbean community[5] in terms of discrimination, employment and housing, while others[6] suggest an analogy to levels of psychological distress. A major difficulty with this tradition is the tendency to overgeneralize the migrant experience across generations and ethnic groups and between states.[7]

Other studies refer to Irish migration as a nineteenth-century phenomenon of 'involuntary labour' and concentrate primarily on post-Second World War mobility from southern Europe, the Maghreb and New Commonwealth countries.[8] According to this view, large-scale labour migration, engineered in many cases by direct state intervention, was actively promoted in order to relieve labour bottlenecks, structural changes in the labour market and demographic patterns.[9] The process of migration from the 'periphery' to the 'centre' ended in the 1970s with the collapse of the expansionary boom,[10] thereby partially accounting for the omission of contemporary Irish migration.

The difficulty with this tradition is that by explaining migration narrowly as the importation of unskilled and semi-skilled labour it ignores the extent to which Irish migrants have always included among their ranks skilled, university, medical, professional and petty-bourgeois who left because of scarcity of employment at home, and higher salaries and better life styles abroad.[11] Globalization of the world economy, characterized by a new international division of labour (NIDL), has exaggerated growing polarization between jobs at the high and low-paying ends of the labour market and, in contrast to manufacturing-based economies, increased concentration in key localities[12] – factors which are particularly relevant in explaining contemporary Irish migration. Indeed, as the anti-immigration lobby has grown across Europe and the United States, gates have opened for the Irish. Racial tensions and fears are partially responsible, but it is equally clear that this new policy has developed in response to heightened global competition and a deepening skills crisis in the United Kingdom and elsewhere in Europe and in the United States.

This chapter aims to examine the political and economic factors of contemporary Irish migration in terms of structural changes within the Irish and global economies. Given Ireland's status as a late-developing semi-peripheral economy, significant migration is likely to remain an essential characteristic of the Irish economy into the next century. The emergence of an identifiable new international division of labour, accompanied by the creation and subsequent enlargement of the European Community (EC) have accelerated the evolution of an integrated economic system embracing all of western Europe.[13] This process will exaggerate the peripheralization of the Irish economy, with significant implications for its class and labour-market structure, and continuing migration. Ireland's high birth rate produces large numbers of under- and unemployed well qualified school leavers and graduates with marketable language skills. In contrast, expanding areas of the European, US and other advanced capitalist economies are experiencing falling birth rates and serious skill shortages. Despite the EC view that post-1992 will encourage 'fluid exchanges' of labour, with skilled persons moving all over the Community, thereby constituting particularly significant net migration movement, the more likely impact for Ireland will be a clearly defined 'one-way outward flow' ensuring that Ireland remains a labour-exporting economy.[14]

Characteristics of Irish late industrialization

The Irish Free State's first decade was marked by reliance on orthodox fiscal measures of competitiveness, 'access for capital' and controlled government spending, and on traditional agricultural exports for growth. These measures had little impact on either unemployment or migration, both of which remained high. Despite some immediate improvement in the volume of industrial production between 1932 and 1938, the combined forces of Fianna Fáil's autarkic policies, the economic war with Britain and the international depression impacted negatively on economic growth. Export volumes, prices and markets collapsed, increasing the country's dependence on international markets. Average earnings in 1937 were 9 per cent below the 1931 level, and, in spite of increases in industrial employment, 145,000 were registered as unemployed in 1938.[15] Eighteen thousand people emigrated annually between 1936 and 1946, rising to 42,000 per annum between 1956 and 1961.

Seán Lemass's 'Programme for Economic Expansion' in 1958 dispassionately dismantled the prevailing strategy. The adoption of a more aggressive role for the state in the 1950s, encouragements to foreign capital and acceptance of free-trade policies spurred rapid economic growth, and raised living standards and expectations in the 1960s.[16] Domestic conditions improved so significantly that the population decline registered over the previous 100 years was reversed – 1961 recorded the lowest population level of 2.8 million – and the early 1970s recorded a slight net immigration. Ireland was rapidly transformed from a traditional and agricultural society into an industrial and urbanized one.

Lemass's politicized package of economic growth, social progress and industrial stability was similar to the Keynesian-inspired approach adopted by other capitalist states after the Second World War. The strategy, however, proved inadequate for resolving fundamental problems: little indigenous manufacturing and virtually no commercial exploitation of national resources; small-scale and inefficient agriculture; poor dispersal of resources; weak infrastructure. These defects were compounded in the 1970s and 1980s by shrinking state revenues, a surging national debt, rising interest rates and inflation, collapse of home demand, a decline in both agricultural and manufacturing output, rising unemployment, and international factors, including the 1973–4 and 1979 oil-induced crises, and alterations in international capital formations. Demographic factors – (brief) net immigration, population increase, expansion in the number seeking work, and migration from rural to urban areas (giving Dublin one-third of the state's population) – converged with labour-force changes to produce a labour-market situation that was, in an increasingly depressed economic climate, explosive.

Initially the dominant influence on industrial expansion was the rapid growth in high-technology export-oriented foreign manufacturing, which accounted for 34 per cent of manufacturing employment, over half of industrial production and 80 per cent of non-food manufactured exports in 1980.[17] In the following decade there was a noticeable shift towards new technological sectors, expanding Ireland's attractiveness to telecommunica-

Table 8.1 Employment and unemployment in Ireland, 1926–91 (000)

	Agriculture	Industry	Services	Total	Labour force	Unemploy-ment
1926	653	162	406	1,220	1,300	79
1936	614	206	415	1,235	1,331	96
1946	568	225	432	1,225	1,289	64
1951	496	282	438	1,217	1,262	45
1961★	360	252	405	1,018	1,076	59
	(380)	(259)	(414)	(1,053)	(1,108)	(56)
1971	272	320	457	1,049	1,110	61
1981	196	363	587	1,146	1,272	126
1991	155	318	648	1,121	1,331	210

★There is a discontinuity in the data at 1961; the figures in parentheses are comparable with earlier years. Because of the difficulties of measuring unemployment over a long period, the pre- and post-1961 unemployment figures should be treated as comparable.

Source. K.A. Kennedy, T. Giblin and D. McHugh, *The Economic Development of Ireland*, Routledge, London, 1988, p143; Tansey, *Sunday Tribune*, 3 November 1991.

tions and financial investors. Despite a sharp rise in output, exports, productivity and profits, and other financial indicators, throughout the 1980s, unemployment soared, in line with growing international acknowledgement of the phenomenon of jobless or job-deficient growth.[18]

The exodus from agriculture continued, manufacturing collapsed – the collapse was particularly evident in Dublin, where the number employed fell by 36.7 per cent between 1961 and 1981 – while the service sector grew, with a strong performance in commerce, insurance, finance and public administration. Fewer people were at work in 1991 than in 1926 (see Table 8.1). In this context, official unemployment statistics, based on the Labour Force Survey, must be measured against the 40,000-plus on varying schemes, those discouraged from working, eliminated from social welfare or migrating.[19] A 1988 Combat Poverty report showed that one-third of the population lived below a low-poverty line owing to unemployment and low pay. A 'dual economy', with persistently high levels of unemployment, migration and endemic poverty, residing side-by-side with booming economic indicators inspired relatively little public debate.

In the post-Lemass era the primary influence has remained modernization theory's premise that Ireland needs to integrate itself more fully with global expansionism in order to acquire the accoutrements of industrialisation. This premise has embraced neoclassical economic assumptions. In Ireland's case it has meant encouraging foreign capital investment, favouring free-market zones (Anglo-Irish Free Trade Agreement, 1966; EC membership, 1973; EMS membership, 1981; EC integration, 1992), accommodating capital-intensive export-oriented development, tying education to industrial requirements and keeping labour costs down.[20]

Endorsement for this strategy has been across the political and social-partner divide. Ironically, it was a 1982 government-sponsored review of industrial strategy which highlighted key defects. The review argued that foreign companies in Ireland were involved primarily in 'low-skill assembly and testing operations with minimal research and development, little independent marketing capacity, limited decision-making functions, and limited supply linkages with the rest of the economy'. Expatriation of profits, amounting to over 10 per cent of GNP in 1989, exaggerated the precariousness of Irish economic performance and potential growth.[21] In the context of global economic restructuring, Telesis warned that Ireland was in danger of becoming a labour-intensive, low-cost, low-wage production centre while high-wage knowledge-intensive activities would be concentrated elsewhere. In the light of public concern about the repatriation of profits by foreign companies, poor economic performance, and catastrophic levels of structural unemployment and migration, debate has subsequently broadened to include consideration of the problems and dangers of peripheralization and late development.

Class structure and migration

Rapid industrialization between 1950 and the mid-1970s has accounted for the most spectacular shift in the Irish class structure. The transformation from a class structure based on family property to one based on skills and educational opportunities has been more rapid and more state-inspired than in most Western societies. In the process the massive decline in agricultural and unskilled manual employment has not been adequately met by expanding, new opportunities for skilled manual and non-manual employment in the public and service sectors.

When growth in manufacturing and construction slackened in the 1970s the government responded with employment measures that rested principally on the use of the public sector. As in previous decades, these openings did not compensate for job losses in terms of either numbers or skill level. Several studies anticipated that, taking account of the number of new entrants to the labour market, 30,000 new jobs would have to be created annually in order to provide full employment by 1986.[22]

In so far as social mobility was a major social force in the 1960s and 1970s, it was available only to those for whom the expanding opportunities in education were already accessible. Breen *et al.* argue that industrial development and expansion provided certain avenues of upward social mobility for a limited time and a limited number. The return to escalating and structural unemployment in the 1980s polarized mobility into two main alternatives: upward mobility for the middle class or unemployment. Approximately one-third of the population survive solely on state subsidy, a position made more untenable given gloomy economic projections and declining state revenues. Ironically, the impact of state policies and industrialization has produced a rigid class structure with growing class polarity, inequality and social immobility, which further undermines the Lemass belief that the 'rising tide would raise all boats'.[23]

These developments underscore the correlation between social structure,

Table 8.2 Irish migration, 1979–91

1979–80	8,000
1980–81	+2,000
1981–82	1,000
1982–83	14,000
1983–84	9,000
1984–85	20,000
1985–86	28,000
1986–87	27,000
1987–88	32,000
1988–89	46,000
1989–90	31,000
1990–91	1,000*

* CSO, estimate subject to census revision in 1991.
Source: *Census*, 1986, CSO, Dublin.

labour force, trends in unemployment and migration. Put simply, Ireland's 'class structure reflects the selective process of emigration . . . as much as it does growth in new opportunities'.[24] In the 1960 and 1970s male migration predominated, accounting for the image of Irish migrants as rural, semi- or unskilled labourers.[25] The economic upturn of the 1960s and 1970s resulted in brief net immigration, recording a rise of 104,000 between 1971 and 1981.[26] Since 1981 the steady rise in unemployment has been matched by a return to migration. A modest resumption was evident in 1979–80, but considerable restrictions on US immigration, and mounting unemployment and inflation in the United Kingdom and most other European economies, were negative determinants at that time. Mass migration recommenced about 1984, reaching a peak of 46,000 in 1988–9 (see Table 8.2). Over the decade an estimated 25 per cent of graduates left for new opportunities, while the unskilled have been forced either to float between destinations or to remain at home, contributing to a large, permanent underclass in Ireland. Consequently, official statistics citing only 1,000 people migrating between 1990 and 1991 conceal the class nature of Irish migration.

Contemporary Irish migrants tend to be highly educated, with commensurate skill levels, to come mainly from an urban environment and to be predominantly young – concentrated in the fifteen-to-twenty-four age group – single and mobile. Analysis of 1980s migrants to the United Kingdom by gender show that males formed a significant majority, possibly reflecting the decline in manufacturing and construction – traditionally bastions of male employment – while female employment was available in the new service sector.[27] Between 1971 and 1988 the small increase in total employment (4 per cent) was mainly attributable to the 27 per cent rise in female employment, centred on the financial and insurance sector, and professional services.[28] Since 1984 there has been a noticeable increase in migration among school leavers in general and third-level graduates in particular. Employment and unemployment remain primary explanations,

Table 8.3   Pattern of first destinations (Ireland and overseas), 1985–90: primary degree (%)

Outcome	1985	1986	1987	1988	1989	1990
Further study/training schemes/work experience	44	42	39	37	38	40
Unemployed	5	6	4	3	3	5
Employed	49	50	56	58	58	53
Left Ireland	16	20	26	26	25	19

Source: HEA, *First Destination of Award Recipients in Higher Education*, (1990), 14, 21.

but respondents to surveys indicate a complex pattern of reasons which also include studying, wider experience and career opportunities, the social conservatism of Irish society – stimulated by a negative reaction to the results of the constitutional referenda on the 'right to life' (1983) and divorce (1986) – and natural mobility away from family and community, which in a small closed society like Ireland virtually necessitates migration.[29]

So noticeable has the change been in the characteristics of migrants that one leading commentator warned of an outflow of 'an inordinately high proportion of highly qualified people' tantamount to a 'brain drain',[30] and possibly leading to a skill shortage in the medium to long term. For this group, migration, which peaked in 1988–9, presented a more realistic option than for less qualified labour. In the year to April 1991 (i.e. 1990 graduates) 19 per cent of primary and 24 per cent of higher-degree holders migrated in harmonization with the fluctuating labour-market demand of certain disciplines. The small decline in graduate migration between 1989 and 1990 was matched by a rise in unemployment and a return to further study (see Table 8.3).[31]

This high skill level is reflected in the widening pattern of employment registered for Irish migrants to the United Kingdom after 1984. They remain disproportionately employed in skilled manual (26 per cent), non-manual (24 per cent) and semi-skilled (19 per cent) work, with some notable departures from previous generations. The 1980 generation shows distinct movement into administrative, professional and managerial occupations. For women the most significant development is their reappearance in the professional category, after an absence of thirty years, and their disappearance from nursing (see Table 8.4).[32]

Expansion in private and state education, and state and EC-sponsored work experience and training schemes, have broadened and developed overall skill levels but also distorted the actual level of under- and unemployment among school leavers, graduates and adult labour. There is little doubt that desire for further study or training is an essential response to global competition, international trends requiring higher qualifications, and greater access to education. Nevertheless, it is clear that this desire fluctuates in tune with the pace of global and domestic economic growth and with the demands of the labour market. In other words, persistent high unemployment is a major factor influencing further education and training schemes, the corollary of which is that the government uses these schemes to massage

Table 8.4 Irish immigrants to the UK by year of entry, gender and occupational group pre-1955 to 1984 (%)

Group	Pre-1955	1955–64	1965–74	1975–9	1980–3	1984+
Male						
I	6.7	4.3	11.7	10.6	21.5	12.9
II	3.6	5.1	3.5	13.7	15.4	–
V	7.6	12.7	6.9	7.6	–	9.7
VI	4.0	3.8	5.3	6.3	–	4.3
XI	13.0	6.9	7.6	7.0	12.5	9.5
XII	13.9	11.0	10.2	13.2	9.7	15.7
XIV	14.2	17.7	18.7	19.4	21.7	37.1
XV	8.2	11.8	21.6	–	–	–
Total No.	40,231	61,840	24,325	6,559	4,200	15,858
Female						
I	1.2	1.8	1.7	16.1	22.9	11.1
II	16.8	16.6	28.7	26.2	38.7	26.4
IV	1.9	–	–	–	–	5.6
V	4.7	6.4	3.6	–	–	3.3
VI	18.3	19.9	23.0	17.6	8.0	25.6
VII	2.1	9.0	13.8	–	16.9	6.4
IX	4.4	36.0	20.9	27.5	13.4	16.0
Total No.	35,369	46,855	19,353	3,474	2,367	10,434

Key. Occupational Group I Management/Administration, II Education, Health, Welfare, III Literary/Artistic, IV Professional, V Managerial, VI Clerical, VII Selling, VIII Security, IX Catering/Cleaning, X Farming/Fishing, XI Non-metal Processing, XII Metal Processing, XIII Printing/Assembling, XIV Construction/Mining, XV Transport, XVI Miscellaneous.

Source: *UK Labour Force Survey*, Office of Population Censuses and Surveys, London, 1988.

the unemployment figures downwards. School leavers have been especially affected by these domestic trends and the downturn in the UK economy. Their third-level participation rates soared in the 1980s, from 21 per cent in 1980 to 36 per cent in 1990, in line with their unemployment levels, which rose from 8 per cent to 18 per cent.[33]

Throughout Western Europe, in the post-Second World War period, semi- and unskilled labourers have moved into manual wage labour, following 'the movement of indigenous labour into a variety of semi- and highly skilled non-manual jobs, especially in the tertiary or service sector of the economy'.[34] The UK labour market has been a principal destination for Irish (rural) migrants, particularly in the light of the absence of sufficient employment growth in Ireland for semi- and unskilled employment following the contraction in agriculture. Reacting rationally to severe economic decline and labour surplus at home, as well as widening differentials in welfare payments, they left in their thousands. In the United Kingdom 'unemployment among . . . [the Irish] was very small compared with the British work force as a whole.'[35]

The rapid expansion of the London economy in the 1980s confirmed traditional patterns; young, low-skilled or unskilled socially immature labour was most heavily employed in construction, metal processing and administration for men, and clerical, education and health, and catering, for women. The wide availability and reportedly high wages of the 1980s London building boom would have contributed to the large numbers of unskilled Irish males migrating and in construction. Distance, stringent qualification requirements, quota restrictions, poor language skills and an unfamiliar social and community environment placed other European countries, the United States and Australia beyond reach. Consequently, low-skilled Irish migrants were disproportionately represented in the United Kingdom, often leading commentators to suggest that discriminatory practices were being invoked by employers. The sharp rise in unemployment levels among post-1980 Irish migrants to the United Kingdom to an average 20 per cent for males and 15 per cent for females reflected the insecurity of their labour-market status. The collapse of the UK boom by 1990 has effectively eliminated this destination, intensifying their transient, casual place in the labour market and inflating unemployment levels in Ireland.

Changes in the global and Irish economies in the 1980s and 1990s have polarized and magnified the class differences in Irish migration patterns. There is no homogeneous group of people identified as migrant labour who fill predetermined positions in the international labour market. Thus the view of Irish migrants as only those who do poorly in low-skilled, low-pay, non-promotional employment is too stereotyped and ignores fundamental class divisions among Irish migrants. Likewise, there have been different migrations of Irish labour, between which comparability is misleading.

State policy

In the nineteenth century most economists believed that Ireland suffered from chronic 'overpopulation'. Senior and Whately urged state assistance to encourage and aid migration in the 1830s in preference to workhouse relief. After the Great Famine, controlled state supervision of migration to Canada, the United States, Australia and New Zealand was widespread. Between 1818 and 1906 over 400,000 people were assisted by state, colonial and private funds and by remittances, equalling a total of £36 million. According to Fitzpatrick, with the surplus population removed, the mean income and duration of employment of those remaining rose; migration was viewed positively, undermining the need for economic development.[36]

This conviction was endorsed years later by Alexis Fitzgerald, a senior member of Fine Gael, in his response to the 1954 report of the Commission on Emigration and other Population Problems, wherein he argued that migration was not a

> sign of national decline . . . [nor should] policy . . . be over-anxiously framed to reduce it . . . High emigration, granted a population excess, releases social tensions which would otherwise explode and makes possible a stability of manners and customs which would otherwise be the subject of radical change. It is a national advantage that it is easy for emigrants to establish their lives in other

parts of the world not merely from the point of view of the Irish society they leave behind but from the point of view of the individuals concerned whose horizon of opportunity is widened. . . . High emigration might in the circumstances be a sign of our vitality.[37]

This view seems to have been shared, if not in public at least in government memos. The exodus of 100,000, mostly male, from Ireland to the United Kingdom between 1939 and 1945 enabled record unemployment to fall from 15 per cent to 10 per cent. Although the problem posed by a 'potentially dangerous labour surplus' was solved by its departure, it resurfaced in anticipation of the end of the war. Lemass sought to use this financial and labour threat to influence de Valera towards an expansionist policy. In this he was influenced by the Assistant Secretary of External Affairs, F. H. Boland, who warned of the 'danger of social revolution' in Ireland following the 'British authorities' [desire] to rush all these workers . . . [(who have no doubt imbibed a good deal of "leftism" in Britain)] . . . back to this country as quickly as they can . . .'.[38] The anxiety raised by this 'doomsday' scenario faded, however, once it became clear that British post-war reconstruction and superior welfare benefits would retain existing labour. In so doing it again undermined pressure to pursue an expansionary strategy.

Other explanations saw the migration experience as miserable, lonely and, for women, sexually threatening. The *Freeman's Journal* of 1908 accused migrants of giving 'up more than they know . . . [and choosing] . . . tawdry, uncertain splendours . . .'.[39] This attempt to draw a correlation between poverty and spirituality was also evident in Fitzgerald's 'Reservation' when he referred to migration as a

> vocation for the nation . . . In order of values, it seems more important to preserve and improve the quality of life and thereby the purity of that message which our people have communicated to the world than it is to reduce the numbers of Irish emigrants.

Two conclusions can be drawn: Irish migrants voted with their feet either to preserve traditional Ireland for their remaining relatives and friends or to reject unreservedly de Valera's dream of 'a people . . . satisfied with a frugal comfort and devoted . . . to the things of the spirit'.[40]

Despite public disquiet about migration, there was also public complicity. Those left behind enjoyed a higher standard of living than would have been possible, given the country's economic performance, if revenue was required to finance unemployment and other welfare benefits for the escalating unemployed. Commenting on the Commission of Emigration's report, Geary and McCarthy acknowledged that people were not prepared to make sacrifices to end migration:

> The forced cessation of emigration would lead to heavy unemployment, a lowering of wage rates and a reduction of the average standard of living. It is very doubtful if the people would freely consent to pay the price of stopping emigration . . .[41]

In addition, migration influenced employment chances by depleting key age categories; this created a 'relative shortage of people to fill . . . positions of seniority and responsibility . . . [leading to] an exceptionally rapid rate of promotion of young people to senior posts'.[47] The *Irish Banking Review* could therefore justifiably argue, in 1958, that migration provided a 'useful safety valve'.[43]

These explanations managed to sidestep traditional assumptions about the link between legislative autonomy and economic growth.[44] Those who sought to improve their standard of living did so from individual choice and not because of any indictment of Irish economic performance. This view was echoed by Department of External Affairs memos of 1947 which pinpointed 'those obscure, traditional, psychological factors' rather than economic necessity.[45] Acceptance of economic factors clearly carried economic and political implications.

The adoption of an interventionist policy in the 1950s under Lemass marked the rejection of what Lee calls the 'escapist school of policymakers'.[46] Instead the Irish state pursued a positive and appreciative view, accepting that it was 'reasonable' in the circumstance to migrate in search of a decent livelihood. In line with other states of the Western European periphery, the export of a proportion of the (surplus) population was viewed as a means of overcoming relative backwardness or underdevelopment, assisting the spread of the capitalist mode of production and increasing industrial employment.[47] Suggestions that restrictions on the exodus of key workers should be introduced were rejected in preference for an interventionist role by the state, either silently condoning or actively encouraging migration. Like the Turkish state in the 1960s and 1970s, Irish governments have subsequently facilitated migration as a means of alleviating social and political tension, providing additional skills and experience, and earning income through remittances and tourism. During the 1980s governments used financial and political resources to widen migrant opportunities and services.

A key element of this strategy has been the extraordinary level of government and media attention to lobbying and reporting on US immigration policy, which now favours skills over family ties. This approach was taken to extremes during 1991, when a Fianna Fáil senator initially sought to negotiate a special postal arrangement for thousands of US Morrison visa applications and, failing that, flew to the United States in order to circumvent an Irish postal dispute. Computerization of the leaving certificate results process and the speeding up of university placement acknowledgements have occurred partly in order to facilitate easier access to UK third-level educational institutions, which unlike Irish ones are free under EC regulations and short of students. Educational policy has deliberately sought to equip prospective graduate migrants by extending modern language teaching beyond Irish and French to include German and Spanish.

As argued above, the collapse of indigenous manufacturing has not been met by past economic performance or current government strategies, which are directed at high-technology industries and the financial sector. While global and domestic demand for highly skilled labour will continue, albeit at fluctuating levels, less skilled Irish labour has been most susceptible to unemployment. Deindustrialization, the reduction in unskilled manufacturing in favour of services, and economic crisis in, *inter alia*, the United Kingdom in the early 1990s, have effectively cut off this accessible option, giving way to historic levels of unemployment. The structural nature of unemployment is particularly acute, but so also is the structural basis of Irish migration.

The new international division of labour and Irish migration

The long wave of economic expansion from the end of the Second World War to the early 1970s was the most rapid and sustained period of development in recorded history, with world capitalist output doubling between 1952 and 1968.[48] Underpinning and sustaining the success of that expansion, a large supply of labour was pulled in as 'post-war Europe had exhausted or was unable, for ideological or demographic reasons, to further draw on its traditional internal labour reservoirs'.[49] Labour from southern Europe, the Maghreb and Turkey was actively facilitated and encouraged, through formal and informal arrangements, to migrate as 'temporary' guest workers to north-east Europe by respective host and sender countries.[50] Recruitment of labour from outside national boundaries is a further phase in the 'internationalization of the labour market'.[51]

Migrant labour had particular advantages; capital could recruit 'ready-made' labour power without having to meet its costs of production. Migrants were initially recruited into low- and semi-skilled manual sectors, in particular construction, manufacturing and services, which had been vacated by indigenous labour moving into higher-skilled non-manual employment. The majority of migrants subsequently moved into positions in key sectors integral to capitalist expansion and accumulation, becoming a permanent part of the economic structure.[52] In this respect there was, argues Cohen, a structural necessity for migrant labour.[53]

The post-1970s, in contrast, have been characterized by a global economic slump, the magnitude of which has not been overcome by reference to trade or business cycle models. The decline in the rate of economic growth reduced the rate of growth of world output in the 1980s to less than half that of the 1960s, and that of world trade even further. The severity and protracted nature of this crisis has triggered a fundamental restructuring of the world capitalist economy, incorporating the following features: (1) growing integration via world trade, seamless international financial markets and cross-border investments by transnational corporations (TNCs); (2) geographical extension of the market to new areas, e.g. South East Asia, Africa, and South America; (3) intensification of markets within societies and the opening up of new markets in developing societies; and (4) a shift in the power balance, particularly acute in the aftermath of the collapse of 'communism' and the Gulf War. These developments occurred side by side with a strategy aimed at accelerating the rate of profit or capital accumulation through rearranging the relations of production, and reorganizing the labour process. Transnational corporations, controlling the main technologically advanced sectors of the global economy, succeeded in circumventing and superseding national boundaries and barriers and in creating mutually dependent state–corporate partnerships.

In contrast to post–Second World War expansion, the structural needs of late capitalism no longer include continuous imports of unskilled migrants. The relative or perhaps absolute decline in manufacturing and the advance of microtechnology suggests that 'the presence of a large manual labour force has ceased to be a prerequisite of industrial production'.[54] Globalization has shifted the emphasis from the import of labour to the export of capital, making it possible to subdivide commodity production and the production process. With developments in transport and communication, complete or partial production can occur wherever the most profitable combination of capital and labour exists.[55] This emergence of a new international division of labour has heightened the transnational character of the labour process, creating a world market for labour and production sites.

Because the range of economic tasks is not evenly distributed throughout the world system, a hierarchy of occupational tasks is established. Knowledge-intensive sectors with their emphasis on high levels of skill and greater capitalization are reserved for core states, while low-skill, labour-intensive activities dominate peripheral and semi-peripheral regions. This bisection has been assisted by advances in deskilling, enabling minimal levels of skill to be learnt easily. The 'capitalist world–economy essentially rewards accumulated capital, including human capital, at a higher rate than "raw" labor [*sic*] power . . .', thus escalating global inequality between dominant and dependent economies.[56]

The impact of these developments on labour is striking, reproducing on a global level changes already witnessed in the structure of the Irish labour market: (1) a shrinkage in agricultural employment in advanced capitalist countries, (2) stabilization of or a slight drop in manufacturing employment in these same economies, (3) an increase in information–related employment and (4) growth in the strategic world cities of service employment.[57] Recognition of a practically inexhaustible supply of disposable low-skill labour in developing countries has enabled and encouraged transnational corporations to concentrate labour-intensive production there, displacing migrant labour at home while producing complex political and social contradictions. In the 1980s the racially inspired demands of the anti-immigrant lobby across Europe coincided with the requirements of the new international division of labour and capital to find alternative, cheaper labour. This simultaneously raised a political dilemma for states possessed of a settled migrant community with guaranteed 'rights' in a period of increasing unemployment. In these endeavours, states were partially defended and aided by EC regulations seeking to 'police' frontiers. In the post-1970s unskilled migrant labour in Western Europe was no longer a structural necessity.

The transformation of the Common Market into an integrated political and economic supra-state has prioritized the need for an 'internal market' of capital and labour. The Single European Act and other EC policy measures endorse the right of the European citizen to move freely, prohibit any discrimination on grounds of nationality and seek to provide absolute harmonization across, *inter alia*, qualifications, labour markets and the right of entry.[58] Integration will encourage 'fluid exchanges' of labour, with skilled persons moving all over the Community, thereby 'constitut- ing [a] particularly significant net migrating movement'.[59] These initia- tives confirm the determination by European capital to create a 'transnational space within which the circulation of workers can be regarded as one of several flows, including capital, goods, services and information'.[60]

A key assumption of migration studies is that the basic causes are poverty, overpopulation and a stagnant economy. While many peripheral countries have these problems, not all have significant migration. In Ireland's case, persistent unemployment, poor economic prospects and state initiatives have contributed to a 'culture' of migration. Sustained efforts to internationalize the Irish economy have linked Irish migration with devel- opments in the international labour market. In this respect, as Sassen argues, 'it may be that particular forms of incorporation into the inter- nationalisation of production coalesce with basic causes to promote emigration'.[61]

It is in the context of concerted policy efforts to transform hitherto autonomous and unequal European economies into a single global player that EC efforts to break down barriers to labour mobility and recruit- ment must be seen. In turn, they cannot be isolated from global econ- omic restructuring; thus EC strategy for economic growth is linked with establishing a dominant role for itself *vis-à-vis* Japan and the United States within the world economy. This means increased emphasis on high technology and valorization production aimed at the control and management of the global economy. An obstacle to this strategy is the recognizable shortage of highly skilled labour. These developments impinge on Ireland in two interrelated ways: migration and the economy.

Conclusion

The resurgence of mass migration from Ireland in the 1980s coincided with growing under- and unemployment among Irish graduates at home and an economic take-off and a growing skills shortage in the UK, US and other advanced capitalist economies. A fall in British population and increased graduate migration have forced UK employers to intensify their recruit- ment of skilled Irish labour to compensate for their own depleting labour pool. These problems were highlighted in a *Guardian* survey which showed that 49 per cent of UK graduates would prefer to work abroad after completing their studies.[62] Similar reports from the United States confirm that:

> the existing gap in work skills could widen to a chasm; [the] rapid decline in the numbers of young people now entering the work force, . . . [caused by the]

1970s baby bust, coupled with rising illiteracy and school drop-out rates, could produce a shortfall of 23 million American workers by the early 1990s.[63]

In circumstances of rapidly expanding needs of the financial, service and construction sectors, the labour needs of which cannot be met domestically, Irish labour has provided a reasonably local, white, English-speaking alternative. Not surprisingly, almost 18 per cent of the Irish population were living elsewhere in the EC in 1989, the highest figure for any member state.[64] 7   The demand for high skilled graduate migration from Ireland is set to continue. EC measures to 'complete the internal market' through skilled labour mobility – on a permanent, temporary or exchange basis – is an essential solution of anticipated labour market imbalances, particularly in the light of evidence that intra-European migration is declining in all member states of the Council of Europe.[65] The German IAB Prognos study on occupational trends until 2010 forecast an increase of 3.4 million jobs in highly skilled occupations, and a loss of 2 million unskilled and low-skilled jobs.[64] Eurostat predictions in 1988 of a 6 million fall in the EC labour force aged fifteen to twenty-five years between 1990 and 2000 must be seen alongside the fact that, with 28 per cent of its population under fifteen years, Ireland has the youngest Western European population, with the exception of Turkey.[67] These factors converge to the benefit of Irish graduates, albeit the impact of migration from Eastern Europe is unclear. Alarm about a possible skill shortage in Ireland will not mitigate the greater demand for labour across the EC and United States, prompted by a demographic and a 'qualitative' skills gap – the latter being the difference between the qualifications possessed and those required. The net effect is likely to be outward rather than inward migration.

The down side of economic restructuring is the decline in unskilled and semi-skilled manufacturing employment via the impact of the new international division of labour. This does not necessarily mean that all such jobs will be 'eliminated from Western European capitalist economies, if only because not all sectors and processes employing such labour can be exported'.[68] Construction and a wide range of service industries are examples. Nevertheless, coupled with the overall decline in manufacturing and agriculture both in Ireland and in other potential host countries, unskilled Irish labour is particularly vulnerable, as recent UK events illustrate. A resumption of large-scale migration of unskilled manual workers as has occurred in the past is unlikely; not only is demand for this type of labour diminishing but an increasing proportion of service employment requires minimum communicative ability.[69]

The new international division of labour, with its demarcation between knowledge-intensive and labour-intensive sectors and localities, will accentuate Ireland's peripheral status in the global economy. The lack of sufficient highly skilled employment in Ireland is a reflection of the predominance of small companies in low-technology industrial sectors, poor investment in R&D and foreign capital's investment strategy. Firm size affects the ability to offer high salaries, good promotion prospects and career development and further training.[70] The exodus of skilled

professional, technical and managerial labour confirms survey data showing a strong correlation between skill or occupational level and career
aspiration.[71] Transnational corporations have chosen to retain R&D at the
core and to locate low-skilled assembly-type production in Ireland, poach-
ing or asset-stripping high-quality technical and scientific skills in the
process. The tendency of the new international division of labour will be
to intensify the split between core and periphery by draining highly
skilled labour out of the latter, concentrating growth sectors in key core
cities (of which London is one), and producing an array of specialized
services, including financial services. The strategy behind the Financial
Services Centre, established in Dublin in the late 1980s, corresponded to
these global developments by endeavouring to catapult Ireland to the
status of a core city of the emergent information economy. Politically the
concept was a means of attracting back highly skilled migrants, albeit
there is a lack of control over returnees.

The decline in manufacturing and agriculture is a function of economic
restructuring and not simply a moment of crisis. The historical pattern
which showed a correlation between economic growth and unemployment is not part of this new configuration; Irish profits and productivity
have climbed since the mid-1980s but overall employment has fallen,
producing the phenomenon of job-deficient growth. The collapse in traditional manufacturing employment has disproportionately affected males in
contrast to expanding foreign and service sector preferences for females.
With the contraction in low-skill employment in key host destinations,
such migration is effectively closed. Rising mass unemployment in
Ireland, impacting on an already polarized social structure and labour
market, appears likely.

Public attention has focused on the possibility of a skill shortage, offering contradictory scenarios affecting different skills and qualifications, and
its impact on economic take-off. This has led to questioning whether the
Irish state should underwrite the educational cost of skills that are used
principally by other (core) economies.[72] Related issues have, however,
received less attention: the effect of a loss of skilled labour on the labour
market and labour mobility generally; the implications of declining
domestic employment and migration opportunities for unskilled and
semi-skilled labour. O'Malley's argument that the rapid industrial growth
of the 1960s and 1970s was an 'exceptional experience . . . a temporary
phenomenon . . . which eventually passes' widens the debate
significantly.[73]

Opinion polls reveal a deep ambiguity about migration, ranging between anger, acceptance and compliance.[74] Popularized explanations have
steered away from asking whether migration is an irrevocable structural
result of peripheralization and the new international division of labour or
a victim of specific (and hence alterable) politico-economic policies.
Because of the implications of the latter, there has been a long-standing
effort at official level to describe migration as positive and attribute blame
to cultural and islandic factors or natural phenomena:

196   *Ellen Hazelkorn*

What we have now is a very literate emigrant who thinks nothing of coming to the United States and going back to Ireland and maybe on to Germany and back to Ireland again. . . . The world is now one world and they can always return to Ireland with the skills they have developed. We regard them as part of a global generation of Irish people. We shouldn't be defeatist or pessimistic about it. We should be proud of it. After all, we can't all live on a small island.[75]

This chapter has argued, in contrast, that migration is a 'rational' response to Irish underdevelopment and internationalization of the economy and labour market. Global economic restructuring has witnessed 'persistent, indeed deepening, income inequality among the regions and political jurisdictions into which the world–economy is divided'.[76] Within this structure, surplus highly skilled Irish labour will continue to be exported to core economies, facilitated by government initiatives, augmenting the international labour market for particular specialized non-manual skills. Bleak migration and employment prospects for low-skilled Irish illustrate the essentially class nature of migration and, in so far as they challenge traditional images, argue against overgeneralizing the migration experience.

Notes

1. 'Ireland' refers to the Republic of Ireland or, prior to independence in 1922, to the island of Ireland.
2. See, for example, S. Castles, and G. Kosack, *Immigrant Workers and Class Structures in Western Europe*, Oxford University Press, London, 1973; S. Castles with Heather Booth and Tina Wallace, *Here for Good: Western Europe's New Ethnic Minorities*, Pluto Press, London, 1984; Bobby Gilmore, 'Emigration begins before you climb on the boat', in J. Mulholland and D. Keogh, eds., *Emigration, Employment and Enterprise*, Hibernian University Press, Cork and Dublin, 1989, pp. 46–51; Tom O'Connor, 'Irish Youth in London', research report, Action group for Irish Youth, London.
3. Karl Marx, *Capital* 1, International Publishers, New York, 1967, pp. 697–712; Friedric Engels, *The Condition of the Working Class in England*, trans. W. O. Henderson and W. H. Chaloner, Stanford University Press, Stanford, Cal., 1958, pp. 104–7; see Ellen Hazelkorn, '*Capital* and the Irish Question', *Science and Society*, 44, 3, 1980, pp. 326–56.
4. Tom O'Connor, *The London Irish*, Strategic Policy Unit, London, 1987; see also Bronwen Walter, *Irish Women in London*, Strategic Policy Unit, London, 1988; London Strategic Policy Committee (Race Equality Policy sub-committee), 'The Irish Community', unpublished, 1986; Gearoid O'Meachair and Ada Burns, 'Irish Homelessness: the Hidden Dimension', Cara Homeless Project, London, 1988.
5. Cf. Robert Miles and Victor Satzewich, 'Migration, racism and "postmodern" capitalism', *Economy and Society*, 19, 3, 1990, p. 337.
6. For example, Marie O'Shea, Introduction, Report by Brent Irish Mental Health Group, n.d.
7. E. Hazelkorn, *Irish Immigrants Today: a Socio-economic Profile of Contemporary Irish Emigrants and Immigrants in the UK*, Polytechnic of North London, London, 1990; Ellen Hazelkorn, 'Irish labour and British capital: evidence from the 1980s', in Galway Labour History Group, eds., *The Emigrant Experience*, Galway Labour History Group, Galway, 1991.

8. John Salt, 'International labour migration: the geographical pattern of demand', in J. Salt and H. Clout, eds., *Migration in Post-war Europe: Geographical Essays*, Oxford University Press, London, 1976, pp. 80–125; John Salt, 'International labour migration in Western Europe: a geographical review', in Mary M. Kritz, Charles B. Keely and Silvano M. Tomasi, eds., *Global Trends in Migration: Theory and Research on International Population Movements*, Centre for Migration Studies, New York, 1981, pp. 133–57; Robin Cohen, *The New Helots: Migrants in the International Division of Labour*, Gower, Aldershot, 1987; Lydia Potts, *The World Labour Market: a History of Migration*, trans. Terry Bond, Zed Books, London and Atlantic Highlands, N.J., 1990.

9. Demetrios G. Papademetriou, 'International migration in North America and Western Europe: trends and consquences', in Reginald Appleyard, ed., *International Migration Today 1, Trends and Prospects*, UNESCO and Centre for Migration and Development Studies, Paris, and University of Western Australia, Nedlands, 1988, pp. 311–80.

10. John Salt, 'Contemporary trends in international migration study', *International Migration*, 15, 1987, pp. 241–51.

11. Kerby A. Miller, *Emigrants and Exiles: Ireland and the Irish Exodus to North America*, Oxford University Press, New York and Oxford, 1985, p. 569; cf. Miles and Satzewich, 'Migration'.

12. Folker Frobel, Jurgen Heinrichs and Otto Kreye, *The New International Division of Labour*, Maison des Sciences de l'Homme, Paris, and Cambridge University Press, Cambridge, 1980; Saskia Sassen Koob, 'The new labour demand: conditions for the absorption of immigrant workers in the United States', in Charles W. Stahl, ed., *International Migration Today 2, Emerging Issues*, UNESCO and Centre for Migration and Development Studies, Paris, and University of Western Australia, Nedlands, 1988, pp. 81–104.

13. Proinnsias Breathnach, and John Jackson, 'Ireland, emigration and the new international division of labour', in Russell King, ed., *Contemporary Irish Migration*, Geographical Society of Ireland, Dublin, 1991, pp. 1–10.

14. James Wickham and Peter Murray, 'Filling the Bath and forgetting to put the Plug in? Irish Graduate Emigration and the new European Labour Market', Trinity College Employment Research Unit, Dublin, 1989, unpublished.

15. Kieran A. Kennedy, Thomas Giblin and Deirdre McHugh, *The Economic Development of Ireland in the Twentieth Century*, Routledge, London, 1988, pp. 45–6.

16. Sean Glynn, 'Irish immigration to Britain, 1911–51: patterns and policy', *Irish Economic and Social History*, 8, 1981, pp. 50–69; Robert E. Kennedy Jr, *The Irish: Emigration, Marriage and Fertility*, University of California Press, Berkeley, Cal. 1973, pp. 74–5.

17. Breathnach and Jackson, 'Emigration', p. 4.

18. Paul Tansey 'Irish industry's profits boom and rise is set to continue', *Sunday Tribune*, Dublin, 21 August, 1988; 'Ireland takes the prize for job-deficient growth', *Sunday Tribune*, Dublin, 3 November, 1991.

19. Figures based on the 'live' register of people 'signing on' at employment exchanges, cite a much higher number of unemployed: 270,000, or 21 per cent, at the end of 1991.

20. Eoin O'Malley, *Industry and Economic Development: the Challenge for the Latecomer*, Gill & Macmillan, Dublin, 1989, pp. 8–10; Paul Bew, Ellen Hazelkorn and Henry Patterson, *The Dynamics of Irish Politics*, Lawrence & Wishart, London, 1989.

21. Breathnach and Jackson, 'Emigration', p. 5; Telesis Consultancy Group, *A*

Review of Industrial Policy, NESC, Dublin, 1982, pp. 149–55.

22. Brendan Walsh, *Population and Employment Protections, 1971–86*, ESRI, Dublin, 1975.

23. Richard Breen, Damian F. Hannan, David B. Rottman and Christopher T. Whelan, *Understanding Contemporary Ireland*, Gill & Macmillan, Dublin, 1990.

24. Christopher T. Whelan, Richard Breen and Brendan J. Whelan, 'Industrialisation, Class Formation and Social Mobility in Ireland', unpublished conference paper, Nuffield College, Oxford, 1990, p. 4.

25. Robert Kennedy, *The Irish*, p. 81; Pauline Jackson, 'Migrant women: the Republic of Ireland, 1987', EC, DG: Employment, Social Affairs and Education, Brussels, 1987, p. 7.

26. P. J. Drudy, 'Irish population change and emigration since independence', *The Irish in America: Emigration, Assimilation and Impact*, Cambridge University Press, Cambridge, 1985, pp. 76–8.

27. Hazelkorn, *Irish Immigrants Today*.

28. Rosheen Callandar, 'Women and Work – the more Things Change . . .?', unpublished, 1989.

29. See National Economic and Social Council, *The Economic and Social Implications of Emigration*, NESC, Dublin, 1991.

30. J. J. Sexton, 'Recent changes in the Irish population and in the pattern of emigration', *Irish Banking Review*, autumn 1987.

31. Higher Education Authority, *First Destination of Award Recipients in Higher Education: a Composite Report*, HEA, Dublin, 1987, 1988, 1989, 1990.

32. Hazelkorn, *Irish Immigrants Today*.

33. Department of Labour, *Economic Status of School Leavers*, Dublin, 1985, 1986, 1987, 1988, 1990; Richard Breen and Brendan Whelan with John Costigan, *School Leavers, 1980–85*, Department of Labour, Dublin, 1986.

34. Miles and Satzewich, 'Migration', p. 313.

35. Glynn, 'Irish immigration', p. 67.

36. David Fitzpatrick, *Irish Emigration, 1801–1921*, Economic and Social History of Ireland, Dublin, 1984, pp. 17–9.

37. Alexis Fitzgerald, Reservation No. 3, *Reports of the Commission on Emigration and other Population Problems, 1948–54*, Dublin, 1954.

38. Quoted in J. J. Lee, *Ireland, 1912–85: Politics and Society*, Cambridge University Press, Cambridge, 1989, pp. 226–7.

39. Quoted in Lee, *Ireland*, p. 376; see also pp. 374–87.

40. Eamonn de Valera, St Patricks Day speech, 1943, in Maurice Moynihan, ed., *Speeches and Statements by Eamonn de Valera, 1917–73*, Gill & Macmillan, Dublin, and St Martins Press, New York, 1980, pp. 466–9.

41. R. C. Geary, and M. D. McCarthy, Addendum 2, in *Reports of the Commission on Emigration*.

42. Brendan M. Walsh, *Ireland's Changing Demographic Structure*, Gill & Macmillan, Dublin, 1989, p. 16.

43. 'Favourable aspects of the Irish economy', *Irish Banking Review*, December 1958, p. 8.

44. See David S. Johnson and Liam Kennedy, 'Nationalist historiography and the decline of the Irish economy: George O'Brien revisited', in Sean Hutton and Paul Stewart, eds., *Ireland's Histories: Aspects of State, Society and Ideology*, Routledge, London and New York, 1991, pp. 11–35.

45. Lee, *Ireland*, p. 377.

46. Lee, *Ireland*, p. 386.

47. Robert Miles, 'Labour migration, racism and capital accumulation in Western

Europe since 1945: an overview', *Capital and Class*, 29, 1986, p. 59.
48. Castles with Booth and Wallace, p. 20.
49. Cohen, *The New Helots*, p. 120.
50. Papademetriou, 'International migration', p. 343.
51. Miles, 'Labour migration', p. 55.
52. Miles, 'Labour migration', p. 71.
53. Cohen, *The New Helots*, p. 31.
54. Roger Ballard, 'The political economy of migration: Pakistan, Britain, and the Middle East', in Jeremy Eades, ed., *Migrants, Workers, and the Social Order*, ASA Monographs 26, Tavistock, London and New York, 1987, pp. 17–8.
55. Frobel, Heinrich's and Kreye, pp. 13, 34–7.
56. Immanuel Wallerstein, *The Modern World-System*, Academic Press, New York, 1974, p. 350.
57. Cohen, *The New Helots*, p. 251.
58. Commission of the European Communities, *Completing the Internal Market. White Paper from the Commission to the European Council*, COM (85) 310 final, Milan, 28–9 June 1985; Jean-Claude Séché, *Freedom of Movement in the Community*, EC, Brussels, 1988.
59. Wickham and Murray, 'Filling the bath'.
60. Saskia Sassen, *The Mobility of Labour and Capital: a Study in International Investment and Labour Flow*, Cambridge University Press, Cambridge, 1988, p. 3.
61. Sassen, *The Mobility of Labour*, p. 4.
62. Quoted in the *Irish Times*, Dublin, 11 September 1989; see also Ian Shuttleworth, 'Graduate emigration from Ireland: a symptom of peripherality?', in King, *Contemporary Irish Migration*, pp. 83–95.
63. Michael Kiernan, Studying the forces shaping the workplace will get you a better job', *U.S. News and World Report*, 25 September 1989, pp. 61–2.
64. Commission of the European Communities, DG: Employment, Industrial Relations and Social Affairs, *Employment in Europe*, COM (91) 248 final, Luxembourg, 1991, p. 85.
65. Damien A. Courtney, 'Demographic Trends in Ireland and Western Europe in the 1980s', Dublin, 1991, unpublished.
66. EC, *Employment in Europe*, p. 131.
67. J. J. Sexton, 'The Economic and Social Consequences of Emigration', Dublin, 1991, unpublished.
68. Miles, 'Labour migration', p. 71.
69. EC, *Employment in Europe*, p. 87.
70. Shuttleworth, 'Graduate emigration', p. 86.
71. For example, see James Walsh, 'To go or not to go? The migration intentions of leaving certificate students', Discussion Paper 2, Carysfort College, Dublin, 1984, unpublished; Derek Forrest, *Managerial Emigration*, Irish National Productivity Committee, Dublin, 1967; Shuttleworth, 'Graduate emigration'.
72. See, for example, Eamonn de Valera, speech in Dáil Éireann, 12–13 July 1928, in Moynihan, *Speeches and Statements by Eamonn de Valera*, p. 154; Brendan Walsh, 'Emigration: some policy issues', *Irish Banking Review*, summer 1989; James Wickham, The over-educated engineer? The work, education and careers of Irish electronic engineers, *Journal of Irish Business and Administrative Research*, 10, 1989.
73. O'Malley, *Industry and Economic Development*, p. 265.
74. See *Irish Times*, 21 June 1989; *Irish Independent*, 4 February 1987; MRBI/*Irish Times*, 28 November, 1989.

75. Brian Lenihan, *Newsweek* interview, quoted in *Irish Times*, 13 October 1987; cf. Seamus Martin, 'Comely maidens dancing skilfully at the crossroads', *Irish Times*, 17 October, 1987.

76. Giovanni Arrighi, 'World income inequalities and the future of socialism', *New Left Review*, 189, 1991, p. 39.

9 White skin, white masks: psychological distress among the Irish in Britain

Liam Greenslade

I am talking millions of men [*sic*] who have been skilfully injected with fear, inferiority complexes, trepidation, servility, despair, abasement. [Aimé Césaire]

Introduction: the people that God made mad

Background and point of departure

This chapter is concerned with the high prevalence of mental illness among Irish people living in Britain. Rates per 100,000 of the population for mental hospital admissions in England and Wales in 1971,[1] and repeated for England in 1981,[2] showed that Irish people, from both the Republic and Northern Ireland, had and continue to have the highest rates of admission to mental hospital of any migrant or ethnic/racial group. In particular, rates for Irish women were the highest of all groups, being more than double that for English-born women in the same periods.

What I intend to do is review the psychological, epidemiological and morbidity data relating to Irish people both as migrants and in their home country from a historical and a contemporary perspective. In pursuing this task I hope to accomplish two things: (1) to suggest that the incidence and characteristics of mental illness among Irish people can best be understood in theoretical terms derived from the work of Fanon on the effects of colonialism[3] and (2) to generate awareness among both Irish and English people regarding the serious and pressing nature of the problems facing the migrant community in England. In pursuing these aims, my intention is, first, to present the data relating to mental illness among the migrant Irish population, in England and elsewhere; second, to outline the work of Fanon on the psychopathological effects of the colonialist discourse, and, third, to offer an analytical framework that addresses the specific conditions of Irish people and which offers some alternative for developing a therapeutic approach.

Before commencing this project, however, in order to avoid confusion later, I would like to begin by stating some of the premisses that condition both the tone and content of the chapter.

A socio-psychological perspective on mental illness

Illness, even in the physical sense, is a socially constructed notion that has consequences independent of the biological organism.[4] The tendency to utilize a medical model of illness in regard to social psychological and behavioural dysfunction directs attention on to the individual and away from the social, historical, political and economic circumstances that surround the sufferer. This person then becomes a victim, of a disease entity, of bad genes, of a weak constitution, and remedies are sought for these personal factors, and both attention and resources are directed away from the surrounding socio-historical milieu in which the person's dysfunction occurs.

It is my belief that the vast majority of mentally ill people are not 'ill' in the sense proposed by the medical model of illness and its social practices. What such people are, in fact, are the physical manifestation, the 'symptoms', of the oppression, contradictions and pathologies in the society in which they live. They are a consequence that cannot be cured at the level of the individual. As a result, energies directed towards the treatment of such people, on the basis of a medical model that ignores the wider context, is misdirected, since it can never be more than a form of social control, the adaptation of human beings to the existing perversity of their experience.

A social psychological perspective of the kind that I am advocating seeks to circumvent this shortcoming in our understanding of madness, not merely by refuting the concept of mental illness, as some theorists have attempted,[5] transforming it into a purely sociological process,[6] or recasting its description in sociological terms.[7] Rather the aim is to grasp the idea of madness, in both its social and its psychological aspects simultaneously, by recognizing that, although it is primarily manifest as a phenomenon at the level of the individual, that individual does not exist in the abstract.

The position advocated here is not a simple one, but it can be stated simply. Levels of madness in a given society are a direct function of the contradiction between the socially organized nature of experience and the ideological means of rendering that experience intelligible. In this view, madness arises within a community when the members of that community experience a disjunction between the practices and processes of everyday life and the means they have at their disposal for articulating in a coherent and intelligible manner their experience of these activities. Such people are not merely alienated in the classical sense of the term, they are in fact alienated from their very experience of the world, since all experience is understood ideologically.

Power plays a crucial role in this analysis. But it must be remembered, as Foucault[8] has pointed out, that power does not merely function to oppress or destroy, it also functions to produce and reproduce. The psychologically oriented studies of madness in the family of Laing and his colleagues[9] and the Palo Alto Group[10] go some way to illustrating this point. The power to produce madness by the imposition of the pathological constraints implicit in the double bind[11] is wielded in an unconscious fashion by the non-mad parents and other family members. It arises outside of the institution of the family in the contradictions and double binds that the family members confront in their gender, race, class and other practical social relations, separately or in combination.

In the social psychological view adopted here, the practices typical of the family micro-system are regarded as operating analogously at the level of the macro-system of society as a whole. Institutions do not operate directly upon individuals to induce madness. Rather, it is the contradictions within and between institutions and ideological apparatuses (e.g. education, the legal system, the economic base, religion, etc.) that are left to individuals to reconcile and at the same time preserve an ideologically coherent notion of identity that enables them to function in relation to those institutions and ideological apparatuses. As we shall see later, the question of an 'Irish' identity becomes a crucial factor in understanding the psychological conditions of the Irish migrant in Britain.

Britain and Ireland: colonialism and after

My second premiss concerns the relationship between Ireland and England. It is my view that Ireland is the nearest equivalent in Europe to a developing country. A former colony of Britain – in fact perhaps the first part of the offshore empire – Ireland has over its history suffered conditions of colonial violence, oppression and expropriation, underdevelopment and clientism comparable with any former British colony in the developing world.[12]

With part of it still engaged in a struggle for liberation from British imperialism, the Irish economy and infrastructure have depended for their survival on the export of one principal raw material; people. In a period when the population of the developed world doubled, that of Ireland halved. Even today, although Ireland has one of the highest birth rates in Europe, its population is falling, owing to migration.[13]

There is insufficient space here to provide an adequate discussion of the colonial situation with regard to Ireland, or to elaborate in detail the consequences of post-colonial Anglo-Irish relations as they are encountered by Irish migrants to England. What I intend to do, however, is propose a number of factors arising directly from the country's colonial history that have a bearing upon Irish experience, both at home and abroad. The first and foremost of these are the economic consequences of colonialism. Typical of all colonial powers, the British in Ireland systematically underdeveloped the productive economy of the country, tying it primarily to the production of unfinished materials and agricultural goods which were expropriated on terms determined by the colonial power.

The now familiar methods of colonial terror and intimidation were inflicted first upon the Irish: the institutionalization of English as the dominant language, the settlement and exclusion of natives from parts of their country, the characterization of natives as savages, unfit to govern themselves, as children, as non-rational, as primitive.[14] When persuasion and economic control failed to persuade the Irish of their colonial status, violence was used to destroy their confidence.

Perhaps the greatest act of violence, and the one with most relevance to the present argument, came during the middle of the nineteenth century in the form of the Great Famine. By this time a nationalist bourgeoisie had developed in Ireland that had become increasingly vociferous in its demands for an independent Ireland. Civil disorder threatened colonial rule, and its saviour came in the mass starvation and emigration that followed from the Great Hunger of 1845–9. Typically portrayed as a natural disaster, as are contemporary famines in Ethiopia and elsewhere, the effects of the Famine bore less relation to an ecological catastrophe than to a logical outcome of colonial rule, which the British exploited for their own ends.

The consequences of the Famine have lasted until the present day. It is estimated that between 1845 and 1849 a million and a half Irish people died and a further million emigrated. Caught in an economic double bind that resulted in mass starvation, for the Irish emigration became the only viable means of survival. It is important to understand Irish migration in this way. For Irish people emigration is not a course they follow voluntarily. It is forced upon them by economic conditions of which the Great Hunger is but an extreme example. The return of Irish people to their homeland and the sharp decline in Irish migration during that period in the 1970s when the Irish economy entered a boom phase witness the unwillingness of Irish people to migrate.

This sortie into economic history sets the context of the present chapter, which is primarily concerned with what happens to the Irish as a result of their economic and political conditions as a colonized people. These conditions go hand-in-hand with an ideological and cultural point of view. With migration forced upon them by economic vicissitudes beyond their personal control, the Irish suffer the effects of a unique double bind: that of being a culturally a First World subject, with all the expectations and assumptions that entails, caught in economic and ideological relations typical of the Third World.

Neither staying at home nor migration is capable of resolving that double bind, and the price of it, we shall see, is paid in an inestimable amount of human misery and suffering.

The 'mad' Irish

There is insufficient space to discuss here the problem of mental illness in the Republic of Ireland. This is, in fact, the subject of another paper.[15] Suffice to say that it has a long history[16] and high, if not the highest, rates of incidence and prevalence in the world.[17] So much so that some illnesses, most notably schizophrenia, have been described as endemic.[18] The lifetime expectancy of hospitalization for schizophrenia in Ireland has been estimated at 4 per cent, as compared with 1 per cent for most other countries.[19]

Table 9.1   Age-standardized rates of admission to mental hospital
for all diagnoses per 100,000 population aged sixteen or over, by
country of birth, England, 1981

Country of birth	Males	Females	All
Irish Republic	1,054	1,102	1,080
Northern Ireland	793	880	838
England	418	583	504
Afro-Caribbean	565	532	548

Source: From R. Cochrane and S. Bal, 'Mental hospital admission
rates of immigrants to England', *Social Psychiatry*, 12, 1977, pp.
23–35.

Many attempts have been made to account for the prevalence of insanity
in Ireland, from the genetic to the sociological,[20] but, to date, none has
found conclusive support. It has been said, in fact, that if the high prevalence of schizophrenia in the Irish Republic could be explained, then so
could that disease itself.[21]

The prevalence of madness at home is implicit in my characterization of
madness among the migrant Irish. But it should not be regarded as an
explanation of it. As we shall see, the English data simply do not support
the postulation of a simple, causal relationship. This is not to say that the
two are not related – I believe them to be so – but their relationship is as two
distinct effects of the same causal factor; the contextualized results of a
legacy of colonial history.

Mental illness among Irish migrants

In the most recently reported study[22] it was shown that Irish people resident
in Britain had the highest rates of first and subsequent admissions to mental
hospital of any migrant group. For all causes and all admissions, people
born in the Irish Republic had twice the rate of admission of the English-
born, and a rate 50 per cent higher than that of the next highest group. The
relevant data are shown in Table 9.1, where figures for both the English-
born and the Afro-Caribbean community, a relatively much more studied
group, are included by way of comparison. The considerable discrepancy
between the rates for both Irish-born groups and the others in these data is
remarkable. What is more remarkable is that this severity of incidence has
been the subject of almost next to no subsequent investigation.[23]

The rates of principal diagnoses for all admissions for men and women in
the same period for the selected groups are shown in Table 9.2. A number
of facts emerge from this table. First, Irish people, whether born in the
Republic or in Northern Ireland, have the highest rate of admission for
every diagnosis except schizophrenia. Another point to note is the overrepresentation of Irish people in the categories of depression and alcohol-

Table 9.2   Rates of mental hospital admission per 100,000 population for selected nativity groups, by diagnosis and gender, England, 1981

	Country of birth							
	Republic of Ireland		Northern Ireland		England		Caribbean	
Diagnosis	M	F	M	F	M	F	M	F
Schizophrenia[a]	158	174	103	111	61	58	259	235
Psychoses	36	50	28	52	16	27	28	40
Depression[b]	197	410	143	266	79	166	65	152
Neuroses[c]	62	111	44	80	28	56	6	25
Personality disorder	62	80	50	52	30	35	22	42
Alcohol abuse[d]	332	133	261	90	38	18	27	9
Drug abuse	13	8	17	8	5	3	13	0

(a) Schizophrenia includes paranoia.
(b) Depression: affective psychoses and depressive disorders.
(c) Neurosis includes 'neurotic depression'.
(d) Alcohol abuse: psychosis, dependence, and non-dependent abuse.

Source: Cochrane and Bal, 'Mental hospital admission rates'.

related disorders. Men and women born in the Republic of Ireland have rates of admission for depression approximately two and a half times those of their native-born counterparts. The rates for people born in Northern Ireland are nearly double those of the English-born. For depression the rate of admission for women born in both Northern Ireland and the Irish Republic is approximately twice that of their male compatriots.

For alcohol-related disorders men and women born in the Republic of Ireland respectively suffer approximately nine times and seven times the rate of the English-born, with men and women of Northern Irish origin suffering seven and five times the native-born rate.

The published figures for rates of admission by diagnosis do not appear to be standardized by age, which makes comparison and interpretation difficult for a number of reasons. I do not, therefore, intend to spend too much time discussing them. I would, however, like to make one or two observations before passing on to discuss other migrant Irish data.

Although the rates for schizophrenia are high, they are perhaps less than expected, given the extent of the problem in Ireland. Other studies[24] have shown the Irish to be underrepresented in the schizophrenic population in England. In the Cochrane and Bal study the category of depression includes affective psychosis and that of alcohol abuse includes alcohol psychosis. When placed alongside the issue of endemic schizophrenia among the indigenous Irish, there is a possibility that these sub-categories have been misapplied in the case of migrants as a result of ethnic stereotyping by English practitioners. There is evidence that Irishmen are diagnosed alcoholic by British psychiatrists in preference to schizophrenic and that alcoholism in Irishmen can mask schizophrenic symptoms.[25]

The extensive Cochrane and Bal study compares well, however, with another study conducted by Dean *et al.* in south-east England.[26] This showed admissions for alcoholism to be 5.3 and 2.4 times the expected number for Irish men and women respectively, with schizophrenia admissions being 2.4 and 4.0 times greater than expected. This study also compared admissions with those in the Republic of Ireland. Dean *et al.* found that migrant admissions were significantly lower than might have been expected from admission rates in Ireland.

Except for a drop in the incidence levels for people from Northern Ireland, the findings reported for Irish people by Cochrane and Bal show a level of stability over the preceding decade. Overall rates of hospitalization for people from Northern Ireland and the Irish Republic were more than twice the native-born rate in 1971.[27]

Elsewhere, Malzberg's investigations in New York state showed that the Irish-born had rates of admission for alcoholic psychoses and dementia praecox 3.39 (men 3.03, women 4.78) and 1.46 (men 1.70, women 1.23) times those of the native-born population.[28] Other studies in Canada showed the Irish again to have high rates of hospitalization for schizophrenia, exceeded only by those for migrants from Poland and the Soviet Union.[29]

Mental illness in the non-hospitalized migrant Irish community

One might suppose that excessively high and seemingly stable rates of incidence lasting over a decade might provoke some further investigation and/or prompt a search for further explanations within the community as a whole. This, unfortunately for Irish people, has not been the case. Only four studies[30] have addressed the question of psychological morbidity in the community as a whole. This dearth of research is the more worrying when, at the same time as high rates of incidence were being identified, other research was showing a gross overrepresentation of Irish-born people in the figures for attempted suicide.[31]

Attempts to assess levels of psychological symptoms among the non-hospitalized Irish community that might account for the hospitalization rate have been largely unsuccessful. Neither Cochrane and Stopes-Roe nor Der and Bebbington could find indicators in the community that might predict the observed hospitalization rates.

Stopes-Roe and Cochrane compared Irish migrants with those from India and Pakistan (both groups which have considerably lower rates of hospitalization for mental illness, compared with either the Irish or the native-born). They found that in terms of psychological well-being, as measured using Langner scale scores, the Irish occupied an intermediate position between the two groups, a finding that would not have been predicted from the incidence data.

McNicholl's study compared Irish migrants who had been referred to statutory alcohol services with a control group who had not. As might be expected, he found that the non-referred group exhibited better psychological adjustment to life in England than the referred group.

Of these studies, which are not without their methodological and other difficulties, it is that by Cochrane and Stopes-Roe which is the most comprehensive and which provides the most intriguing results. Based on 1971 hospitalization and census data, reported in an earlier study by Cochrane,[32] it sought to test a series of hypotheses by the comparison of Irish people resident in Ireland, English people resident in England and migrant Irish people in England who were matched on age, sex and residential area. Cochrane and Stopes-Roe assessed psychological symptoms, using the Symptom Rating Test (SRT)[33] and the twenty-two-item scale of distress developed by Langner.[34] Other measures included proximity and contact with close family, social isolation, migration difficulty and acculturation (measures of ties with Ireland, integration at work, return visits, etc.).

It was found that the migrant group had the lowest SRT and Langner score means, indicating better psychological adjustment than either of the non-migrant groups, were slightly less socially isolated and more likely to be downwardly socially mobile. This study found no significant relationships between social mobility, urban or rural origin, marital or employment status and levels of psychological symptoms, all of which have been hypothesized at some time or other as playing some role in mental illness among migrants.[36] One finding was reported which directly contradicted a stated hypothesis regarding the relationship between psychological stability and acculturation. Namely, in Cochrane and Stopes-Roe's migrant group, there was a distinct tendency for those oriented more towards England and less towards Ireland to have higher psychological symptom scores. They note, 'It appears that, for males at least, maintaining strong ties with the home country is associated with psychological stability.'[36] Support for this finding appears in the McNicholl study, where it was found that the non-referred group were significantly more acculturated towards Ireland, even when age was taken into account.

Causation and selection in migrant madness

Two hypotheses are commonly advanced to account for high rates of mental hospitalization among migrant groups; the social selection hypothesis and the social causation hypothesis. The former suggests that high rates are the result of the overrepresentation of psychologically unstable individuals among migrants, the latter that mental illness is a result of the stresses of migration and post-migration adjustment. Support for both these hypotheses has been forthcoming from examinations of different migrant groups at different times.[37]

Unfortunately, the Irish population in England corresponds with neither hypothesis. If the selection hypothesis applied, then, given the incidence and prevalence of mental illness in Ireland, we would expect to find comparable rates of mental illness among migrants to England. As stated above, significantly lower than expected admissions were found for Irish migrants by Dean *et al.* First admission data for the principal causes of

Table 9.3 First mental health admission rates for selected conditions per 100,000 population aged fourteen or over, by country of birth/residence, 1971

			England and Wales			
			Native-born		Irish-born	
	Ireland					
Cause of admission	M	F	M	F	M	F
Schizophrenia	88	68	16	17	31	45
Depressive psychoses	58	90	13	22	17	40
Alcohol-related	121	25	9	2	81	11
All diagnoses	395	358	157	195	312	330

Source: R. Cochrane and M. Stopes-Roe, 'Psychological disturbance in Ireland, in England and in Irish Emigrants to England', *Economic and Social Review*, 10, 1979, pp. 301–20.

admission among Irish migrants in 1971, presented in Table 9.3, show markedly lower rates when compared with the indigenous Irish population.

Although overall rates are comparable, it would appear that Irish people suffer illnesses differentially in England and Ireland, suggesting that migration itself plays some role in inducing illness not allowed for in this hypothesis. At the same time, one would expect to see higher levels of psychological symptoms among the general population. These have not been found.

The social causation hypothesis fares somewhat better in the face of the Irish evidence, although even that faces some important difficulties. Again, we would expect to find higher rates of psychological symptoms among the migrant population *vis-à-vis* the native-born. They do not occur. Secondly, we would expect predisposing symptoms to have fallen off over time as the migrants adjusted and came to terms with the new society. In fact Cochrane and Stopes-Roe found the opposite. Length of stay was significantly and positively correlated with symptom levels in their study. Other factors often cited in support of the social causation hypothesis, such as changing culture, language, customs, etc., are much more drastic for other migrant groups yet do not produce anything like equivalent levels of hospitalization.

That neither hypothesis seems to find adequate support in the case of the Irish led Cochrane and Stopes-Roe to postulate the existence of two populations of Irish migrants. They argue that 'another group of Irish immigrants living in England, but not readily accessible to sample surveys, accounts almost entirely for the high level of psychopathology recorded in official statistics'.[38] This neat suggestion seems to solve the problem once and for all. It simultaneously explains (away) the incidence of mental hospitalization among Irish migrants and, implicitly, moves the problem out of England and back to Ireland. The subtext of the 'two populations' hypothesis goes something like this:

1 Ireland has the highest rates of mental hospitalization in the world.
2 Ireland also has the highest rates of emigration of any European country.
3 The prevalence of insanity and the rate of emigration are related, in the

sense that a disproportionate number of psychologically stable people quit the population, leaving behind a disproportionate number of the mentally ill.
4 However, the cultural availability of migration as a social option and the ease with which it can be accomplished, particularly to England, mean that some people who are psychologically unstable in Ireland are able to effect migration before their illness requires hospitalization.
5 These people, who constitute a minority of migrants, find the stresses of migration difficult to cope with, their symptoms become florid, and a cycle of mental hospital admission and readmission begins.

This reconciliation of the social selection and the social causation hypotheses has a certain elegance to it. However, it begs several crucially important questions:

1 Why does Ireland have the highest rates of mental hospitalization, particularly for schizophrenia?
2 What is the relationship between emigration and madness in the homeland?
3 Why do the patterns of diagnosis differ between migrant Irish and indigenous Irish?
4 Why do people from Northern Ireland, which has low indigenous rates of hospitalization, have rates of admission in England comparable with those of migrants from the Republic of Ireland?
5 What of second-generation Irish people, known to have high rates of hospitalization elsewhere in the world but who disappear in the British statistics?

In the final section of this chapter I shall attempt to address some of these questions, but before doing so I should like to elaborate a general theoretical position deriving from the work of the Martinican psychiatrist Frantz Fanon (1925–61) on the psychological effects of colonialism.

Frantz Fanon and the colonized psyche

Frantz Fanon: a brief life

Born in the French colony of Martinique in 1925, Fanon trained in France to be a doctor. He published his first book, *Black Skin, White Masks*, which dealt with the psychological effects of racism upon black people in France, at the age of twenty-seven. As a specialist in psychiatry he was assigned, in the 1950s, to a hospital in Algeria. He became a revolutionary and a Marxist during the Algerian people's struggle for independence and was an active freedom fighter. He utilized his psychiatric training both to treat and to theorize the psychopathologies he encountered, coming to see them as a direct function of colonial oppression and the pathologies of social relations and practices it induced. At the age of thirty-six he was diagnosed as suffering from leukaemia and died in Washington in December 1961.

Colonialism, racism and mental life

For Fanon, colonialism induces in the colonized subject a sense of worth-lessness and dependence that hampers both personal and political auton-omy. This sense derives from both the attribution of negative or inferior qualities to the colonized by the colonizer and the organization of space, labour, social relations and social practices by the latter to systematize and concretize both the sense of inferiority in the former and the practical relationship of superiority/inferiority between the two. He contends that 'It is the racist who creates his own inferior.'[39]

The racist colonial order accomplishes the creation of inferiority in a variety of ways. It divides its world up into compartments which imply its own lines of force, which are maintained in place by violence and the threat of violence embodied in the police force and the military. The spaces occupied by the colonialists and the colonized are, he contends, not comp-lementary but contrasting. The former is spacious, brightly lit, clean, well maintained and structurally sound. The native space is overcrowded, dirty and poor. Except to provide the services necessary to the maintenance of the colonial space, the native is largely excluded from it.[40]

However, this exclusion brings with it a kind of resistance, bred of fear. As Fanon notes, 'The colonized exerts a considerable effort to keep away from the colonial world, not to expose himself [*sic*] to any action of the conqueror'.[41] Yet in each encounter the native is reminded of the superior-ity of the colonizer, his power, his wealth, and this contrasts starkly with the native's own position. However, as he observes:

> It is not enough for the settler to delimit physically, that is to say with the help of the army and the police force, the place of the native. As if to show the totalitarian character of colonial exploitation the settler paints the native as a sort of quintessence of evil.[32]

Native society becomes characterized by the settler as a place where values have disappeared or never existed. Representing an absence of values, the native is also a negation of them. For the colonist the native is destructive, the enemy of civilized values, 'the unconscious instrument of blind forces'.[43] The inhuman qualities of the native are embodied in the character of the beast. The native is represented and described in animal terms, incapable of self-government and of industry without supervision.

In addition, the cultural and spiritual life of the native is devalued. Native traditions and customs, religions and myths are read as '. . . the very sign of that poverty of spirit and their constitutional depravity'.[44] The indigenous culture is overtly and subtly subverted by the institution of colonial values through education and religion, forced conversion and the outlawing of native customs, and by the institutionalization of the colonial language as part of the discourse of power. Complementing this process, the settler begins to rewrite the history of the colonized land. Colonization becomes a process of making history itself. Just as the colonized land becomes an extension of the mother country, so does its history. All that existed before the colonist's advent was barbarism and savagery. The exploitation and appropriation inherent in colonization are written out of history, to be replaced by a Manichaean struggle of order over disorder and the gradual, inevitable extension of the civilizing process to the colonized world.

Language plays a crucial role in this process. As Fanon put it:

> Every colonized people – in other words, every people in whose soul an inferiority complex has been created by the death and burial of its local cultural originality – finds itself face-to-face with the language of the civilizing nation; that is, with the culture of the mother country.[45]

Displaced by the loss of a language in which to express aspirations or construct a coherent identity, adapting the borrowed words of the colonialist's tongue to encapsulate the fragmented experience of the present, the native lives a schizophrenic existence.

The native is caught in a constant battle between language and culture as each one becomes more or less orientated towards the past or the present, to the community or the economy. Cultural identity, to the extent that one can talk of this, undergoes a constant process of fragmentation as a result. To be a colonized speaker of a colonial language is to undergo the experience of taking on a foreign culture while remaining in your own. To gain mastery over that language, to make it work for one's own ends, is to alienate oneself even further from the culture of origin; to reject it is to risk consigning oneself to an historical backwater.

What, then, are the effects of the colonial process upon mental life? Fanon argues that we must understand colonialism not simply as an economic or political process; it is also a psychological and ideological one.[46] Caught in a context in which all significant factors had previously been within the scope of his or her own cultural experience, in which some sense of control could be achieved, the colonized subject has two choices: to resist or to identify. Neither option is an enviable one. As Fanon observes:

> Because it is a systematic negation of the other person and a furious determination to deny the person all attributes of humanity, colonialism forces the people it dominates to ask the question constantly: 'In reality, who am I?'[47]

The existential dilemma of the colonized subject, as Fanon's work both on those who chose to resist and on those who were induced to identify shows, permeates all levels of psychic life, from the conscious to the unconscious. Trapped in 'the tight links of the chains of colonialism',[48] the native is forced to internalize an anger that the colonist forbids expression. It emerges in dreams of action and physical prowess, of aggression and the release of the body from physical constraint. It also appears in violence against the colonized subject's own kind, a feature commonly identified in the Irish at both the political and the personal level.[49]

While the native recognizes and experiences the violence of the colonial regime, and his or her own relative powerlessness in the face of it, he or she also envies it, and through envy identifies with it. He or she wishes to substitute for the settler – if not to be him, then certainly to replace him. This identification is encouraged by the ideological apparatus that the colonial power institutes.

These collective apparatuses, popular media, religion, education, and so forth, incite the native to give up his or her cultural identity and become like the colonizer. In its extreme it can create an internal dichotomy so strong that pathology ensues almost automatically. Fanon cites the experience of black Antilleans, where the African spirit is repressed in consciousness to be replaced by the symbol of the white master. He notes:

> Little by little, one can observe in the young Antillean the formation and crystallisation of an attitude and a way of thinking and seeing that are essentially white . . . Because the Antillean does not think of himself as a black man; he thinks of himself as an Antillean. The Negro lives in Africa. Subjectively, intellectually, the Antillean conducts himself like a white man. But he is a Negro.[50]

At every level the colonized subject is induced to devalue and reject his or her own culture and adopt the values of the colonial power. S/he is confronted by a series of dichotomies that oppose the positive qualities of the Other (the colonial) with the negative qualities of the self. The native lives an ambiguity that is extraordinarily neurotic, identifying his or her own nativensss to the degree that s/he is wicked, sloppy, malicious, instinctual and uncivilized; everything opposite is a property of the Other.

This internalized opposition creates, in Fanon's analysis, two important characteristics that emerge at the level of the subject. The native's consciousness and sense of identity need to find their validation in the Other, while at the same time being tinged by an historical sense of inferiority resulting from the need to do so. The native has to recognize his or her inferiority in order to achieve self-validation but, at the same time, a secure identity eludes him or her because total identification with the Other is impossible; the colonized can never become the colonist, at best s/he can only replace him or her.

The colonized subject experiences a double bind, but it is important to note that the constraining term in this bind is not personal but social. It is the very organization of colonial society that induces the bind, that forces a choice between two states which are equally insufficient while at the same time making them vital for psychological survival.[51] Such a society becomes itself pathological, what Fanon terms a 'society of comparison'[52] in which the subject compares him or herself not with the colonist but with other natives 'against the pattern of the white man'.[53]

Such a culture uses its people as agents of their own pathologies. Describing the situation in his native Martinique, Fanon makes the following observation: 'The Martinican is a man [*sic*] crucified. The environment that has shaped him (but that he has not shaped) has horribly drawn and quartered him; and he feeds this cultural environment with his blood and his essences'.[54]

Colonialism and the psychological life of migrants

The effects of upbringing and socialization within such a society are not cast off upon leaving it. At one level the double bind is made clearer while at another it becomes more obscure. Recognizing the inferiority of his or her own society, the migrant makes the choice of leaving it. At the same time a choice is made to 'climb up' into the society of the colonial. Neither of these choices is, however, without its consequences.

While the fragile identity of the colonized subject can, in large part, be preserved intact and unquestioned in the native land, on migration the migrant is confronted with the substantiality of his or her own identity. Every time he or she speaks or appears in public in the new homeland his or her national identity will become, to a greater or lesser extent, a focus of attention. The migrant will be reminded of the differences which exist between him or her and the majority of individuals in the new environment. At the same time adapting to these differences, accepting their inevitability and coming to terms with them will invoke a distance between the new situation and the old.

As Fanon points out,[55] the native is a 'phobogenic' object in the eyes of the colonist. The individual migrant from a colonized culture has to overcome the practical difficulties of this object status which emerge at a number of levels, from the interpersonal and the institutional. S/he has to cope with outright racism at the hands of the majority: discrimination, patronization, exploitation, stereotyping. Two strategies present themselves in dealing with such things: the migrant must either make him or herself more like the colonist, more acceptable to him, or must find some other way to disappear within the host culture.

Again a double bind emerges. The migrant must choose between giving up one cultural identity, exchanging it for another, or minimizing the contact between the new and the old. Both choices are insufficient. The first is rarely possible; the relation between the colonial power and the colonized subject is not equivalent; the latter will always be inferior in the eyes of the former and will always be forced to recognize his or her inferiority. The colonized cannot become the colonist because the structure of the relationship will not permit it. Conversely, contact between two cultures in the same spatial and economic environment can be limited only so far. The migrant can bury him or herself in the migrant community only to a certain extent. At certain crucial points, in the workplace, in education, etc., s/he will have to emerge to deal with the majority population, at which points the cultural or racial inferiority presupposed in the colonial relationship will be made manifest.

The colonized migrant in the 'mother' country cannot win. At best s/he can only resist the worst effects of the institutionalized, historical relationship between the two cultures. Attempts at assimilation are rebuffed or treated with a certain specific kind of contempt. Attempts to preserve the native culture intact are regarded as open acts of defiance and a denigration of the host culture. Every instance of contact with the colonist Other is potentially fraught with anxiety for the migrant. To be accepted s/he must act in accordance with the stereotypes the host culture imposes, as long as they are the 'positive' ones, of the happy-go-lucky, easy-going and cheerful native. At the same time the migrant learns to recognize that s/he is an object of fear, an unpredictable and violent natural force, in the eyes of the colonist. Any attempt to diverge from the positive model will be interpreted as evidence of the truth underlying the negative one. The ambiguity of such experiences is, as Fanon contends, 'extraordinarily neurotic'.[56]

Whatever strategy is chosen, the migrant is prevented from forming or preserving a stable cultural identity autonomously. S/he is always caught in a pathological double bind over which s/he has little or no control. Deprived of the context of resistance in the homeland that provides, to some extent, a stable basis for identity, the migrant can only opt for an identity that someone else, the Other, has created for him/her. To do so means assimilating and internalizing the pathological projections of the colonist's assumptions and fears and to risk further alienation from his/her own experience. In other words the migrant must be, as Fanon observes 'for ever in combat with his [*sic*] own image'.[57]

Mental illness and the Irish: towards an understanding

In this section I shall attempt to assimilate mental illness among the migrant Irish with the work of Fanon discussed in the previous section.

I do not think I need to labour the point that the last five centuries of Irish history illustrate each and every one of the phenomena described by Fanon, plus a few more besides. From the Pale to the Settlements, from the outlawing of Catholicism to the more recent punishment of Irish schoolchildren for using Gaelic in the classroom, through the representation of Irish people as simians to the promulgation of jokes about their 'stupidity', from the institution of primogeniture to the establishment of the 'big house' system and the protection accorded to absentee landlords while the mass of the people starved, Irish history is a monument to the institutionalization of native inferiority and powerlessness, to the systematic docking of cultural roots.[58]

Of course, the Irish were not rendered wholly passive in this process. Alongside the tradition of colonialist pacification is another one of struggle and resistance that continues to the present day. But in understanding the present problem it is not this tradition which can assist us, since, as Fanon's work shows, the nature and efficacy of resistance is itself conditioned by the inferiority imbued by colonialism.

The Irish migrant to England occupies a peculiar position in the class and ethnic structure of the country. Having a longer tradition of 'voluntary' migration to England than most other migrant communities, being of the same skin colour as the host population, speaking the same language, and having a shorter distance to migrate, it might be thought that the Irish migrant would have several distinct advantages over other, more recent, migrant groups. However, by whatever measure of economic or social advantage one chooses to use, it is clear that Irish people in England fare no better than other migrant groups.[59] In fact on some measures, such as mental hospitalization and mortality, they fare considerably worse.[60]

Arriving with the whole baggage of a colonial past on his or her back, the Irish migrant comes to England in search of opportunity and a more economically stable way of life. He or she may also be escaping from the more repressive aspects of Irish life, traditionalist Catholicism and family values. There may also be the possibility of joining friends who have already made the trip successfully.

I do not wish to dwell upon the economic, demographic and social conditions of Irish people in Britain. They have been dealt with more extensively elsewhere.[61] This is not to say that their importance is to be underestimated or considered irrelevant to my argument. On the contrary it is precisely because their social, demographic and economic position differs so little from those of the new migrant communities that many of the problems they encounter arise.

One feature of Irishness in England is its relative invisibility. This arises in two ways. English racism focuses upon colour of skin rather than ethnicity. In this milieu the Irish are literally invisible until they open their mouths. There are two other senses in which the Irish are invisible. The first arises from an administrative decision of the British government during the 1950s to render them so by treating Ireland as part of the British Isles as a means of avoiding subsequent problems when immigration from the New Commonwealth had to be controlled. In previous waves of migration, during the nineteenth century, the Irish had been as visible and subject to as much surveillance as black migrants are today.[62] The second, which is what Fanon's work would predict, comes from an implicit decision of those Irish who came in the post-war period 'to keep their heads down and their mouths shut'.[63]

A second feature of Irishness in Britain that might be predicted from Fanon is concern for and ambivalence about cultural identity which split it along lines taken from the colonists' discourse. This ambivalence is most manifest in the attempt to preserve what is both 'good' and 'different' about that identity while rejecting or recasting what is 'bad' and 'different' about it. The concern manifests itself most strongly in an interest in the authenticity of individual identity.

The preservation and importance of traditional Irish activities such as sport and dancing reflect this concern, as evinced by the number of pages devoted to them in the principal Irish migrant newspapers and the number of Irish migrants who participate in them. Conversely, one often finds complaints in the letter columns of those same papers about the 'needless' resurrection of past injustices inflicted upon the Irish by the British.[64]

A recent study by Kells of the immigrant Irish in London gives flavour to these contentions.[65] Bearing in mind that her respondents are middle-class, and thus relatively privileged and mobile in relation to the large mass of Irish people in Britain, their conceptions of Irish identity and their hold upon it are no less ambivalent and tenuous than might be predicted from Fanon's characterization. Her respondents articulate a whole series of contradictions about their own position and the Irish in general. For them, the Irish are seen as being, among other things, open, spontaneous, informal, warm, imaginative and unpretentious. On the negative side they are seen to be moody, untrustworthy, drunken and volatile.[66] Middle-class Irish women saw Irish people as having stronger 'feelings' than the English but less ability to articulate them. Many saw the Irish as spiritual, contrasting that with English secularism.

Kells' respondents also had some comments to make on the question of authenticity and Irish identity. Northern Irish Protestants saw the Catholic Irish as the 'real' Irish; one middle-class informant regarded the working-class Irish as the genuine article. The implications for their own authenticity are not discussed but are, I think, obvious. Some regarded second-generation Irish as inauthentic, using the term 'plastic Paddies' to character-ize them. Others resented the 'hi-jacking' of Irishness to further political aims and those people who had 'become more Irish' (i.e. who made a point of emphasizing their ethnic identity) on migration.

Kells' respondents are by no means representative of the Irish in Britain as a whole. As middle-class subjects they are given far greater opportunity to express themselves on the topic and more space in which to do so, by the very nature of their lives. Nonetheless the ambivalences and contradictions they express, and which she notes, reflect precisely the dilemma that Fanon describes in the Antillean, namely the constant need to address oneself to the question 'Who am I?' only to find that a coherent answer is elusive. Furthermore, despite their relatively privileged position, Kells' informants were aware of discrimination and concerned about the reaction of English people to them as Irish people.

Another study which emphasizes the problem of Irish identity in England, conducted by Pink, concerns itself with the entry of a working-class Northern Irish Protestant, George, into a middle-class English con-text.[67] George's experiences are worth noting, since they illustrate, in a number of different ways, Fanon's idea that the colonist's objectification of the colonized supersedes any rational notion the colonized may have of themselves.

Brought up in an 'Orange' household, he regards himself as British, but on arrival he discovered that he is in fact Irish:

> When I first came over I was aware of being Irish because I felt different from everyone else who was English. I tended to think that everyone looked upon me as being the Irish guy, rather than George, and saw me as being Irish rather than me.[68]

Elsewhere, and ironically, he experiences some of the phobic treatment meted out to Irish people as a result of events in Northern Ireland. George is working in London at the time two British soldiers are killed after inter-rupting a nationalist funeral in Belfast. He recalls his experience as follows:

> I got a lot of hassle at work from people because I was Irish and they resented what had happened. That was really bad, because I came from Belfast they associated me with the violence and I got a lot of verbal abuse and got roughed up a bit.[69]

George's experience is particularly telling in the present context, since administratively and politically he is in fact British. It is only on arrival in England that his Irishness becomes a question. The position of Protestant Northern Irish is analogous to that of the Antilleans in Fanon who can regard themselves as French, and thus not black in the Negro sense, as long as they remain in Martinique. It is only when they come to France that they discover their blackness and its consequences.[70] This analogy may go some way towards accounting for the high mental hospitalization rates of people from Northern Ireland in England, which contrasts with the relatively low rates, by Irish standards, there.[71]

Alcoholism, depression and schizophrenia constitute the largest problem areas met by Irish people in Britain. All these are represented in a series of interviews with former mental patients published by Brent Irish Mental Health Group in 1986.[72] While again these accounts of experiences are not claimed to be representative, each of them in its different way fits in with what might be expected from Fanon's work. Some of the interviewees left for England to escape from personal and social problems that had developed in Ireland, only to find their difficulties exacerbated. Others came as a result of poverty, only to suffer problems once here.

They recount a variety of experiences in an equal variety of ways, but they also share some common aspects. One is the experience of prejudice and the discovery of themselves as 'thick Paddies'. Another is loneliness and isolation, even within the Irish community, which some interviewees regarded as a problematic environment in itself, owing to its inwardness. Their vulnerability to stress is evident from their accounts; breakdown could be induced by the death of family in Ireland, the stress of dealing with authority or officialdom, the absence of familiar social contacts in England.

Despite their difficulties, these troubled people express cogent insights in the conflictual status of the Irish in Britain. As one interviewee, Sean, put it; 'The English have a preconception that the Irish are thick, they put us down and laugh at us . . . It creates conflict, so the Irish live in closed communities, they feel isolated'.[73] Another, Brendan, put it this way: 'That is the reason why Irish people have problems. They tend to keep themselves to themselves'.[74] Common themes emerge throughout these accounts; the homesickness for and the estrangement from the homeland, the sense of 'things being different there now', the unfriendliness of the new context and its strangeness, the need for other people and the fear of being alone, the sense that no one listens. What comes across is the sense of isolation, of loss, of grief.

At this point I would draw to your attention two facts, one of which I have already mentioned. The first is the finding that levels of psychological symptoms are correlated with orientation towards life and length of stay in England.[75] The second comes from another study which shows that in England schizophrenia among Irish men is highly and negatively correlated with levels of 'ethnic density'.[76] In short, in regions where relatively few Irish-born people live, the rate of schizophrenia among Irish men is much higher than in areas where they constitute a larger proportion of the population. They were the only group of migrants tested where this proved to be the case.

What I am getting at here should by now be obvious. The very culture that proves so pathogenic in its homeland[77] seems to protect people from the worst effects of migration. Paradoxical as it may seem this, again, is precisely what Fanon's theory would lead us to expect. As he put it, 'As long as a black man is among his own, he will have no occasion, except in minor internal conflicts, to experience his being through others'.[78] As the work of Laing, Bateson and others has shown, at the level of its principal symptoms this is precisely what schizophrenia is.[79] It is the total, existential and ontological, sense of being for others, of having no sense of being for oneself.

In an important respect, because of the cultural, political and ideological effects of a colonial history, no Irish person, migrant or not, has a full cultural or existential sense of 'being for oneself' and thus every Irish person is potentially subject to psychological pathology. At the level of the collective, political unconsciousness,[80] every Irish person is orientated towards being for the colonial, and hence English, Other. The direct and immediate effects and consequences of living in a 'society of comparison' are removed on migration. But they are partially reconstructed within the migrant community, where being 'too Irish' whatever that may mean, can bring disapproval.[81] But even this regulation is a small price to pay compared with the consequences of being isolated and thus losing all sense of being for oneself.

The point I am making – and you may regard it simply as assertion – is that psychopathology is inherent in every Irish migrant for the theoretical reasons mentioned. Its realization is dependent largely upon factors outside the individual migrant's control, as is its simultaneous substantiation in the psyche, conscious or unconscious, of every Irish person. Isolation from the community is a principal, but not the sole, factor in its emergence. This isolation can take many forms and can occur in the workplace, in the home or in everyday social relations. The conditions inducing migrant isolation are manifold, and choice plays little part in them. From the worker who has to go where the work is and not where his or her community is, to the mother forced into the solitary confinement of the home and domestic labour, to the elderly too impoverished or infirm to participate actively in social relations, these are just some of the more obvious manifestations of what is a general social condition.

Irish people sustain themselves through their communities, in formal and informal gatherings, through the 'craic' in pubs, through the gatherings of 'lads' after work and at weekends.[82] Alcohol plays an important part in these activities, for two reasons. First, it is ever present in the places where Irish people meet to sustain their sense of community, many of which are available to them without cost. Second, considered as a drug, alcohol serves analgesic functions; it dulls the pain, of toil, of homesickness, of estrangement, of loss. In company, it smooths the path of interaction. But it is not without its consequences, for the Irish or anyone else who uses it in that way, as the data above suggest.

The Irish have accepted the myth of themselves as prone to drink, and it is precisely that – a myth. Where statistical data exist, they show that the Irish drink less and are more likely to abstain from alcohol than other national groups.[83] Alcohol becomes pathological for Irish people when it becomes a substitute for community instead of a component of it, when the

analgesic function supersedes the social one. In this sense they are no
different from any other people. Except for the fact that their circumstances, historical and current, make the presence of community more
necessary while at the same time making isolation more likely.

For the second generation, the children of Irish migrants, the position
is simultaneously easier and more difficult. The absence of research on
second-generation people of Irish descent forces me to limit my comments.
Isolation, in the sense of a deeply felt or experienced, classical alienation is, I
would hypothesize, characteristic of these people. They belong completely
to neither one culture nor the other and are caught between their parents'
heritage and their present context, rendered invisible and inaudible from the
point of view of recognition. Such people, and I am one of them, have to
come to terms with life as best they can, adapting to circumstances in which
in some senses they have more choice than their parents and in others less.
In concluding these speculations about the conditions of second-generation
Irish people, I would recall Kells' respondents' comments on the 'plastic
Paddies' of the second generation: even membership of second-class community is not straightforwardly available to them.[84]

Curious journey: conclusions and points of departure

I regard myself as Irish for many reasons, not least because it coheres an
identity about myself which, for class and other reasons, in my present
context helps to make sense of the world in which I live. It enables me to
realign my sense of myself in the present with my experiences in the past. It
ennobles, in an odd sense, my self-perceived status as the victim of forces
based on a cultural and economic system beyond my control. In the
understanding and development of a cultural and personal identity the
exercise of personal choice plays very little part in the class system of British
society; but, where one can exercise it, one does. It is better to identify with
a culture that has produced a James Joyce or a Brendan Behan, a Shane
McGowan or a Bobby Sands, than with one whose heroes have been
effaced from the collective memory or who conclude their lives dead on the
pavements of New York or recuperated in the firmament of bourgeois
popular culture.

When I talk to first-generation Irish people about my work on the
physical and mental health of Irish people, three things happen, sometimes
simultaneously, sometimes consecutively. There is astonishment at the facts
I reveal about how bad it is to be Irish in England in terms of mortality and
madness, there is a fascination which is both morbid and self-concerned,
and there is resentment that someone 'not Irish' should be the source of this
information. In such interactions the very dilemma of Irish people is
summed up: the externally imposed ignorance of their own condition and
its causes, perverse pride arising from confirmation of their given identity as
history's martyrs, and anger directed not at the causes of their lot but at the
reminders of it.

In my experience, the bulk of expatriate Irish people seek explanations for the information I present to them in terms of stereotypes and conditions they have had imposed upon them and which they have partly accepted: their drinking, their Celtic temperament, their unhealthy diet and life style, their ignorance, and so on and so forth. What they rarely do is look to their historical relationship with England as a cause of their problems, even those whom one might regard as 'politicized'. Like all colonized subjects their anger is directed, in the first instance, at themselves, because, as history has taught them, explicitly or implicitly, taking it out on the English has no effect. The latter's consolidation of the power relation is so complete that anger expressed in that direction is pointless; there can be no negotiation, only interminable struggle in which one either chooses to participate or does not. For whatever reasons – and it is without criticism that I say this – for many people the costs of participation are too great to bear.

The solution to the problem of mental ill health among Irish migrants, and indeed among the indigenous Irish, that derives from the view presented here does not lie in accommodating to a received historical destiny or a colonial culture. It is in fact encapsulated in a Gaelic expression that is also the name of a political party, and I borrow it not to express an allegiance or advocate anything other than what the words themselves express. It is simply *Sinn Fein*, 'ourselves alone'.

In short, it is only Irish people who can do anything about the mental illness that appears to be endemic to their culture, both at home and abroad. They have to rid themselves of their historical inferiority by developing strategies that reflect the conditions and circumstances of the present. Self-determination, in this context, means more than Home Rule. It means grasping and understanding the present in order to go beyond it. The work of Fanon, developed precisely in a context where that was going on, can only point to such a solution, which is not a terminal point but rather a beginning. It entails the recapturing of historical circumstances in order to create a future, which is not the insertion of the colonized in the place of the colonist but a fundamental restructuring of the relationship between the two.

In view of the fact that my exposition of Fanon was by no means complete, I feel it apt that the last word on the matter should go to him:

> It is through the effort to recapture the self and to scrutinize the self, it is through the lasting tension of their freedom that men [sic] will be able to create the ideal conditions of existence for a human world.[85]

Notes

1. R. Cochrane, 'Mental illness in immigrants to England and Wales: an analysis of mental hospital admissions', *Social Psychiatry*, 12, 1977, pp. 23–35.
2. R. Cochrane and S. Bal, 'Mental hospital admission rates of immigrants to England: a comparison of 1971 and 1981', *Social Psychiatry*, 24, 1989, pp. 2–11.
3. F. Fanon, *The Wretched of the Earth*, trans. C. Farrington, Penguin, Harmondsworth, 1967; *Black Skin, White Masks*, trans. C. L. Markmann,

Paladin Books, London, 1970; *A Dying Colonialism*, trans. H. Chevalier, Penguin, Harmondsworth, 1970.

4. P. Conrad, 'On the medicalisation of deviance and social control', in D. Ingelby, ed., *Critical Psychiatry*, Penguin, Harmondsworth, 1981.
5. T. Szasz, *The Myth of Mental Illness*, Paladin Books, London, 1972.
6. T. Scheff, *Being Mentally Ill*, second edition, Aldine, New York, 1984.
7. E. Goffman, *Asylums*, Penguin, Harmondsworth, 1968; *Stigma*, Penguin, Harmondsworth, 1968.
8. M. Foucault, *Discipline and Punish*, Penguin, Harmondsworth, 1979.
9. R. D. Laing and A. Esterson, *Sanity, Madness and the Family*, Penguin, Harmondsworth, 1964; A. Esterson, *The Leaves of Spring*, Penguin, Harmondsworth, 1970.
10. G. Bateson, *Steps to an Ecology of Mind*, Paladin Books, London, 1973.
11. A. Wilden, *The Rules are no Game: the Strategy of Communication*, Routledge, London and New York, 1987.
12. R. Crotty, *Ireland in Crisis: a Study in Capitalist Colonial Underdevelopment*, Brandon, Dublin, 1986.
13. U. Kockel, and I. Shuttleworth, *Aspects of Irish Immigration in the 1980s*, APRU Discussion paper 90/3, Applied Population Research Unit, 1990.
14. L. Curtis, *Nothing but the same old Story: the Roots of anti-Irish Racism*, Information on Ireland, London, 1984.
15. L. Greenslade, 'A Culture of Madness: Schizophrenia in Modern Ireland', paper presented at the fourth Workshop in Social Science, University of Liverpool, May 1991.
16. W. J. Corbet, 'On the increase in insanity', *Am. J. Insanity*, 50, 1893, pp. 224–38; T. Drapes, 'On the alleged increase of insanity in Ireland', *J. Ment. Sci.* 40, 1894, pp. 519–48; W. R. Dawson, 'The relation between the geographical distribution of insanity and that of certain social and other conditions in Ireland *J. Ment. Sci.*, 57, 1911, pp. 571–97; D. H. Tuke, 'Increase of Insanity in Ireland', *J. Ment. Sci.*, 40, 1894, pp. 549–58.
17. D. Walsh, 'Hospitalized psychiatric morbidity in the Republic of Ireland', *Brit. J. Psychiatr.*, 114, 1968, pp. 11–14; A. O'Hare and D. Walsh, 'Further data on the activities of Irish psychiatric hospitals and units, 1965–1969', *J. Ir. Med. Assoc.*, 67, 1974, pp. 57–63.
18. E. F. Torrey, M. McGuire, A. O'Hare, D. Walsh and M. P. Spelman, 'Endemic psychosis in western Ireland', *Am. J. Psychiatry*, 141, 1984, pp. 966–70.
19. D. Walsh, 'Epidemiological methods applied to an Irish problem', in D. Leigh and J. Noorbakhsh, eds. *Epidemiological Studies in Psychiatry*, World Psychiatric Association, London, 1974.
20. D. Walsh, 'Two and two make five: multifactoriogenesis in mental illness in Ireland', *J. Irish Medical Assoc.*, 69, 1976, pp. 417–22.
21. E. F. Torrey, *Schizophrenia and Civilization*, Jason Aronson, New York, 1980.
22. Cochrane and Bal, 'Mental hospital admission rates'.
23. L. Greenslade, 'From Visible to Invisible: a Historical Perspective on the Health of Irish People in Britain', paper presented at the Society for the Social History of Medicine annual conference, St Katherine's College, Liverpool, July 1990; M. Pearson, M. Madden, and L. Greenslade, *Generations of an Invisible Minority*, Institute of Irish Studies Occasional Paper 2, Institute of Irish Studies, Liverpool, 1991.
24. C. Bagely, 'A comparative study of mental illness among immigrant groups in Britain', *Rev. Ethnics*, 1, 1970, pp. 24–36; A. W. Clare, 'Mental illness in the Irish emigrant', *J. Irish Medical Assoc.*, 67, 1974, pp. 20–4.

25. C. Bagely and A. Binitie, 'Alcoholism and schizophrenia among Irishmen in London', *Br. J. Addict.*, 65, 1970, 3–7.
26. G. Dean, H. Downing and E. Shelley, 'First admissions to psychiatric hospitals in south-east England in 1976 among immigrants from Ireland', *Brit. Med. J.*, 282, 1981, pp. 1831–3.
27. Cochrane, 'Mental illness in immigrants'.
28. B. Malzberg, 'Mental disease among Irish-born and native whites of Irish parentage in New York State, 1949–51, *Ment. Hyg.*, 47, 1963, pp. 12–42.
29. H. B. M. Murphy, 'Mental Hospitalisation Patterns in twelve Canadian Subcultures', mimeo, 1968; 'Sociocultural factors in schizophrenia: a compromise theory', in J. Zubin and F. A. Freyhan, eds., *Social Psychiatry*, Grune & Stratton, New York, 1968.
30. R. Cochrane and M. Stopes-Roe, 'Psychological disturbance in Ireland, in England and in Irish emigrants to England: a comparative study', *Economic and Social Review*, 10, 1979, pp. 301–20; M. Stopes-Roe and R. Cochrane, 'Mental health and integration: a comparison of Indian, Pakistani and Irish immigrants to England', *Ethnic and Racial Studies*, 3, 1980, pp. 316–41; G. Der and P. Bebbington, 'Depression in inner London', *Social Psychiatry*, 23, 1987, pp. 73–84; D. McNicholl, 'Migration Factors related to the Psychological Adjustment of the Irish in Britain, M.Sc. dissertation, University of Leicester, 1990.
31. A. W. Burke, 'Attempted suicide among the Irish-born population in Birmingham', *Br. J. Psychiatry*, 128, 1976, pp. 528–33.
32. Cochrane, 'Mental illness in immigrants'.
33. R. Kellner and B. F. Sheffield, 'A self-rating scale of distress', *Psychological Medicine*, 3, 1973, pp. 88–100.
34. T. S. Langner, 'A twenty-two item screening score of psychiatric symptoms indicating impairment', *Journal of Health and Social Behaviour*, 3, 1962, pp. 269–75.
35. C. Zwingmann and M. Pfister-Ammende, *Uprooting and after*, Springer-Verlag, New York, 1973.
36. Cochrane and Stopes-Roe, 'Psychological disturbance', p. 315.
37. Zwingmann and Pfister-Ammende, *Uprooting and after*.
38. Cochrane and Stopes-Roe, 'Psychological disturbances', p. 316.
39. Fanon, *Black Skins, White Masks*, p. 65.
40. Fanon, *The Wretched of the Earth*.
41. Fanon, *A Dying Colonialism*, p. 111.
42. Fanon, *The Wretched of the Earth*, pp. 31–2.
43. Fanon, *The Wretched of the Earth*, p. 32.
44. Fanon, *The Wretched of the Earth*, p. 32.
45. Fanon, *Black Skins, White Masks*, p. 14.
46. Fanon, *The Wretched of the Earth*.
47. Fanon, *The Wretched of the Earth*, p. 200.
48. Fanon, *The Wretched of the Earth*, p. 42.
49. T. P. Coogan, *The IRA*, Fontana Books, London, 1980.
50. Fanon, *Black Skins, White Masks*, pp. 104–5.
51. Wilden, *The Rules are no Game*.
52. Fanon, *Black Skins, White Masks*, p. 151.
53. Fanon, p. 153.
54. Fanon, *Black Skins, White Masks*, p. 153.
55. Fanon, *Black Skins, White Masks*, p. 107.
56. Fanon, *Black Skins, White Masks*, p. 136.

224   *Liam Greenslade*

57. Fanon, *Black Skins, White Masks*, p. 138.
58. F. Harrington and P. Finnegan, *Factors in the Genesis of Stress and Mental Ill Health among the Irish in Britain*, Irish Mental Health Forum, London, 1988.
59. T. Connor, *The London Irish*, London Strategic Policy Unit, London, 1987.
60. Pearson *et al.*, *Generations of an Invisible Minority*.
61. J. A. Jackson, *The Irish in Britain*, Routledge, London, 1962; K. O'Connor, *The Irish in Britain*, Torc, Dublin, 1974; Connor, *The London Irish*; L. Greenslade, M. Pearson and M. Madden, *Irish Migrants in Britain*, Occasional Papers in Irish Studies 3, Institute of Irish Studies, Liverpool, 1991.
62. Greenslade, 'From Visible to Invisible'.
63. Connor, *The London Irish*, p. 19.
64. Irish Support and Advice Centre, *Annual Report*, ISAC, London, 1990.
65. Mary Kells, 'The Relevance of Ethnicity in 1990: the Case of Contemporary Irish Immigrants in London', paper presented at the third Workshop in Social Science, University of Liverpool, May 1990. See also, Mary Kells, '"I'm myself and nobody else": gender and ethnicity among young middle class Irish women in London', 'Irish women and Irish migration', in Volume 4 of *The Irish World Wide*, forthcoming.
66. Kells, 'The Relevance of Ethnicity', p. 6.
67. S. Pink, 'From Belfast to London: a Case Study of Identity and Ethnicity amongst young Migrants from Northern Ireland', M.A. dissertation, University of Manchester, 1990.
68. Pink, 'From Belfast to London', p. 42.
69. Pink, 'From Belfast to London', p. 39.
70. Fanon, *Black Skins, White Masks*.
71. Torrey, *Schizophrenia and Civilization*.
72. Brent Irish Mental Health Group, *The Irish Experience of Mental Ill-health in London*, BIMHG, London, 1986.
73. Brent Irish Mental Health Group, *The Irish Experience*, p. 16.
74. Brent Irish Mental Health Group, *The Irish Experience*, p. 19.
75. Cochrane and Stopes-Roe, 'Psychological disturbance'.
76. R. Cochrane and S. Bal, 'Ethnic density is unrelated to incidence of schizophrenia', *Br. J. Psychiatr.*, 153, 1988, p. 363–6.
77. N. Scheper-Hughes, *Saints, Scholars, and Schizophrenics: Mental Illness in rural Ireland*, University of California Press, Berkeley, 1979. Greenslade, 'A Culture of Madness'.
78. Fanon, *Black Skins, White Masks*, p. 77.
79. R. D. Laing, *The Divided Self*, Tavistock, London, 1959; Bateson, *Steps to an Ecology of Mind*; M. Roth, 'Diagnosis and prognosis of schizophrenia', in G. D. Burrows *et al.*, eds., *Handbook of Studies on Schizophrenia* 1, Elsevier, Amsterdam, 1986; K. Schneider, *Clinical Psychopathology*, trans. M. W. Hamilton, Grune & Stratton, London, 1959.
80. F. Jameson, *The Political Unconscious*, Methuen, London, 1981.
81. Kells, 'The Relevance of Ethnicity'.
82. Pink, *From Belfast to London*.
83. R. Lynn and S. Hampson, 'Alcoholism and alcohol consumption in Ireland', *J. Irish Medical Assoc.*, 63, 1970, pp. 39–42; Pearson *et al.*, *Generations of an Invisible Minority*.
84. Kells, 'The Relevance of Ethnicity'.
85. Fanon, *Black Skins, White Masks*, p. 165.

Acknowledgements

This chapter is a revised version of a paper originally presented at the British Sociological Association annual conference in March 1991. Financial support in its preparation was provided by Declan Kelly PLC, to whom grateful thanks are extended. Further thanks for their help, support and patience during its production must also be given to Janet Ditchfield, Ulrich Kockel, Mark McGovern, Peter Shirlow and the staff and customers of Mulligan's and the Ducie Arms, Manchester. Responsibility for errors is my own.

10 Irish studies: a historical survey across the Irish diaspora

Nessan Danaher

The recent growth and expansion of Irish studies, in the United States, Canada, Australia and Britain especially, have served various useful purposes. Partly, this development has served to dispel ignorance, suspicion, misconception and apathy, be these traits among the various host communities or among the Irish themselves. In the cases of all the areas settled by Irish migrants over the last 150 years, there is evidence of a common residual strand of anti-Irish prejudice; there is also some evidence in most of attempts to develop an Irish dimension within education provision. Transient though these attempts may have been, they were nonetheless of value at the time, and deserve respect, given the time in and circumstances under which they operated. In the late twentieth century, governments' educational policy perspectives developed more positively, especially perhaps in Britain, with recognition being accorded to an Irish dimension by local and national government, and by the Roman Catholic Church authorities. (This chapter does not attempt to develop a perspective in regard to Irish Protestant migrants; the intention is deliberately to examine the majority Catholic experience.) This recognition, and the creation of vibrant centres of Irish studies at various levels of education, and the national Irish studies associations, have helped the overall rate of development, as has the creation of new learning and teaching resources. Although much still needs to be carried out, and resources (especially money) are sparse, the lines of development are there and will, hopefully, prosper in the future.

Irish studies seem to have become an important part of the ethnic and social identity process for the second-generation Irish, and as such need thoughtful, responsible fostering so that a positive experience emerges in educational as well as personal terms for students at all levels. In 1980 a percipient article by Ivan Gibbons, a pioneer of the 'new wave' of Irish studies in Britain, pinpointed three fundamental reasons why Irish studies courses should be offered in the context of adult education. These three factors are valid in a wider educational sense and could be applied to any standard national curriculum in an area of Irish migrant settlement, whether it be in the UK or elsewhere. They therefore deserve closer examination and can briefly be summarized as follows:

1 Despite extensive, topical media coverage of Ireland and Irish affairs, the average English citizen apparently had little or no knowledge of the background to the critical events; this ignorance was often compounded by suspicion, misunderstanding and apathy.
2 Educational institutes committed to responding positively to the educational needs of ethnic minorities should, surely, be catering for the largest and longest-settled such group in the UK, namely the Irish. Gibbons went on to comment that there 'was indeed a vacuum needing to be filled because of the increasing sense of identity that many Irish people in Britain were feeling in the mid-1970s, largely as a result of the Northern troubles. This was evidenced by mushrooming interest in traditional music and Irish language amongst other forms.'
3 There was evidence that second-generation Irish school pupils, despite an emotional affinity with the land of their parents, had little cultural or historical knowledge of the country.[1]

Each of the above phenomena reflects certain historical perspectives; furthermore, the experiences described are in most instances common to Irish migrants in North America and Australia as well as Great Britain.

'Ignorance, suspicion, misconception and . . . apathy'

Gibbons could easily have extended his first argument into two associated areas: the characteristic features of the anti-Irish stereotype and the quality of media treatment of Ireland, both currently and in the past.

The historical pattern of prejudice against the Irish, not just in Britain but also in other English-speaking areas, is so manifest as to be beyond dispute. Whatever the Irish may themselves have contributed to the negative stereotype, the evidence of sustained prejudice speaks for itself. Modern scholarship by authors such as N. Lebow and L. P. Curtis[2] deals more than adequately with deep-rooted denigration and prejudicial images. In fact there is ample evidence of endemic anti-Irish hostility in standard works covering Irish settlement in Britain, North America and Australia. The theme is also evident in biographical material, as well as in fictional portrayals.

As might be expected, the evidence suggests that the negative image travelled with English/British settlers on their way to the then colonies. O'Tuathaigh, in a model analysis of the problems of integration for the Irish in nineteenth-century Britain, remarks, 'That this antagonism was an odd compound of religious, social and political elements, of the rational and the irrational, is not in dispute.'[3] Writing almost half a century ago, Handley commented tellingly on Scottish native attitudes to Irish newcomers in the 1798–1845 period: 'Those who felt it derogatory to their position to indulge in physical violence found an outlet for their animosity against the Irish in all sorts of verbal abuse and mockery.'[4] He continued:

it was the cumulative effect of such abuse appearing frequently over decades of years that etched with its acid an unflattering picture of the Irishman in the minds of many who might otherwise have been prepared to receive him on probation. As a consequence, the dice were loaded against him from the beginning.

Handley was, of course, a Catholic cleric, and not surprisingly he deals at length with prejudices based on religion; however, considering that he was writing long before the fashionable radical airings of anti-racism, his analysis is well furnished with evidence relating to the stereotypical traits of 'Paddy' – for example, the frequently repeated theme of the interplay between Irish gullibilty and cunningness – or 'heads we win, tails you lose'. The similarity with European images of blacks is striking; it is also echoed in antisemitic lore of the 1930s, where Jews are at once conniving capitalists and conspiratorial communists.

Writing some sixteen years later, J. A. Jackson reached similar conclusions: 'Economic, political and religious motives often lay behind the attack on the Irishman as the representative of a foreign and execrated religion . . . the twentieth century Irish migrant to Britain experiences the inheritance of past rancours.'[5] Jackson cites court cases of the 1950s and '60s where Irish persons were either forced or encouraged to leave the country; the *Irish Post* of the late 1980s and early '90s carried similar reports (e.g. in London, Camden Council's housing department's refusal to house Irish families).

The same pattern of prejudice is easily traceable in accounts of Irish settlement in the then British empire. Kerby Miller, speaking of pre-1780s Irish migration to North America, noted that 'Presbyterian indentured servants often fared little better than their Catholic peers';[6] epithets quoted by Miller in original descriptions of Ulster Protestant settlers include 'lazy', 'dissipated', 'poor', 'uncleanly', 'unwholesome', 'disgusting', 'pernicious' and 'pugnacious'. Not surprisingly, Catholics in the post-Famine migration movements reaped an even more abundant harvest of abuse. Miller prefaces his detailed evidence thus:

> Frightened by the growth of what seemed to be a permanently impoverished proletariat, the nation's upper and middle classes adopted increasingly harsh attitudes towards unskilled labourers, whose failure to rise in a purportedly open and egalitarian society could now be 'explained' conveniently by reference to their predominantly Irish origins, Catholic religion, and intemperate and unruly habits. Cultural antipathies often so reinforced economic cleavages as to preclude even the most elemental forms of justice or charity.[7]

Another American commentator, specializing specifically on questions of ethnicity and nationality *vis-á-vis* the Irish in the United States before *c.* 1865, noted that the Irish endured a double dose of negative stereotyping; whilst 'Anglo–American perceptions of the Irish doubtless owed something to traditions in language derived from their English cultural inheritance and reinforced by the continued passage of literature and language from Britain to America,'[8] the particular and developing internal situation in the United States *c.* 1840–65 led to even more sophisticated and permeating stereotypical assumptions.

The Canadian experience was similar. In a compilation concerning the Irish in Canada, Donald Power underlined this similarity between English, American and Canadian magazines and newspapers in both the nineteenth and twentieth centuries:

> Through an examination of political cartoons and comics, it can be shown that the Irish were generally portrayed in negative ways and that, for a long time, in an attempt to denigrate them, they were represented as members of a sub-human species, similar to apes, baboons, orang-utangs and gorillas.[9]

A useful brief and well illustrated summary of the pictorial evidence is to be found in a recent British publication by Liz Curtis.[10]

Another ex-British colony, Australia, provides further material to support the developing argument. O'Farrell's impressive history cites convincing evidence that the Irish in Australia were credited with being inferior in both racial and religious terms; 'like the Aborigine, the Irish were primitive, backward, outmoded, the butt of impatience and contempt'.[11] As in Britain and the United States, in terms of employment opportunities 'the general drift is clear: the Irish believed they were discriminated against, and to some extent they were'.[12] O'Farrell goes on to mention media mendacity against the Irish in the 1920s and '30s, partly as a reaction to the attitude of the Irish government of the time to the Empire. In 1980 Kirkaldy, another commentator then working in Australia, produced a well rounded piece entitled 'The return of the Irish joke'. He concluded:

> The Ireland of Irish jokes exists only in English minds. They are attempts to rationalise and explain a crisis in a part of Britain that few Englishmen really understand. . . . The images and stereotypes displayed in Irish jokes are a major factor in promoting English incomprehension and insensitivity regarding these realities and are, therefore, an important part of what is a continuing British tragedy.[13]

The contention here is that the Irish joke is the late twentieth century's version of earlier anti-Irish stereotyping, the difference being that it is not confined to the literate classes, as was much nineteenth-century prejudice, but instead is purveyed to the widest possible audience via prime-time television slots.[14] Of much greater significance are the questions thrown up by the freeing of incarcerated groups like the Birmingham Six, the Guildford Four and the Maguire Seven: is it possible for someone of Irish extraction to receive fair treatment at the hands of Britain's media, law enforcement agencies and legal system? Clearly, being Irish in Britain can have its disadvantages (witness the massive non-prosecution rate of Irish individuals detained under and hence harassed by the Prevention of Terrorism Act). This disadvantage also extends to the second generation, with implications for both the process and the content of education.

Kirkaldy's contribution deftly relates patterns of historical prejudice to current affairs considerations. The relevance to Irish studies is twofold: the current troubles have led to continued media distortion, dishonesty and misinformation; these in turn have created problems for second-generation Irish in Britain in terms of developing a positive sense of self-identity.

Whilst indicating problems created by British media coverage of Northern Irish affairs, Gibbons did not allude to the associated problem, namely the poor quality, on the whole, of popular media coverage of the topic, and the serious problems of selectivity, objectivity and censorship thereby created. The shortcomings caused by both official and covert manipulation have been adequately catalogued by Liz Curtis and Elliott. Elliott was an academic working at the Mass Communications Research Centre (Leicester University), where he produced a UNESCO-commissioned report on comparative media treatment of Northern Irish affairs. His research indicated that the British press deliberately set out to heal the physical, and especially the psychological, wounds, inflicted on British society by IRA bombings. He termed this process 'social cauterization'; indeed, after the Guildford bombings, noted Elliott, 'the British media orchestrated a process of social cauterisation for which there was no parallel in Ulster'.[15] The research explored issues such as the trivialization of material, the reliance on biased, pro-British government information sources, and the absence of any analysis. Inevitably, whatever good this process may have done for the psyche of the ordinary person in the street, the same process must surely have caused problems for children and adolescents of Irish descent attempting to develop a positive sense of identity for themselves. Where Irish newspapers were in general more open and sceptical, and concentrated less on ephemera, 'in Britain, scepticism of the official account was rarely shown'.[16] Elliott also commented on the manner in which contemporary media reports of the troubles served to support the traditional negative stereotypes analysed earlier. The sources of violence were portrayed as products of 'terrorism, the result of inexplicable asocial forces';[17] of sectarianism, which was widespread and was, again, inexplicable; and of feuding, which was explicable but unreasonable.

These findings by Elliott were supported by Liz Curtis in her important study of the propaganda surrounding reportage on Ireland. Her research, aptly subtitled 'the British media and the battle for hearts and minds', listed more than forty television programmes on the North which have been banned, censored or deliberately delayed.[18]

Against such a background of manipulation and news management, it is hardly surprising that research interviews carried out with second-generation Irish children in London and Birmingham should have shown that the pressures brought to bear on them by biased media treatment of Northern Irish topics have led to problems in the process of ethnic identity.

The London survey was carried out in four Catholic schools, two primary and two secondary. The questions involved considerations of whether or not an Irish dimension should feature within curriculum policy and content, and teaching staff attitudes to such questions. Joan Inglis interviewed 127 pupils and twenty-seven staff; particularly interesting were the answers of the nine Irish-born staff and the four teachers of Irish descent. The answers given by these thirteen teachers can, for present purposes, be analysed specifically in order to assess how they reacted to certain key issues:

1 Five said they would avoid any mention of Irish matters because of the

troubles; two of these remarked on a high degree of antipathy towards the Irish from English colleagues because of this issue.

2 Four staff felt that children should assimilate (as simple as that).

3 Four staff felt that children did suffer a loss of identity and, in some instances, incurred a sense of inferiority.

4 Two remarked on the absence of Irish names from junior-age (five-to-eleven) reading schemes, while noting the presence of Asian and Afro-Caribbean names.

5 One teacher mentioned that non-Irish colleagues had objected to a primary-level religious studies (Roman Catholic) scheme (Veritas) because of its use of Irish personal and place names. I myself have found evidence of similar reactions in junior schools in the East Midlands.

6 Four teachers did feel that Irish dancing should feature on the curriculum. I think this would represent goodwill whilst in effect being unsupported tokenism.

7 No teacher interviewed felt that second-generation Irish children should be seen as an integral part of a multi-cultural education programme. After reviewing the children's statements, Inglis remarked of the telling of Irish jokes (i.e. anti-Irish jokes) that 'the damage it is causing in the Irish community can be seen in the children's comments'. Inglis concluded, 'what was revealed to me was the "near death" of Irish culture in England, especially in the area of education . . . and, more hopefully, the efforts of some individuals and groups to promote the Irish culture in this country to the equal status it merits with all other cultures'.[19]

On the effects of the political situation, she found that 'the effects of the Northern Irish situation could be seen in the attitudes of some Irish teachers (almost a fear), in their reluctance to promote Irish culture'.

These conclusions were reinforced four years later by the findings of extensive fieldwork carried out among second-generation Irish children in Birmingham. On the basic assumption that low-status minority groups invent strategies to counter the resulting negative psychological consequences, Philip Ullah set out to find out whether if the Irish fitted this picture.[20] Did the second-generation Irish experience identity problems? If they did, how did they cope? Given the historical background of negative stereotyping, did children of Irish descent suffer embarrassment and shame, or did they develop a sense of pride as a counterbalance? Of his first investigation (1981) Ullah remarked, 'the main premise of the study is that to be Irish, or of Irish descent, in Britain today is to be a member of a negatively defined group'. This finding underlines the fact that anti-Irish prejudice (or racism, to use the current terminology of the debate) is not merely a past historical phenomenon.

Ullah's research went on to declare that it was clear that the implications of the effects of minority group membership applied to all low-status groups, regardless of colour. On the issue of whether pupils of Irish descent experienced the syndrome of cultural marginality, he concluded that they appeared to synthesize competing identities by adapting to two cultures.

Interestingly, a report in a national educational journal in the early 1980s confirmed Ullah's and Inglis's findings. Dr K. C. Thomas, of Nottingham University, in the process of a 'stereotyping' exercise held in a multi-racial East Midlands eleven-to-sixteen school, noted that 'the English came out best, the Pakistanis and Irish the worst . . . media coverage of Northern Ireland's troubles could account for the negative view of the Irish'.[21]

These findings are worth closer examination in the context of Gibbon's second point, where he considers the educational needs of the Irish community if that community is defined as an ethnic minority group.

Culture, ethnicity and education policy

The at times acrimonious debate about whether or not the Irish constitute an ethnic group has simmered on during the last decade. At this point it should be made clear that I myself subscribe to the view that the Irish clearly constitute an ethnic minority group as far as residence in Britain is concerned. The definitions of ethnicity used to reach this conclusion are those of Morris and de Vos.[22]

It is the links between culture, ethnicity and education that offer a way forward. 'The possession of a distinct culture provides one of the most important identifying characteristics of an ethnic group'.[23] Minority groups usually enjoy less influence than dominant groups over policy-making and resource acquisition. Government policy, especially in the field of education, determines whether cultural diversity is eliminated, modified or encouraged. In America and Australia, as in Britain, an Anglocentric cultural norm was (in the past) deliberately fostered.

> Schools were consciously seen as one of the most effective instruments of achieving the cultural assimilation of ethnic children, not only through immersion in the ways of the majority, but also by the elimination of their native cultures.[24]

Even when assimilation is publicly eschewed as government policy, multiculturalism can be used as a cover for the fragmenting of ethnic cultures into meaningless residues, where their impact on the majority and transmission to the minority become doubtful. A typical method of indirect assimilation is the discouraging of ethnic minority languages, so hastening the disintegration of the minority culture. Interestingly, Irish language activists in Britain have campaigned for the last two years for Irish to be included as a recognized optional language in the new British national curriculum (i.e. the compulsory fare for all in public state education from five years to sixteen). Whilst the language should be maintained and supported, this campaign may well have represented a misdirection of effort in that Irish cannot be regarded as a community language on mainland Britain, that is, a widely used tongue like Punjabi, Gujarati and Urdu. By comparison, far less of a campaigning effort seems to have been made in terms of developing an Irish dimension in the curricular areas of history, geography and literature. Happily, colleagues in educational and community organizations maintained enough pressure to see a worthwhile

Irish dimension emerge in the final programme for history in the national curriculum (discussed at greater length further on).[25]

The idea of benevolent government policy towards minority groups is basically a post-1965 phenomenon. It is pertinent to look at nineteenth and early twentieth-century Irish migrant experience to see what agendas, if any, had been set prior to the last quarter-century. Instructive examples can be gleaned from Irish experience in Canada, the United States, Australia and Britain. Similar experiences over recognition, educational resources and practice emerge. While it is clear that early state education was not designed to meet minority needs, such state efforts are significant – for, in effect, they record official attitudes to the Irish migrants in those countries.

The North American experience

In Canada, as early as 1830, concern was being shown about the dangerous ideology being imported by US teachers into Canadian establishments. Davin, writing in 1877 in *The Irishman in Canada*, noted that:

> at this time many of the school teachers were from below the line, and children were taught false history and inspired with passions hostile to the present state; nor was it until 1846 that a stop was put to this abuse of confidence by men characterised as 'anti-British adventurers'.[26]

It must be assumed that Davin, given his brief, was making reference to republican ideals, which were clearly anti-British and may possibly have emanated from Irish-Americans inimical to British colonial sensibilities.

A compilation detailing the Canadian Irish experience conveys some revealing insights into the education of the Irish and their descendants in Canada. As well as the looming presence of the Church – in matters educational and otherwise – Patrick O'Flaherty, growing up in early twentieth-century Newfoundland, recalled the curriculum thus:

> . . . what astonishes me now is how thoroughly Ireland had been expunged from it. No Irish geography, history or literature was taught. We knew nothing of such Irishmen as John Kent, John Valentine Nugent and Patrick Morris, who played prominent roles in Newfoundland's fight for self-government in the nineteenth century, and whose biographies might have left us with a sense of pride.[27]

O'Flaherty expanded on his theme, and detailed a series of missed opportunities in history whereby Irish personages and themes could have been legitimately treated. Regarding a particular text used as standard history, he commented that the author:

> silently allowed the Irish to be absorbed into the nationality of their oppressors. All this we eagerly drank in. The school curriculum was, in fact, that of a successfully colonised people. Nothing is more typical of a long-colonised race than to kiss the boot that treads it down. We children dutifully learned English history and literature [which, he continues] carries with it the baggage of national pride and an implication of racial and cultural superiority.[28]

The presumption must be that this was part of a similar pattern across the

Canadian experience, and may help to account for the Canadian Irish Catholic's penchant for non-extremist positions on most political topics.

Nicolson discusses the part played in the urbanization processes by the Roman Catholic Church in Victorian Toronto.[29] A strict, all-embracing code covered most aspects of daily life, with Catholic ideology determining behaviour in all situations. However, in contrast to O'Flaherty's account, Nicolson remarks that 'with Irish novels, popular history and cheap religious literature available, a number of Irish Catholic bookstores sprang up in the City; this led to an increased pride in nationality and linked nationality to religion'.[30] He concluded that 'the Church fostered a pride in being Irish and educated the family to live and work with self-respect in a Protestant city'.[31] The nationality referred to would seem to be based on cultural and religious criteria, and not forms of ethnic or political consciousness which might have had awkward ramifications for the Catholic Irish Canadians in their relations with their fellow citizens.

South of the border, educational matters appear to have led to a wider variety of disputes and community pressures. Referring to mid-nineteenth-century prejudice by the Know-nothings, Knobel remarks:

> Religious, fraternal, or political, the institutional forms of ante-bellum nativism were interconnected. . . . Active participants consistently agitated for a Protestant atmosphere in the public schools, for exclusion of Roman Catholics from public office, for more stringent enforcement of the naturalisation laws[32]

as well as for a tightening of citizenship procedures. Nativism, says Knobel, was anti-Irish only in the sense that it derived from anti-Catholicism.[33] However, in the wider context of the societal stereotype, the home-produced American image of the Irish was virtually censorious and very widely agreed upon, and American materials (perhaps surprisingly) more often chose negative descriptives than did English-produced materials.[34] A brief examination of a cross-section of local, state experiences fills out the picture; disputes centred on funding, and curricular areas.

A detailed account by Dennis Clark of educational experiences of the Irish in Philadelphia throws an interesting light on experiences apparently shared by the Irish elsewhere in the United States.[35] The pre-eminence of clerical influence, the proselytizing by Protestants, and the direct action of the Catholic Church in ameliorating social conditions, all meant that Catholic American educational activity could be characterized by 'clerical leadership, voluntarism, religious separation, social service and cultural simplicity.'[36] The joint influence of school and church was decisive for the Irish in the process of adjustment to new conditions; Clark describes the development of an alternative school system as being 'amongst the most dynamic features of the city's life in the 1850s and 1860s'. He comments further: 'the educational systems, both formal and informal, permitted the maintenance of ethnic tradition and the alignment of immigrant aspirations. This was more true of the parochial – than of the public – school network.'[37] What is left unclear is exactly what ethnic tradition was being maintained.

The situation in Chicago as described by Ellen Skerrett indicates that, although the Irish were regarded as the most 'American' of the city's ethnic groups, the strong underlying Protestant orientation of the public schools until the last decades of the nineteenth century was an inhibiting factor for Catholics. In their own schools, however, according to Skerrett, the teaching sisters, while they:

> did not denigrate Irish identity, neither were they particularly conscious of it . . . the nuns felt no need to foster ethnic identity in either their convents or their schools. Indeed, the study of Irish history was not incorporated into Chicago's English-speaking parochial schools until 1904 and then only because of an organised campaign by the Ancient Order of Hibernians . . . while efforts at promoting Irish history, language, music, and art made some headway, the Gaelic movement as a whole failed to catch on.[38]

Skerrett offers two reasons for this pattern: as the nuns were Irish or Irish-American, there was no need to do anything specific with the curriculum; also, second-generation Chicago Irish began to see Irish community bodies as associated with the 'shanty Irish' and therefore militating against upward mobility. Furthermore, whatever the elements of Irish history that were integrated into the curriculum turned out to be inappropriate to the needs and experiences of second-generation Irish Americans.

The main aspects of the Philadelphia experience were mirrored in that of San Francisco. Burchell details the disputes over funding and Protestant cultural dominance.[39] On the key underlying issues of social, ethnic and psychological identity Burchell's comment goes to the core of these questions:

> Every immigrant had to make up his or her mind what parts of the ancestral culture should be retained, what elements of the new society adopted . . . There was a need to retain the psychologically useful and to jettison what was irrelevant to life in a new home. Individuals would disagree on the precise amount of cultural divestment that was necessary . . . whereas the attitudes to parochial schools show that they were regarded by a majority as necessary to group identity and security . . .[40]

There was no such unanimity on other issues, such as the need for an Irish 'ethnic' newspaper, or a purely 'ethnic' popular theatrical tradition.[41]

The process of *loosening* cultural ties and ethnic roots for the Irish-Americans was assisted also by the nature of the learning materials in use. Writing as early as 1956, Wittke commented on disputes in the 1850s and 1880s about history textbooks and noted that 'as late as 1920, Edward F. McSweeney of Boston, speaking for the Friends of Irish Freedom, complained heatedly of the Century Dictionary's definition of the word "brutal" in connection with a reference to the Irish'.[42]

The topic of textbooks is also covered by Clark's portrayal of the educational experience of the Philadelphia Irish. He comments:

> the subject matter used was inappropriate for the initiation of youth into a world of accuracy, literacy and regulated behaviour . . . It can safely be assumed that children did not learn much of their own social backgrounds or of the community conditions of their city in the schools.[43]

Similar trains of thought are discernible in relevant fictional material.

Perhaps the most enduring Irish-American youth in fiction is Studs Lonigan. When Studs, almost fifteen years old, is leaving St Patrick's Grammar School the priest's valedictory address to the departing pupils concentrates on the implications of their being Catholics, without any mention of the Irish connection. Oddly, although the opening of the story is set in 1916, there is not even a hint of the significance of that date in the context of Irish nationalist hagiography. As one notable historian of Irish America puts it, 'In the course of the twentieth century the American Irish passed through an identity crisis and in doing so lost their psychological dependence on Irish nationalism.'[44]

What conclusions, then, can be reached about the effects of their educational experiences on the second-generation Irish in America? Wittke, writing in 1956, stressed the Irish sense of belonging, of being American, and commented that 'their constant preoccupation with the causes of their native land may have been partly responsible for the fact that they developed no distinct Irish culture in the United States or any consistent program of "Irishism" '.[45] Most of the Irish were seen as being in the famous melting pot, enjoying upward mobility. This view is developed by McCaffrey, who states that 'the American Irish took their biggest leap forward in social and occupational mobility after World War II, with education providing the springboard'.[46] Was there a hidden cost to this advance, a cost in terms of social identity and religious practice? We await further study of the parallel experience in post-war Britain: how many of the children of Irish descent benefited from the famous Butler Education Act of 1944? One beneficiary has made the implications of that Act in Northern Ireland very clear. In her autobiography, Bernadette Devlin stresses the liberating effects of the 1944 Act for deprived Catholics who, like herself, were offered better opportunities.[47] Perhaps this helps to account for the sober appreciation of the high quality of a number of the young personnel in the Provisional IRA in the now famous leaked British army intelligence report by General Glover, featured on the main BBC news analysis programme *Panorama* in 1987.

As to the American experience, there is a broad measure of agreement among the authors cited on the proven positive virtues of the Catholic parochial educational system. In particular, two strands are notable: the high level of achievement in parochial schools *per se* and in terms of the public schools' standards; and also the success in producing teachers, especially women teachers, not only for the parochial schools but for the public schools as well. Where there has been some debate is over the issue of the contribution of Irish-American Catholics to the wider intellectual life of the United States.[48] McCaffrey concludes that 'lack of confidence and opportunity more than inadequate educational institutions retarded the advance of Catholic intellectualism'.[49] The post-1945 opportunities of educational development offered in the GI Bill of Rights was the underlying guarantor of this development.

If the educational achievement of the Irish-American was secure by the third quarter of this century, what of their sense of Irish identity? Both Skerrett and Burchell have revealing insights to offer on this issue. Writing of the San Francisco Irish in the 1848–80 period, Burchell concludes that a 'cultural pluralism' of both shared and exclusive values emerged. Full-scale assimilation did not occur, partly because of nativist hostility and partly because the immigrants did not want it to occur.[50] Burchell's conclusion is that 'the central core of Irish experience in the city was whole and satisfactory', even given the large numbers of Irish in city institutions (prisons, almshouses, hospitals and asylums) and despite the persistence of bitter controversies over schooling. Of the Philadelphia situation, Clark concludes by emphasizing the factor of increasing urban pluralism, and the positive achievement of affirming democratic values represented by the two freedoms – of religious conscience and of association.[51] Neither of these examples indicates in any detail what the situation became in respect of Irish identity. Skerrett, deliberating on the Chicago experience, concludes that 'far from limiting mobility or assimilation, the parochial institutions created by the Irish hastened their integration into the larger society'; the parishes and schools 'met their special needs as American Catholics'.[52] However, she alludes to the conclusions of McCaffrey – that residents of urban Irish neighbourhoods were religiously and emotionally, but not culturally, Irish. Skerrett goes on to quote McCaffrey's contention:

> that the vast majority of American Irish have been severed from their historical roots by Catholic education. Not only did Irish American Catholic educators ignore the Irish dimension of their heritage but they emphasized a Catholic culture that was devoid of ethnic identity.

The evidence examined above would appear to lend weight to McCaffrey's conclusions. Was the American Irish educational experience repeated in other geographical areas, in Australia and Great Britain?

The Australian Irish experience

The whole question of the 'Irishness' of Catholic schools in Australia is dealt with directly, and from the outset of his discussion, by O'Farrell. He notes bluntly that:

> a hard look at the historical realities (as distinct from the nostalgic inventions) suggests that neither the church nor the school authorities, nor the Irish Catholic population, took much interest in Irish cultural values, nor tried to impart them, except in regard to religion. One clear strand of evidence of this lack is the occasional (they were greatly discouraged) efforts of Irish culture enthusiasts (or fanatics) to get such Irish culture introduced into the Catholic school system.[53]

He offers several examples to justify his conclusions. The United Irish League, founded in 1901, stayed in existence for only five years. Operating in New South Wales, it succeeded in attracting only twenty-seven out of 350 Catholic schools to its Irish history and language classes; in 1904 some 400 out of a total of 32,000 Catholic pupils sat Irish history examinations. The emphasis on religious matters, together with the rest of the standard curriculum, left little time for things Irish. Although some of the textbooks used did convey a little of a sense of Irishness, O'Farrell suggests that the leading Catholic colleges 'shared that element of snobbery in the social classes to which they belonged, or aspired, which looked down on anything Irish as inferior, grubby and common – attitudes held, and communicated, even by teachers Irish themselves'. Even in the schools for the offspring of the poor Irish, the deliberate policy and practice of training pupils for future employment as manual labourers or domestic servants had the effect of being anti-Irish, given the representation of the Irish in the Australian poverty statistics. O'Farrell concludes that 'the whole atmosphere of such schooling confirmed a *status quo* in which the Irish were on the bottom'. To make matters worse, Irish-born teachers of higher socio-economic standing exhibited such disdainful attitudes to the Irish slum children that the latter were sometimes imbued with a deep hatred of persons and things Irish. Even where an element of choice existed, as in school concerts, only a brief, token Irish representation emerged (O'Farrell quotes research by Louise Mazzaroli). Similar trends will be noted when the situation in Britain is analysed. However, it may be necessary to temper O'Farrell's conclusions in two respects:

1 Given the internal history of Australia's origins and existing attitudes of hostility towards the Irish, the low figures quoted for active participation in an Irish educational dimension may represent a rather modest victory rather than an overwhelming defeat.
2 The inimical attitudes of 'successful' Irish towards their poorer confreres and the latter's cultural habits, not only in Australia but elsewhere, need some analysis and explanation in terms of psychological pressures.

In an article which examines the post-colonial personality, Kenny, a psychotherapist, throws some interesting light on the Irish–English relationship: Kenny defines 'personality' as a 'fluid evolving process within which individuals and communities may channel themselves and move towards the future'. He posits that Irish–English relations represent 'complementary interactions'; in other words, 'those where the actions of both sides are very different, but yet mutually fit one another in a jig-saw fashion. Such a pattern is often developed by people who have endured long-term insecurity and uncertainty.'[54] The following table, from Kenny, presents the ideas succinctly:

English	Irish
Dominant	Submissive
Exhibitionism	Spectatorship
Succouring	Dependence

Whereas some nations experience symmetrical interactions, marked by rivalry, competitiveness and mutual emulation, the English–Irish interaction is complementary (as defined above). Kenny suggests:

The English dominated and the Irish eventually submitted. The English exhibited their power and the Irish were the captive audience (spectators). Helplessness and dependency were engendered in the Irish with the concomitant evocation of succourance (e.g. famine soup kitchens) from the English.

This process can result, says Kenny, in 'constriction', the deliberate decision by individuals to limit their horizons in order to improve their ability to cope. He extends the idea from the individual:

> we may also postulate that for a nation faced with continuing defeat at the hands of its oppressors (including colonisation, deprivation, famine, poverty, etc.) and living with an ever-present hated authority (together with the guilt, shame, sense of inferiority, anger and frustration that arise from defeat and failure), a type of NATIONAL CONSTRICTION could be seen to be taking place in an attempt to cope with living in an impossible situation.[55]

Possibly, this psychological phenomenon would have travelled with the migrants, and would continue to operate in a host society such as Australia which still functioned, either by inheritance or by virtue of colonial rule, as a British cultural entity. The WASP syndrome so often associated with United States had its counterparts elsewhere. O'Farrell, indeed, has commented on the influence over a forty-year period of Dr Alexander Leeper, of Melbourne University, who 'moulded student minds and the public atmosphere towards hostility to Irish Catholicism'.[56] Leeper, an Irishman, was a proficient and widely effective Protestant Anglo-Irish ideologue. Also raised by O'Farrell is the unsound assumption of the 'Irishness' of Irish Catholic teachers.[57] (This point receives further attention below.)

The experience of the Irish in Britain

The experience of the children of the Irish migrants in Britain echoes that of the North American and Australian situations with respect to both the content of the curriculum and the nature of learning resources. Lees's well known study of Irish migrants in Victorian London had a chapter on education aptly entitled 'The reforging of an Irish Catholic culture'. As in the American examples, the teaching profession represented 'an avenue [that] had been opened up by the Church for the movement of Irish migrants into the middle class'.[58] The fare for most pupils, however, was only basic; the well known 'three Rs' plus a fourth – religion. For the minority (10 per cent) who studied any history at all 'Irish history was excluded.'[59] Even though certain sets of texts were modelled on series produced for the Irish market, Catholic schoolbooks 'defended and exalted the *status quo*. . . . The political *status quo* was accepted too. . . . Ancient and biblical history took precedence over news of modern events.' Lees concludes that 'it may be surmised that those who passed through church schools had their Catholic loyalties reinforced and grew in familiarity with the norms and messages of the Church'.[60]

There are parallels to the London experience in Scotland. Handley details attempts in the 1850s to introduce into Scottish Catholic schools sets of textbooks produced by the Irish National Board of Education. Scottish Protestant objections were understandable but unnecessary, for Handley clearly illustrates that these materials presented no threat to Protestant ideology; a senior member of the board had set out to 'purge the educational curriculum of those classbooks that he believed not only assumed an attitude of tolerance towards the Catholic Faith but taught the Irish pupil that love of his motherland was one of the first virtues of a citizen'.[61]

Not surprisingly, then, it is possible to identify a trend which started in the 1880s and 1890s in England, Scotland and, as seen above, in Australia, namely the provision of opportunities, outside the standard compulsory diet, for second-generation Irish children to learn something more about their heritage, apart from religion. The forms these enterprises took varied; in Australia it was through the medium of special essay-writing competitions, and optional history courses, offered in the schools themselves. In London and other parts of Britain, and in Scotland, alternative structures were created and maintained, structures that today would probably be termed adult and community education.

There is a fascinating account of the growth of this movement in a rare work by William Patrick Ryan, written in 1894, with the slightly misleading title of *The Irish Literary Revival: its History, Pioneers and Possibilities*.[62] Whilst dealing with the turn-of-the-century renaissance in Irish and Anglo-Irish literature, it also details graphically the growth and development of what today would be termed Irish studies classes. A simple time line, listing locations with active programmes, gives some idea of this fruitful outpouring:

1880/81	Southwark Junior Irish Literary Club
1884	Belfast Young Irish Society
1884	Liverpool Irish Literary Institute
1893	Bradford Irish Literary Society
1893	Bolton Irish Literary Society
1893	Manchester Irish Literary Society
1893	Newcastle Irish Literary Society

Circa 1890 there was a similar body to the Liverpool Irish Literary Institute, operating in Bootle; in any case, John Denvir had been organizing various cultural and educational enterprises in the Lancashire area since the 1850s. There were also the various Gaelic League offshoots, for example two classes in Leicestershire in 1902, an area rarely associated with such developments. These enterprises furnish evidence of a reasonably widespread network of informal, committed, organized and active self-help groups. Probably the 'centre of excellence' was the Southwark Junior Irish Literary Club. The guiding spirit in Southwark and south London was Francis A. Fahy, who, with colleagues, co-ordinated existing small local efforts and developed educational and cultural activities in a professional as well as enthusiastic manner. Ryan indicates the contemporary atmosphere:

> Notwithstanding the political ferment, thousands of Irish children in London were growing up Irish in nothing but name. Now came an effort to make them Irish of the Irish, to teach them Irish history and many things kindred, to brighten their minds with national songs, stories and traditions to develop their now dim Celtic talents.[63]

Shorn of romantic gloss, the effort described was businesslike (and remarkably similar to some of the local education authority-backed initiatives which were still a century away).

Fahy's organizing ability was extensive, and voluntary, many of the resulting programmes taking place on Sunday afternoons, not unlike the supplementary schools run by Asian, black and East European cultural and educational groups at the present time. Ryan commented that Fahy's paperwork and planning were 'suggestive of a Government department in their minuteness and complexity, and illustrate quite a system of Irish national education'.[64]

These developments led in turn to other new departures. In January 1893 supportive adults increasingly felt the need of 'a congenial Irish centre, as intellectual as they could make it'.[65] The outcome was the founding of the Southwark Irish Literary Club. The club's aims, 'the cultivation of Irish history, art and literature, and the providing of a medium of social and intellectual intercourse for Irish people of both sexes',[66] were topical in their consciousness of the gender factor. Programmes and activities included lectures, essays, concerts, plays, creative writing, liaison with external media, the publication and sale of cheaply priced printed material, a collection of lectures for use by similar groups without facilities, and the development of a lending library. As usual, then as now, 'though the active workers were never a large number, [the work] was carried out with unfailing spirit through many years of political tension, scanty finances, and trying circumstances of other kinds'.[67] This ferment of activity was compounded by the parallel activities of the Gaelic League and the Irish Texts Society. As early as 1892 moves were afoot to set up an Irish Publishing Company, a departure supported by the Southwark activists, but one which ultimately proved to be abortive.[68]

These developments in London, together with similar departures in the traditional areas of Irish settlement in the north-west and north-east of England, were accompanied by equally impressive activities in Scotland. Handley remarked pointedly, 'One form of cultural education that has appealed to a number of adolescent and adult Irish, and descendants of Irish, in the west of Scotland is the study of the Gaelic language and civilisation.'[69] In 1898 the Glasgow branch of the Gaelic League was founded; by 1903 it was organizing a most impressive *feis* (festival of music, song, dance and verse), encompassing all the functions nowadays carried out by Irish dancing, music and language classes, and for all age groups. By 1900 there were already seventeen branches of the Gaelic cultural movement in the west of Scotland. 'In addition to language lessons, activities included choir practice, juvenile writing and arithmetic classes, dramatic club rehearsals and performances, native-dancing classes, Irish history classes, and tuition in lace-making.'[70] Handley's list represents a programme that a modern educational institute would be proud to offer. Despite the political effects of early twentieth-century Anglo-Irish relations, and the normal variations in enthusiasm and activity caused by changes of personnel and similar factors, Handley was able to trace the continuation of a network of valid activities up to the early 1940s. (Since the late 1980s Feis Glasgow has even been revived.)

Given the sometimes bitter history of Anglo-Irish relations after 1921, and adverse British public reaction to events such as Irish neutrality in

World War II, it is hardly surprising that there was an ebb tide to match the flood tide of Irish cultural activities. Outside areas that enjoyed sophisticated levels of organization there must have been some residual awareness of Irish heritage which was passed on to second from first generation, even if it later succumbed to other dominant cultural strains. One of the best of the very few autobiographies of the poor Irish migrant in Britain is that of Tom Barclay, born of famine migrants in Leicester, in great poverty, in 1852. His memoirs offer some revealing insights into what was known and could be passed on in terms of cultural trans-mission, despite severe socio-economic adversity. Barclay was sent out to work at the age of eight and succeeded in educating himself to the stan-dard of university college extra-mural classes. His story has much to tell; for present purposes, his reflections on his parents' aptitudes and abilities indicate that migration and poverty did not necessarily lead to the death of the spirit and intellect:

> Mother taught me to spell and read. . . . she could read Dr Gallacher's sermons in Irish. . . . How she who read English with difficulty could read those sermons, though in Roman characters . . . is something I do not understand. . . . she was well acquainted with the old legends of Oisin, the Fin, and Cuchullan, and the Gobawn Sayr, and could sing and recite a goodly number of old Irish songs and poems.[71]

Barclay's father, who was of a tough disposition and apparently typical of his harsh situation, was also able to transmit value and worth: 'he had read Byron and Burns and Tom Moore, but I often wonder how he acquired some twenty numbers of a periodical called *The Celt*. . . . it was a "Young Irelander" periodical I believe. . . .'[72] Clearly, parents were in a position to pass on some elements of cultural knowledge.

Barclay, who died in 1933, also commented on anti-Irish attitudes he experienced as a child, in the 1850s and '60s. I myself have interviewed elderly second-generation Irish people, born in Leicester and now in their nineties, who report the same sort of taunts being flung about in the 1920s and '30s, usually a combination of religious and racial/national prejudice. Evidence to date concerning Leicester-born children of Irish descent in Catholic schools in the 1880 to 1950 period echoes the Australian experience described by O'Farrell: token selections of Irish/Catholic hymns, songs, poems, readings and so on at certain appropriate times of the school term. Tellingly, the staff lists of one school, for the period 1886–1904, have twenty-nine out of fifty surnames which are definitely Irish;[73] of the twenty head teachers who served between 1886 and 1991, ten were definitely Irish.[74] These teachers' names may represent first or second-generation Irish; many of the children were certainly of Irish background, according to census and oral history evidence; when the head teacher who produced the centenary history of the school in 1986 was asked to comment on any possible significance, no reply was forthcoming. Once the names had been indicated to him he observed that an Irish factor in the historical staffing of the school had never occurred to him.

Material similar to other than Barclay's work offers evidence of prejudice against children of Irish descent; these works are spread out across the last four decades. Bill Naughton's memoirs and what appears to be an autobiographical novel[75] offer clear instances of prejudice by teachers in Catholic schools and in the wider community in the 1915–20 period. Contemporary material offers similar themes; for example, Maude Casey's 1987 story about a second-generation teenage girl growing up in England,[76] and Brian Keaney's story of a teenage boy of Irish descent growing up in east London in the 1960s.[77] The theme of English–Irish culture clash emerges clearly, with the repeated message of the preponderance of the religious interest in the Catholic schools in which the stories are set. The general preoccupation of Irish Catholic parents and the Church from 1944 onwards was with funding, preserving and maintaining the Catholic sector in state education; there is an interesting personal account of this period by Anne Higgins, a teacher born of Irish parents in Manchester in the 1930s, who describes the main cultural influences in her life, and her changing sense of identity *vis-à-vis* her Irish roots.[78]

Policy perspectives

The various historical, biographical and literary resources alluded to above reach their apogee, as it were, in the only full formal report to be issued by the Catholic education authorities which reflects on the Irish dimension in British education. Gibbons's article, discussed in the introduction, noted that, whilst responding positively to the needs of ethnic minority groups, his institution appeared to be ignoring the needs of the Irish community, 'the largest ethnic minority not only in north Hammersmith' but 'in Britain as a whole'.[79]

This is not the place for a discussion of British educational policy towards ethnic groups over the last three decades, but it should be noted that, in the process of change from an attitude assuming assimilation in the 1960s, local education authorities (LEAs) were beginning to advocate an approach based on multi-cultural awareness, and, in a minority of cases, with the added political zest of anti-racism. At no stage were approaches and policies across the country either completely in place or uniform in philosophy and practice. Sympathetic sounds and in some cases action towards the Irish were emerging in the early 1980s in London (especially in Brent, Haringey and Islington), Manchester and Birmingham. The Commission for Racial Equality (CRE) and the then National Association for Multi-racial Education (NAME) both made positive sounds.[80] By the mid 1980s the two most thorough reports concerning the Irish were adopted by the Greater London Council (GLC) and the Inner London Education Authority (ILEA). Given the prevailing political winds of 1980s Britain, it is perhaps not surprising that those few councils which had enacted policies were forced either to dilute or to abandon them; in the cases of the GLC and the ILEA the Thatcher-led Conservative governments would settle for no less than the outright abolition of the institutions themselves.

Where did this leave the question of recognition for the Irish? A closer examination is needed of the Catholic education authorities' report referred to above.

Recognition by the Catholic education authorities in Britain

Until 1984 there were legitimate grounds for complaint about the lack of official Catholic recognition of the Irish dimension. Because of the historical politico-religious relationship the Catholic Church in Britain generally appears to have preferred a 'low profile' and to avoid controversy: one writer has remarked on the Church's policy of 'playing it cool' in terms of educational politics in the 1950s. Hornsby-Smith has remarked that 'the successful consolidation of the Catholic schools system might possibly have been bought at the cost of any distinctive character or educational contribution'.[81]

Also, historic class divisions existed within the Church's membership between old established upper-class English worshippers and the more recent working-class Irish arrivals.[82]

In his 1973 study of Irish assimilation Ryan remarked that 'the vast majority of priests in London are English-born and among them in dealing with Irish emigrants there exists an unwritten and unacknowledged law: "Thou shalt not create an Irish ghetto"'. In practice, this often means that a priest makes no concession at all to the fact that the majority of his congregation are Irish; indeed, said Ryan, 'there is no evidence that ethnic associations or the Church constitute an obstacle to assimilation among the Irish in Britain'.[83] He went on to remark that 'the emphasis has been placed more on integrating Irish immigrants into the English church irrespective of its nature than on integrating the social cleavages between Irish and English Catholics'.

This issue was examined in detail by Hornsby-Smith and Lee in the late 1970s. They reported that English and Irish Catholics differed in terms of national identity, culture and social class. They offer evidence that as early as the nineteenth century English bishops opposed the provision of Irish priests for Irish immigrants in England; only in the early twentieth century did Irish priests arrive in significant numbers. More important, Hornsby-Smith and Lee comment that the 1944 Education Act probably did not unite Roman Catholics of all classes because of the number and size of Roman Catholic independent schools for the upper middle classes.[84]

In 1978 Hornsby-Smith produced a sociological study of Catholic schools wherein he delivered a critical appraisal of injustices in Church educational institutions. He mentioned the valid moral criticisms that can be made about the strong independent sector and the resulting perpetuation of elitism through socio-economic privilege; this is especially pertinent as the Catholic community has a higher than average proportion of independent schools and places. He also commented on the persistence of social class inequalities of educational opportunity, questioning whether Catholic schools were doing enough to reduce structural inequalities, especially in the light of their strong grammar school traditions.[85]

In both the above areas it is suggested that the second-generation Irish are suffering disadvantage. Hornsby-Smith, in the same 1978 study, remarked, 'One unintended consequence of a policy of Catholic schools for Catholic children may very well be that they are failing to participate in society's attempts to assimilate large numbers of coloured immigrants and their children.'[86]

There is almost an implication here that white pupils, a category which would include the Irish, were being assimilated quite successfully. The unfortunate stress on the assimilation of the second generation no longer holds true of Catholic education (see below) but it does suggest that little thought, if any, was given to the ethnicity of other second-generation groups before this date.

Two other documents, both pamphlets emanating from the Catholic Teachers' Federation, are similarly paradoxical; while they include positive and useful definitions of multi-cultural education they contain complacent claims that Catholic education has always been conscious of multi-cultural issues if only because of the multi-cultural intake of Catholic schools in the past.[87] The 1982 Racial Tensions Enquiry pamphlet would indicate that, in terms of practice, Catholic schools were perhaps neither better nor worse than the average state school in terms of multi-cultural policy and practice. In terms of specific recognition of the Irish dimension, the 1982 pamphlet simply remarks – and in parentheses – '(Celtic, Roman, Norse and Norman cultures have in the past also contributed to our historic British culture)'. The 1983 pamphlet simply lists the Irish as one of the eleven non-British groups whose education has been the responsibility of the Church.

The Catholic Church's 1984 report

The most recent report on Catholic education in a multi-racial society appeared in 1984.[88] It was based on two years' work actively involving fifty Catholic schools in England and Wales, as well as a number of colleges of education and seminaries. It should be noted from the outset that the report is based on thorough and sympathetic understanding of all contemporary issues in multi-cultural and anti-racist education, and in many ways it is an exemplar of what such an education policy document should be. For example, the report examines crucial issues such as institutional racism, the hidden curriculum, the importance of school policies, the relevance of multi-cultural and anti-racist education in schools of limited cultural diversity (e.g. all-white schools) and the importance of in-service staff training.

For obvious reasons, it might be expected that Catholic Schools could and should lead the way in terms of establishing the Irish dimension. In the mid-1970s one child in eleven in England and Wales attended a Roman Catholic school; there were then over 900,000 pupils in just over 3,000 Catholic schools, staffed by over 44,000 teachers.[89] According to the new 1984 report on multi-cultural education in Catholic schools, only two out of the fifty primary and secondary schools visited had less than 10 per cent of pupils of Irish origin, while the vast majority had between 20 per cent and 50 per cent of children from Irish backgrounds.[90]

In terms of staff awareness of these children's needs and of relevant curricular renewal the report is critical indeed, remarking that 'this particular dimension of education has received even less attention than approaches which deal directly with the history, traditions, culture and religion of the Afro-Caribbean and Asian communities'. This report would also appear to confirm the concern that has been raised in this chapter with regard to the malevolent effects of anti-Irish racism and the inhibitions produced by a consciousness of the Northern Ireland situation: 'we encountered some reluctance to deal with Irish issues because of the political controversy surrounding Northern Ireland. . . . There seemed to be little attempt in most schools to help children reflect on the prejudice encountered by the Irish Community in the past.'[91] It is to be regretted that the report sees anti-Irish prejudice as a thing of the past, for, despite the degree of assimilation and integration, it is still very much alive. Another and rather odd feature of the final draft of the report is that the references to the Irish have been grouped together in an appendix; in a previous draft these references were logically interspersed among the relevant sections. The effect has been to decontextualize the Irish experience within the report itself; this is unfortunate, as the approach to the Irish dimension contained in this appendix does not attempt to relate it to the overall picture of multi-cultural and anti-racist education. (When I questioned one of the HMIs, government inspectors, associated with the report about the last-minute alterations I was informed that the answer lay with the Bishop's Commission which was responsible for the final version. Readers must draw their own conclusions . . .)

The Catholic Church's 1984 report states, honestly but depressingly, that:

> it would be fair to say that the headteacher who commented, 'My parents were Irish, but I don't set much store by it,' spoke for the prevailing attitude. We encountered almost no evidence of the use of Irish literature, music or drama in the curricula of either primary or secondary schools. . . . Surprisingly, we found that Irish history was rarely taught.

Despite the overall discouraging tone, the section on the Irish attempted a positive conclusion: 'In our opinion an argument can be put forward to show that Irish culture provides a valuable source which should have a place alongside others in an attempt to broaden the educational experience.'[92] Although in Britain, late 1991, there is now a compulsory national curriculum (in state schools), happily there is, within the suggested programmes for history, a reasonably sufficient set of opportunities to develop Irish-related themes. It is to these, and the question of resourcing them in the classroom, that the last section of this chapter turns.

Teaching resources and revisionism

That there is a need for revision in the writing of history is perfectly obvious; as new information becomes available new interpretations emerge. Before looking briefly at current issues concerning the 'revisionism debate', it is instructive to go back a century in time and examine the teaching force and its accompanying pedogogy in Ireland and in places of Irish settlement. Whilst it may be unfashionable (perhaps even suicidal) to quote Pearse, his comments about the education system in Ireland at the turn of the last century are relevant to these considerations: 'A compulsory programme imposed by an external authority . . . is what we have in Ireland.'[93] In his famous essay criticizing the education structures, 'The murder machine', Pearse argued, convincingly, that the system in Ireland was designed to 'repress' and to 'tame'. 'The English are too wise a people to attempt to educate the Irish, in any worthy sense. As well expect them to arm us.'[94] The whole system, he argued, from junior school to university, was a kind of 'servitude'.[95] In terms of cultural domination, Pearse's points are defensible and accurate. The point was made succinctly by Hyde in that other famous essay, 'The necessity for de-anglicising Ireland'.[96] Hyde stressed that the thrust of his message was not a protest at imitating what was best in the English system 'but rather to show the folly of neglecting what is Irish'. He went on to indicate that this argument did not just affect nationalists but Unionists also; today many in Northern Ireland are actively exploring that dimension mapped out by Hyde in 1892.

The significance of Pearse's and Hyde's strictures are that the contamination, as they would see it, extended to the Irish diaspora also. In Australia, the United States and Britain many Irish-born teachers had been educated, and sometimes trained, in Ireland. Inevitably they brought with them the implanted attitudes described. 'Irishness' was assumed, rightly or wrongly, in the Catholic school context.[97] Miller has pointed out that the organizations which personified the late nineteenth-century cultural review in Ireland, the Gaelic League, the Gaelic Athletic Association and Sinn Féin, had non-traditional structures and methods. Their bases tended to be urban, much of their clientele still rural; their literature, despite declared intentions, 'was largely emulative of British literary tastes'.[98] The evaporating ancient forms of culture were being replaced by one which 'complemented contemporary economic processes by reordering social life and homogenising popular culture'. Emigration, exacerbated by changing conditions after the Famine, fed on itself and further sapped social and cultural vitality.[99]

Awareness of these issues was not confined to Catholics and nationalists. A commentator in the *Irish Review* in 1913 produced a piece entitled 'Irish schools: an exhortation' in which, analysing the growth of Protestant national consciousness, he noted:

> Irish schools, however, do not play their part in this work. . . . many parents send their children to be educated in England . . . and the result is that the Irish boy sent to be educated at an English school is placed in an environment less favourable than that to which he rightfully belongs, and the parents who so treat him are doing him an irreparable wrong.[100]

As early as 1835 Alexis de Tocqueville, on his well documented tour of Ireland, had commented:

> Not only do the Irish nobility live away from their homeland; not only do they spend abroad the money their country earns; they have their children educated in England, no doubt for fear that a vague instinct of patriotism and youthful memories might one day attract them to Ireland.[101]

Again in 1913 the *Review* carried a pithy piece entitled 'Irish history in English magazines' by Miriam Alexander. Today it would be labelled 'anti-revisionist'; it is introduced thus: 'Ireland is in one respect unhappily unique. She alone, of all the countries in the world, has had the misfortune to bring forth sons who, for their own ends, do not scruple to traduce her.'[102] Whilst the tone of the article may be emotional and defensive, it would be unreasonable to dispute much of the factual manipulation it goes on to describe. A similar trend can be detected in modern material produced, for example, for the 'Irish Question' option of the Schools History Project. Specifically, texts such as MacDonald's 'The Irish Question', the original Schools Council material for the course, and the printed support material for the BBC Radiovision film strip unit, all exhibit a tendency to purvey a balance of equal iniquities, a balance which frequently flies in the face of the full factual picture. (For example, the BBC booklet repeatedly quotes exact numbers of Protestants killed in massacres by Catholics; it repeatedly fails to do the same for Catholics killed by Protestants.) Very few school materials deal fully and openly with 'the Famine'; questions regarding, for example, food exports from Ireland and the possibility of government intervention are easily dismissed by reference to contemporary *laissez-faire* economic doctrine. Statistical analysis of casualty figures in treatments of the current troubles consistently exaggerates the responsibility of nationalists and evades discussion of the figures for Catholics murdered in sectarian outbreaks.

A study by Mary Hickman considered thirty-three British textbooks, mainly secondary school history, from seven sets by mainstream educational publishers. She concluded that:

> It is clear that the texts do more than perpetuate prejudice via the presentation of racial stereotypes. The model of explanation utilised enables a systematic bifurcated characterisation of relations between Britain and Ireland. The essential feature of that characterisation is the dichotomy drawn between Britain as superior and Ireland as inferior. This is the core of the racism against the Irish which is perpetuated by the model of explanation which underpins the accounts of Anglo-Irish relations in the school texts.[103]

Perhaps this genre of textbook writing can be epitomised by one particular example, from the American historian Garrett Mattingly, who pointed to deliberate myth creation in relation to 'the story spread by the English almost from the Armada Year, that the Spaniards who came ashore were spontaneously murdered by the Irish'.[104]

To overcome some of these problems, various educational conferences were held in the 1970s and 1980s, on a tripartite basis (Dublin, Belfast and London). Designed to fit in with an Anglo-Irish aura of *rapprochement*, they attempted with some success to bring teachers and historians of different traditions together. They resulted in greater opportunities for meeting and working together, but most of the effort and outcome was probably, and understandably, concentrated on Northern Ireland, and between the north and south of the island. There have been developments across the Irish diaspora, in particular the founding of the various international bodies for Irish studies, the American Conference for Irish Studies (ACIS), The British Association for Irish Studies (BAIS) and the Canadian Association for Irish Studies (CAIS). In the main, money, effort and resources have tended to gravitate towards higher education, on the assumption that a cascade, or trickle-down, model will lead to better informed and equipped teachers. The questionable premise here is that Irish Studies graduates will necessarily become teachers and that, if they do, they will be enthusiastic about developing Irish Studies.

Some useful material has been, and is being, produced (e.g. the Irish Cultural Studies pack for junior ages;[105] the new materials emanating from the Joint Education Committee of BAIS and the Irish Studies Institute at Liverpool University). The new British national curriculum presents positive opportunities for developing Irish dimensions across most of the age ranges in the proposed History programme.[106] In the United States (but not in Canada) educational suppliers have good printed and audio-visual materials for use with eleven-to-eighteen-year-olds;[107] these tend to concentrate on the Irish as part of the immigrant structure in the United States and have validity in courses elsewhere.

There are also some very useful materials produced in Ireland which have served well in secondary courses where they have been employed. Particularly notable are books such as *The Celtic Way of Life*[108] and *The First Settlers in Ireland*,[109] both of which can usefully be used in a British context; another strategy is the limited comparative study, such as that of Viking Dublin and Viking York, and the contrasting treatment of the sites by the respective local and national governments. While both Irish and British textbooks will almost all have some limitations, it is simply untrue to argue that suitable materials are not available.

Of long-term underlying importance for material on Anglo-Irish relations is the relatively new approach, as exemplified by Professor Kearney and other recent writers, where British history really does mean just that, where the archipelago, with all its Celtic fringe of Scotland, Wales and Ireland, is sensibly and sensitively incorporated into a balanced account of affairs that does not afford opportunities for Anglocentric cultural domination.

Attempts to produce a notionally neutral account of Anglo-Irish relations have been made. ILEA produce a three-part unit for this topic, comprising teacher and student texts plus a student notebook; the final version appeared to differ from that issued as trial materials in that it was 'cleansed' before publication (or so reliable rumour has it) by an acceptable (i.e. revisionist) historian whose identity is unknown. The story may be apocryphal, but it is understandable, given the sensibilities involved.

Apocrypha are important for our sense of understanding sensitive issues.

Senior BAIS members heard informally from a reliable source that the senate of one British university, asked to endorse an Irish Studies programme, erupted in dismissive guffaws. This was a rare documented example of a scenario where anti-Irish prejudice emanated from the suppos-edly well educated, and to this day the astonished supporters of Irish Studies who witnessed the scene are still unwilling (or psychologically unable) to name the institution involved. It is no secret that within the ranks of Irish Studies enthusiasts there are stresses and strains over such obvious issues as funding, job opportunities and competing institutions. Happily, the BAIS, with four sub-committees that are theoretically equal and represent higher education, adult/community education, compulsory (junior and secondary education) and the Irish language, has maintained more than a facade of unity since its inception in 1985.

In fact, moderation, that hallmark of respectability, is perhaps used to stifle what should be the widest possible range of debate. One commenta-tor, Desmond Fennell, has aptly and amusingly defined the stances taken in debate on Irish topics of significance as those of the 'Nice People' and the 'Rednecks'.[110] The reputation of most Irish historians as 'revisionists' led to the now famous incident over the Terence McSwiney lectures, sponsored by the Greater London Council and deserted by Dr Laffan, of University College Dublin, because of the coincidental hunger strike about to begin at the Maze prison (1986). One British-based Irish Studies lecturer sums up the situation thus:

> The Irish have found solace in reminding themselves of their victimised past. The past is where a small nation was colonised and crushed by a ruthless oppressor. In their own lives they may well be ridiculed at work for being Irish. . . . A reading of traditional Irish nationalist history helps to place their experiences in context. It gives people pride in their past, and thus national self-respect. Irish studies classes at adult education level thus take on the role as centres for cultural reinforcement.[111]

This role is not necessarily inimical to an open, pluralist and democratic approach to Irish studies teaching. Much relies on the professionalism of the course leader. It would certainly be naive to point the finger at Irish Studies for subjectivity; the History syllabus in Britain's new national curriculum deliberately espouses an element of Anglocentricity, an element that no student can escape from.

Is there a future for Irish studies?

It is beyond the scope of this chapter to address that question in detail as far as North America and Australia are concerned. Certainly, from the evi-dence available, higher education provision in Irish studies in these areas, as in Britain, is more than ample, despite the transient nature of some American courses.[112] Is there anything that distinguishes any particular approach at this level? Two factors appear pre-eminent, and both rely on the ability of tertiary-level operators to liaise externally: specifically, to the community, Irish and otherwise, via adult education, and to the ordinary school pupil following the general curriculum in the compulsory sector.

With regard to the latter, the joint BAIS–Liverpool Institute initiatives referred to are crucial. The latest situation reports (August 1991) indicate sound progress in relation to primary and junior schools, secondary schools, Irish Studies from sixteen-to-eighteen, in-service training for teachers, and education for mutual understanding in Northern Ireland. Clearly, much relies on the continuation of this work, especially that which is available to all students (i.e. between the ages of five and sixteen), as Britain has a most discouraging paucity of takers for post-sixteen education compared with the United States, Japan and most other European countries.

Of equal importance is not so much higher education *per se* as access to that service. As Mary Hickman has emphasized, 'What is often the case is that Irish Studies forms the catalyst, and the confidence giver, to bring Irish people into Higher Education.'[113] Hickman, Director of the Irish Studies Centre at the University of North London, the erstwhile North London Polytechnic, makes clear in the centre's mission statement that the educational process it offers is truly rooted in the surrounding community, and is not just available to those of an Irish background. Both Liverpool and North London emphasize the associated importance of continuing and maintaining the Irish studies components in compulsory education.

At the twenty-fifth anniversary conference of ACIS in Dublin in 1987 it was accepted that Irish Studies in US tertiary colleges were at risk because of the vagaries of appointments, despite the wide range of opportunities available.[114] Perhaps the answer for all the areas of the diaspora lies with adult, community and continuing education. Although this is sometimes threatened by governments' policies and drives for thrift, an analysis of provision in the United Kingdom and the United States throws up some interesting comparisons.

The ACIS *Guide to Irish Studies* (1987) noted that there were in total 445 courses available, compared with 356 in 1982. The great majority were in universities. The availability of Irish studies in the community college context (allowing for the fact that in the United States community colleges have higher status and can offer more prestigious certification than in the UK) was by comparison quite limited (five institutions in Pennsylvania, nine in New York state, two in Massachusetts, two in Chicago, three in Washington, D.C., one in Los Angeles, plus five in various locations – a total of twenty-seven institutions altogether).[115] Nevertheless, it may be the case that there is room for expansion in Irish studies in the context of the community college programmes, and via local cultural lobbies, such as the Irish Cultural Society of Garden City, N.Y., which runs a modest lecture programme, organizes imaginative school competitions and publishes an informative newsletter.

By comparison, the 1982–3 *Guide to Irish Studies* in London alone offered, within the context of adult/community education, ten Irish studies courses, six Irish literature courses, sixteen Irish language classes, seven Irish dancing classes and five traditional music courses. The situation in London today is broadly similar, and there are also active, on–going, organized Irish studies programmes in the provinces (Leicester, Coventry, Birmingham, Newark on Trent, Manchester, Liverpool and Merseyside, Bradford, Newcastle upon Tyne, Wolverhampton and Luton). The Irish Studies Workshop at Soar Valley Community College in Leicester offers annual programmes in Irish Studies, language and ceili dancing, as well as in–service professional training and an annual national conference on 'Irish dimensions in British education'.

This type and style of provision is obviously popular, is professional and competent, and in an increasing number of cases offers optional certification with access to higher educational opportunities. As this chapter has attempted to identify common strands in the experience of the people of the Irish diaspora, it is perhaps fitting to end with the conclusions of an American colleague. These conclusions, whilst particular to her location, have a general application:

> . . . it comes as a surprise that the resurgence of interest in Irish identity places such little emphasis on Catholicism. . . . Whereas the old identity was almost wholly Catholic-centred, the new one seeks its roots in Irish history, literature, music, and art. While the rekindling of Irish identity is a cause for celebration, the new version may prove to be as narrow and brief as the old.[116]

Perhaps the final cautionary observation should come from another noted American commentator, the fictional Mr Dooley, who engaged in the following exchange with his regular colleague, Mr Hennessy.

> 'Do ye think th' colledges has much to do with th' progress iv th' wurruld?' asked Mr Hennessy.
> 'D'ye think,' said Mr Dooley, ''tis th' mill that makes th' wather run?'[117]

Notes

1. Ivan, Gibbons, 'Irish studies in west London', *Adult Education*, 53, 2, 1980, pp. 101–3.
2. For a useful discussion of historical stereotyping see R. N. Lebow, 'British historians and Irish history', *Eire* VIII, 4, 1973, Irish American Cultural Institute; *White British and Black Irish: the Influence of Stereotypes on Colonial Policy*, Institute for the Study of Human Issues, Philadelphia, Pa., 1976; L. P. Curtis, *Anglo-Saxons and Celts: a study in anti-Catholic prejudice*, Conference of British Studies, Bridgeport, Conn., 1978; *Apes and Angels: the Irishman in Victorian Caricature*, David & Charles, Newton Abbot, 1971.
3. M. A. G. O'Tuathaigh, 'The Irish in nineteenth-century Britain: problems of integration', in Roger Swift and Sheridan Gilley, eds., *The Irish in the Victorian City*, Croom Helm, London, 1985, pp. 13–35, at p. 20.
4. J. E. Handley, *The Irish in Modern Scotland*, Cork University Press, Cork, 1947, p. 133.
5. John A. Jackson, *The Irish in Britain*, Routledge, London, 1963, pp. 154–6.
6. Kerby A. Miller, *Emigrants and Exiles; Ireland and the Irish Exodus to North America*, Oxford University Press, Oxford, 1985, p. 162.
7. Miller, *Emigrants and Exiles*, p. 322.

8. Dale T. Knobel, *Paddy and the Republic: Ethnicity and Nationality in Antebellum America*, Wesleyan University Press, Middletown, Conn., 1986, p. 38.
9. Donald Power, 'The Paddy image: the stereotype of the Irishman in cartoon and comic', in Robert O'Driscoll and Lorna Reynolds, eds., *The Untold Story: the Irish in Canada* I, Celtic Arts, Toronto, 1988, p. 37.
10. Liz Curtis, *Nothing but the same old Story: the Roots of anti-Irish Racism*, Information on Ireland, London, 1984.
11. Patrick O'Farrell, *The Irish in Australia*, University of New South Wales Press, Kensington, N.S.W, 1986, p. 72.
12. O'Farrell, *The Irish in Australia*, p. 160.
13. John M. G. Kirkaldy, 'The return of the Irish joke', *Quadrant*, May 1980, p. 14.
14. R. Taylor, 'Images of the Irish', *New Society*, 28 November 1974, pp. 556–7.
15. P. Elliott, *Reporting Northern Ireland: a study of the News in Britain, Ulster and the Irish Republic*; Part III of *Media and Ethnicity*, UNESCO, Paris (typescript at Centre for Mass Communications Research, University of Leicester), 1977, chapter 2, p. 32.
16. Elliott, *Reporting Northern Ireland*, chapter 2, p. 33.
17. Elliott, *Reporting Northern Ireland*, chapter 5, pp. 3–4.
18. Liz Curtis, *Ireland: the Propaganda War*, Pluto Press, London, 1984, pp. 279–90.
19. Joan Inglis, 'The Irish Community in London: a Question of Identity', Dip.Ed., Southlands College, 1979, p. 7.
20. The most accessible source for Phillip Ullah's research results is his article entitled 'Second-generation Irish youth: identity and ethnicity' in *New Community*, journal of the Commission for Racial Equality, XII, 2, 1985, pp. 310–20.
21. From a report by D. Spencer entitled 'Pupils show bias against Irish', *Times Educational Supplement*, 23 March 1984.
22. Cited in Nessan Danaher, 'Irish Dimensions in British Education, with particular Reference to Multi-cultural and Anti-racist Education', M.Ed. dissertation, University of Leicester, 1984, p.5.
23. J. J. Smolicz, 'Culture, ethnicity and education: multi-culturalism in a plural society', in J. Megarry *et al.*, *Education of Minorities: World Yearbook of Education*, Kogan Page, London, 1981, p. 18.
24. Smolicz, 'Culture', p. 19.
25. Nessan Danaher, feature article on Irish dimensions in history in the new national curriculum, *Irish Post*, 23 June 1990, pp. 18–19.
26. Nicholas Flood Davin, *The Irishman in Canada*, 1877 reprinted, Irish University Press, Dublin, 1968, p. 474.
27. O'Driscoll and Reynolds, *The Untold Story: the Irish in Canada*, I, Part X, Language and Culture, p. 727.
28. O'Driscoll and Reynolds, *The Untold Story*, pp. 727–8.
29. Murray W. Nicolson, 'The education of a minority: the Irish family urbanised', in O'Driscoll and Reynolds, *The Untold Story* II, pp. 759–84.
30. Nicolson, 'The education of a minority', p. 774.
31. Nicolson, 'The education of a minority', p. 780.
32. Knobel, *Paddy and the Republic*, p. 136.
33. Knobel, *Paddy and the Republic*, p. 137.
34. Knobel, *Paddy and the Republic*, pp. 35–6.
35. Denis Clark, *The Irish in Philadelphia: Ten Generations of Urban Experience*, Temple University Press, Philadelphia, Pa., 1973, pp. 90–1.
36. Clark, *The Irish in Philadelphia*, p. 94.
37. Clark, *Irish in Philadelphia*, p. 94.

38. Ellen Skerrett, 'The Catholic dimension', in Lawrence J. McCaffrey *et al.*, *The Irish in Chicago*, University of Illinois Press, Chicago, 1987, pp. 43–4, at p. 47.

39. R. A. Burchell, *The San Francisco Irish, 1848–80*, Manchester University Press, Manchester, 1979, p. 182.

40. Burchell, *The San Francisco Irish*, p. 175.

41. Burchell, *The San Francisco Irish*, pp. 175–7.

42. Carl Wittke, *The Irish in America*, Louisiana State University Press, Baton Rouge, La., 1956, p. 100.

43. Clark, *The Irish in Philadelphia*, p. 93.

44. L. J. McCaffrey, *The Irish Diaspora in America*, Catholic University of America Press, Washington, D.C., 1976, p. 158.

45. Wittke, *The Irish in America*, p. 293.

46. McCaffrey, *The Irish Diaspora in America*, p. 158.

47. Bernadette Devlin, *The Price of my Soul*, Pan, London, 1969, pp. 59–70, 73–4, 84–5, 106.

48. For example, see Wittke, *The Irish in America*, pp. 238–9, and Skerrett, 'The Catholic Dimension', pp. 45–6.

49. McCaffrey, *The Irish Diaspora in America*, pp. 167–8.

50. Burchell, *The San Francisco Irish*, p. 178.

51. Clark, *The Irish in Philadelphia*, p. 105.

52. Skerrett, 'The Catholic dimension', p. 55.

53. O'Farrell, *The Irish in Australia*, pp. 185–6.

54. V. Kenny, 'The post-colonial personality', in M. P. Hederman and R. Kearney, eds., *The Crane Bag Book of Irish Studies* 9, 1, Wolfhound Press, Dublin, 1985, pp. 70–8, at p. 70.

55. Kenny, 'The post-colonial personality', p. 71.

56. O'Farrell, *The Irish in Australia*, p. 190.

57. O'Farrell, *The Irish in Australia*, p. 187.

58. Lynn H. Lees, *Exiles of Erin: Irish Migrants in Victorian London*, Cornell University Press, Ithaca, N.Y., 1979, pp. 2–3.

59. Lees, *Exiles of Erin*, p. 204.

60. Lees, *Exiles of Erin*, p. 205.

61. Handley, *The Irish in Modern Scotland*, p. 207.

62. William Patrick Ryan, *The Irish Literary Revival: its History, Pioneers and Possibilities*, published by the author, London, 1894, chapters II and VII.

63. Ryan, *Irish Literary Revival*, p. 12.

64. Ryan, *Irish Literary Revival*, p. 14.

65. Ryan, *Irish Literary Revival*, p. 15.

66. Ryan, *Irish Literary Revival*, p. 16.

67. Ryan, *Irish Literary Revival*, pp, 16–17.

68. Ryan, *Irish Literary Revival*, pp. 66–7.

69. Handley, *The Irish in Modern Ireland*, p. 228.

70. Handley, *The Irish in Modern Ireland*, p. 233.

71. Tom Barclay, *Memoirs and Medleys: the Autobiography of a Bottle Washer*, Edgar Backeus, Leicester, 1934, p. 23.

72. Barcley, *Memoirs and Medleys*, p. 10.

73. M. B. Burrill, *Sacred Heart School, Leicester, 1886–1986: Centenary*, published by the school, 1986, p. 5.

74. Burrill, *Sacred Heart School*, p. 76.

75. Bill Naughton, *On the Pigs Back, an Autobiographical Excursion*, Oxford University Press, Oxford, 1987, pp. 92–3; *One Small Boy*, Alison & Busby, London, 1957, p. 149.

76. Maude Casey, *Over the Water*, Women's Press, London, 1987, p. 3.

77. Brian Keaney, *Don't hang about*, Oxford University Press, Oxford, 1985, pp. 6, 29, 95.
78. Mary Lennon, Masie McAdam and Joanne O'Brien, *Across the Water: Irish Women's Lives in Britain*, Virago Press, London, 1988, pp. 146–55.
79. Gibbons, 'Irish studies in west London'.
80. Danaher, 'Irish Dimensions', p. 65.
81. Michael Hornsby-Smith, *Catholic Education, the Unobtrusive Partner: Sociological Studies of the Catholic School System in England and Wales*, Sheed & Ward, London, 1978, p. 4.
82. Rev. Liam Ryan, 'Assimilation of Irish Immigrants in Britain', Ph.D. thesis, St Louis University (University Microfilms International No. 74-24, 138), 1973, pp. 104, 107.
83. Ryan, *Irish Literary Revival*, p. 198.
84. M. Hornsby-Smith, and R. M. Lee, *Roman Catholic Opinion: a Study of Roman Catholics in England and Wales in the 1970s*, Department of Sociology, University of Surrey, 1979, from p. 19.
85. Hornsby-Smith, *Catholic Education*, pp. 38–42.
86. Hornsby-Smith, *Catholic Education*, pp. 39–42.
87. A. Flynn, 'Racial Tensions Enquiry – Catholic Schools', Catholic Teachers' Federation, Solihull, November 1982; T. O'Donovan, 'Multicultural Education and Catholic Schools', Catholic Teachers' Federation, Solihull, autumn 1983.
88. A. Cosgrave, ed., *Learning from Diversity: a Challenge for Catholic Education. Report of the Working Party on Catholic Education in a Multiracial, Multicultural Society*, Catholic Bishops' Conference of England and Wales, London, July 1984 (for distribution later that year; page references are to the typed final draft text).
89. Hornsby-Smith, *Catholic Education*, p. 3.
90. Cosgrave, *Learning from Diversity*, p. 82.
91. Cosgrave, *Learning from Diversity*, pp. 82 f.
92. Cosgrave, *Learning from Diversity*, p. 77.
93. Patrick Pearse, *The Murder Machine, and other Essays*, Mercier, Cork, 1976, p. 19.
94. Pearse, *Murder Machine*, p. 6.
95. Pearse, *Murder Machine*, p. 7.
96. Douglas Hyde, 'The Necessity for De-anglicising Ireland' (1892), in *Language, Lore and Lyrics: Essays and Lectures*, Irish Academic Press, Dublin, 1985.
97. O'Farrell, *The Irish in Australia*, p. 189.
98. Miller, *Emigrants and Exiles*, p. 422.
99. Miller, *Emigrants and Exiles*, p. 423.
100. E. Creagh-Kitson, 'Irish schools – an exhortation', *Irish Review*, 3 March 1913–February 1914, pp. 1–7.
101. Alexis de Tocqueville, *Journeys to England and Ireland*, 1835, ed. J. P. Mayer, Anchor Books, New York, 1968, p. 113.
102. Miriam Alexander, 'Irish history in English magazines', *Irish Review*, 3, March 1913–February 1914, pp. 42–51.
103. Mary Hickman, 'The Problematic Irish: an Analysis of the Presentation of Britain's Relationship to Ireland in School Texts, to demonstrate the Transmission of Knowledge about Britain's Colonial Relationships', Southbank Polytechnic', M.Sc. thesis, University of London, 1979, p. 74.
104. Garret Mattingley, *The Defeat of the Spanish Armada*, Penguin/Pelican, London 1962, p. 386.

105. Tom Arkell, ed., *Irish Cultural Studies: a Teaching Pack*, Trentham Books, 151 Etruria Road, Stoke on Trent, ST1 5NS, 1988.
106. Danaher, feature article, *Irish Post*, 23 June 1990, pp. 18–19.
107. Social Studies School Service Catalogues, 10200 Jefferson Boulevard, room R81, P.O. Box 802, Culver City, Cal. 90232–0802, USA.
108. Curriculum Development Unit, *The Celtic Way of Life*, O'Brien Press, Dublin, 1976.
109. Roger Austin, ed., *The First Settlers in Ireland: Evidence from Mountsandel*, Resource Centre, University of Ulster, Coleraine.
110. Referred to in N. Evans, 'Nice people and rednecks: Irish studies in Britain', *Planet*, 80, April–May 1990, pp. 87–93.
111. Jonathan Moore, 'Historical revisionism and the Irish in Britain', in N. Danaher, ed., *Irish Dimensions in British Education: Report on the Sixth Annual National Conference of 11 February 1989*, Irish Studies Workshop, Soar Valley College, Leicester, 1990, pp. 9–10.
112. Mary Hickman, 'The Irish studies scene in Britain: perceptions and progress', in N. Danaher, ed., *Irish Dimensions in British Education: Report on the Sixth Annual National Conference of 11 February 1989*, 1990, pp. 4–8.
113. Hickman, 'Irish studies scene in Britain', p. 4.
114. Hickman, 'Irish studies scene in Britain', p. 4.
115. Maureen O'Rourke-Murphy, ed., *The ACIS Guide to Irish Studies*, American Conference for Irish Studies, New York, revised third edition, 1987.
116. Skerrett, 'The Catholic dimension', p. 55.
117. Finley Peter Dunne, 'Colleges and degrees', *Mr Dooley's Opinions*, Heinemann, London, 1902; pp. 199–204.

Index
